Acclaim for

An Introduction to Christology

"*An Introduction to Christology* makes a significant contribution to 'doing theology,' and most especially to 'doing Christology.' I deeply believe that this is one of the most important and ongoing quests for all of us as believers! I pray that this book will assist many in that quest for years to come."

The Most Rev. John R. McGann, D.D.
Bishop of Rockville Centre

"Highly informative, this book sifts contemporary scholarship about Jesus, kneads it with questions arising from faith, and cooks the two together to produce nourishing bread for the mind and the heart. The author's moderate and competent judgments chart a clear path through biblical and conciliar questions. Written in straightforward prose and simple style, this book indeed makes Christology accessible to intelligent beginners."

Elizabeth A. Johnson, C.S.J.
Professor of Theology
Fordham University

"Luttenberger's work in Christology accomplishes with astonishing clarity the two distinct but unified tasks of an introduction: it explicates the process, method, and character of the discipline itself, and it represents the elementary content and language of the discipline in relation to the problems that it responds to. This book keeps these distinct dimensions in close interactive contact with each other throughout.

The book is distinguished by its constant appeal to experience to illuminate the meaning of technical terms, a patient effort to reappropriate the traditional christological language by means of close attention to Scripture, to Jesus research and the pluralism of Gospel interpretations of Jesus, and to a clear exposition of the logic of the genesis of classical christological doctrines. It provides a first foundation in Christology by explaining how these historical sources have combined to determine the language of the discipline.

This resource is perfect for those who are approaching Christology for the first time. It will also be useful for teachers of Christology who will find many clear explanations of technical terms. When read in conjunction with the Gospels and the early history of christological development this book will be an excellent text for use by religious educators in all settings."

Roger Haight, S.J.
Weston Jesuit School of Theology
Cambridge, Massachusetts

"A fine resource for those who are engaged in the professional task of teaching theology, this book is also written for all who seek to find a deeper personal understanding of Jesus Christ. Taking as its point of departure the Gospel question "Who do *you* say that I am?" it guides readers through a clear and sound synopsis of the biblical and post-apostolic development of the foundational christological questions, providing insight into the issues and questions involved. At each step in the discussion the author provides a series of questions, inviting the reader to enter personally into the dynamic process of doing Christology. In the author's words, "If 'Who do *you* say that I am?' is the ultimate question posed to every Christian, then engaging the reader in the task of answering that question is the ultimate goal of this book."

Donald J. Harrington, C.M.
President, St. John's University

WHO DO YOU SAY THAT I AM?

An Introduction

to Christology

in the New Testament
and Early Church

GERARD H. LUTTENBERGER, C.M.

Nihil Obstat: Rev. Msgr. Francis J. Schneider, J.C.D.
Censor Librorum
January 4, 1998

Imprimatur: Most Reverend John R. McGann, D.D.
Bishop of Rockville Centre
February 4, 1998

Dedication

To Philip and Kathryn Luttenberger,
my beloved parents,
who, by their loving word and example,
were the first persons to help me appreciate
God's love, alive for us in Jesus, the Christ

Preface to the Second Edition

The 2012 edition of *An Introduction to Christology,* self-published at CreateSpace.com, is almost an exact replica of the original text, published in 1998 by Twenty-Third Publications. As a result, it might better be referred to as a "third printing" rather than a revised edition, since the primary reason for my self-publishing the text was simply to keep it in print, to continue to offer it to professors who encouraged me to provide them with the text for use in their courses, and to present it to readers of a new generation who wish to engage in the process of "doing Christology". However, in preparing the text for republication, I have made several changes which would best be described as editorial. I list them especially for the benefit of professors who have used the first edition and may wish to use this second edition in conducting their classes.

The most obvious change, of course, is the publisher and the ISBN. Four other changes may, however, be of significance to professors who have previously used the text. First, Scripture texts in this edition are taken from the New American Bible, revised edition, whereas the first edition of *An Introduction to Christology* used the NRSV. Second, the wording and formatting of the headings within the chapters of the text have been changed to make the interrelationship of the various divisions and sub-divisions of the chapters clearer, and in some cases more accurate. Third, the pagination, particularly with regard to Chapters 8, 9, and 10, is slightly altered (due to formatting). Finally, there are several minor editorial changes in wording and punctuation. I trust that these changes will be helpful to all who use or continue to use this text as an aid in the ongoing process of "doing Christology".

Gerard H. Luttenberger, C.M.

Acknowledgments

Many persons contributed to my taking up the task of writing a book in Christology. First and foremost, the Rev. Joseph P. McClain, C.M., a friend and scholar, awakened within me a love for the intellectual and spiritual values of doing Christology more than forty-five years ago. From another point of view, many of my students, by their questions, challenges, and interest in Christology, sparked within me the desire and the courage to embark upon the adventure of writing a book in this field.

After I had resolved to compose this book, a number of other persons offered significant support. Among them are Msgr. Francis Schneider of the Diocese of Rockville Centre who offered many helpful suggestions after graciously reading the original manuscript; Neil Kluepfel, the publisher of the first edition, who responded to my proposal of a book with wonderfully encouraging enthusiasm; Dan Connors, Gwen Costello and Alison Berger, who in various ways guided me with their editorial expertise; and my brothers in the Vincentian Community, who day by day shared my interest, struggle, and delight in moving this book to completion.

More recently, a second group of persons have both encouraged me and also assisted me in the effort to self-publish the text after it had gone out of print at Twenty-Third Publications. Among them, I would like to offer a special word of thanks to Ramon Lazarraga of Dayton University, who awakened within me the desire to keep the text available to professors and students and then suggested the possibility of publishing the text with Create-Space.com. Finally, I am indebted to Joseph Tufano and Roger So of St. John's University, Queens, New York, for contributing their time and expertise in assisting me in the many steps required to bring the work to final production.

To each of these persons I am most grateful. Without their support and encouragement this book would never have been written, much less moved to what is now a Second Edition.

TABLE OF CONTENTS

INTRODUCTION

"Who do people say that I am?" (Mk. 8:27), Jesus asked his disciples at the lakeside near Caesarea Philippi. The question was pointed. The disciples were being invited to express their sense of Jesus' identity, having experienced his preaching and his wonders (or miracles) for some time. At first Jesus led the disciples to rely on "tradition," understood broadly as "that which has been 'handed on' by others." Such tradition could be thought of as genuine insight or merely opinion; but in either sense, it constituted the explicit understanding of Jesus that people offered to one another as they tried to make sense of who he was. Hence, the disciples responded: "Some say John the Baptist, others Elijah, still others, one of the prophets." (8:28).

To borrow from the insight of others, however, even if it was insight generated by an incipient faith, was not enough for Jesus. To relate to him, the disciple must take personal responsibility for his/her understanding of Jesus. Hence Jesus pressed the question: "Who do *you* say that I am?" (8:29). Simon Peter accepted Jesus' challenge and replied: "You are the Messiah." Peter had come to know Jesus through many interpersonal experiences, and obviously had thought about who Jesus was. Since Jesus presented himself as a religious leader in Israel, Peter reflected upon Jesus in the context of his own faith experience of Yahweh, God of Israel. In that context, "Messiah" was the best way Peter could bring to full conscious expression his own experience of Jesus, including his sense of the way Jesus related to others and of the way Jesus spoke to and touched his mind and heart. In this affirmation, "You are the Messiah," Peter certainly said something about Jesus' identity. But more personally, Peter gave expression to *his own* experience of Christ, an experience made possible, in part, by Peter's openness in faith. This "confession of faith," this naming of Jesus, stood forth at that moment of Peter's life as an exciting moment of fuller awareness of Jesus within the growing interpersonal relationship between Jesus and this first of the disciples.

The development of the dialogue between Jesus and the disciples at Caesarea *and* the ways it prompted Peter both to reflect upon the faith-expressions of others and also to enunciate his own faith-consciousness, deserve further comment. It is evident from this narrative that no one relates to Jesus in isolation; there is always a collective opinion, a "Community of Beliefs," which precedes, and in some way begins to shape, one's experience of Jesus. These beliefs, handed on by the community, are themselves the testimony of the personal encounters which others have had with Jesus. They invite persons who hear of Jesus and who come to know these beliefs, to seek Jesus, to be curious about him, to expect something of him (in this case, to expect some special wisdom, some healing, some avenue to God).

But if these beliefs are to affect one personally, the individual must enter into relationship with Jesus and come to express a *personal* understanding of him, drawn from living encounters with him. Again, in this case, Peter moves further than the others in his understanding of Jesus as he names Jesus "Messiah" (that is, one sent by God to establish God's final kingdom among humankind). It is not Peter's last insight into the mystery of Jesus, to be sure, but it is a fuller insight and clearly a truly personal one. It marks a deepening of Peter's understanding of Jesus, constituting a milestone in Peter's journey of faith.

Each Christian is the beneficiary of multiple understandings and beliefs concerning Christ. They are not without significance; they shape the beginnings of the growing Christian's relationship with the Lord. But "Who do *you* say that I am?" is the ultimate question which the Lord poses to each disciple wishing to walk the journey of faith in the hope of finding deeper meaning and more abundant life in communion with him. "Who do *you* say that I am?" is the ultimate question every Christian is asked by Jesus. It is a question which, because of its ultimacy, needs to be asked again and again as life and one's relationship with Christ progress. It is the question which, because it draws us into ever deeper communion with Christ, leads to eternal life.

This book attempts to address and to foster the development of every Christian's response to two questions. The first, the preliminary question is "Who do people say that I am?" This question will invite the reader to gather the testimony of centuries of Christians who have gone before us. This testimony is truly valuable. To be valuable for us, however, it must be regarded as more than simply factual, objective, historical data. Rather, it must be looked upon as expressions of *genuine personal experiences* which real people have had of Christ in their own journeys of faith. This testimony must be seen as the product of persons who strove to express their experience and understanding of Christ as adequately as they could. Understood in this manner, their witness necessarily challenges us to meet the Lord in similar, even more profound, ways.

The second question to be addressed by this book, the ultimate question, is "Who do *you* say that I am?" It *presumes* that we are walking toward Jesus with others: Gospel writers, Christian leaders, popes, bishops, theologians, saints, faith-filled laity -- people of faith of the past and of the present. It *presupposes* that we are taking seriously the living relationship which they have had with Jesus and which they offer to us. But it demands much more. It demands that *we* meet Christ too; and that we meet him in *ongoing* ways as we journey through life, negotiating its many turns. It demands that we attain some depth in *our* experience of Jesus as we walk with our ancestors in our journey of faith. And it demands that we speak *from our own minds and hearts* about who Jesus is *for us*, how he has become a partner in our daily life, and what he gives that no other can give. We may have to wrestle with both tradition and our own experiences to express all this clearly. But such wrestling is worth all the effort it entails, for it is a significant aspect of keeping this relationship in our minds and hearts, a significant part of valuing and fostering the growth of the relationship itself. If "Who do *you* say that I am?" is the ultimate question posed to every Christian, then engaging the reader in the task of answering that question is the ultimate goal of this book.

From a broader perspective, this book is an essay in Christology; or more precisely, it is an exercise in doing Christology. The distinction between Christology and doing Christology needs to be made clear. It proceeds from a basic conviction, shared by many contemporary theologians, of precisely what Christology is. Christology is a *process of interpreting and reinterpreting one's faith experience* of God, alive for us in and through Jesus of Nazareth. As such, Christology is more than a study; it is a personal reflective *process*, stimulated and energized by one's personal sense (in faith) of having experienced the saving God in and through Jesus. It is a process which is ongoing as one seeks to deepen one's relationship with that God in and through a deeper, interpersonal relationship with Christ. For the Christian, salvation (the experience of healing, of light, and of abiding love beyond that which finite reality can offer) is continually fostered by, and ultimately depends upon, this relationship. Hence, engagement in the process of understanding or interpreting one's experience of God alive in Jesus is a saving and life-giving task which every Christian must be involved in.

To speak of doing Christology as a *personal* task, however, does not mean that it is a *private* task. Identifying "personal" with "private" and "individualistic" is an unfortunate characteristic of late 20th century and early 21st century American culture. Today's Americans are programmed to think of individual rights as the *sole* way of survival, when in actual fact, communion with one another, collaboration, and efforts to work in harmony are equally necessary for survival, the survival both of the individual and of the community, of the nation and of the world itself. The biblical axiom: "It is not good for man (human beings) to be alone" (Gn. 2:18) is as true today as it was in the early centuries of Jewish history. Human life, education, scientific and medical advancement, personal and societal safety, economy, and the development of the arts all depend on people walking together and sharing insights. Personal growth and enrichment depend as much upon mutuality as they do upon individual initiative.

Similarly, our understanding of God, of Jesus, and of salvation is no less dependent upon shared experience, insight and conviction.

"It is not good for humans to be alone." We who share the same human needs, trials, and destinies need the support and insight of one another's support and insight to find meaning in our personal experiences of God, God's healing, God's enlightenment, God's life. Hence, God addresses us both *personally* and also *as a family* - and when God does so in Christ, God addresses us as *Christian* family. As a family, we enlighten and advance one another's understanding of the God who lives deeply within us all. For this reason, doing Christology needs to be a personal but not a private or individualistic task. Rather, it is a task which we need to share with our Christian ancestors and our present day companions in the faith.

Another way of understanding the familial or communal dimension of the task of doing Christology is to see it as an endeavor which belongs properly to the People of God as a whole. We belong to this People by the very fact that we have been touched by God in Christ just as these people have been touched. These people, past and present, gathered together, we name "Church." More than a building, the word Church refers to a people assembled together in one faith and in the one Spirit of Christ. The Latin word *ecclesia* means "Church" precisely in this sense of "assembly of God's People." The task of doing Christology belongs to the entire assembly of God's People. Hence it is in this sense of Church, *ecclesia*, the assembly of God's People, that we affirm that the task of doing Christology must be both personal and ecclesial.

Given this understanding of the nature of Christology, together with the ultimate significance of Jesus' question, "Who do *you* say that I am?," addressed to all disciples, we can now define more fully the goals and the plan of this book.

First, this volume will attempt to lead the reader to understand the dynamic, personal, and ecclesial nature of Christology. To accomplish this goal, it will seek gradually to unfold the rich heritage of beliefs which continues to shape the Christian family. In doing so, it will underscore the fact that, and the manner in which, this heritage grew out of the constant prayer, the faith-filled struggles, and the personal experiences which Christians of the past progressively sought to bring to explicit consciousness and clear understanding. It will adhere to this process, being governed by the conviction that what has proven to be meaningful, insightful and life-giving to our ancestors in the faith will likewise offer meaning, insight, and life to contemporary believers.

Secondly, and concomitantly with the effort to accomplish the first goal, this book will seek to guide the reader in giving his or her own answer to the question which Christ addressed to Peter: "Who do *you* say that I am?" Fortified with a fuller understanding of the Lord as he has become known and is experienced by the Christian community of two thousand years, each believer should find him or herself ready and able to respond to that question as a challenge and an opportunity offering fuller faith and life in communion with Christ in the struggles of today.

The plan of the book, divided into four parts, will unfold as follows: Part I is foundational. It consists in only one chapter. This chapter will establish in fuller measure the perspectives which will guide the work. It will place the nature and work of Christology in the context of the whole of theology. In doing so, it will distinguish and interrelate the various dynamics and elements which make the doing of theology, and therefore the doing of Christology, a profoundly personal and ecclesial task. And so, this chapter will provide the necessary background for giving more exact definition to the specific nature and purpose of this text.

Part II seeks to unfold and understand Christology, both as an accomplishment and as a dynamic process, during the New Testament Era. It comprises chapters 2 through 4. Chapter 2 presents the Christologies (not one, but four) of each of the Gospels. It seeks not only to provide light and insight into the tradition which the New Testament churches handed on, but also to offer some initial insight into the processes, the efforts of doing theology, which led to these traditions. Chapters 3 and 4 focus on the churches (also not one, but four) which generated the saving images and understandings of Christ elaborated in the Gospels. These chapters will offer greater insight into the process of doing Christology via the example of the apostolic churches.

Introduction

Part III focuses more immediately upon the historical life and ministry, the death and resurrection of Jesus as witnessed by the original disciples. It seeks to discern more exactly the manner in which these disciples had experienced Jesus and to identify more clearly that Jesus who stands at the origin of the beliefs of the post-resurrection faith communities and of the Gospels which they, in turn, produced. The content of these chapters will encompass four aspects of the life of Jesus: Jesus' preaching the arrival of the reign of God (Chapter 5); Jesus' working of miracles (Chapter 6); Jesus' crucifixion and death (Chapter 7); and Jesus' resurrection in glory (Chapter 8). The effort of each of these chapters (5 to 8) is twofold: (1) to unfold the meaning of Christ and the Christ event as they are recorded in the biblical Tradition, and (2) to hold in relief the movement from experience, through reflection, to belief as it occurs in the lives of the first disciples.

In reflecting upon chapters 2 through 8 (parts II and III), the reader will note that they stand in a dynamic relationship to one another. They seek to unfold the established beliefs of the New Testament churches through a process of continually reaching backward, from developed beliefs of the church to the experiences which originated those beliefs. As will become clear, this process is discernible through several stages, involving the experiences of the post-resurrection communities as well as the experiences of the original disciples. For this reason these chapters move from the expositions of the four Evangelists (Chapter 2) through the experience of the New Testament churches living in Christ (Chapters 3 and 4), to the developing Christology of the early disciples who first experienced and sought to understand Jesus (Chapters 5 through 8). Thus these chapters, taken *as a whole* (as well as individually) will provide insight, not only into the *content* of the New Testament tradition, but also into the *process* of doing Christology, the process by which that tradition developed, the process which lies at the basis of all further christological development, personal and ecclesial.

Part IV seeks to unfold the development of Christology after the New Testament era. It focuses, however, chiefly on the issues and on the subsequent development of christological understanding which the Church experienced during the fourth and fifth centuries, the so-called "Classical Period" of Christology. It seeks to understand those issues and their resolution both in the context of the first four ecumenical councils and also in the context of contemporary christological thinking. It will illustrate how change in culture and language not only affect previous christological doctrine, but also require further processing if Christian faith is to remain alive and authentic. The goal of this part is threefold: (1) to foster insight into the Tradition as it developed during this period, (2) to offer possibilities for understanding that Tradition coherent with contemporary questions and insight, and (3) to provide further insight into the dynamics of doing Christology, the task of the Church and of every Christian today.

This part consists of two chapters, each dealing with refined philosophical efforts to understand Jesus. The first, *Understanding Jesus: Human and Divine* (Chapter 9), seeks to initiate the Christian quest for fuller insight into the reality of Jesus' true Self in relationship to God and to human beings. The second, *Understanding Jesus: One Person Uniting Eternity and Time* (Chapter 10), recounts the Church's pursuit of the question of Jesus' Self as it became more clearly focused upon the personal center of his unity, and begot questions concerning his self-knowledge, freedom and sinlessness. In order to present these questions and the Church's evolving responses to them with some clarity, each of these chapters will focus primarily upon these issues and insights as they have developed in their immediate historical contexts. Then, having accomplished this primary task, each chapter will attempt to bring these same questions and insights into a contemporary setting, refracted in the light of the Christology of the contemporary Church.

In summary, this book should be read as an exercise in the Christian task of doing Christology. It views this task as unfolding in two stages. The first stage will attempt to involve the reader in a personally engaged inquiry into the question, "Who do people say that I am?" The goal of this first stage will be to lead the reader as a disciple of Christ to investigate, and to find personal meaning in, the Christian Tradition. The second stage of this task will attempt to engage the reader in reflecting upon the center of his or her own relationship with Christ by calling for a personal response to the direct and ultimate question "Who do *you* say that I am?" The goal of this stage will be to lead the reader to work through much personal reflection, surrounded by prayer, so that he or she might give ever-developing, enlightened, fully ecclesial, and deeply personal responses to the Lord, and thereby experience fuller life in his name.

PART
I

Foundations for

Doing Christology

CHAPTER 1

What Is Christology?

Various writers give a wide number of definitions of Christology. Some define it as the "study of Christ," with the understanding that this study is part of theology, the "study of God." The notion of study creates the impression that a body of knowledge already exists and the expectation that much information needs to be gathered and assimilated.[1] The process is complete in that, after the study, one supposedly can feel confident that one has mastered the field, in this case, mastered at least the essentials of what there is to know about Jesus.

Others define Christology as "thinking about" or "reflecting upon" Christ.[2] The words "thinking" and "reflecting" imply much more activity than does the word "study." The implication is that the student of Christology will be much more actively engaged in the process of coming to understand Christ and that the student's thinking is important in Christology.[3]

In this text on doing Christology, I will define Christology as *"the process of interpreting one's faith-experience of God, alive for us in and through Jesus, the Christ."* It is the purpose of this chapter to explain this definition and each of its elements. To do this, however, we must first understand the nature of theology, for doing Christology is simply one aspect of doing theology as a whole.

The Nature of Theology

What is theology? Etymologically, the word theology has its origin in two Greek words: "*Theos*" (God) and "*Logos*" (Word). Theology is "Words about God" or "the study of God." (As can readily be seen, this definition parallels the first definition of Christology given above.) Such analysis and the definition which flows from it, however, can easily be misconstrued. They lead to an understanding of theology in which God is conceived as an object of study, implying that the student might study God, thought of as a distinct knowable being, much as he or she, with little personal engagement, might study any other object of curiosity or interest. How often have we studied history, or biology, or physics in that manner, with little effect on our everyday lives!

There is no doubt that we could study about God in such an impartial manner. That study would, then, become an effort to discern what other persons think about God, how they perceive God, without our entering into any relationship with God ourselves. As valid as that approach to theology might be, however, it is quite different from the inquiry about God undertaken by a person who is engaged in the task because he or she has a living and personal relationship with God which he or she wishes to explore.

Clearly, then, there needs to be another way of defining theology, one which more readily highlights the personal involvement of the individual engaged in the study. The celebrated definition of St. Anselm of Canterbury (d.1109) provides a lead toward such a definition. This saint-theologian described theology as *"faith seeking understanding."* The starting point of theology, according to this definition, is faith. In defining theology Anselm presumes that the one seeking understanding is a believer, someone who is personally aware of God, of God's presence, of God's healing, of God's love. This person, already gifted with living faith, wishes to describe, to make sense of, and to express his or her awareness and experience of God.

The individual wishes to understand and to express his or her faith-experience of God because that experience is both engaging and mystifying. On the one hand, it embraces the individual deeply with a sense of being healed, enlightened, comforted, supported, and loved; yet, on the other hand, it is different from any other experience of healing, insight, comfort, or love which he or she has had. Further, in some ways, this experience seems to be very fleeting, but, in other ways, it is more dependable than any other personal experience. The desire to understand, to express, and to interpret the experience of God flows from the engaging nature of the faith-experience itself. And persons of living faith are driven by that experience to engage in theology.[4]

Contemporary theologians take their lead from Anselm's definition but tend to draw out the implications of this definition more explicitly. One way of doing so is by defining theology as *"the process of interpreting one's faith-experience (knowledge, awareness) of God."*[5]

This definition does two things. First, it clearly indicates that theology is *a process*, not a body of truths. So long as there are believers, there will be need of further understanding and interpretation. By describing theology as a process, we recognize that theology is ongoing, open-ended, never finished. It can meet new situations, manage new questions, face new challenges. To be sure, it seeks enlightenment from the past, but more importantly, it is open to the future. As long as there are believers, both erudite and ordinary, there will be persons who need to process their faith-experience of God in further understanding, explicit articulation, and developing interpretation.

Second, this definition chooses the word *interpreting* over the word *understanding*. Certainly, theology is the process by which a person seeks to understand his or her faith-experience. But that understanding involves making sense of what God desires and/or is doing in the present; that understanding needs to make explicit the implications of God's action for human initiatives and behaviors, both in the present and for the future. The word interpreting is meant to bring out these facts: first, that *human initiative* is involved in seeking to understand the experience of God; and second, that this human initiative seeks *to translate the impact of God's presence and movements into meaning, energy and power for human action* with God in the world of today. The crucial question for each age is "What is the meaning of God's gracious presence, inspiration, healing, and love for human life and action in today's world?" To discover that meaning demands that the believer interpret, interpret carefully, and interpret well the experience of God, given in faith.

The nature and role of theology are to foster among persons who experience God the capacity to engage effectively in that kind of reflection which affords enlightened understanding and insight into action for the advancement of personal life, social life, and human history as a whole.[6] It is in this sense of interpretation that we define theology as *"the process of interpreting one's faith-experience of God."*

Faith - Theology - Beliefs

Crucial to the definition of theology is the meaning given to the reality called faith. At times, Christians have used the term faith synonymously with the terms doctrine or teaching. Such is the case when they speak of "the deposit of faith" and of "handing on the faith." If we understand faith to be identical with doctrine, then *"faith seeking understanding"* is hardly different from efforts to make sense of doctrine. Neither is it much different from the study of (teachings about) God. We have already shown that such an understanding of theology serves to remove the inquirer from playing a significant role in doing theology.

A careful reading of the Scriptures, however, yields a more personally centered understanding of faith. There it most frequently describes, not a body of truths, but a personal disposition of an individual's mind and heart. More specifically, it describes a disposition of trust in, of openness to, of readiness to commit oneself to a person deemed worthy of unconditional trust, whether that person be Yahweh or Jesus. For example, in the book of Genesis we read that Abraham believed, he entrusted himself to Yahweh's call, and he received the promise that he would become the Father of many nations (12:1-9). Likewise, in each of the synoptic Gospels we read of a woman suffering from an incurable hemorrhage and finding healing simply by entrusting herself to Jesus. Jesus praises her, saying: "Daughter, your faith has saved you. Go in peace and be cured of your affliction" (Mk. 5:34).

These two passages (and there are many others like them) are a good illustration of the personal and subjective character of faith. Abraham is not said to have believed a set of doctrines about God;

rather, he entrusted himself directly to God, responding to God's presence and call. It was not doctrine but the experience of God himself that was compelling. Similarly, the woman did not confess a series of doctrines; rather, she expressed trust in Jesus, committing her hope for healing into his hands. "If I but touch his clothes, I shall be cured" (Mk. 5:28). Faith is "personal awareness of the presence of God," "a personal disposition of mind and heart in which one commits oneself to another who is deemed worthy of unconditional trust."[7]

This personal disposition which the Scriptures name as faith embraces several dimensions of human activity. On the passive side, it includes a fundamental awareness of God, an awareness of Someone quite different, more deeply engaging, than any other. It is experienced as *"being grasped by God"* and even as *"being led forward by the profound Presence of an engaging and mystifying Other."* On the more active side, faith consists in an *abiding openness* to that God, wherever and whenever God discloses God's Self. This active dimension of faith gradually deepens, leading the person to embrace an attitude of *surrender* to God and a *readiness to commit oneself* to that God, however God chooses to lead him or her forward into the future.[8] Finally, in its fullness, faith involves *actual commitment* to God, the free choosing to walk in the way in which one discerns that God is leading. Such commitment is born of the conviction that responding to God's initiatives will lead to the fullest healing, inspiration or light, love and peace that a person could desire in this life.[9] It is this understanding of faith that is presupposed in defining theology. It is this kind of faith that seeks understanding and that cries out for meaning and interpretation.[10]

But, if faith refers primarily to a disposition of mind and heart, a disposition of personal awareness of and commitment to God, how does one arrive at doctrine and teachings? How is it that we are given to speak of "the faith" as if faith comprised a body of truths? The answer to these questions is fairly simple, but nonetheless significant. In the effort to understand and to interpret the experience of God, the believer necessarily speaks words and makes judgments. Though the words and judgments may be inadequate, they will, nonetheless, say something about the experience and something about the One of whom the believer has become aware. They will express personal convictions about the encounter between God and the believer, about the consequent transformation within the believer, and also about the nature of God. These words, judgments, and convictions about God and the experience of God are best termed "beliefs."[11] They cannot be proven by any empirical method; they are simply verbal expressions and convictions which are intended to reflect a specifically religious, and in many ways incomparable, experience. Since they are convictions, and convictions flowing from faith, they are rightly called beliefs.

It should be noted that beliefs have both a divine and a human origin. They have their origin in God in that they are, at root, generated by God's having engaged the individual and God's having disclosed God's Self to the believer. Yet they have a truly human origin in that they consist of human words and images which the believer chooses, in an attempt to express as accurately as possible the profound, mysterious experience of God, which is so difficult to describe. Beliefs originate in God's Self-disclosing presence and love for the believer, but are enunciated by the individual only after careful personal reflection. They are, therefore, the products of theology, products of the very human process of interpreting one's experience of God in faith.[12] It is these products of theology, these beliefs, that we are referring to when we use phrases like "the faith," or "the deposit of faith."

Being products of the human processes of reflection and articulation, these beliefs have the capacity "to stand alone"; that is, they have the capacity and tendency to stand apart from the person who enjoyed the experience of God and who expressed in word something about that experience. In this sense, they attain a certain objective status. They can be handed on just as one can hand on statements of mathematical principles or verifiable conclusions from an experiment in physics. Yet, unlike the principles and conclusions of mathematics and physics, the statements of beliefs cannot be verified by repeating an experiment or reworking a formula. Rather, they depend totally on the encounter with God in faith, an encounter which is not within the control of the individual, an encounter which depends on God's free gift of God's Self to the believer. Beliefs are objective in that they stand outside of the individual and can be handed on; but they always refer back to an experience which is not simply objective, but rather resides in the depth of a personal subject. It is this highly personal origin of beliefs which makes theology and its product a deeply personal science and endeavor.

One further aspect of beliefs deserves comment: beliefs can be true or false. Beliefs are true in so far as they accurately express and interpret the experience of God from which they flow; they are false if, and in so far as, they misrepresent that experience.[13] Since any individual is capable of misconstruing his or her awareness of God, sincere religious persons seek the confirmation of their beliefs by sharing and refining them with other religious persons. If they are Christian, they will seek to measure and confirm their beliefs by referring to the teachings (beliefs) of the Church, the teaching of the apostles, and the belief statements of Sacred Scripture, and ultimately, the beliefs of Jesus himself. This is so even though the experience of God has its own truth and validity; for statements of belief (sometimes referred to as religious truths) are so dependent upon human capacities of understanding, articulation, and interpretation that they demand human cooperation on a large scale so that one may be sure that such beliefs adequately express and accurately interpret the encounter with God.[14]

Personal Faith - Community of Beliefs Tradition

Certitude regarding the truthfulness of beliefs is, at least in part, derived from their confirmation by other believers. But what enables other believers to evaluate an individual's personal and unfolding relationship with God? Only their own personal experiences of God and their corporate agreement in the articulation and interpretation of these experiences can give them the capability of justly and correctly making such an evaluation. The reason for this flows from the following: first, God, being Ultimate Reality, is necessarily one. Therefore, the God who discloses God's Self is ultimately the same, having the same nature and disposition for all.[15]

Second, all persons will exhibit similar basic needs and strivings which finite creation cannot satisfy. And, therefore, the saving action of God in response to these needs will have similar patterns and effects upon human experience.[16] Third, all persons of the same culture and language share the same imaginative and expressive powers with which they communicate and interpret all their experiences. Hence, they will be able to express their personal encounters with this saving Reality in a manner intelligible to all persons within the confines of their cultural and linguistic environment. In this way they will be capable of judging the adequacy and meaningfulness of one another's statements of belief and also become united as a community of faith and a community of beliefs.[17]

It should be noted that this community of faith and beliefs arises out of the personal faith of each member and not simply out of their sharing a group of already articulated understandings and convictions. Nevertheless, as with all beliefs, once a community expresses itself in commonly held beliefs, these beliefs attain a certain objective status. They will then serve to guide the life and further sustain the religious experience of the members of the community. Further, they can be utilized to evaluate newer beliefs which arise both from within and from outside the community. Finally, they can be handed on in teaching, and so become tradition. In this way, they become instrumental in shaping the religious attitudes and religious life of future generations. Though, fundamentally personal faith precedes beliefs, in this latter sense the tradition of beliefs precedes personal faith, inviting persons to faith and calling it forth.[18]

Some examples of the foregoing will serve to clarify the point. Often we may think of the Scriptures as sacred writings embracing unquestionable truths about God and commands from God, all given to us by God. As such, they are handed on and have become the standard, the norms, by which the Jewish community (using what Christians refer to as the Old Testament) and the Judaeo-Christian community (using both Old and New Testaments) measure themselves. These writings and the beliefs which they contain serve to guide the religious life of these communities, to renew that life in worship, and to shape the religious and human behaviors of future generations.

The Scriptures themselves support such usage. The book of Exodus reports that, after hearing the law which Moses communicated from God, the people responded: "Everything the Lord has commanded, we will do" (19:8). Likewise, in a Christian context, the author of the Second Letter to Timothy urges his reader:

> Remain faithful to what you have learned and believed, because...from infancy you have known the Sacred Scriptures, which are capable of giving you wisdom for salvation through faith in Christ Jesus. All Scripture is inspired by God and is useful for teaching, for refutation, for correction, and for training in holiness, so that one who belongs to God may be competent, equipped for every good work. (II Tim. 3:14-17).

It would be difficult to find a more complete description of the value of a community's written tradition, and the shared beliefs which that tradition encompasses.

Nevertheless, one must ask: "Where did these writings, and the beliefs expressed in them, come from? Did God actually hand them down?" The answer is somewhat complex. Contemporary biblical theologians recognize that, from one point of view, these writings originated in the living faith and interpretative initiatives of their human authors. From another point of view, however, they derived from smaller portions of written materials which the biblical authors received from the communities with which they shared faith. For example, each of the four Gospels was written by collecting, organizing and editing many independent and pre-existent written traditions; namely, passion narratives, resurrection narratives, collections of sayings of the Lord, miracle stories, parables of Jesus, and so forth.[19] Before any of these materials were put to writing, however, the tradition which they communicated was handed on orally. These oral traditions reflected the personal faith and original teaching of the Apostles and earliest disciples. Ultimately these traditions originated in Jesus' own experiences of the God he named *Abba,* and in the beliefs, the teachings, and the convictions in which Jesus articulated his understanding and interpretation of these experiences.[20]

Where did these writings and the beliefs which they contain come from? They came from God in that they originated principally in Jesus', but also in the Apostles', the community's, and the authors' experience of God and God's self-disclosure. And they came from human beings and human initiatives in that they originated principally in Jesus', but also in the Apostles', the community's, and the authors' efforts to interpret the experience for themselves and for others. Each stage of this development shows deepening insight and refinement of beliefs within the community. Yet each stage also exhibits clear fidelity to the original experience of the Apostles and of Jesus himself.

The tradition captured in the sacred writings, then, points in two directions. It points backward in time to the original encounters with God enjoyed by those who stand as the foundational persons of the community (e.g., in the Christian community, Jesus and the Apostles). It points forward in time, providing a basis and standard in and through which subsequent generations are formed in the religious values of the community. With regard to the latter, this tradition calls each generation into a communion of faith with its founders and leads it to discover and to interpret correctly, in its own experience, the God whom the community has known to be so vitally engaging. Originating in the faith-experiences of a community's founder(s), the community's tradition and its commonly held beliefs become a vital element in the development of the faith-life of all its members throughout its history.

Receptivity with regard to the tradition, however, does not exhaust the individual's relationship to the historic community and its beliefs. Members formed by the tradition also contribute to the growth of this body of beliefs as they encounter God in face of the new challenges of a new day. For, on God's side, the divine Reality continues to address each individual as human life and history continue to unfold. And, on the human side, each individual will find himself or herself continually enlivened and inspired by God and God's saving presence. While remaining faithful to the previously established tradition, these believers will also be challenged to interpret their sense of God's movements in language and actions particularly suitable for their own day. They will have the honor, and be given the responsibility, of contributing to the community's beliefs as people of religious depth, continuing to walk together in the power and presence of God.

Personal Faith and the Transcendent Object of Faith

In this brief description of the elements which make up the task of theology, we have striven to clarify our understanding of a number of terms: faith, theology itself, beliefs and the community of beliefs, and tradition. We have defined faith as a disposition rendering the individual capable of perceiving the presence of God and providing that person with the readiness to commit himself or herself to God. We have spoken of God as giving light or inspiration, healing, love, and peace as no other can. Theology has been defined as the process of interpreting one's faith experience of just such a God.

Yet many do not affirm the existence of such a God. Some think of God as "a Being who is quite distant, yet One who operates much like humans do but with much more power." Pagan antiquity thought of the gods in just such a manner. Others prefer not to speak of God at all. We cannot presume, then, that the meaning we intend by the term "God" is absolutely clear. Yet a proper understanding of what we mean when we speak the name God is pivotal for a right understanding of theology. For, if we are not precise about what we mean by God, how shall we know we are referring to the same kind of experience when we speak of interpreting one's experience of God in faith?

The most generic way of describing God, the Other experienced in faith, is by naming God "the Transcendent."[21] Literally, the word transcendent comes from two Latin words meaning "to climb across" or "to go beyond the limits." Human beings continually strive to go beyond the limits. Explorers of space sought to put a man on the moon and, later, to create a space station revolving about the earth. Medical science seeks ever new ways of avoiding disease and of increasing the human life-span. Athletes seek to break records; artists seek to create newer and more expressive works of art; ordinary families seek to improve their standard of living beyond that enjoyed by their parents. Human beings constantly strive to go beyond the limits of life as they know it.

Behind these efforts to transcend life as people have known it lies a deep dissatisfaction with the present. Life does not afford freedom from suffering, lasting peace, abiding love and acceptance, or liberation from the threat of death. Suffering, violence and war, rejection and hatred, sickness and death are universally perceived as evils we would wish to be free of.[22] Hence, the desire for freedom from these evils or, from a more positive standpoint, the longing for fullness of life continues to well up from the human spirit. Yet nothing in this world can free human beings from these evils, at least not in any certain and abiding manner. Nothing in the world as we know it, nothing created, not even the sum of created realities, can calm or satisfy this longing and desire. This insatiable and universal longing may be called the desire for transcendence, a longing to live beyond the limits of this world, beyond existence as it is given in this world. It speaks of an openness for the infinite. It is a longing for the Reality which will satisfy without limit, or, in other words, a longing for transcendent Reality.[23]

The experience of God in faith is an experience of a Presence affording a sense of healing, inspiration and insight, wisdom, peace and love, life -- beyond the limits of that which created, finite reality, even in the best of circumstances, can offer. This experience may be given at particular times and places, but it is always an awareness of reality, meaning, comfort which far exceeds the limits of those times and places. It is an experience of the presence of transcendent healing, light, peace, and love. As such, it provides comfort, hope, and renewed energy for life and for fostering the very values we find so threatened in everyday existence. The experience of God in faith is best described as an experience of the Transcendent.

Several aspects of this experience deserve further note. First, an essential characteristic of the experience of the Transcendent is its graciousness. The experience comes as gift. It cannot be turned on or controlled. It is always freely given. It is far beyond what anyone could produce, even by the most noble deeds. It arises only out of the freedom of the One who bestows it. Hence it may be given the name of "Supreme Love."

Further, the experience of the Transcendent is always transformative. Persons who experience this deep Presence, which brings with it profound healing, or unexpected insight and inspiration, or an embracing sense of being loved and valued, or any number of transcendent saving gifts, find that their lives change.[24] They have Someone always present to live for. They have a Partner leading them onward to a richer life here in this world and beyond. They have a Person worthy of their unconditional commitment.

An example will clarify these points. The Book of Exodus recounts the story of Moses being drawn to contemplate a burning bush. As Moses watched, the bush, radiating warmth and light, did not cease to burn (3:2b). Moses was led to investigate the spectacle further. The sacred author then recounts the following:

> When the Lord saw him coming over to look at it more closely, God called out to him 'Moses! Moses!'.... 'I have witnessed the affliction of my people in Egypt and have heard their cry of complaint against their slave drivers so I know well what they are suffering. Therefore, I have come down to rescue them from the hands of the Egyptians and lead them out of that land into a good and spacious land.... Come now! I will send you to Pharaoh to lead my people, the Israelites, out of Egypt.' But Moses said to God 'Who am I that I should go to Pharaoh and lead the Israelites out of Egypt?' He answered, 'I will be with you.' (3:4-12).

In this narrative we note all of the aforementioned characteristics of the experience of the Transcendent. The Presence, call, and promise are not only beyond the limits of the bush but they are also beyond the limits of Moses' wildest imagination. Further, the experience is given freely, surprisingly, as gift. Moses does not create it nor does he control it. Further still, the experience brings a promise of salvation from the evils that surround these people, a promise of rescue from oppression and entrance into fuller life.[25] And finally, the experience is transformative. It changes Moses' life and fills him with energy and courage to act on behalf of his people. Moses has been gifted with an experience of the Transcendent. He has experienced God in faith.

As we read this account, however, we need to avoid taking it in an overly literal way, as if we had an exact transcription of God's words within the narrative. In light of what we have said above, we can readily recognize that the written account hands on statements of beliefs: the beliefs of the author reflecting the beliefs of the Israelite community. Ultimately these convictions rest upon a more foundational series of beliefs, that is, Moses' own expressions and interpretations of his original and his subsequent experiences of God. The original faith-awareness of Moses would be less specific, though not less engaging, than the narrative portrays. Moses himself would have clarified the original experience as the intentions of God and further experiences of God unfolded through time. Hence, the narrative is already the product of much theologizing. Nevertheless, this narrative, this series of beliefs, clearly reflects an authentic experience of the transcendent God and conveys valid insight into the nature and intentions of the Transcendent itself.[26]

The Nature of Christology

We have defined Christology as *"the process of interpreting one's faith experience of God, alive in and through Jesus, the Christ."* At this point, we can unfold the elements of this definition more fully. Doing so will enable us better to understand the goal of this book and the plan of the following chapters.

Like all theology, Christology originates in the faith experience of God. The specific focus of Christology rests on the fact that the community of Christian believers, and anyone personally engaged in doing Christology, have come to experience God, the Transcendent, in and through Jesus, the Christ. We say *in* Jesus, because persons have come to awareness of the Transcendent in the *very person* of Jesus. To decide how that awareness has come about and what meaning derives from it is one of the tasks of the following pages. We say *through* Jesus, because persons have come to experience God and God's transforming light and love through the *words and actions* of Jesus, and through *the events* (such as the baptism, temptations, the passion, death and resurrection) of Jesus' life. We will see that experiencing God acting and giving God's Self through Jesus preceded experiencing and recognizing the ways God united God's Self with and lived in Jesus. So also, the beliefs which emerged out of experiencing God through Jesus preceded the beliefs which emerged out of the later awareness and recognition of God's living in Jesus. In either case, however, the specific focus of Christology arises from the experience that the saving and self-giving presence and love of the Transcendent became fully revealed and mediated in and through Christ and the Christ-event.

Further, like all theology, Christology is a process of *interpretation*. Throughout their experiences, those who knew Jesus first-hand necessarily interpreted the faith experiences which they enjoyed in and through him. Some questioned "'Where did this man get all this? What kind of wisdom has been given him? What mighty deeds are wrought by his hands! Is he not the carpenter, the son of Mary...?' And they took offense at him" (Mk. 6:2b-3). Yet others met God at various levels acting through Jesus and hence named him Rabbi, Teacher, Prophet, and Messiah. Later Christians, experiencing even more deeply God's saving presence in and through Jesus, called him Son of God, Lord and Savior. Each name gave witness to the believer's encountering God through and even in Jesus. And each name represented an attempt to understand God, God's action in Christ, and Jesus himself alive in God.

Further, early disciples saw that experiencing God in Jesus called for new *commitments*. It was necessary to interpret the consequences of accepting God's self-gift in Jesus. One such interpretation is given by Peter on the first Pentecost. After his moving proclamation of Jesus' resurrection, his audience asked:

> 'What are we to do, my brothers?' Peter said to
> them 'Repent and be baptized'.... Those who
> accepted his message were baptized.... They devoted
> themselves to the teaching of the apostles and to the
> communal life, to the breaking of the bread and to
> the prayer (Acts 2:37-42).

Early Christians interpreted the experience of God in Jesus as demanding that they adhere to Christ's word, forgive others, love their enemies, accept the cross in their own lives, and live in hope of a personal resurrection. The Transcendent deserves absolute trust; so also, God alive in Jesus calls forth the unconditional commitment of one's life. The community of faith, therefore, doing Christology, necessarily interpreted and expressed its experience of God alive in Jesus. It did so in forming beliefs marked by significant convictions regarding the way of life to be lived in fidelity to the gift it received in him and through him.

Finally, like all theology, Christology is a *process*. To say this is to say, once again, that it is not just the presentation of facts, data, opinions, or revered truths. It is a process in which the individual engaged in the study seeks to interpret his or her own experience of God, in this case the experience of God filtered through the words and deeds, the life, death and resurrection, the mediatorship and personal presence, of Jesus. The process, in its first stage, involves meeting God and Jesus in the community of beliefs handed on by the Church and finding God alive within these many interpretations of God's saving presence. In effect this involves giving answer to the question: "Who do people say that I am?" In its second stage, the process involves meeting Jesus in the present, personally, and responding to the question "Who do *you* say that I am?" The process at this latter stage involves gathering the responses of past and present, and searching for the meaning of God's self-gift, ever present in Jesus, for today. Doing so requires that one listen to these responses as they resound in oneself and within the contemporary community of believers. Doing so also requires that one allow these new and renewed interpretations to carry one forward in fuller commitment and discipleship.

Christology is the process of interpreting one's faith experience of God alive in and through Jesus, the Christ. We are now about to engage in that process. Before entering upon the journey, however, it will be important for the reader to identify, to reflect upon, and to bring to expression, his or her personal experience of the major themes of this chapter. Such efforts are integral to the doing of theology and are a necessary prelude to the doing of Christology. They are indispensable components of living faith, the task of every Christian who seeks life and meaning in relationship with God and God's Christ.

The following questions are intended to facilitate this task. The questions may also be used to initiate discussion, a sharing of one's beliefs.

Questions for Reflection

1. How have you understood the nature of faith prior to this reading? How do you understand the nature of faith now?

2. What is your understanding of God? How, in your experience, have you detected the presence of God? What, in your experience, might lead you to understand God as transcendent?

3. How has your faith been fostered and shaped by the beliefs of the community of faith of which you are a member? In what ways has the community's tradition led you to experience God? How have you grown to refine your understanding of some of these beliefs through your life?

4. How do you understand the nature of theology? What do you see as your role in doing theology?

5. How do you understand Christology? What are your hopes and expectations for doing Christology?

PART
II

Christology in the
New Testament
Churches

The Early Christians' Experience and Understanding of Christ

CHAPTER 2

Four Gospel Images of Christ: The Shape of the Biblical Tradition

Often we think of the four Gospels as the starting point of Christology. They provide the data about Jesus, his mission, his apparent defeat but then genuine victory, together with his effect upon his disciples before, during, and after his death and resurrection. We think of Christology as a process of seeking to understand and to unfold the consequences of Jesus' life and mission, his cross and his manifestation as the risen One *precisely as he and his life are recorded* in the sacred texts. Christology begins with the theologian taking these texts in hand and interpreting them for his own generation. In this sense, these Scriptures precede and provide the basis for every effort to do Christology.

It is true that the sacred writings provide a necessary dimension[1] of the starting point for doing Christology with respect to the efforts of every theologian living after the New Testament era. However Christology itself does not begin after the composition of these sacred books. Rather, these writings themselves are the examples and the fruit of the earliest processes of doing Christology. As such, they constitute for future generations models both of what Christology entails and also of how the process of doing Christology should be accomplished.

The purpose of this chapter is twofold. First, it aims to show that the four Gospels, while offering a basically similar core image of Jesus, intentionally yield four very distinctive perspectives or shadings of that image. Second, it seeks to relate this material, the images of Christ and the Christian understandings which they represent, to the elements and dynamics of doing Christology as described in Chapter 1 above. The latter section will include some preliminary reflections on the relationship of the Gospel images of Christ to the development of personal Christian faith. The chapter will conclude (as did the previous chapter) with a series of questions for reflection. These are intended to aid the readers both to process this material meaningfully for themselves and, further, to enter into the process of doing Christology personally for their own advancement in the life of faith and discipleship.

Four Gospels - Four Images of Christ

The four Gospels clearly give us an account of the life, ministry, death and resurrection of the same Jesus. They each tell of the baptism, preaching, and teaching of Jesus, of his wondrous healing of both physical and spiritual ills, of his compassion for the marginalized and abandoned of Israel, of his growing conflict with the religious authorities of his day, and of his trial, crucifixion and his subsequent appearances[2] as the risen One.[3] In these basically similar accounts, however, one notices immediately some dissimilarities. Matthew and Luke add "infancy narratives" describing the announcement of the births of John the Baptist and Jesus, the births themselves, and something of the earliest years of Jesus. The Fourth Gospel, which carries the name of John, adds a "prologue," reflecting upon the divine origin of Jesus as Word of God. Further reading reveals an abundance of differences in the portrayal of Jesus, none of which contradicts the core image described thus far, but all of which create very distinctive perspectives on the person of Jesus, the tone of his teaching, the exercise of his ministry, and the ways in which the disciples ultimately came to understand him. It is these differences in perspective which we are about to describe.

The Christ of the Gospel of Mark[4]

The Gospel of Mark is clearly the shortest and the most direct of the four Gospel accounts of Jesus' life and ministry. This in itself underscores its uniqueness and distinctiveness in its presentation of Jesus.

THE MARCAN JESUS: HEALER AND EXORCIST

One cannot help but be struck by how quickly the Gospel moves to present Jesus as healer and exorcist. Already in the first chapter we read of Jesus casting out demons, healing Simon's mother-in-law's fever, cleansing a leper, and working many other cures so that people "brought to him all that were ill or possessed by demons" (1:32b). So promising and engaging was Jesus in this ministry that Mark notes immediately: "The whole town was gathered at the door" (1:33). Even when Jesus sought quiet and prayer, his disciples pursued and found him, exclaiming: "Everyone is looking for you" (1:37), so much so that "it was impossible for Jesus to enter a town openly. He remained outside in deserted places, and people kept coming to him from everywhere" (1:45). In the opening scenes of this Gospel, Jesus is presented to us as a very compelling figure. People were immediately drawn, with confidence, by his ready power to heal.

A further succession of stories, in rapid sequence, intensifies the image of Jesus as healer-exorcist. The second chapter begins by telling of Jesus healing a paralyzed man and forgiving his sin (2:1-11). Next, Jesus is presented curing a man suffering from a withered hand (3:1-5). Finally, the author emphasizes the magnetic strength of Jesus: "A large number of people came to him also from Jerusalem, from Idumea, from beyond the Jordan, and from the neighborhood of Tyre and Sidon. He told his disciples to have a boat for him because of the crowd, so that they would not crush him" (3:8f). One gets the sense that everybody knew of Jesus; everybody rushed to him and found marvelous healing through him.

Subsequent chapters depict Jesus' works of healing and exorcizing reaching an even greater magnitude. His power extends also to non-Israelites; he heals persons in what would be deemed the most impossible situations. Jesus is presented as performing an exorcism on behalf of a man living among pagans in Gerasene territory (5:1-20). The man could not be subdued; he had been shackled and chained, but he broke the chains. The man was afflicted not by one spirit, but by so many, so much so that the spirit was named Legion. So great was their number that it took two thousand pigs to provide a new home for them when the man was cured. Yet, once Jesus acted in his behalf, people found this man fully dressed and perfectly sane.

In a similar manner, Jesus heals the daughter of a synagogue official (5:21-24, 35-43) while she is "at the point of death" (5:23). He cures a woman suffering from hemorrhages for twelve years, after every recourse to doctors had only made the condition worse (5:25-34). He frees the daughter of a Syrophoenician woman from a demon (7:24-30) and a man from the district of the Ten Cities (Gentile territory) of hearing and speech impediments (7:31-37).

The Marcan Jesus, then, emerges quickly and with mounting energy as a powerful healer. Anyone who read this Gospel could not but marvel at this power; anyone afflicted in any way could not help but be drawn to seek his healing strength, his readiness and ability to cure every infirmity. It is precisely this Jesus who, Mark wishes to assure the reader, is present forever with us. For Mark's image of the risen Christ remains distinctive within the four Gospels. The Marcan Christ, alive for us forever, instructs his disciples: "These signs will accompany those who believe: in my name they will drive out demons, they will speak new languages. They will pick up serpents (with their own hands), and if they drink any deadly thing, it will not harm them. They will lay hands on the sick, and they will recover" (16:17f). The risen Christ, alive in his Church, is Jesus healer and exorcist.

THE MARCAN JESUS: FAITHFUL AND SUFFERING SERVANT
In addition to highlighting Jesus' role of exorcist and healer, the Gospel of Mark, with equal clarity, offers another, more paradoxical image of Christ: Jesus is the *faithful and suffering Servant of God*.[5] The author announces this perspective right from the beginning: his is the Gospel of "Jesus Christ, Son of God" (1:1).

The designation "Son of God," for Mark, needs to be understood in its biblical context. Many Christians will understand the term

"Son of God" first and foremost as reflecting the belief that Jesus is "begotten of God" and "sharer in God's own divine nature." That understanding of the term "Son of God" flows more from fourth-century Christian philosophical-theological reflection than from first-century biblical-theological understanding. The designation, "Son of God," according to biblical usage means "chosen one" and "faithful servant."[6] In that sense, it had been applied to the people Israel (Ex. 4:22f; Hos. 11:1), to the king of Israel (Ps. 2:7; II Sam. 7:14) or to any devout and law-abiding Jew (Sir. 4:10). The title is repeated at Jesus' baptism when the voice from heaven proclaims: "You are my beloved Son; with you I am well pleased" (1:11). Here the proclamation reflects the beginning of the Isaian "Servant Songs,"[7] oracles which culminate in praise of the sinless servant who atones for the people's sins. The reader, therefore, is immediately invited to understand Jesus as the "faithful and beloved servant of God."

Again, events move quickly in Mark's account. The servant, at first described as gifted with healing power, is also presented as laboring under suspicion of authority and as causing ever deepening conflicts. Already in the second chapter, the author places Jesus in the midst of struggle four times in quick succession. Jesus had pronounced forgiveness of sin over the paralytic. Some Scribes, sitting in the crowd asked themselves: "Why does this man speak that way? He is blaspheming. Who but God alone can forgive sin?" (2:6f). Next, Jesus is presented dining with Levi, a tax collector. Some Pharisees noticed this and remarked to Jesus' disciples: "Why does he eat with tax collectors and sinners?" (2:16). Then Mark notes that Jesus and the disciples had not adopted the practice of fasting. "People came to him and objected: 'Why do the disciples of John and the disciples of the Pharisees fast, but your disciples do not fast?'" (2:18). Further on, the author recounts the fact that Jesus' disciples plucked off the heads of grain while walking through a field on the Sabbath. The action engendered the rebuke: "Look, why are they doing what is unlawful on the Sabbath?" (2:24). Finally, the growing conflict reaches a crescendo when the Pharisees watch to see if Jesus would cure on the Sabbath. He does so and the author tells us: "The Pharisees went out and immediately took counsel with the Herodians against him to put him to death" (3:6). Jesus' very faithfulness to God sparks threats of persecution. The reader cannot miss the image: Jesus is the faithful Servant of God, suffering rejection from the beginning. In a sense, it is "his most personal and deepest identity" to be both faithful to God and also to be persecuted for that fidelity.

But these first manifestations of Jesus' being subject to rejection are only the tip of the iceberg. His relatives think he is mad (3:21), and the Scribes accuse him of healing *by means of demonic power* (3:22). He is rejected at Nazareth (6:1-6) and the author soon recounts the tale of the death of John the Baptist, letting the reader see in this event an ominous anticipation of Jesus' own fate (6:17-29). Finally, the mystery of the destiny and identity of the Marcan Christ is made absolutely clear as Jesus qualifies and corrects Peter's brief insight of faith in his naming Jesus "Messiah." At that point Jesus himself, in the first of three predictions of his Passion,[8] "began to teach them that the Son of Man must suffer greatly and be rejected by the elders, the chief priests, and the scribes, and be killed, and rise after three days," much to his disciples' disbelief and dismay (8:27-33). Like his Sonship, so his Messianic mission of bringing about the kingdom of God is bound to the way of the cross.

The culmination of this movement comes, of course, at the moment of Jesus' passion and death. The distinctiveness of Mark's image of Jesus as faithful Son and suffering Servant of God shines forth in the very starkness with which he portrays Jesus' final moments.[9] Jesus' prayer in the garden is especially painful. His cry to the Father seems unanswered; he is "forced" to leave the garden supported only by his steadfastness and resignation (14:41f.). The pain is compounded by the continued disbelief of the Apostles, by Peter's denial, and eventually by the desertion of all his disciples. Mark alone underscores the completeness of that abandonment by telling the reader of an enigmatic young man, wearing nothing but a linen cloth, who followed Jesus. When Jesus' adversaries seized this disciple, he "left the cloth behind and ran off naked" (14:51). Mark's intent seems to be to contrast the disciples' initial response to Jesus, in which *they left everything* (their nets, their families) *to follow him* (1:18,20), with their final response to Jesus, in which a last disciple *leaves everything behind to get away from him*![10] As a result, Jesus endures the double trial, often given to unrelieved silence,[11] having nowhere to go, no one to turn to, to secure an effective defense. He is left to endure the crucifixion alone, further degraded by a quick succession of words of rejection, mockery, ridicule, and abandonment: from passers-by (15:29), from the chief priests and scribes (15:31), and from the criminals crucified with him (15:32). Jesus is the epitome of one destined to suffer.

For the reader, Mark's portrayal of Jesus leads to only one conclusion: the way to salvation is to walk with Jesus, enduring personal rejection, abandonment, persecution, and the cross. Although it may be difficult to affirm with perseverance, Jesus is the faithful Son of God by being the true Suffering Servant of Yahweh. It is this distinctive way of envisioning Christ, one which Jesus' disciples find so hard to accept, that Mark affirms unconditionally in the words of a non-disciple, a Roman centurion: "Truly this man was the Son of God" (15:39). With those words, Mark brings us back to where he started. Having set out to tell us the Good News of Jesus, the Son of God, he unfolds a progressively, ever more painful story, and concludes by telling us what being faithful to God, what being a "Son of God" truly means.

The Christ of the Gospel of Matthew

The Christ of Matthew is obviously the same Jesus whose life, ministry, death, and resurrection is recounted by Mark. Matthew's Jesus also heals, casts out devils, suffers, dies and rises. But Matthew underscores aspects of Jesus' origins, life, and ministry which, at best, lie in the background in Mark's account. It is the uniqueness of Matthew's Christ which we seek to highlight.

MATTHEW'S JESUS: SON OF DAVID, KING OF THE NATIONS
The reader first notes that Matthew introduces his Gospel with a genealogy followed by an infancy narrative.[12] The first verse of the Gospel speaks of Jesus' human origin: he is the Son of David, the Son of Abraham. David is mentioned five times (1:1,6,17) in the genealogy. Joseph, father of Jesus, is addressed as "Son of David" in the annunciation to him of Christ's birth (1:20). At the outset,

Matthew's Christ is tied tightly to Jewish history and to the Davidic line. About to fulfill the role of the anointed Kings of Israel, Jesus is the royal Messiah, the anointed one come to establish the final and long-awaited kingdom of Israel.[13]

The reader of Matthew's Gospel, however, quickly notes an expansiveness to Christ's reign. His kingly identity is recognized and honored not just by Jews (Joseph, Mary, shepherds) but by Gentiles, that is, by all nations. Unique to Matthew is the story of the Magi, non-Jews, who seek the newborn king and worship him.[14] Unique to Matthew also is the manner in which he introduces Christ's public ministry, Jesus being "a light to the Gentiles" (4:15f.; see Is. 8:22-9:1). This universal expansiveness of Jesus' reign and light is highlighted in growing measure in the Gospel proper, not only in Jesus' praise of the Roman centurion (8:10) and in his exorcism of the Gaderene demoniacs (8:28-30) - events also recounted in Mark - but in his prophecy that the kingdom of God will be taken from the Priests, Elders and Pharisees and given to others (8:11f; 21:43). Matthew's Christ is born with a universal stature, destined to rule both Jew and Gentile alike.

THE MATTHEAN CHRIST: NEW MOSES, NEW LAWGIVER

The most distinctive feature of Matthew's Jesus is set in relief by the author's recasting of Israel's revered mediator of the divine Law, Moses. For Matthew, Jesus is the successor to Moses; he is the New Moses, the New Lawgiver, bringing the New Law to and for the new Israel. This image of Christ is set forth in striking relief in the infancy narrative itself. Jesus is sought by Herod who wishes to kill the newborn, is taken to Egypt by his parents under divine guidance, and when it becomes safe to return comes out of Egypt to establish the new promised land (2:1-23). One is reminded of Moses whose life was threatened shortly after his birth, who found protection in Egypt, and, by divine guidance, led God's People forth to the promised land (Ex.2-15).

The theme introduced in Matthew's infancy narrative becomes the early focus of the Gospel proper. Unlike Mark, Matthew chooses to sum up Jesus' work of healing and exorcism with a brief statement (Mt. 4:23f). Instead, Matthew's first descriptions of

Jesus' ministry stress Christ's teaching mission, his labor of unfolding the New Law of the New Kingdom (5:1-7:29).[15] And so, like Moses who received the Law on Mt. Sinai (Ex.19-24), Jesus ascends the mountain (Mt. 5:1) and begins to teach the crowds.[16] And Jesus truly delivers a New Law: not the wealthy but the poor (in spirit) are blessed; not the warrior or the victor, but the meek, the peacemaker, and the persecuted are blessed; not the comfortable, the untroubled, but those who mourn are blessed.

The newness of this Law, moreover, requires a new and fuller responsiveness on the part of the disciple. The New Moses makes this very clear in an overriding statement: "Unless your holiness surpasses that of the Scribes and the Pharisees, you shall not enter the kingdom of heaven" (5:20). He then specifies: not only murder and adultery are forbidden; but one must resolve anger and control lust before these passions lead to visible offenses (5:21-30). Not only must one love one's neighbor, but one must love, and even pray for, one's enemies as well (5:43f).

This deeper responsiveness, however, is not without reason. The Matthean Christ counsels his disciples that all are children of the same heavenly Father. Only by loving as that Father loves, only by being complete as he is complete, can one truly share his life and be part of his household (5:45-48). More is required of the disciple who seeks to live under God's reign, but more is promised also. In living by this Law, one will become fully alive as God is alive; one will live by the love which is God.

Further, the Matthean Christ surpasses Moses in a second way. Not only is he Mediator of a New Law, but also he mediates that New Law in a new way. In this regard, Matthew's Christ teaches using the antithesis: "You have heard it said in the past..., but I say to you...."[17] Whereas Moses and the prophets always spoke of the Law or the Word of God being given to them, Jesus presents the Law as coming from his own authority. He is not simply Law-giver but Law-maker. He assumes an authority which no leader of Israel had ever assumed before him (7:28f). Hence, both in the content of his teaching and the manner of his teaching, Jesus is truly the *New Moses, the New Lawgiver, par excellence!*

In this light, several other characteristics of this New Lawgiver should be noted. First, in giving this New Law, Matthew's Christ does not disregard the former law. He came, not to abolish the Law but to fulfill it (5:17). Hence, the Matthean Christ cites the Scriptures (Old Testament) more frequently than does the Christ of any other Gospel. He verifies his intention and his mission to bring the old covenant to full stature.

Second, this Christ frequently nuances the Law for his audience. It is not just the poor, but the poor in spirit, who are blessed; not just the hungry, but those who hunger and thirst for justice who will receive their fill.[18] Disciples of Matthew's Christ are *not obliged to pay taxes* for the upkeep of the Temple or for the support of the Roman government, but *they are instructed to pay them to avoid controversy or offense* (17:24-27). And, given the legitimate authority of the Scribes and Pharisees, they are counseled to observe what the latter command, but to avoid following their example (23:1-2). As ideal and transforming as the New Law is, the Matthean Christ gives it much nuance, showing careful sensitivity to the concrete issues facing his hearers.[19]

So significant is the New Law for the disciple's life under God's reign, that the Matthean Christ takes several steps to secure its continued mediation. After Peter's confession of faith at Caesarea-Philippi, where the Marcan Christ simply responds with a teaching that the Son of Man must suffer, the Matthean Christ affirms Peter (calling him "blessed" by the heavenly Father) and gives Peter the "keys to the kingdom," with authority to "bind and to loose" (16:16-19).[20] Further, while instructing the disciples about the constant need to forgive one another, he seeks to ensure fidelity by laying down a process for administering fraternal correction and by pledging that whatever the Church binds or looses on earth will be bound and loosed in heaven (18:15-35).[21]

The reader of Matthew's Gospel cannot but see the New Law as central to Matthew's account and see Jesus clearly as the divine Lawgiver. That Law and Jesus' ministry are meant to guide the disciple safely and effectively in the deeper ways of living God's life under God's reign. It is that Law, enunciated by him who is both the new King of Israel and Light to the Gentiles, which holds all persons together in the life of Jesus' God and Father. And so Matthew, presents Jesus in this image as the lasting way in which the risen Christ addresses his followers. For while the Marcan Christ commissioned the disciples to heal, the Christ of Matthew, in full power, returned to the mountain with these final instructions: "Make disciples of all nations,...teaching them to observe all that I have commanded you. And behold, I am with you always, until the end of the age" (28:18-20).[22]

Jesus is the New Moses, giving the New Law to all who hear him. Through the authority he bestowed on Peter and those gathered with him, the Matthean Christ guides all peoples and unites them with himself. In that way, all can live under God's reign and be one in sharing God's life.

The Christ of the Gospel of Luke

The Christ of Luke's Gospel presents himself to us from still another perspective. In Luke's Jesus, one meets, not primarily the faithful and suffering Servant of Yahweh, not primarily the powerful healer and exorcist, nor principally God's chosen universal King and Lawmaker, but God's prophetic advocate of the poor, the anointed prophet of God's own compassion and mercy. Luke's Jesus depicts the joy of salvation as emanating from the generous living and sharing in Godly compassion and merciful forgiveness.[23]

THE LUCAN CHRIST: PROPHETIC ADVOCATE OF THE POOR[24]
Jesus has come to bring mercy to and to call forth justice for the poor. This dimension of Jesus' mission resounds throughout the first two chapters, the infancy narrative, of this Gospel. Like that of Matthew's Gospel, this narrative serves as prologue and preview of the book proper. And so, Luke anticipates the mission of Jesus in the canticle of praise placed on the lips of his mother:

> My soul proclaims the greatness of the Lord.... He
> has thrown down rulers from their thrones but has
> lifted up the lowly. The hungry he has filled with

good things; the rich he has sent away empty. He
has helped Israel his servant, remembering his
promise of mercy (1:46a, 52-54).

And Luke continues the theme in the canticle of Zechariah,
father of John the Baptist:

Blessed be the Lord, the God of Israel, for he has
visited and brought redemption to his people.... He
has raised up a horn for our salvation...to show
mercy to our fathers.... And you, child, will be
called prophet of the Most High, for you will go
before the Lord to prepare his ways,...because of the
tender mercy of our God by which the daybreak
from on high[25] will visit us.... (1:68-78).

Luke's Christ is destined to express the compassion and mercy
of God.

The fulfillment of this vision of Christ and his mission plays out
clearly in the Gospel proper. Luke's record of Christ's initial
proclamation regarding the presence of the reign of God contrasts
with the account in Mark (1:15) and Matthew (4:17) because it is
directed toward the poor: "The Spirit of the Lord is upon me. To
proclaim Good News to the poor he has anointed me" (4:18).[26] The
contrast continues: Luke's Christ, like Matthew's, teaches that God
blesses the poor and the hungry but, unlike the Christ of Matthew,
does not qualify these terms. Thus, Luke leaves his reader to
understand that God, through Jesus, intends his blessing precisely
for those suffering from material poverty and physical hunger.[27]

Luke's image of Christ as champion of the poor becomes
sharper as Jesus counsels his listeners to "invite the poor, the
crippled, the lame, the blind" to their banquets instead of inviting
the wealthy, for then, indeed, "will you be blessed because of their
inability to repay you. You will be repaid at the resurrection of the
just" (14:13f).[28] In fact, one's attitudes toward and treatment of the
poor have eternal significance. In this regard, the Lucan Christ is
especially stern with the wealthy who neglect the poor (16:19-31)[29]

but unambiguously affirms the salvation of those converts who are generous with their possessions (18:24-30; 19:1-10; 21:1-4).[30] Whereas poverty had once been seen as a sign of God's displeasure, the Lucan Christ firmly communicates his twofold conviction that poverty can leave one freer to enjoy God's blessing and that God, in Jesus, is working to alleviate the lot of the poor.

THE LUCAN CHRIST: PROPHET OF GOD'S COMPASSION AND MERCY

The image of Christ as prophetic advocate of the poor, while central to the vision of the author of the third Gospel, is in fact an expression of a much deeper image. Luke's Christ is primarily the prophet of God's unlimited mercy and compassionate forgiveness. For Jesus, God's mercy is unconditional; it transforms sinners into saints; it extends to all in need and is measured only by need and repentance. This message is made clear as Jesus, dining with Simon the pharisee, instructs him about the source and genuineness of the loving actions of a penitent woman. She loves much because she has been forgiven much. Mercy has transformed her (7:36-50)[31]. The message unfolds further in the parable of the "Good Samaritan" (recorded only by Luke alone).[32] This story challenges all who hear it to recognize that true mercy, God's mercy, must be extended to foreigners as well as to one's countrymen (10:25-37). Finally, only in Luke does Jesus tell the stories of the woman searching for the lost coin and of the father eager to bestow forgiveness on his returning wayward son. Both narratives intend not only to evoke a sense of God's relentless and unconditional mercy, but also to challenge the hearer to find joy in forgiving others in like manner (15:9f, 31f).[33] Because mercy is the most salient feature of the Lucan Christ's disposition, Luke leaves us with a picture of the compassion of Christ on the cross, pledging the repentant thief: "Behold, I say to you, this day you will be with me in paradise" (23:43).[34] The very being of Christ, established forever in his death, is compassionate mercy. It is through compassion and mercy that Jesus, the prophetic voice of God, announces and brings about the reign of God in the new age.

THE LUCAN CHRIST: A PERSON OF PRAYER

Concomitant with his overriding concern for the poor and the neglected, the outcast and the sinner, the Lucan Christ is characterized by a profound and constant attentiveness to God. Again, more than in any other Gospel, the Christ of Luke's Gospel stands out as a person of prayer.

Already in the infancy narratives, Jesus is pictured as being deeply occupied with his transcendent Father. He is offered to God in the temple and is understood by Simeon as having a unique God-given destiny (2:22-35). At the age of twelve, remaining in the temple without his parents' prior knowledge, he confounds Mary and Joseph with the question: "Why were you looking for me? Did you not know that I must be in my Father's house?" (2:48-50).

It is not surprising, therefore, that prayer stands forth as a most frequent and significant activity of Jesus. It provides an indispensable avenue for his developing communion with God; it becomes the principal context for the decisions which he makes concerning his unique ministry. All his important decisions find their origin in prayer. He receives confirmation of his vocation while praying after his baptism (3:21-22). He enters the desert, a place of meditation and of confrontation with Satan, thereby deepening his vocational commitment (4:1-13). Before choosing his closest followers, he spends the night in prayer (6:12). As Jesus' ministry unfolds, personal prayer provides the occasions for his speaking with his disciples of his forthcoming passion (9:18), for his transfiguration and his conversation with Moses and Elijah concerning his exodus[35] to be accomplished in Jerusalem (9:28-36), and for his instructing his disciples on prayer itself (11:1-4). Finally, as his time on earth is about to end, he speaks of having prayed for Peter and for the disciple's fidelity (22:32). He makes his way to the garden to pray "as was his custom" (22:39-42), and ultimately hands his life over to God with a prayer from the cross: "Father, into your hands I commend my spirit" (23:46). Not only is the Lucan Jesus a "Man for others," a "Prophet of God's compassion and mercy"; he is also, and more deeply, a "Man of God." In prayer, he found the inspiration and the origin of the ministry of care which touched and healed the hearts of many. In prayer he found communion with his God, whom he named "Father."

THE LUCAN CHRIST: ANOINTED BY THE SPIRIT OF GOD

Finally, Luke's Christ, more than the Christ of any other Gospel, is fashioned and empowered by the Spirit of God,[36] the Spirit who often appears in the context of prayer. For Luke, the Spirit is decisively active at Jesus' conception.[37] The virgin conceives because, in the angel's words to Mary, "the Holy Spirit will come upon you and the power of the Most High will overshadow you" (1:34f.).[38] That Holy Spirit strengthens Jesus for ministry at his baptism (3:22) and fills him and leads him into the desert (4:1) where he is tempted, struggling with his calling (4:1-13). The Spirit directs him and renews him more deeply for his ministry (4:14), inspiring him to initiate his ministry with a proclamation of the new age of God's reign (4:18-21). That same Spirit empowers him to recognize and praise the ways of God (10:21)[39] as that new age unfolds. Hence the Lucan Jesus assures his disciples of God's eagerness to share the Spirit with them if only they would ask (11:13),[40] and he declares that the Spirit will give them courage to remain faithful under trial (12:12).[41]

For Luke's audience, there could be no doubt that the words and work of Jesus originated in the Spirit of God. His readers would have to understand that the Spirit inspired Jesus in his calling to bring compassion and justice to the poor, merciful forgiveness to all. The reader could not miss the fact that Jesus' prayer enabled him to receive this Gift of God, not only for Jesus' benefit, but for the accomplishment of Jesus' God-given ministry and God-given destiny. No wonder then that the centrality of the Spirit and the gift of forgiveness are underscored with finality as the risen Christ pledges to send this Spirit, the promise of the Father, upon his disciples as he approaches the moment of his ascension into heaven (24:48f.).[42] For Luke, Jesus, anointed and empowered by the Spirit as the prophet of God's compassion and mercy, the advocate of the poor, is God's emissary sent to share that same Spirit of power, mercy and justice with all who believe.

The Christ of the Gospel of John

By far the greatest diversity in imaging Jesus appears, not from contrasts drawn between the Gospels of Mark, Matthew and Luke, but by noting the radical differences between the Johannine description of Jesus, on the one hand, and the descriptions offered in the synoptic Gospels, on the other. For the reader of the fourth Gospel is introduced to the mystery of Christ, not at his baptism (as in Mark), nor through an unfolding of his genealogy (Matthew), nor by way of the accounts of his conception and birth (Matthew and Luke), but through a reflection upon the eternal God, God's pre-existent Word and God's action in the world through that Word. Where the synoptics emphasize Christ's origin in history, humanly conceived though the action of God's Spirit, the author of the fourth Gospel stresses Christ's origin in eternity, divinely pre-existing, being in himself God's eternal and creative Word and Wisdom[43] (1:1-3). The human Jesus is the Word of God made flesh (1:14). "As the Father's only Son," he reveals God's glory, God's visible saving presence and power;[44] he enjoys in himself the "fullness of grace and truth," God's loving mercy;[45] and he is truly divine, one with the transcendent God himself.

Hence, the fourth Gospel begins where the synoptic Gospels leave off. The Johannine Christ is introduced quickly, with a multiplicity of titles, as he enters his public ministry. He is recognized immediately as the "Lamb of God" who takes away the sin of the world (1:29, 36), Son of God (1:34, 49), Rabbi (1:38, 49), Messiah (1:41) and King of Israel (1:49), names which the disciples of the synoptic Gospels only gradually came to apply to Jesus. The author of the fourth Gospel, however, presumes his readers are familiar with these understandings of Jesus. The intention of this author is to lead the reader to a deeper understanding of the mystery of Jesus' identity. Therefore, in response to the disciples' curiosity in asking, "Where do you dwell?" (1:38), Jesus invites them to "come and see" (1:39), ultimately promising: "You will see the sky opened and the angels of God ascending and descending on the Son of Man" (1:51). In that statement, the author of the fourth Gospel clearly declares the intention of his writing: There is a previously unrecognized depth to Jesus which he wishes to lead the reader to appreciate.

THE JOHANNINE CHRIST: PRE-EXISTENT WORD, ETERNAL WISDOM

The Johannine author uses several interwoven themes and images to unveil the identity of Jesus. First, Jesus is the manifestation of *God's pre-existent Word, the eternal and creative Wisdom of God,* in human flesh. He is not just God's emissary sent to deliver the Word of God (in Mark), nor is he simply the supreme Lawgiver, able to communicate this word on his own authority (in Matthew), but he is that Word in itself, the embodiment of God's own creative Wisdom.[46] As Wisdom is God's firstborn, poured forth from above before the creation of the world (Prov. 8:22-31), so Jesus tells Nicodemus that he himself is the one who comes from above, able to speak the words of God and to give the Spirit of God (Jn. 3:13, 31ff). As Wisdom spreads a table, and calls from the heights to one who lacks understanding: "Come, eat of my food and drink of the wine I have mixed! Forsake foolishness that you may live; advance in the way of understanding" (Prov. 9:2-11)[47], so Jesus, speaking with the Samaritan woman at Jacob's well, claims: "Everyone who drinks this water will be thirsty again; the water I will give will become in him a spring of water welling up to eternal life" (Jn. 4:13-14).[48] He restates his identity in the "bread of life" discourse: "It was not Moses who gave you bread from heaven; my Father gives you the true bread from heaven. I am the bread of life; whoever comes to me will never hunger, and whoever believes in me will never thirst" (6:32-35). And just as Wisdom, present at the creation of light (Prov. 8:22 with Gn. 1:3), is the aura of the power of God, the splendor of everlasting light (Wis. 7:25-26) and a guiding light which freed Israel from the dark oppression of the Egyptians (Wis. 10:15-17),[49] so the Johannine Jesus claims not only to embody but also to be saving Wisdom and penetrating light: "I am the light of the world. Whoever follows me will not walk in darkness, but will have the light of life" (Jn. 8:12).

THE JOHANNINE CHRIST: REVELATION OF GOD'S GLORY

A second interwoven and complementary theme which speaks of Jesus' identity in the fourth Gospel images Jesus *as the revelation of God's glory,* the revelation of God's presence in saving power. The distinctiveness of John's perspective shines forth clearly in that the Jesus of the fourth Gospel works not miracles or wonders, but signs. The goal of these signs is not so much to evoke wonder or amazement,[50] or to reveal the kingdom,[51] but to manifest God's glory residing in the person and action of Jesus. Thus, Jesus transforms water into wine, performing "the first of his signs...and so revealed his glory" with the result that "his disciples began to believe in him" (2:1-11). He heals the son of a royal official (4:46-54), cures a paralytic (5:1-18), and anticipates the new Passover by crossing the Sea of Galilee and by multiplying loaves (6:1-21)[52]. Each sign either leads to fuller belief in Jesus (4:50, 53; 5:15; 6:14-15), or becomes the reason why some refuse to believe (5:9b-16; 6:41, 52, 61-66). This moves Jesus to challenge even Peter's fidelity, to which Peter responds: "Lord, to whom shall we go? You have the words of eternal life. We have come to believe and are convinced that you are the holy one of God" (6:68-69).

In the same pattern, and with mounting controversy,[53] the Johannine Christ shows that he is Light for the world (already proclaimed in the previous chapter[54]) by giving sight to a man blind from birth (9:5-7). Finally, the Wisdom theme, Christ's work of manifesting God's glory, and the divided reactions to him, reach a climax in a quick succession of events. First, Jesus claims: "I am the resurrection and the life; whoever believes in me, even if he dies, will live; and whoever lives and believes in me will never die" (11:25-26). He then reveals the glory of God in raising Lazarus (11:4,40-44). Finally, and almost predictably, he either receives an acknowledgment of faith (11:27, 45) or becomes the object of a concerted plot to kill him (11:46-53). For the Johannine author, however, there is only the truth: Jesus is the revelation of God's glory, God's visible saving power for all who believe.

THE JOHANNINE CHRIST: THE **ONE WHO IS**
A third image distinguishing the Johannine Christ from the Christ of the synoptics emerges in Jesus' naming himself as "I AM," the same divine name Yahweh revealed to Moses (Ex. 3:14).[55] In this vein, Jesus states "I AM...the bread of life" (6:35), "...the light of the world" (8:12), "...the gate" (10:7,9), "...the good (model) shepherd" (10:11,14), "...the resurrection and the life" (11:25), "...the way, and the truth, and the life" (14:6), and "...the true vine" (15:1). Jesus makes clear the importance of these statements in a dialogue with his adversaries, affirming that "unless you come to believe that I

AM, you will surely die in your sins" (8:24). If doubt should persist, his death will confirm that identity: "When you lift up the Son of Man, then you will realize that I AM" (8:28). His is an identity which transcends history: "Before Abraham even came into existence, I AM" (8:58). The Johannine Christ is the *transcendent saving God of Israel's history.*

The three distinctive characteristics of the Johannine Jesus that disclose his profound identity in God unfold further and show themselves to be even more deeply interwoven, in the second half of the fourth Gospel (chapters 13-21), the portion which biblical theologians refer to as the "Book of Glory."[56] As the author allows the revelation to deepen, it becomes clear that Jesus' pledge that he will not leave his disciples orphans but will come back to them (14:18) foretells the very personal manner in which Jesus is and will remain the transcendent source of salvation for all who believe in him. This pledge of ongoing personal presence serves to unify the distinctive characteristics of the Johannine Jesus. This can be illustrated in three steps.

First, Jesus invites the disciples to be one with him, living in him and letting him live in them, by living in his love (15:4-5,9). This call expresses the heart of the invitation of Wisdom, the image in which Jesus has been promising nourishment and life from the beginning. Thus Jesus/Wisdom is the very model of love: "Love one another as I have loved you" (13:34).[57]

The love which reveals the heart of Wisdom, however, needs further qualification. It is not merely a romantic love, but love unto sacrifice. The disciples are called to die with Christ for one another (15:12f). At the same time, Jesus sees the disclosing of this way of love to his disciples as an act establishing deep bonds of personal union between himself and them. In revealing the depth of his love, he entrusts himself to them, regarding them clearly as friends not servants (15:15). What is more, in this love one sees and experiences God for, as Jesus has told Philip, the one who sees Jesus sees the Father (14:8-9). It is not surprising, then, that this invitation and command of love and of sacrifice unto death is voiced again, this time by the risen Lord to Peter as a prerequisite for

Peter's commission to lead Christ's disciples (21:15-19).[58] The eternal Word of God, the Johannine Christ, tells the disciple that the way to everlasting communion with him and with the Father is the journey of Christlike love. In that love the disciple, even now, lives in the presence of Jesus, eternal Wisdom.

Second, the Johannine Jesus, as the Christ of Luke, promises the Spirit whom the Father will send in his name (14:15-17, 26; 16:12). But unlike the Lucan Christ, the Christ of the fourth Gospel also sends the Spirit of himself (15:26; 16:7).[59] That Spirit will be within the disciples and will remain with them. He will remind the disciples of all that Jesus (Wisdom) has taught (14:26), and will guide them in the way of truth, especially in times of struggle and trial (16:12f), as the name "Advocate" indicates.

For the Johannine author, Jesus "hands over his Spirit" already in his death as "blood and water" flow from his side (19:30,34), and bestows this Gift in full measure on the evening of the day of the resurrection. Appearing in the upper room, Jesus, in full power, breathes forth the Spirit upon the disciples with the commission to forgive sin (20:19-23). And so the Spirit becomes fully alive within the disciples, uniting them with Jesus in an abiding manner. Through that Spirit, Jesus himself remains personally active, the living and saving Word for his disciples in every age and circumstance.

Third, if Jesus worked signs of glory, showing forth the saving presence and power of God in his ministry, so in his passion and death he is to show his glory all the more. This is the "hour of his glorification" (12:23f, 28f.), the moment of his being lifted up with the result that "when it does happen you may believe that I AM" (13:19), the moment when he will receive the glory he had with the Father "before the world began" (17:1-5). Thus, the Johannine Christ continues to identify himself as "I AM." As soldiers, inquiring about Jesus of Nazareth, come to arrest him, he, unlike the Suffering Servant of Mark who is resigned and often silent, stands before these soldiers with strength, stating, "I AM (HE)," causing the soldiers to collapse in their weakness before him (18:4-8).

As it is with each of the Johannine themes depicting Christ, so the revelation of Christ's glory and of Jesus' identity in God, HE WHO IS, also reach their apex in the resurrection narratives. After the disciples (Thomas being absent) see and recognize Jesus as Lord, Thomas himself meets the risen One only to be firmly challenged: "Put your finger here and see my hands..., be not unbelieving, but believe." Belief, at this point, requires full recognition of WHO JESUS IS. Hence Thomas confesses Jesus' identity: "My Lord and my God" (20:27f), expressing the full flowering of a Johannine disciple's faith. At Cana, the disciples began to believe in Jesus, who showed forth his glory in an initial sign. In the upper room, the disciple believes fully as Jesus' glory is fully revealed.

For the author of the fourth Gospel, Jesus is Lord and God, the eternal Word/Wisdom who reveals and is one with the Father, the transcendent God and saving presence, forever alive, bringing eternal life to all who believe. The reader of this Gospel cannot but recognize his transcendent saving presence. He is personally present even now within every disciple in the power of his living love and the energy of his Spirit, uniting all with HIMSELF WHO IS. Hence, the Gospel ends with an affirmation from the lips of Jesus, not just in behalf of the Eleven, but in behalf of every reader: "(Thomas,) have you come to believe because you have seen me? Blessed are those who have not seen and have believed" (20:29f).

The Gospel Images of Christ
and Doing Christology

Having analyzed the four differing ways in which the four evangelists have viewed Jesus, we can now return to the question of the nature of Christology. Our effort here will be to make explicit some of the elements and dynamics of theology implicit in the work of the evangelists, the fruit of which we have just considered. What we intend here is simply a first step; we will continue these efforts throughout this study. In this chapter we will seek to highlight the theological dynamics operative in the evangelists' inspired yet deeply personal activity as they crafted four distinct portraits of

Jesus: 1) that of beliefs and tradition; 2) that of the personal experience of the transcendent which lies at the origin of images of God and Christ; 3) that of the transforming nature of the experience of God; and 4) that of the unity of Christ and of faith within the various images.

IMAGES OF CHRIST - BELIEFS - TRADITION

In light of the analysis of the nature of theology as delineated in Chapter 1 above, the articulated images of Christ presented by each Gospel would best be described as beliefs. They express, not an initial faith experience of Christ, but a faith experience already reflected upon, correlated to a variety of themes within the Jewish tradition and interpreted in the light of that tradition. These portraits of Christ, therefore, are the fruit of the process of doing theology, or in this case, doing Christology. As such, they illustrate well a significant aspect of that process. The evangelist, a theologian and believer seeking to interpret his faith experience, necessarily relies upon and makes good use of a prior tradition which itself has interpreted and articulated a vibrant faith experience. In effect, what this believer, the evangelist, is doing is coming to explicit consciousness of the fact that the transcendent God, who had acted and revealed the transcendent Self in an earlier age to the believer's ancestors in the faith, has clearly acted again. The believer is explicitly recognizing that that God has acted *in continuity with the past* and yet has acted and revealed the transcendent Self *in a superlative way in and through Jesus*. Doing Christology involves the believer in the process 1) of retrieving a tradition, 2) of allowing it to shape one's understanding in the present, and 3) of updating and expanding that tradition to include the more recent and fuller experiences of God. The process results in the articulation of a fuller, richer, and more compelling set of beliefs reflecting the "contemporary" faith experience of the evangelist and his immediate audience.

IMAGES OF CHRIST - EXPERIENCE OF GOD

Further, it is clear that what drives this process is the fact that the interpreter-evangelist has truly encountered the transcendent God, the saving God, alive in and through Jesus. This is true whether he has met God *in Jesus' action* (e.g., in healing or exorcizing), *in*

Jesus' teachings (e.g., in mediating the new divine Law), or ultimately *in Jesus himself* (e.g., as eternal Word of God dwelling among us). Through Jesus, the transcendent longings of the believer's mind and heart, reaching for light, healing, love, and life beyond what the finite world could give, have found sustained comfort and promise. Through Jesus, self-transcending longings have met the transcendent saving God. The images of Christ seek to interpret and clarify, as well as affirm, the manner in which God has mediated God's own saving presence to the believer. As the believer's needs and longings have taken different shape, so God's responses in the living Christ have also taken different shape. And just as all theology seeks to interpret a believer's personal and living faith experience of the Transcendent using different images and/or descriptions of the Transcendent, so the evangelist has come to interpret a genuinely personal experience of God in and through Jesus, offering differing portraits of Jesus. Hence the writer is truly seeking to express the fact that it is God who has visited the believer in Christ and that God has mediated salvation through Christ in a multiplicity of ways.

IMAGES OF CHRIST - PERSONAL TRANSFORMATION
Further still, the experience of God is always transforming. The healing, the light, and the insight; the comfort, the sense of profound love, the peace of God's presence: all such experiences of God inspire a change in a believer's way of life.[60] Thus, miracles of healing not only affect the believer's physical well-being, but they also open the heart in gratitude, moving and freeing the recipient for discipleship. Proclamation of the New Law not only challenges persons but invites and motivates them to walk concretely in the power of God's reign. The witness of dedicated advocacy for the poor and compassionate mercy for all motivate and empower persons to empty themselves in an inclusive and merciful love reflective of the divine life. The opportunity to place one's wholehearted belief, trust and love in creative Wisdom Incarnate satisfies one's deepest hungers and gives one a taste of eternal life now. The believer is changed by the experience of God in Christ and those changes are reflected in the concrete way of life which the believer subsequently embraces. Each way of encountering God in Christ, each distinctive way of perceiving Christ, has had

transforming effects upon evangelist and disciple alike. Hence these various depictions of Christ capture not only God's visitation of God's people, but also the way people experience themselves transformed by Jesus for fuller life in the world and in the community as he speaks and acts in their behalf.

MANY IMAGES - ONE CHRIST - ONE FAITH
Finally, the fact that each of the four Gospels presents somewhat distinctive images of Jesus suggests that one need not make explicit every aspect of Christ's life, teaching, ministry, and personal identity in order to attain saving insight into him or to encounter the saving God who acts in and through him. Some of the dimensions of Jesus' life and person, highlighted in one Gospel, merely form the background of the other. This fact suggests that genuine faith may legitimately encounter the living God through Jesus in a variety of ways, each way being sufficient in itself as an avenue of God's self-disclosure and saving action. Each way in which Jesus mediates God's love in itself effectively brings the believer into contact with that love. When God discloses anything of God's intentions in and through Christ, it is the one and same God who leads; it is the true God whom one meets. Likewise, in each distinctive action of Jesus, it is the one true Jesus who calls the individual to have genuine faith in him.

The fact that the multiplicity of images each mediate the same Jesus, together with the power resident in him, has relevance for the believer and for the development of personal faith today. For the disciple of today, like the persons comprising the evangelists' audiences, can and will meet Christ in a variety of circumstances. In those circumstances, he or she is likely to be struck by certain ways in which Jesus has acted or by certain teachings which Jesus has offered, but not by other of his actions or teachings. The one image will give the believer genuine access to Christ and to the transcendent God acting in and through him even now. At that moment, the specific manner of envisioning Christ which has such strong appeal is all that is necessary for the disciple to be touched by God and be further transformed in faith.

On the other hand, no one way in which Jesus reveals himself is totally adequate, either as a representation of Jesus or as an image of the transcendent God. Many portraits are necessary to represent the true Christ and the fullness of God's self-revelation in him. Many images are necessary to express the fullness of the Gospel tradition, the tradition which as a whole grounds the development of the beliefs of the Church. Each image refines the other, corrects the other, and amplifies the other.

This fact, too, has relevance for the contemporary believer. Sooner or later, the circumstances of one's life and the particularity of one's deepest needs and longings will change. At that time, the disciple will be asking something new and further of Christ and of the Transcendent. As God in Christ responds, God will act in new ways. The disciple will need and/or fashion a new image of God and of Christ as an expression of his or her further experience of the saving Lord.[61] Ultimately, he or she will come to understand that no image is fully satisfying; for it is not an image which one really seeks but rather salvation through a deepening relationship with the transcendent God in God's Self.[62]

But where is the ecclesial element in "doing Christology?" (We noted in Chapter 1 that all theology is ecclesial.) And why did each evangelist describe Jesus in the particular fashion of his own particular Gospel and not in other perspectives? The foregoing discussion does not answer these questions; rather it raises them. The next two chapters are dedicated to shedding some light on these important dynamics of the process. But before we turn to these issues, we encourage the reader to reflect upon the following questions. Again, they are meant to assist the reader both to process the foregoing material and to become more fully engaged in doing Christology as a personal and faith-filled task.

Questions for Reflection

1. Which of the images of Jesus described in this chapter attracts you the most? Why?

2. Are you aware of other ways (beyond those given in this chapter) in which any of the Gospel writers have described Jesus? If so, what meaning do you find in those descriptions?

3. In what types of situations and/or for what types of audiences would Mark's portrait of Jesus be most apt to inspire faith? What groups of persons would more likely seek Jesus as depicted in Mark? (Please reflect upon and respond to the same questions in reference to the portraits of Jesus of each of the other three evangelists.)

4. What significance do you see in the evangelists' uses of incidents, teaching and images from the Old Testament in their efforts to describe Jesus? What passages taken from the Old Testament have helped you deepen your understanding of Jesus?

5. Have you known anyone who has spoken of a personally striking experience of Jesus? How have they described Christ? How has that experience affected, even transformed, his or her life?

6. What has been your own experience of Christ? How would you express that experience?

CHAPTER 3

The Communities of the Synoptic Gospels: Shaping the Biblical Tradition (1)

The four Gospel portraits of Jesus, etched in the series of images as described in the previous chapter, manifest a striking diversity in their unity and an equally striking unity in their diversity. As articulations of the beliefs of both the authors of the Gospels and also of the readers/hearers of these writings, these Gospel pictures of Jesus indicate that the Christians who embraced the Good News of Jesus were both one and yet diverse in their ways of meeting Jesus and the God who acted in and through him. The shape of the Gospel tradition itself is both one and fourfold. Indeed, it might more properly be said that the Gospels reflect four traditions, four sets of beliefs "handed on," in one.

The focus of this chapter is to examine the manner in which the traditions reflected in each of these Gospels developed. How is it that different portraits of the one Jesus came to be drawn? What resources did the various authors have at hand? Why did the authors cast the same story of Jesus, healing and teaching, crucified and risen, with differing emphases? In sum, what factors and purposes lay behind the actual shaping of these traditions as we now possess them?

The plan of this chapter takes its lead from a set of observations made in chapter 1. There we mentioned that the articulation of one's personal faith, in the form of statements of belief, takes on a public character, becomes a shared expression of faith and unites a community in its faith and life. The community, driven by a common faith articulated in a set of common expressions of that faith, of necessity becomes a community of beliefs.[1] We could presume then that the role of the community in generating statements of belief and in shaping the Gospel traditions would be most significant.

However, we are not left merely to presumption in this matter. Contemporary approaches toward understanding biblical literature in general, and most especially the distinct literary form we know as "gospel," establish clearly that the roles of the various communities of believers are a most significant influence upon the shape of the different Gospel traditions. In this light, current scholarship regards the four Gospels as works of literature written specifically for people of faith by people of faith. It notes that their overall purpose aims at stimulating and strengthening the life of faith and beliefs of committed Christians.

This approach to the Gospels carries with it two immediate implications: First the Gospels cannot be regarded primarily as chronologies or historical records whose purpose would be to present a biographical sketch of the life of Jesus; they are far from being the kind of historical records or journalistic accounts of events of Jesus' own time which contemporary readers might expect. Second, the Gospels cannot be thought of primarily as apologetic writings; that is, writings whose goal is to defend a community's faith and beliefs before nonbelievers. Thus, they are not intended to offer a proof of the supernatural character of Jesus' miracles, nor are they intended to be a demonstration of Jesus' divinity, a would-be effort designed (hopefully) to bring about the conversion of nonbelievers in a compelling manner.

Conversely, this approach does require that we understand the Gospels precisely as writings which, on the one hand, strive to preserve the memory of Jesus for those who have been touched by him, and which, on the other hand, strive to inspire and strengthen the faith of a group of people in their own present struggle. Much of their effectiveness in this regard arises from the fact that these writings are made up of shorter episodes, stories, which might be easily remembered and narrated, stories which have an inspirational, challenging, or consoling impact. Much of their effectiveness also stems from the fact that, in telling these stories, the narrator could easily engage in a process of selecting especially pertinent materials from his abundant sources, adding interpretations and making applications which would help the listener more immediately perceive the relevance of Jesus for his or her own very real, and perhaps trying, situation. Put together as one unfolding story, these narratives, then, would have the capacity to draw the reader into the conscious presence of the Lord, the One Lord whom the reader had affirmed as risen, alive and present to the churches, and whom that same reader sought to recall in his or her present-day crises. In this fashion, these stories become vehicles through which the listener meets the Transcendent God, acting once again, calling, strengthening and sustaining the hearer with ongoing love in and through Christ.

It is with this understanding of the Gospels, then, that this chapter is written. Our effort will aim at unfolding the character of the diverse Christian communities and at discerning their precise influence upon the formation of each Gospel tradition. This effort will provide the perspective and context in which the questions which we asked at the outset of this chapter can be addressed.

This effort, however, will not be as simple as it might first seem. For the early Christian communities did not generate the elaborate and intricately composed writings which we know as Gospels overnight. Rather, as the very complexity of the Gospel writings suggests, these compositions represent expressions of faith which have matured only by passing through a series of reflective stages spanning a significant period of time. Biblical scholars, using what has become known as the "historical-critical" method of interpreting the Scriptures,[2] distinguish three such stages, each with its own importance for, and influence upon, these final statements of belief, the written Gospels themselves. In brief, we can refer to these stages as 1) the time and situation during the earthly life of Jesus,[3] 2) the time and situation within the church during which the early disciples and first Christians spread the "Good News" of Jesus' life, ministry, death and resurrection[4] largely through preaching and catechizing[5], and 3) the situation reflected within the particular Gospel itself,[6] the modifications within the composition of the Gospels which would have been particularly influenced by the time and situation of the churches when each of the four Gospels was composed.[7]

In terms of the historical-critical method of interpreting the Scriptures, then, the purpose of this chapter will focus on the development of the New Testament Christian traditions largely during the third period of its growth, with some attention also being given to the second period. It is during this time that the original revelation given in Jesus was received by diverse communities, reflected upon again and again, and eventually recorded in Gospel form. It is during these periods that the communities, and especially the evangelists in interaction with their respective communities, crafted the specific formulations of the Gospel traditions as we have them.[8]

Mindful of the nature and purpose, as well as the complexities of the formation, of Gospel literature, we can better delineate the overall purpose of this chapter.

Our primary purpose will be to show how the portrait of Jesus, drawn by each evangelist, was specifically tailored to meet the historical needs of each respective Gospel community; or, from another perspective, to show how each community itself influenced the process of interpreting Jesus precisely because of its need for God's saving love in its own distinct historical dilemma and challenges. We are concerned, primarily, with the Gospel communities' roles in *the shaping of the tradition.*

Our secondary, but no less significant, purpose will be to broaden and deepen our grasp of the portraits of Jesus as presented in the previous chapter by highlighting each community's image of Jesus as the Master who shapes disciples, as its Leader who fashions for it a "way of discipleship," as the ever-present living Lord who engages the community in the very fabric of its own concrete journey of faith and life in its very real historical setting in the world. In accomplishing this purpose, we will be building upon the material which we set forth in the previous chapter, material that sets forth *the shape of the tradition.*

As we will see, this latter dimension of each Gospel's portrait of Jesus, the Jesus who fashions a way of discipleship, also corresponds to the specific historical needs of each respective community. It too grows out of and reflects the developing concrete faith-filled life of the community, itself seeking to find salvation in and through Christ in its own day. It is clear then that this secondary aim, more fully and adequately to draw the portraits of Jesus, will serve to show, even more forcefully that the journey of a given community's life played a significant role in its interpreting its experience of God alive in and through Jesus and in its crafting images of the Lord. At the same time, this effort will serve to underscore the fact that a true portrait of Jesus always involves, not only images of Jesus in relationship to "the One Who sent him," but also Jesus' living, engaging and effective relationship to "those to whom he has been sent."

The plan according to which we will develop this chapter, then, will consist in by describing each of the communities for which the synoptic Gospels were written.[9] After introducing each Gospel by noting the various dates and places of composition of that Gospel, together with the sources which each evangelist had at his disposal in constructing his work, we will offer a description of the life-setting of the specific community or communities of believers for which the particular Gospel was composed. Here we will attend especially to the diverse needs, challenges and struggles which each community had to face in order to preserve and deepen its faith-life in communion with its crucified and risen Lord.[10] Second, we will seek to unfold the relationship of the life-situation of the community and its struggles to the portrait of Jesus which the particular evangelist crafted in its behalf, showing how the manner of portraying Jesus served to sustain and foster the faith of the community under consideration. Third, we will show how the evangelist's portrait of Jesus enables the Lord to enter the very fabric of the life of the community, as the Jesus of each specific Gospel defines for each respective community the nature and way of true discipleship, providing it with a series of genuine moral imperatives (binding norms) for Christian living. Finally, we will draw the chapter to a close with some interim conclusions which will serve as a bridge between the two chapters dealing with the roles of the Gospel communities in shaping the four Gospel traditions.

The Marcan Community

The Gospel of Mark was written in and for Jewish and Gentile (non-Jewish) Christians living in Rome.[11] Scholars date the composition of the text prior to the year 70 but after the death of the Apostle Peter (between 64 and 67, during the persecution under Nero).[12] A brief description, therefore, of the Roman Christian community or communities in the late 60's and of their environment at Rome during that same decade will provide significant background for understanding the relationship of the Roman church or churches to the composition of Mark's Gospel.

THE LIFE-SETTING OF THE MARCAN COMMUNITY
A pervasive threat of persecution stood as the dominant characteristic of the life and environment of the Roman Christians during the year 67. The Roman population in general, and imperial authority in particular, held Christians in disregard and looked upon them with an air of suspicion. The fact that Christians had separated themselves from pagan worship played at least some part in this situation. They were readily regarded as irreligious.[13]

The threat of persecution, however, was not merely psychological and social; it was also physical and political. In the year 64, the emperor Nero arrested and persecuted a large number of Christians including Peter and Paul who eventually suffered martyrdom.[14] It would be easy for such an event to repeat itself, especially since the outbreak of war between the Romans and the Jews of Palestine, a war which lasted from 66-70, would have left Jewish Christians in Rome vulnerable to imperial suspicion if not outright persecution in retaliation or revenge.[15]

A second characteristic, and a source of genuine struggle, for Roman Christians concerned their life with one another and with their non-Christian Jewish brothers and sisters. Though Christian communities of Rome consisted largely of Jewish Christians converted by Jewish Christian missionaries (most probably) from the Jerusalem community,[16] these Roman Christian communities did not consist of simply one unified church with a single unified leadership. Rather, many Jewish Christians belonged to separate local house-churches. As a result, these varying communities could profess differing attitudes regarding their own and their Gentile converts' obligations in relationship to their Jewish heritage.[17] Such differences would be intensified as individual communities, through one or two of their more strongly opinionated members, might attempt to influence the beliefs and convictions of members of other groups, thereby instilling painful disharmony both among these Christian communities themselves and also between Christians and Jews with whom the Christian converts were still affiliated.

Further, such disharmony among Christian communities and such tensions between Jewish Christian churches and non-Christian Jews could become politically dangerous. For, while Jewish communities had political and religious acceptance and protection in Rome, Christians, of themselves, had no such status or protection. Hence, when envies, jealousies, or other tensions arose between Jews and Christians, Jewish communities could leave Christians quite vulnerable to imperial suspicion and persecution, simply by excommunicating them from the synagogue or, worse, by betraying them into imperial hands.[18]

Both a sense of imminent persecution at the whim of imperial authorities, on the one hand, and an equally troublesome sense of tension from within various Jewish Christian communities, on the other hand, then, clearly contributed to the overall precariousness of being a Christian in the Roman climate. Both factors of Roman Christian life in the year 67 served to create the context within which Mark composed his Gospel, a Gospel which sought to empower Christian communities to live in fidelity to Christ Jesus and in harmony with one another.

THE MARCAN COMMUNITY AND THE MARCAN PORTRAIT OF JESUS

In the previous chapter we noted that Mark drew his picture of Jesus with decided emphases upon the Lord as Healer/Exorcist and as faithful Suffering Servant/Son of God. Having described the life-situation of the Marcan community, we can readily perceive why Mark underscored these particular dimensions of Jesus' life and mission. On the one hand, the evils of sin, dissoluteness, and the threatening oppression of Roman rule required a divine healer and exorcist if there were to be any hope at all of overcoming such evil. And, in the midst of a society reverencing many "gods," it would be important for Roman Christians to maintain a firm tradition supporting their own faith in Jesus and in Jesus alone, as God's divinely chosen emissary, God's divinely appointed Healer/Exorcist.[19]

On the other hand, the suspicion and rejection of Christians by Roman citizenry together with the constant threat of an outbreak of persecution demanded that Christians face the harsh reality of suffering as the central characteristic of discipleship if they were to survive. By highlighting Jesus as *suffering* Messiah, Mark sought to bolster the Christians' allegiance to their Master, emphasizing the fact that suffering and persecution, far from being *an obstacle to salvation and life*, constituted *the very way to salvation and life*, not only for Jesus but for the disciple. For Mark and for his community Jesus is and must be understood as suffering Messiah, having expressed thereby his fidelity to the Father as the true Son of God. Anyone who wished to come after him "must deny himself, take up his cross, and follow" Jesus (8:34).

THE MARCAN JESUS AND THE WAY OF DISCIPLESHIP[20]

Having recognized the appropriateness of the Marcan portrait of Jesus for the community in Rome, we can now turn our attention to the manner in which the Marcan Jesus calls forth and fashions the life of his disciples. For the image and example of Jesus is of little value unless it effectively shapes and draws forth noticeable patterns of life by which disciples themselves embrace Jesus' life. How does the Marcan Jesus affect the way of life of the disciple? How does this Jesus actively engage his followers so that their lives may be deepened in communion with him?

Scholars have long recognized that Mark presents Jesus instruction of his disciples in two stages. First, Jesus labors to offset an incorrect understanding of himself and of the nature of discipleship (1:1-8:26). Secondly, after disowning inadequate images of his own identity, Jesus begins in earnest to disclose the heart of his identity together with the way of true discipleship (8:27 onward). We will look at each stage of Jesus' teaching, though the second will deserve greater consideration.

Jesus as Healer/Exorcist:
An Inadequate Foundation for the Way of Discipleship
The first stage of Jesus' active efforts to form his disciples is rather peculiar: he performs powerful deeds, but rejects recognition for them. Thus, in the early chapters of the Gospel we read of Jesus' consistent striving to keep his identity secret. Demons recognize him, naming him as the "Holy One of God" (1:24) and "Son of God" (3:11), but Jesus commands them to keep quiet (1:25, 34; 3:12). Jesus heals, but he admonishes all persons to whom he has brought healing to contain their desire to speak of him (1:44); no one should know of the cures he has worked (5:43, see also 7:36). He sends a man whose sight had been restored directly home, instructing him not to go "even into the village" (8:26), while he himself makes concerted efforts to perform his wonders out of the sight of crowds (5:37, 40; 7:33, 8:23).[21]

The effect of all of this is to create confusion among the disciples. They simply do not understand Jesus.[22] And, of course, Mark's intention is to awaken the disciples in Rome to that same fact:[23] Jesus *is* difficult to understand. The true significance of Jesus and of the pattern of his life's journey for the disciples and for their lives is only now about to be disclosed.

Jesus as Suffering Son of God:
The True Foundation for the Way of Discipleship
The second stage of Jesus' explicit challenge to his disciples runs from 8:27 to 10:45.[24] This entire section is unfolded under the perspective of the inevitability of the cross. It consists of three subsections, each initiated by Jesus predicting his forthcoming passion and death.

This portion of the Gospel begins with Jesus first prediction of his passion (8:31-32), is followed by Peter's resistance (8:33), and is completed by Jesus' first challenging instruction to the disciples (8:34b-35). The perspective is sustained through two further predictions of Christ's imminent suffering and death (9:31, 10:33), each followed by further resistances of the apostles (9:33-34, 10:35, 37, 41), and each completed by very pointed commands of the Lord (9:35, 10:38f.). Finally, the entire section concludes with a summary statement which gathers together the entire instruction (10:45), leaving no doubt that Jesus' way must necessarily be the disciple's way: All must live under the shadow of the cross. Thus, Jesus' predictions of his own destiny serve as a prism through which the disciple must understand everything about the life of a follower of Jesus.[25]

These three predictions, moreover, are not merely repetitious; they are developmental: they enable Jesus to apply the meaning of the cross to the varied dimensions of the life of the disciple. Each of the resistances and conflicts among the disciples become opportunities for Jesus to interpret the cross ever more concretely and specifically. In order fully to appreciate this effort of the Marcan Jesus, we will attend to each instruction in detail.

Jesus' **first instruction** is triggered by Peter's bold opposition to any suggestion of the cross of Jesus. In response, Jesus presents his hearers with the overriding principle governing every attitude and every action of the disciple:

> Whoever wishes to come after me must deny himself, take up his cross, and follow me. For whoever wishes to save his life will lose it, but whoever loses his life for my sake and that of the gospel will save it (8:34b-35).[26]

The way of the Son of Man involves a journey to the cross; he finds life through that journey and that cross.[27] The disciple of the Marcan Jesus must follow the Lord along the same path.

To offset any possibility of the disciples' taking this teaching lightly, Jesus concludes by stressing the eternal significance of this teaching:

> Whoever is ashamed of me and of my words in this faithless and sinful generation, the Son of Man will be ashamed when he comes in his Father's glory with the holy angels (8:38).

Indeed, how one lives one's life in the present, amidst all its challenges - and particularly for the Roman Christian in the midst of temptation to escape rejection and persecution by hiding their Christian identity - has everlasting import. And yet, so as not to end on a negative note, the author quickly recalls another word of Jesus: "I solemnly tell you, there are some standing here who will not taste death until they see that the kingdom of God has come in power" (9:1).

Jesus' **second instruction**, triggered, on the one hand by the disciples' inattentiveness to, and fear of, his second prediction of his passion, and, on the other hand, by their excessive concern about their being regarded as "the greatest" (in Jesus' kingdom) leads the Marcan Jesus to apply the cross specifically to the disciples' attitudes toward self-seeking and self-promotion: Anyone who wishes to be first must be the servant of all (9:35) even to the point of serving the most insignificant little child (9:36f).[28] Willingness to walk the path of servanthood and to be regarded as insignificant constitutes, paradoxically, the true way of greatness. In the midst of a community vulnerable to envy and jealousy, indeed an envy and jealousy which apparently led to the betrayal of Peter and Paul, this instruction is no mere "pious saying," no mere counsel for those wishing to ascend to the extraordinary heights of holiness; rather it is an instruction regarding the very integrity and survival of the community, an instruction directed toward safeguarding the very life of the individual and the community as such.

The subsequent reflections of the Lord also must be understood in light of the cross and by way of Jesus' perspective of that "self-denial" which allows for true servant-love.[29] In this framework, the Marcan Jesus continues by reaffirming the pre-Mosaic prohibition of divorce (10:1-12), a practice which was quite acceptable in the Roman society which surrounded the community. The thrust of the teaching is that God empowers partners (10:9) to live servant-love for one another. A true disciple must draw on that power rather than assert a (lesser) self over against his or her partner. Similarly, servant-love must lead one to welcome the most insignificant members of the community, those who, like little children, have absolutely no status and can offer one no recompense for what they receive. One must be willing to be the servant of the lowly and the powerless (10:13-16). And finally, such love calls one to share one's wealth with the needy rather than to seek self-affirmation or a sense of personal worth and esteem from accumulating and controlling riches (10:17-22).[30]

For the evangelist, service of others and being a servant of Christ is the only way to follow Jesus. To embrace the difficulty and hardship which such service entails is, concretely, to embrace the reality of the cross, while to serve the needy and the powerless, resisting the tendency to seek the promotion of one's own status and esteem, is truly to deny one's (false) self and to find one's true self. Such service of others heeds the overriding injunction which Jesus gave the disciples at the beginning of this section (8:34b-35); such a way of life is truly to live under the shadow of the cross. For Mark's community especially, such attitudes will offset the tendency toward divisive self-assertion which inevitably begets tension and even can lead to betrayal.

Jesus' **final instruction**, triggered on the one hand by James' and John's ignoring Jesus' final prediction of the cross and, on the other hand, by their bold request for privilege, leads the Marcan Jesus to a final effort of linking the call to take up the cross with the challenge to embrace a life of humble service.[31] In this instance, Jesus instructs the disciples, intent on being one with Christ in glory, not only that *they most certainly will drink of the cup of Jesus' suffering* (10:38f) but also that, in order to rank first, *they must be the servants*, the slaves, of all. Then, to draw each of these elements of authentic discipleship together, Jesus presents himself

-67-

as model and as reason for his counsel: "For the Son of man came not to be served but to serve and *to give his life* as a ransom for many" (10:45). The implication is twofold: (1) Jesus' identity precisely as a divine figure (Son of Man) is characterized, not by worldly power or status, but by an attitude of humble service, his suffering being the fullest expression and realization of that service; and, therefore, (2) the way of greatness for the disciple necessarily involves the same posture of humble service of others which will be challenged and solidified in enduring the cross.

Thus, through a triple prediction of his passion, followed by misunderstanding and resistance on the part of his disciples and concluded with Jesus' pointed instructions to those disciples, the Marcan Jesus supports and shapes the life of the community of Rome, leading his followers along the way of discipleship. Though in many ways, Jesus' instruction has perennial value, it penetrates the core of the struggle of Mark's community and calls the disciples to walk the only way in which that community would be able to preserve life in Christ and attain its salvation.

Jesus' Imminent Return:
The Sure Hope of Discipleship
The way of discipleship in all of the Gospel communities involved walking in fidelity with the certain hope that Jesus would return and would bring his followers to share in the victory of his death and resurrection. Each community held that expectation deep in its heart, finding in it a profound source of strength for endurance and fidelity to the Lord. At the same time, each community understood and expressed that expectation differently; each found that expectation and the way of life it engendered colored by the situation in which it lived.

The Marcan community, living prior to the fall of Jerusalem, expected an imminent return of the Lord. It remembered that Lord's predictions both of the fall of Jerusalem and also of his final return; but, unlike the communities of the other three Gospels, it understood them as referring to basically one twofold event:[32] After

-68-

Jerusalem would fall, certainly a calamity for Roman Jewish Christians, Jesus would return in glory, turning calamity into the ultimate of saving, liberating events.

In the thirteenth chapter of his Gospel, Mark presents Jesus addressing his disciples concerning the events surrounding these L last days. In doing so, he brings the call of walking "under the shadow of the cross" face to face with its most challenging, but promising, circumstances. Jesus' counsel to his disciples, in anticipation of the last days is quite straightforward. Recognizing that human anxiety for safety and security will be intensified in these days of life-threatening stress, the Marcan Jesus warns his disciples to "be on guard," to "be careful not to be deceived by false Messiahs"[33] (13:5), repeating the counsel six times (13:5, 9, 21-23, 33, 35, 37)[34] Further, the disciples must anticipate being tried by the Jewish Council (the Sanhedrin), an exhortation which calls us to remember that the disciples listening to Jesus and the disciples at Rome were truly *Jewish* Christians, dependent upon their Jewish status for civil recognition and security. Especially sobering would be Jesus' warning: "Brother will hand over brother to death, and the father his child; children will rise up against parents and have them put to death" (13:12). The community knew that that had happened both within Jesus' own lifetime and within the Roman community several years earlier.

In the midst of such human and religious disarray, the further advice of the Marcan Jesus is to pray (13:18).[35] The promise of such vigilance and prayer is that the Holy Spirit will strengthen one who is brought to trial (13:11-12), perseverance to the end will bring salvation (13:13), and the Son of Man will return in power and glory to gather the faithful together in God's victory.

Yet, life under the shadow of the cross, even in anticipation of Jesus' imminent return is not to be understood merely as a relatively passive waiting. For, in a series of final instructions, the Lord gives direction to the life of the Marcan disciples concerning their mission to the world. They are counseled twice to meet Jesus in Galilee: once by Jesus himself at his last meal with the disciples (14:28) and a second time by a "young man" sitting at Jesus' vacant tomb after his resurrection (16:7).[36] Hence, while continuing to live under the shadow of the cross and while continuing to bear a servant's love for all, the disciples are also charged with proclaiming the Good News of Jesus "to every creature" (16:17). In that mission they also come to experience the living presence of the Lord, who works with them and accompanies them with signs and wonders (16:20).

The Marcan Jesus, then, clearly lives and speaks in a manner most apt to draw the Christian community of Rome to salvation, precisely because it, like he, as faithful servants of God, lived under the shadow of the cross. The community knew and continually rediscovered that life under the shadow of the cross was, not just the way of Jesus, but necessarily its own way as disciples. Mark has tailored his Gospel, his portrait of Jesus, and his account of Jesus' pastoral approach to his disciples in tones that clearly address persons struggling to walk together in such faithfulness to Jesus and with him to the Father. By remembering Jesus, by recalling his words and by heeding his counsel, the community, even in its most challenging moments, found itself deeply alive in his name.

The Matthean Community

The Gospel of Matthew was written in and for Jewish and Gentile Christians living in Antioch. Scholars date the composition of the Gospel within the ten-year period of the 80's.[37] A brief description of the community of Antioch within that time span will provide us with the necessary background both for uncovering the relationship of this community and its needs to the particular portrait which Matthew drew of Jesus and also for fuller insight into the ways in which this church developed its life though relating to that same manner of experiencing Christ.

THE LIFE-SETTING OF THE COMMUNITY OF MATTHEW[38]
The Matthean Community in which and for which this Gospel was written was, like the Community of Mark, a church of both Jew and Gentile. Unlike the Marcan Community, however, the Church which received Matthew's Gospel, had already survived the destruction of the Jerusalem Temple and the fall of that city to the

Romans. Persecution was not so likely at this time; therefore, this Gospel was written for a group that knew a fair degree of stability and peace.

The fruits of this stability were numerous. The group enjoyed fairly wealthy members as well as poor persons. It had time for reflection and careful study of the Law. As a matter of fact, the evangelist himself was most probably a Scribe, well-versed in the Law, one who was quite familiar with the teachings of the Rabbinical School at Jamnia.[39]

At the same time, this was a community which seems to have had even stronger inclinations toward a moderately conservative stance with regard to the Mosaic Law than did the community of Mark. As a result, the party of the Pharisees,[40] the Jewish leaders closely associated with the academy at Jamnia, exerted a powerful influence upon the Antiochene Jewish Christians (who still observed the Mosaic law), often hindering their ability to discern clearly the distinctive ways and freedom of true Christian discipleship.

Finally, the community in Antioch was populated by an ever-increasing number of Gentile converts. The community naturally regarded this event as a wonderful blessing. However, the corresponding decrease of numbers of Jewish converts understandably caused pain and bewilderment among the Jewish members of the Antiochene church. After all, Jesus himself was Jewish; how could it be that the greater number of his followers would be Gentile?

Thus, the rather peaceful and stable community of Matthew was not without its unique problems and challenges in its efforts to follow Jesus. First, how to extricate itself from the interference and dominance of Pharisaical Judaism and the burdensome restrictions which the Pharisees at Jamnia placed upon the community and its growth in Christian vision and life? Second, how to deal with its own need to remain faithful to its Jewish roots as God's chosen people, and even to Jesus, himself a Jew, as it became more and more a Gentile community? And to how justify such a concerted effort toward the evangelization of the Gentiles, an effort which seemed contrary to the stance of the historical Jesus? Third, how to respond to the widespread diversity in the community, the mix of rich and poor, the variety of opinion, the variations among its members in intensity and fidelity in Christian living? Fourth, where to find the true voice and teaching of Jesus, a center of unity in the midst of all of these challenges? Where to find a voice and a teaching strong enough and acceptable enough to hold the community together in Christ when such challenges could easily overturn its stability? And fifth, how to understand and to respond to life given the fact that Jesus had not returned with the fall of Jerusalem? The community at Antioch clearly was not without its challenges and struggles. Such was the community for which the evangelist, known by the name of Matthew, wrote.

THE MATTHEAN COMMUNITY
AND THE MATTHEAN PORTRAIT OF JESUS

Matthew gathered recollections and materials particular to his own tradition, material commonly referred to as "special Matthew" (M), together with two larger written documents, the Gospel of Mark and a collection of sayings of Jesus.[41] His Gospel manifests an elaborate structure, reflective of his own scholarship, being divided into prologue (infancy narrative, chapters 1 and 2), followed by five distinguishable "books," each composed of a narrative section followed by a discourse (chapters 3 to 25),[42] and completed by the passion (chapters 26-27) and resurrection (chapter 28) narratives. As we have already noted, the author has clearly cast Jesus as "Son of David" (Jewish) and Light to the Gentiles (seen even in his infancy as the Magi come to worship him). But most significantly, we have underscored the fact that Matthew's Jesus stands in clear relief as Teacher of the New Law. He is the New Moses, the Divine Lawgiver.

At this point, it is easy to understand why the author selected these images of Jesus. The original members of the community were converted Jews who held a moderately conservative disposition toward the observance of the Mosaic Law. Therefore, it would be important to show that Jesus taught fidelity to the Law, claiming that not one particle of the Law would be cast aside (5:17-

18), and yet it would be equally important to put in clear relief the fact that Jesus also taught a way of life which would take one beyond what Moses commanded (5:21-22, 27-28,...). Jesus' respect for the Law would heighten his credibility among Matthew's audience; Jesus' capacity to reinterpret that Law would lead that same audience to a richer religious life. By exercising the role of divinely inspired and appointed Teacher of a New Law, the Matthean Jesus captures the confidence of his disciples within the community at Antioch, engages them in expansive growth, and shapes their lives so that they can live authentically in his Name. How he does that concretely will be the topic of the next section.

THE MATTHEAN JESUS AND THE WAY OF DISCIPLESHIP[43]

The way of discipleship advocated by the Matthean Jesus centers upon fidelity to the New Law, the Law unfolded by Jesus himself as the New Moses. The author describes Jesus' efforts of unfolding that New Law, quite extensive in itself, as well as his tasks of engaging his disciples in this New Way, in chapters 3 through 25 of his work. We will highlight five dimensions of this effort of the Matthean Jesus as the author paints Jesus' words and deeds with an eye upon the specific needs of the Antiochene Church.

Discipleship: Freedom From Pharisaical Influence

First, the New Moses frees the disciples from the restrictive domination of the Pharisees and their stifling interpretation of the Law. Thus, Jesus comforts the anxious disciples with the affirmation (as mentioned above) that he has come, not to abolish but to fulfill the Law (5:17-18) while also challenging them to move beyond the teachings of the Pharisees: "Unless your holiness surpasses that of the Scribes and Pharisees, you shall not enter the Kingdom of Heaven" (5:20). In that light, he prods the disciples to a higher level of morality, beyond controlling physical violence to restraint from even verbal abusiveness toward others (5:21-22), beyond chastity in action to chastity and reverence for the person even in one's mind and heart (5:27-28, 31-32), beyond fidelity to oaths to honesty and simplicity in all speech (5:33-37), beyond retaliation and revenge to a readiness to resolve animosities through dialogue and mutual good-will (5:38-39), and beyond love of neighbor (which even the pagans do) to love and prayer for one's enemies (which is God's way of acting) (5:43-48).

Further, it should be noted that Jesus, in giving this teaching and placing himself above Moses, contextualizes each statement with the phrases "You have heard that it was said.... But I say to you...." Biblical scholars call attention to the fact that the passive voice of the first phrase ("it was said") reflects the Jewish manner of avoiding use of the divine Name; the meaning actually is "Yahweh said." Thus Jesus assumes the role of Yahweh's spokesperson, standing for Yahweh himself. By that manner of speaking and acting, Jesus affords his hearers both with clear reason to ignore the Pharisees and also provides them with a rule of life which will draw them into deeper communion with God.[44] For ultimately they are "to be perfect just as (their) heavenly Father is perfect" (5:48). They are to live by the life of God and these norms spell out the ways in which that life will flourish.

Finally, not only does the Matthean Jesus advance the Law beyond the teaching of the Pharisees, he also liberates his disciples from several strong Jewish traditions. He shows that even the Sabbath is not absolute, claiming to be Lord of the Sabbath (12:1-8).[45] He denies the binding force of the Jewish food Laws, and calls attention to the fact that the Pharisees actually nullify God's Law by means of their own, very human, traditions (15:1-20). He heals physical infirmity even on the Sabbath and points out that the Pharisees, ignoring the plight of the cripple, would not hesitate to rescue an animal from peril on the Holy Day (12:9-13). He releases a paralyzed man from sin and frees the man to walk, confounding the Pharisees as they accuse Jesus of blaspheming (9:1-8).[46] Finally, in a crescendo of liberating statements, Jesus solemnly warns his followers to be wary of the "leaven" of the Pharisees (16:5-12)[47] and utters scathing condemnations of them toward the end of his ministry (23:13-36). In sum, the Matthean Jesus counteracts every influence which the Pharisees have upon the disciples at Antioch, bringing a Law demanding greater holiness while providing fuller freedom. The way of discipleship for the Matthean community consists in living by the New Law of Christ.

Discipleship: Inclusion of and Mission Toward the Gentiles
A further and most significant challenge which confronted the Matthean community of the 80's, as mentioned above, centered upon the growing number of Gentile converts. Matthew's Jesus, through parables and commands, moves beyond the teaching of the Marcan Jesus in order to address precisely this issue.

Thus, while the community remembers that Jesus, during his earthly ministry, commissioned his disciples not to go "into pagan territory or enter a Samaritan town" but rather to go "to the lost sheep of Israel" (10:5-6), it recalls his parting commission to "make disciples of all nations...teaching them to observe all that (he) had commanded" with the promise that he would be with them always in this task. (28:19-20).[48] To strengthen the community in its readiness to receive the Gentile converts, Matthew also recalls Jesus' surprise and joy at the faith of the Roman centurion (8:10) together with his prediction that "many will come from the east and the west and will recline...at the banquet in the kingdom of heaven" (8:11). To ease the community's pain over the loss of further Jewish converts, Matthew continues as Jesus states: "But the children of the kingdom will be driven out into the outer darkness where there will be wailing and the grinding of teeth" (8:12). Further, with the same purpose of strengthening the community in accepting the influx of Gentiles while consoling them over the deafness of their Jewish brothers and sisters, Matthew presents Jesus' parable of the tenants of the vineyard in which the Matthean Jesus goes beyond the Marcan Christ, proclaiming: "Therefore, I say to you, the kingdom of God will be taken away from you and given to a people that will produce its fruit" (21:43)[49].

Disciples of the Matthean Christ are to walk with and to know Jesus by letting go of the security of ethnic singularity and isolation. They are to live in Christ by being expansive and inclusive in their love. They are to share their many gifts, and especially the gift of the Gospel with all, regardless of differences of ethnic and racial origin which so easily can hinder the growth of love.

Discipleship: Openness to Diversity
A third area of struggle for the community touched upon its

diversity within itself. Diversity is not disunity, but often can be an occasion for disunity and conflict. The Matthean Jesus, with pastoral concern, attends to this reality within his flock.

Thus Jesus, the divinely appointed Teacher supports reverence for the rich as well as the poor (5:3,6) even calling attention to the fact that Joseph of Arimathea, the disciple who obtained Jesus' body from Pilate for burial, was a rich man (27:57). He recognizes many gifts within the community, such as gifts of prophecy, healing, exorcising (10:8,19-20,41; 23:34) but cautions against false prophets and wonder-workers (7:15-23; 24:5,11) stating, as a guideline, that "by their fruits you will recognize them" (7:16, 20). He urges the community not to be precipitate in seeking to be rid of apparent lax members "lest one root out the wheat with the weeds" (13:24-30, 36-43).

Complexity may be a problem for the community; it is not, however, a problem for Jesus. He deals with these situations with a great deal of pastoral nuance.[50]   Disciples of Matthew's community, too, are to live with pastoral openness and tolerance in communion with their Lord, developing these qualities and virtues which constitute the certain way to harmony and peace within a diversified community.

Discipleship: Reliance Upon Peter, a Center of Unity
A fourth area involving both teaching and action on the part of the Matthean Jesus, and a further, most significant development in his addressing the question of the influence of the Pharisees, focuses upon Peter and the central role he enjoys in Matthew's community. The Lord, having warned the disciples to be wary of the leaven (teaching) of the Pharisees (16:12), supplants their authority with the authority of Peter (16:13-19). After this disciple confesses, with profound faith, that Jesus, the Son of Man is the Christ, the Son of the living God,[51] Jesus names him "rock" on which Jesus shall build his church, gives him "the keys to the kingdom," and declares that he shall have the power "to bind and to loose."

Each phrase of Jesus' proclamation to Peter is significant. 1) The solid rock upon which a house can withstand all storms is the

Word (teaching) of God (7:24-27). Peter is that rock; he is Christ's delegate, ministering to the community the Word and teaching of God in its contemporary unfolding. 2) The "keys to the kingdom," the power to open and to shut the entryway into the kingdom, is the capacity to teach the right way to gain admittance into the kingdom, the capacity to teach clearly the way to do God's will (see Is. 22:15-25). Peter, therefore, replaces the Pharisees, the Jewish magisterium, who "lock the kingdom of heaven before human beings....and do not allow entrance to those trying to enter" (23:13). Peter constitutes a new Christian magisterium. 3) The power to "bind and to loose" is the authority to declare what is permissible and what is forbidden. Peter supplants the Jewish magisterium in determining what is lawful and what is not lawful, for the Jewish magisterium has been judged irrevocably incompetent for Christ's saving mission. Thus, in Peter, the community has a sure guide to the teaching of Jesus and is forever free of the intervention of the Pharisees.[52] It has a source of unity to guide it through all the dangers that a new and different age could bring.

The community, its leaders, and Peter himself, however, are not left without guidelines for the exercise of this authority. In the discourse (18:1-35) which follows the narrative of Peter's commission, the Matthean Jesus gives the community a series of instructions on how the community and its leaders should guide the church. It must exercise authority with genuine humility (18:1-5) taking great care not to mislead the innocent (18:6-9). It must seek out the wayward and the sinner (18:10-14) and do its utmost to foster the conversion of the recalcitrant (18:15-20). And, governing all its actions, it must extend God's mercy again and again, knowing no limit in this regard (18:21-35), for if it is to live by the life and love of God (5:48), it too must show God's abiding love characterized by mercy. Thus, in communion with Peter and its leaders, the disciples are to find the ongoing teaching and guidance of Jesus. With these authorities, they can feel safe to move forward into the future, while preserving a morality representative of life in the kingdom of God.

Discipleship: Faithful and Active Waiting
Until the Lord Returns

A final question which the Matthean community, as distinguished from the community of Mark,[53] needed to answer concerned Jesus' "failure" to return after the destruction of Jerusalem as earlier Christians had expected. The Christian who had been urged to be ready for the Lord's return now found he had more time. Will Jesus return? How is the Christian called to live in the interim? The Matthean Jesus guides the community in its reflection upon these issues in several stages. First, he clearly separates the questions of the destruction of the Temple and the fall of Jerusalem from the question of the final return of the Son of Man. The disciples of Matthew's Gospel ask Jesus a clearly twofold question: "Tell us, when will this happen (the destruction of the temple, predicted in the previous verse) and what sign will there be of your coming and of the end of the age?" (24:3), to which Jesus responds in two parts (24:4-28 and 24:29-25:46).

Second, Jesus introduces the notion of a delay in the coming of the Son of Man: The wicked servant who, perceiving that the master is "long-delayed," begins to act shamefully, will be punished severely (24:45-51 at 48); the foolish virgins, lacking sufficient oil for their lamps (that is, lacking sufficiently deepened faith or adequate good works) to meet the "long-delayed" bridegroom, are not prepared when the bridegroom at last does come (25:1-13 at 5); and the servants who receive various sums of money to invest find that the master does not return except "after a long time" (25:14-30).

Third, in view of this "delay," the Lord teaches precisely that the disciple must sustain and deepen his or her faith (as the wise virgins had done), that the good servant of Jesus must invest his or her gifts and increase them (perhaps by spreading the gift of the Gospel) and all disciples must extend themselves in caring for the needy in Christ's name, for "whatever you have done for one of these least brothers of mine, you have done for me" (25:40). The Son of Man will return, perhaps only after a long period, which will seem like a delay. But "when the Son of Man comes in his glory,...he will sit upon his glorious throne and all the nations will be assembled before him." To those who have followed these instructions he will say "Come you who are blessed by my Father. Inherit the kingdom..." (25:31,34).

The Matthean Christ, then, responds well to the needs of the Church of Antioch in the eighth decade of Christian history. Clearly his voice engages his disciples in the very fabric of their concrete lives and struggles. They are given a New Law, the Law of Christ, itself the way of true discipleship. They are to be perfected in God's love as God in God's Self is perfect. They must express a disciple's love by reaching out to persons of every nation, by living together with tolerance and acceptance, by investing their talents and by caring especially for the needy, not fearing difference or diversity, but allowing it to challenge their growth to an even deeper love. And that they may find their way, safely, in the teaching of Jesus, free from any restrictive influence of former traditions, they are given the voice of Peter, Jesus vice-gerent, against whom even "the gates of the netherworld will not prevail" (16:18). Thus, the community of Matthew can live in peace, knowing that Jesus will be with it "all days, even to the end of the world" (28:20).

The Lucan Community

Like the composition of Matthew, Luke's Gospel was written in the mid-80's. Further, Luke, like the author of Matthew, gives clear evidence of dependence upon the Gospel of Mark and upon the collection of sayings of Jesus (Q) as well as a source particular to himself (L).

As we seek to discern the nature of the audience for which Luke has written his Gospel, however, we discover some striking differences between his work and that of both Mark and Matthew: First, while the latter two evangelists wrote for specific and identifiable communities, Luke's work appears to have been composed to strengthen the faith and life in Christ of many communities. In the introduction to his Gospel, acknowledging that many have undertaken the task of writing down narratives of the events of Jesus' life and ministry, death and resurrection, Luke proposes to compile an accurate account "in an orderly sequence for you, most excellent Theophilus, so that you may realize the certainty of the teaching you have received" (1:1-4). The generic name "God-lover" (Theophilus) together with Luke's style of imitating Hellenistic Greek writers and his using a Greek name to designate his readers, show that he has in mind largely Greek speaking Gentile Christians living in a variety (therefore unspecified) of churches.

Second, whereas Mark and Matthew wrote their Gospels in one book (each), Luke composed two books, namely, the Gospel which bears his name and also the Acts of the Apostles. As a result, Luke was able to expand his record of the implications of Jesus' life and ministry, death and resurrection for Jesus' disciples and the church by unfolding them more explicitly in this sequel to his Gospel. This latter book gives account of the expansion of the early church through the missionary efforts, first of Peter but largely of Paul. Thus, we can say that Luke's Gospel was composed, in some manner, with an eye to nourishing the communities described in Acts while both books, necessarily considered as one in purpose, were intended to fortify the life of predominantly Gentile Christian communities of the mid-80's[54] which had been affected, at least indirectly, by Paul's missionary endeavors.[55]

THE LIFE-SETTING OF THE LUCAN COMMUNITIES[56]
Like the Matthean Community of the mid-80's, the Lucan communities had long survived the era of the persecutions under Nero. They were without the authoritative leadership of Peter and Paul, and they found themselves in an interim period between the Lord's first and second comings.[57]

Unlike the community of Matthew, however, they did not have within their midst a strong Jewish-Christian membership. This was a two-edged sword, so to speak. It had the advantage of leaving these communities free from Pharisaical interference and particularly from controversies with regard to observance of Jewish food Laws, but it had the disadvantage of depriving them of firsthand knowledge of their Jewish roots. Without the strong leadership of Peter and Paul, and without a clear sense of their history from and through Judaism, they were, in many ways, communities without a tradition, or at least without ready access to a tradition.

That situation presented these churches with several challenges: 1) How could they attain a sense of their own election in face of the fact that Jesus was Jewish and that the Jews were God's people of choice? How could they sustain a sense that their religious convictions had time-tested and firm foundations, when, in fact, it would appear that their tradition had its origin only a few decades prior to their own conversion?[58] 2) What precisely has Jesus called them to as disciples who live, not Jewish Christianity, nor Gentile Christianity in a Jewish-Christian context, but Gentile Christianity in a purely Gentile world? How adapt to a culture different from Judaic-Christianity and negotiate the challenges and struggles which Christian life in a Gentile culture would demand? 3) How maintain fidelity to Jesus and to his message, given their separation from Jewish-Christian institutions and the passing of the significant apostolic figures, Peter and Paul? 4) How understand the future, particularly in view of Christ's apparent delay in returning? These questions and struggles clearly challenged the author of Luke-Acts as he sought to serve the Gentile churches given to his care. How Luke's composition meets these needs will become clear in the following sections.

THE LUCAN COMMUNITIES AND LUKE'S PORTRAIT OF JESUS

Advocate of the Poor, Prophet of Mercy

As noted in the previous chapter, Luke portrays Jesus as prophetic Advocate of the poor, the marginalized and the neglected, reflected within an overriding perspective of Jesus' being Prophet of God's mercy. This image is especially helpful in drawing the Gentile churches into communion with Jesus, for the Gentile Christians, living in a Gentile world (as distinct from Jewish Christianity) would naturally feel marginalized, second-class, latecomers, the people who were "not of God's choice." Likewise, without having a tradition of being in long-standing relationship with the God of Jesus, without having been gifted with the blessings of God's revelation through the Law and the Prophets, they would have wandered in pagan behaviors and could carry within them a sense of being deeply sinful.[59] Jesus' image, focused on his mediating God's abundant mercy, would offer such people a deep sense of their being welcomed, cared for, and included within the embrace of God's overpowering love.

Anointed by the Spirit, Person of Prayer

Further, Luke's depiction of Jesus as a prophet anointed by and impelled by the Spirit would also have special value for the Gentile Christians. Together with the image of Jesus, a Person of constant and open prayer, this portrait of the Lord would give Luke's Gentile communities the model of a person who had the God-given resources to negotiate a most difficult and challenging environment in his own day. As they faced a world culturally at variance with the world of the historical Jesus, Christ's Spirit, pledged to and given to them, would afford these Gentile disciples a means of encouragement, light and energy to move forward amidst the challenging need to adapt while still remaining faithful to their Lord and Savior.

Jesus: Center of History

Finally, in an even more overriding fashion, Luke draws the Gentiles to feel part of God's embrace by casting Jesus as the center of history, uniting Israel before him with the Gentiles after him. He strives to show that each of these peoples stand as the eternally intended recipients of God's salvation through Christ.[60] Luke seeks to underscore this theme both in his Gospel and in the book of Acts. First he briefly attends to the TIME OF ISRAEL. Thus, in the Gospel, he begins his account by recalling briefly (1:5-3:1) the blessedness of Israel in the persons who represent the best of its people and its piety: Zechariah, Elizabeth, John the Baptist, Simeon and Anna.[61] In effect, he lays out the Jewish heritage which, through Christ, will become the heritage of the Gentiles. In Acts, he presents Peter and Paul as initiating their Easter proclamations with a brief summary of Israel's history in preparation for Jesus.[62] The effect of these proclamations, in Luke's schema, is twofold: They show the Gentiles that Israel was merely the first stage of God's plan, while, at the same time, they provide the Gentiles with a brief catechesis concerning the people who, from God's point of view, are truly their ancestors and roots.

Second, with his presentation of the TIME OF JESUS (3:2-24:51), Luke depicts the Lord as being primarily connected with *all* peoples both *in his ancestry* and also *in his mission*. Thus, Luke traces Jesus' roots back, not only to Abraham, but to Adam, father of all peoples[63], thereby explicitly relating Jesus' ancestry, not only to that of Israel, but to that of the Gentiles also. Further, Luke records the memory of Jesus' inclusive understanding of his mission (beyond Israel). He recounts Jesus' prophetic words at the outset of his public ministry (4:16-30, at 24-27); he highlights Jesus' declaration that the interim between the days of the destruction of Jerusalem and the day of his return constituted the "time of the Gentiles" (21:24); and he concludes his Gospel account with the risen Jesus' commission to his disciples to preach repentance for the forgiveness of sins in his name "to all the nations" (24:47).[64] Jesus himself is the center of history, God's gift to all persons. He unites, in his mediation of the gift of forgiveness, Jew and Gentile in one heritage, making both peoples recipients of one and the same blessings, one and the same saving love, of God.

Third, Luke completes his portrait of Jesus as the "Center of History" by describing the faithful and efficacious efforts of the Apostles, of Paul and of the early Church's missioners and presbyters to continue Jesus' mission during the TIME OF THE GENTILES (24:52-Acts 1:3-28:31). With this sense of their mission, the apostles and other church leaders, ever open to and receptive of Jesus promise of the Spirit,[65] minister under the impulse of that Spirit[66] and mediate the Spirit to their non-Jewish converts.[67] Revering God's Word, they take care to proclaim the Word (just as Jesus delivered the Word), and carefully lead their converts to rely upon that Word for life in Christ.[68] As Jesus healed, so they too work healing wonders in his name.[69] And they gather the community for prayer and for the "breaking of the bread" (2:42-47; 4:23-31; 13:1-3), preserving the memory of Jesus as Jesus had instructed (Luke 22:19b). Jesus, having assumed his place at the center of history, continues his role of drawing the Gentiles into the embrace of God's love through the ministry of the Apostles, of Paul, of missioners and presbyters appointed to minister in his Name.

Thus, through the image of Jesus, the "center of history," Luke effectively builds up the religious self-esteem of his Gentile audience. Gentile Christians have deep roots in God's history of salvation and in a very respected religion. Among all religious persons, they can stand tall. The portrait of Jesus as Advocate of the Poor, Prophet of Mercy, Anointed by the Spirit, Person of Prayer, Center of History mediating God's universal love and blessing to all, serve well to sustain and to fortify Luke's Gentile communities in their quest for fuller life in Jesus. Luke has selected aspects of the life of Jesus especially well-suited for supporting the Christian lives of the specific communities for which he wrote.

THE LUCAN JESUS AND THE WAY OF DISCIPLESHIP

The Way of Discipleship: The Journey to Jerusalem:
Luke presents Jesus explicitly as forming and instructing his followers in the way of discipleship throughout a long section of his Gospel, a section governed by the perspective of Jesus' journey to Jerusalem (9:51-19:27). The journey is described, not simply as living "under the shadow of the cross" (as it was in Mark), but as a "going forth," a "transitus," to glory, a movement through and beyond this world to a fuller life in God.[70] Consistent with this perspective, the risen Lord enlightens the travelers on the Emmaus road with a pointed question: "Was it not necessary that the Messiah suffer these things and [so] enter his glory?" (24:26). Jesus' home is not here, but in the new Jerusalem which he will establish.[71]

The way of discipleship, laid out by the Lucan Jesus, involves following the Lord on this same journey. Thus Jesus reminds the generous inquirer who is willing to follow Jesus wherever he goes, that he has no home in this world: "Foxes have dens and birds of the sky have their nests, but the Son of Man has nowhere to rest his head" (9:57f.). He encourages another to take leave of those, who do not have the spiritual courage to walk with him, and invites him to go forward with him proclaiming God's reign (9:59f). And he insists that every disciple be whole-hearted in his commitment, avoiding all tendency to reconsider former, less than Christian, ways of behavior, for "no one who sets a hand to the plow and looks to what was left behind is fit for the kingdom of God" (9:61f). Like the Lord, disciples must be resolutely determined to "journey to Jerusalem"; they have no lasting home in this world; their life is to be taken up in God, involving total love of God and, in God, total love of neighbor as oneself (10:25-28). Their journey with Jesus is a journey to a fully transformed life.

Along the Journey: Advocacy and Concern for the Poor

Concretely, the journey of discipleship bears clear resemblance to the portrait of Jesus himself. The advocate of the poor enjoins the disciple to welcome all, especially the needy and the foreigner. Hence the Samaritan, himself a foreigner and one who shares his wealth and time in caring for the victim of robbers, merits Jesus' praise and is given as an example of true love of neighbor, the only way of love for a genuine disciple (10:29-37). So also Zacchaeus, a former tax-collector (and therefore a person regarded as "a sinner"), ranks among Jesus' companions and is promised salvation, for he has pledged to give half his possessions to the poor and to repay in a fourfold manner anyone whom he defrauded (19:1-10). And a widow, having only two small coins, stands as a model of discipleship because, in the Master's words: "Others have made offerings from their surplus, but she, from her poverty, has offered her whole livelihood" (21:1-4).[72] The reader could not fail to notice, not only that the journey of discipleship demanded a willingness and readiness to share one's possessions, but that each of those commended by Jesus was a marginalized person (Samaritan, tax-collector, widow). Gentiles, marginalized persons, who share what is theirs, may be better disciples than the religiously accepted and elite, better than those who have reputation, status or power among God's supposedly elect, better than those who had been thought of as "God's chosen people." Gentiles, who share their goods with the needy, are truly on the journey with Jesus to the kingdom which God has promised God's beloved.[73]

Along the Journey: Living in Mercy and Repentance

Second, the prophet of mercy holds before his followers the fact that the way of discipleship is a journey of constant conversion and repentance. This should be no surprise since they are to love God with nothing less than their entire selves and are to focus their love on their neighbor as well as on themselves (10:27). The integrity of such dispositions would require constant conversion. Thus Jesus, frequently reminding the disciples of the call to repentance (10:13; 11:32; 13:3, 5), teaches them both to seek God's forgiveness as part of their prayer (11:4) and also, in the three parables of the lost sheep, the lost coin and the wayward son, to seek out sinners and rejoice at their conversion (15:1-32). In the last parable Jesus describes repentance in terms of his own "Exodus": The son who "was dead" has "returned to life" (15:32), leading his disciples to recognize that, in genuine conversion, one experiences the transforming power of Jesus' own dying and rising. No wonder, then, that Jesus tells the disciples that they must forgive a brother (or sister) as many times as he (or she) expresses sorrow (17:3-4). No wonder then that in his final commission given to his disciples, he, the risen Lord, centers his mandate on preaching repentance and God's mercy to all nations (24:47).[74] In experiencing or fostering conversion and repentance, one enters into the deepest movements of the journey of discipleship; one touches the spiritual center of the disciple's transition from this world to God.

Along the Journey: Being Formed by the Word of God
Further, one dares walk this journey only by relying upon and listening to Jesus. He is in the lead. Hence, although Mary and Martha, both genuine Lucan examples of discipleship, together welcome Jesus into their home *while he is on his journey* (10:38), Mary, who seats herself attentively at the Lord's feet relishing his every word (10:39) enjoys Jesus' singular approval. In comparison to Martha, Jesus affirms that Mary has chosen the better part by listening to and conversing with him (10:41f). In the same light, Jesus insists that it is not worldly status or success that indicate God's blessing, but rather "blessed are they who hear the Word of God and keep it" (11:28f). Hence Jesus takes pains to offer numerous instructions to his followers along the way through sayings, examples and parables (9:51-19:27) and only after "having spoken these things" did he "proceed to enter Jerusalem" (19:28), where he continued to teach daily while "the entire populace was listening to him and hanging on his words" (19:47f; see 21:37f). The way of discipleship, the journey to Jerusalem and beyond, rests upon hearing and heeding the Word of the Lord.

Along the Journey: Constant Prayer
Closely associated with the journeying person's need to listen to God's Word is the disciple's need to be a person constant in prayer.

Therefore Jesus instructs the disciples that prayer must accompany their ministry of proclaiming the "Good News" (10:2), that they must call upon God with persistence (11:5-8), praying always and never losing heart (18:1), and that they must pray with genuine humility and contrition, never asserting themselves proudly before God (18:9-14). Further, he assures them that if they ask, they will receive; if they beckon God's help, the way will be open for them; in a word, if they pray, they will be fully nourished for the journey. Indeed, God knows all their needs and will certainly care for them (12:22-34).

The parable of chapter 11:5-13 is especially powerful in this light: Unlike the man who receives a friend who had *come in from a journey* (11:6) and, finding his cupboard empty, cries out to another friend in utter desperation "Friend, lend me three loaves, I have nothing to offer," the disciple, journeying with Jesus always has everything available to offer. Neither the disciple, nor anyone the disciple wishes to welcome into his or her home need worry about being famished. The follower of Jesus can always call upon the "Father in heaven" with confidence. God, whose capacity to give good gifts surpasses even the most generous human father's capabilities, will listen and will give the disciple the Holy Spirit (11:9-13), the most precious gift of all. Indeed the disciples then will have everything they need for the journey; they will already be living in God![75]

Along the Way: Walking "Daily" in Christ Until He Returns
Like the Matthean Community, and in contrast with the church of Mark, the churches for which Luke writes knew of the fall of Jerusalem and the persecutions which surrounded it, as a past event. Like the Christians of Antioch, they had to reckon with what appeared to be a delayed Parousia. That delay challenged them, as it did the Matthean disciples, to come to understand the meaning and purpose of this interim period, the time between Jesus' ascension and his final coming. Hence the Lucan Jesus, leading the Gentile communities on their journey to Jerusalem and God's life beyond, had to respond to this concern. This he did in two ways.

First, the Lucan Jesus gives a perspective on this delay with regard to his final return.[76] He clearly separates the fall of Jerusalem (21:5-9, 12-24)[77] from the days of his final return (21:10-11, 25-36),[78] calling attention to the fact between these two events lies the "age of the Gentiles" which must be fulfilled first (21:24b).[79] Second, he urges his followers to walk the way of discipleship "day by day," counseling them to take up their cross *daily* (9:23) and to seek spiritual nourishment, their daily bread, *each day*[80] as they pray to their father in heaven (11:3).[81] The reason for this daily effort, part of the Lucan way of discipleship, is that, in spite of a future return of Jesus and the final accomplishment of God's reign, the "kingdom of God is in (their) midst" (17:20f.); disciples have access to the reign now. Hence, Jesus assures his audience in his inaugural address proclaiming Good News to the poor, release to the captives, and sight to the blind (4:18) that: "Today this Scripture passage is fulfilled in your hearing" (4:21). Witnesses of his miraculous cures glorify God, saying "We have seen incredible things today" (5:26). And, lest people become distracted by the expectation of the dramatic establishment of the kingdom in its fully realized form (19:11), the Lucan Jesus urges them to invest their "gold coins" (gifts), for the Master will expect a return on what he has entrusted to them.[82] During the "age of the Gentiles," then, the disciple is to focus on daily living, walking the way of discipleship "day by day," rather than to focus attention on Jesus' final coming. With such daily fidelity, salvation will come to their communities as it had come, "today," to the house of Zacchaeus (19:9). Like the repentant thief, as they approach their final day, they will hear the voice of Jesus saying "Today you will be with me in Paradise" (23:43). In the mind of the Lucan Jesus, it is this day which matters; his return will take care of itself.

The Lucan Jesus, then, is adeptly portrayed with an eye to leading Luke's Gentile churches, having little root in Jewish tradition, into communion with himself and with God's salvific plan from the beginning of history. The images of his being advocate of the poor and prophet of God's mercy are well tailored so as to enable a people, themselves likely to feel or to be marginalized, to be at home and important in God's plan. The image of Jesus' being the center of history, uniting two equally significant phases of one divine plan serves well to give this audience a clear sense of being equally chosen and loved by God, a clear sense of having an ancestry which itself boasts of a firm and blessed tradition. Jesus' call to discipleship, involving the daily task of wholehearted commitment, likewise would help these followers by strengthening their focus directly on their journey with the Lord. Living as Jesus did, with predilection for the poor, the marginalized, the outcast and the repentant sinner, they would sense that Jesus was still alive in their midst and that his mission was unfolding especially through them. Relying upon prayer, the presence of the Spirit and the ongoing ministry of the apostolic word, they would be well prepared to carry Jesus' mission of "preaching repentance in his name to all nations" as they followed Jesus "on the journey to Jerusalem" and into the fullness of the kingdom of God.

Interim Conclusions

Our exploration of the Gospel communities is far from complete. We still need to give attention to the Johannine community which will provide us with a tradition harmonious with, yet complementary to, those of the synoptic communities. Nevertheless, several significant dynamics affecting the shaping of the Gospel traditions have already clearly emerged from our consideration of the synoptic communities. At this point, we will summarize those dynamics briefly, making but two observations, leaving fuller discussion of them for the next chapter.

First, although each of the synoptic Gospels presents decidedly different tones and coloring in its portrait of Jesus, each portrait is carefully attuned to support, to strengthen and to guide the disciples in the midst of their most striking concrete struggles and needs. While the specific design given to the images of Jesus' self-revelation is largely the work of the evangelists who gathered, selected, and organized the materials they received from their own traditions, it is clear that the historical situation of the churches for which they wrote affected the manner in which they chose to present the Lord. No doubt the evangelists were prompted in their tasks of selection and organization by their own awareness that specific images, stories and sayings of Jesus already in circulation offered significant support to their respective communities. Thus, the faith-experience of the communities of disciples and the specific emphases in their beliefs both preceded and also confirmed the writings of the evangelists. In this way, the shaping of the traditions of the synoptic communities emerged from the faith-experience of each community of disciples as a whole, although the evangelists exercised a singular role in that endeavor.[83]

Second, these images, stories and sayings of Jesus focused not only upon Jesus' identity, his living personal relationship, before God, but also upon Jesus' identity, again a living personal relationship, before his disciples. Truly to know Jesus required not only that one ascertain his divine origin and mission, but also that one allow him to lead, to guide, and to call one to conversion of life. Hence, each community developed its own concrete perspective with regard to Jesus' challenge to a "way of discipleship." No doubt these communities did this in conjunction with their recollection of, and desire to remain faithful to, the challenges and injunctions of the historical Jesus vis-à-vis his original followers. However, it also did this cognizant of Jesus' commanding and engaging presence, guidance, and care in its own day. Hence, the images of Jesus' enunciating a specific way of discipleship for each community underscore the fact that to know and understand Jesus is not just to retain and analyze past memories of him, nor is it merely to appreciate him as a distant, uninvolved ancestor, no matter how powerful and good. Rather to know and understand Jesus is to appreciate him as the living Lord challenging each disciple with specific directives in the historical present. To know Jesus fully is to appreciate him as the always present Lord who engages persons in the specifics of their own patterns of life in the context of their own history. Anything less reduces the portrait of Jesus to a picture to be admired on a museum wall. The portraits of Jesus fashioned in each synoptic community are clearly more vibrant and interactive than this. They include not only images which describe Jesus in himself and in his relationship to God, but also images of Jesus directing believers concretely in their personal freedom. The portraits of Jesus reveal a person deeply involved with his followers crafting for them and with them a path of discipleship.

Both of these observations have fuller implications for the nature of Christology and for the task of doing Christology today. Our inquiry into the shaping of the tradition of the Johannine school, with its own history and development, however, promises to broaden, and to provide further grounding for these implications. Hence, we will leave the further pursuit of the questions of the nature and task of Christology to chapter four. Before beginning that inquiry, however, we invite the reader to reflect upon the following questions as ways of processing and personalizing the preceding material.

Questions for Reflection

1. What aspect of Mark's portrait of Jesus appears to you to be most apt to strengthen the community at Rome in its particular struggle? What aspect of Mark's description of the way of discipleship appears to you to be most capable of strengthening the community in its greatest needs? Explain your response to each question. (Please reflect upon the preceding questions in the contexts of Matthew's, then Luke's, Gospels.)

2. How would you explain the evangelists' inclusion of sayings of Jesus and/or events of his ministry in their respective Gospels which do not appear to have an immediate relationship to the particular struggles of the communities for which he wrote?

3. In what ways or on what occasions have you experienced personal need as a stimulus for your efforts to seek Jesus? What images of Jesus have you found most helpful to you in those situations? In what ways has your praying in personal need helped you better understand traditional beliefs concerning the Lord?

4. What elements of Jesus' description of the way of discipleship as recounted in each Gospel would you judge as most significant for your journey with Christ today? for your church's journey? for your nation's journey?

CHAPTER 4

The Johannine Community: Shaping the Biblical Tradition (2)[1]

Having observed the interrelationships of the synoptic communities and their life-situations to the distinct images of Jesus which shine through the Gospels of Mark, Matthew and Luke, we have become familiar with the influences which concrete churches and their particular needs and struggles exercised upon the Gospel portraits of Jesus. We, therefore, can reasonably suspect that the Johannine portrait of Jesus, quite distinct in tone from the portraits found in the other Gospels, developed in a similar fashion. But what were the particular characteristics and the specific struggles of the Johannine community which led the fourth evangelist to picture Jesus in such a profound and exalted manner as we perceive him in the fourth Gospel? How did that community relate its image of the Lord to the call to discipleship? In what ways did the Johannine disciples find both images of Jesus and call to discipleship life-giving? And what does the Johannine portrait of Jesus, viewed both from the perspective of the Lord's own life and also from the perspective of his forming his followers offer us as we strive more deeply to understand and interpret the mystery of God, alive in and through Jesus? Such are the questions which drive our inquiry forward as we seek insight into the shaping of the Christian tradition in the context of the community of the fourth evangelist.

Our plan for this chapter is twofold. First we will seek to describe the interrelationship of the Johannine community to the portrait of Jesus evident in the fourth Gospel. We will follow the outline that we used in the last chapter with one modification: we will introduce an additional subheading under which we will explore the situation and influences of the pre-Gospel community. The reasons for this addition will become clear as we approach that section of our inquiry.

Second, having completed our reflection on all four of the Gospel communities, we will reflect upon the similar dynamics and patterns which all manifest as they process and shape the fourfold traditions. This will lead to fuller insight into Jesus himself, into the nature of Christian beliefs and finally into the process of doing Christology, both in the past and in the present. We will conclude this chapter, as is our custom, with some suggested questions intended to lead the reader more deeply into the process of doing Christology him or herself.

The Johannine Community
Shaping the Fourth Gospel

The fourth Gospel, in its final form (the complete Gospel as we know it), was most likely composed in Ephesus[2] near the year 100[3]. Its audience consisted mostly of Gentile Christians manifesting a notably diverse ancestry. Though some could trace their roots back to Judaism, the origins of many were Samaritan or Gentile. All, however, were united in a profound allegiance to Jesus as the *"Word made flesh,"* the *"preexistent Son of God."* All had definitively severed their relationship to the Jewish synagogue, which had been the home of the earliest Johannine Christians. Like the authors of the three earlier Gospels, the fourth evangelist[4] writes primarily to strengthen and stimulate the Christian faith and life of his readers, a believing community which traces itself back to Jesus through the witness of the "beloved disciple." A description of the life-setting of the Johannine community at the time of the final composition of the fourth Gospel will provide a beginning for understanding the portrait of Jesus which this Gospel offers us.

THE LIFE-SETTING OF THE JOHANNINE COMMUNITY
At the threshold of the second century of the Christian era, Ephesus manifested a sophisticated cosmopolitan and commercial

population. Within it, many religious groups and sects found a home: Jews, whose religious life centered on their synagogue, and Gentiles, espousing a variety of religious convictions. Included among the latter were growing numbers of Hellenistic Gnostics. Within this milieu, the Johannine Christians sought recognition as a respectable religious people and, to some degree, showed themselves to be open to welcome others into communion with them.

Living in peace with such diverse religious peoples, however, was no easy task. Ephesus was the seat of bitter feuds between Christian and Jewish groups, from whose synagogues the Christians had long since been excommunicated. The city also provided an arena for struggles between Christians and pagans.[5] Such conflicts presented serious questions to the Johannine community, seeking, not only to survive, but to be faithful to Jesus, who, it believed, had come forth from God. Among the issues it faced, we can enumerate the following: 1) How to meet the attacks and persecution of their Jewish antagonists? How to deal with other religious groups which surrounded it at this time? 2) How to understand its origins and defend its beliefs, both as a way of vindicating itself against its religious adversaries and also as a way of strengthening its own adherence to Jesus? 3) What does fidelity to Jesus demand of the disciple? 4) Given the fact that Jesus has not yet returned, what can the believer expect regarding the Parousia? How should the community live and move toward the future?

THE JOHANNINE COMMUNITY AND JOHN'S PORTRAIT OF JESUS
Understanding the antagonistic religious environment surrounding the Johannine community at the turn of the century, we can readily appreciate the appropriateness of the author's image of Jesus: Who could question the authority of the "one who has come from above," the "One Who Is," the "preexistent Word made flesh?" In whom else could one find the source of everlasting life? No prophet of Israel, no chosen leader, not even Moses, had such standing before God. One might argue with the Jews about Jesus, but, from the Christian point of view the debate would be "no contest."

Further, that same image of Jesus would enable the Christian to stand strong against the leanings of Gentiles, particularly those who may have had Gnostic tendencies. Jesus, being the eternal Word through whom all things were made, Jesus who himself is Light of the world, would offer the Johannine community insight to withstand non-Christian theories concerning God, creation, and the dualism of light and darkness. The Johannine portrait of Jesus was well tailored to enable the community to meet all adversaries within its environment around the year 100.

But the appropriateness and effectiveness of this image of Jesus for the community at the turn of the century is only one issue. Raymond Brown, in his careful work entitled *The Community of the Beloved Disciple*,[6] has shown that this picture of the Lord had developed decades earlier both as an expression of the community's having incorporated insights from its many and diverse converts and also as a way of responding to challenges from its religious adversaries. Hence many different religious groups influenced the development of the Johannine community and the fourth Gospel.

Among the earliest of these groups were Jewish Christians, particularly disciples of John the Baptist and the person known as the "Beloved Disciple." Soon, however, a number of Samaritan converts as well as Jewish-Christians having a deep "anti-temple" bias exercised an influence upon the community's growth. Finally, a number of Gentiles joined ranks with the community of the "Beloved Disciple," thereby solidifying its openness to all persons, on the one hand, and its distance from its Jewish origins, on the other. To appreciate fully the interrelationship of the Johannine portrait of Jesus and the Johannine community, then, we must attend to its earlier history and to these various groups and religious figures who entered into its complex development. For it was precisely these groups and persons who, in the pre-Gospel period of the community, were responsible for the generation of the image of Jesus which the Johannine community so loved and valued, an image which it found profoundly salvific. Unfortunately, it was this same image which became the cause of bitter controversy with and hostility toward the community's Jewish counterparts.

THE ORIGINS OF THE JOHANNINE PORTRAIT OF JESUS
AND THE DEVELOPMENT OF THE PRE-GOSPEL COMMUNITY

The Johannine Community originated, as did all Christian communities, among Jews who received the good news of God's saving love in Jesus through the preaching and witness of those who had known Jesus and who had seen the risen Lord. Indications that the fourth Gospel took root within a community similar to those for whom the other Gospels were written include the fact that the first disciples to receive Jesus' call in the Johannine tradition (Andrew, Peter, Philip, Nathanael)[7] are also the first to receive Jesus' message in the accounts of the earlier Gospels, although the ordering and timing of their calling are different[8]. Further, the tradition of the miracles of Jesus recorded in the fourth Gospel is similar to that recorded in the other three Gospels even though the narratives surrounding these "signs and wonders" manifest interpretive insights uniquely characteristic of the Johannine tradition. And even more significantly, the titles given to Jesus early in the Gospel (Lamb of God, Rabbi, Messiah, Son of God, King of Israel)[9] reflect titles which circulated among Jewish Christians although no other Gospel would suggest that Jesus would have been recognized by these titles at first sight. The fourth Gospel gives evidence, therefore, of stemming from a tradition first received by Jewish converts to Christianity.[10]

What is especially striking even at the outset of this Gospel, however, is that Jesus promises that these disciples will come to see even greater things than anything they have yet come to know of him as they follow him (1:51-52). With this statement, the Johannine Jesus has launched the disciples on a profound journey of ever deepening insight into himself and his origins, a journey which actually traces the development of the Johannine community itself. It is in light of this promise that the fourth Gospel itself reveals many different persons and groups who comprise the recipients of Jesus' ministry.

The Disciples of John the Baptist
Among the first groups to enter and to fashion the pre-Gospel Johannine church stands a company of the disciples of John the Baptist with the Baptist himself at center-stage. The reader will

note immediately that the Baptist gives testimony to Jesus in this account that is far superior to the testimony he (or anyone else) gives to Jesus in the Synoptic Gospels. Jesus "is the one of whom I have said, 'A man is coming after me who ranks ahead of me because he existed before me'" (1:30, see 1:15); Jesus "who comes from above is above all.... He testifies to what he has seen and heard" (3:31-32). Even at the outset of the Gospel, the precursor proclaims the pre-existence of Jesus. Nevertheless, the Baptist clearly assumes a secondary stance. He states that he is not the Messiah (1:20; see 3:28) nor Elijah, nor the Prophet (1:21). He is unworthy even to untie the sandal strap of the one to come after him (1:27); rather, he must decrease while Jesus must increase (3:30). His sole task is to "make straight the way of the Lord" (1:23), to testify that Jesus is "the Son of God" who will baptize with the Holy Spirit (1:32-34).[11]

The fourth Gospel manifests such a concern for John the Baptist and for his testimony because among the earliest members of the Johannine community stood former disciples of the Baptist. The evangelist (incorporating elements of the tradition which preceded his own writing of the Gospel) wished to show respect for the ancestry of the Baptist's former disciples and to strengthen them in their commitment to Jesus within the setting of the community of the beloved disciple. Hence the evangelist presents their hero, the Baptist, as recognizing and testifying to Jesus, not only as the Messiah, but as "the One from above," the "One who is before all" even though those insights into the origins of Jesus developed in a later period. In this way, the former disciples of the Baptist could discover *in their own tradition,* a strong precedent for affirming these same exalted christological beliefs.

The former disciples of John the Baptist, however, did not join the Johannine community without bringing a richness from their own tradition. Raymond Brown suggests that the community of the Baptist, having originated in close proximity with the Essene community at Qumran, could have shared theological themes which flourished among the Essenes.[12] Such themes would have included the dualistic perspectives of Light/Darkness, Truth/Falsehood, and the spirit of light leading the children of light against the children of darkness. The Johannine identification of the Word with "the true light, which...was coming into the world" (1:9), the light which "shines in the darkness and (which) the darkness could not snuff out" (1:5), the presentation of Jesus as "Light of the world" who gives the "light of life" (8:12), and the Johannine naming of the Holy Spirit as the "Spirit of Truth" (14:17, 16:13) show the transformation of this pre-Christian heritage into the Christology of the Johannine community. The Johannine tradition and the fourth Gospel, then, show attentiveness to the former disciples of the Baptist not only by respectfully remembering the Baptist and his personal witness to Jesus in the development of the Gospel, but also by interpreting the mystery and meaning of Jesus in a manner adapted to the particular background of these disciples. Hence, the Johannine tradition is both stimulated, in an initial movement, by the particular heritage of these disciples and then, in a subsequent movement, is adapted to that heritage.

Significant within this group of early disciples (believers who are of Jewish origin and are disciples of John) is the figure known as the "Beloved Disciple."[13] This person is first designated as "the disciple whom Jesus loved" (13:23-26) in the context of the final meal which Jesus celebrated with his disciples before the feast of the Passover (13:1). Prior to that moment he is described anonymously as "a companion of Andrew" when both disciples first encounter the Lord (1:35-40). Evidently this disciple, an eyewitness, followed Jesus with such singular openness that he came to believe and to understand Jesus more deeply and quickly than did the others. Hence, he alone among the disciples is found at the foot of the cross, where Jesus gives him as son to his mother, thereby naming him his genuine brother (19:25-27). Likewise, this disciple alone, before seeing the risen Lord, recognizes the meaning of the empty tomb and believes (20:2,8). And, finally, he is the first, before Peter, to recognize Jesus at the Sea of Galilee, disclosing Jesus' identity to Peter by announcing: "It is the Lord!" (21:4-7).

For the fourth evangelist, the "Beloved Disciple's" understanding of and belief in Jesus became the model of the understanding and belief of the Johannine community. Not that the disciple held this understanding from the beginning;[14] but he was free enough, and gifted enough, to grow in his understanding of Jesus, as Jesus revealed himself through his ministry. Thus the fourth evangelist claims that his portrait of Jesus rests on the testimony of an eyewitness whose witness is true (21:24).

Samaritan Converts
A second group to enter the Johannine community, a group whose incorporation may have exercised the most significant influence upon the development of the Johannine tradition, consisted in a group of Samaritan converts.[15] The inclusion of these Samaritans also had decided influence on the Johannine community, for the Samaritan believers, like the disciples of John the Baptist, entered the community bringing with them the richness of their pre-Christian faith. This faith centered upon Moses as the one who spoke with God and who came down from the mountain, giving the people of Israel God's commands, his Word and Law (Exodus 3:1-17; 19:1-25). Moses not only was *the one who was sent by God*, but also was *the one who knew God personally*. Whereas the Jews of Judea focused upon God's covenant with David, the restoration of the Davidic kingdom and worship in Jerusalem (the city of David), the Samaritans placed emphasis upon Moses and upon history prior to the era of the Jewish kings. This emphasis subsequently offered the Johannine Christians a specific focus for understanding and interpreting the person of Jesus. It is Jesus who *has seen God*; it is *he* who has *come down, not from the mountain, but from heaven*. Jesus has brought God's Word because Jesus, the Word become flesh, has been with God from eternity. Thus the Samaritan beliefs would have stimulated[16] Christian reflection leading to a deepening of faith within the Johannine tradition, while the same tradition, in an effort to respect and include persons of Samaritan origin, would have accepted their traditions, reinterpreting them in the light of Jesus and his history.

This deepened understanding of Jesus, stimulated by the Samaritan emphasis, also provides insight into the centrality of the Johannine community's use of the Wisdom theme throughout the Gospel. The heritage of Wisdom, the first-born before all creation, the one who leads her hearers to life and nourishes them with food for life (Proverbs 8:1-5, 22-36; 9:1-11), can be easily applied to Jesus who is recognized as the One from above, the One who is the Light of life, the One who is before all. The synoptic traditions, themselves, present Jesus as a wise man, a "Wisdom figure," gathering disciples, teaching by way of parables and guiding others through memorable "wise sayings" (proverbs). The Johannine school, however, having affirmed Jesus as the preexistent One, carries the synoptic traditions further by making Jesus not only a unique teacher of Wisdom, but *Wisdom incarnate*. Thus, this development of the Wisdom theme in the fourth Gospel is easily explained as a corollary of the perspective picturing Jesus the One who is from above, the perspective developed under the catalyst of the Samaritan converts.

Jewish Christians of an Anti-Temple Bias
A third group of believers influential upon the formation of the Johannine tradition consisted of Jewish Christians of an anti-temple bias.[17] The fourth Gospel gives evidence of a group of anti-temple Jews who were responsible for the conversion of the Samaritans.[18] The reader would recognize an anti-temple bias in Jesus himself as he speaks of God's being worshiped neither on Mt. Gerizim (Samaria) nor in Jerusalem (4:21). Indeed, earlier in the Gospel, Jesus replaces water to be used for Jewish rites of purification (2:6), with new wine (2:7-10), anticipating the Eucharist. And more emphatically, after "cleansing" the temple (2:13-17), a dramatic event which the Synoptics place much later in his ministry, Jesus alludes to *his own body as the temple* to be raised up three days after it is destroyed (2:18-21). Contemporary Johannine scholars readily see in the evangelist's early inclusion of these accounts of Jesus' decisive sayings and actions a reflection of the community's early acceptance of a company of Jews opposed to the Temple together with its validation of their convictions. Further, it would have been this "radical" Jewish-Christian group which would have had the freedom from Jewish restraints both to engage and to convert the Samaritans[19] as well as to sponsor patterns of worship within Christianity at variance from traditional Jewish observances, feasts, and rituals.

At this point, it becomes easy to understand, not only the portrait of Johannine Jesus described in the second chapter, but also another significant strain in the Johannine portrait of Jesus, one which highlights Jesus' posture of defensiveness toward, and biting condemnation of, his Jewish adversaries. The Jews claim that they have eternal life through the Scriptures; so Jesus responds by instructing them to search the Scriptures for "even they testify in my behalf" (5:39). The Jews rejoice in the fact that Moses gave them manna in the desert, but Jesus retorts that his Father, not Moses, gives the true bread from heaven (6:32). The Jews insist that they are the children of Abraham; Jesus counters "If you were Abraham's children, you would be doing the works of Abraham. But now you are trying to kill me, a man who has told you the truth that I heard from God. Abraham did not do this" (8:33-40).

As one hears Jesus defending himself, one also hears the Johannine community defending itself in Jesus' name.[20] For in confessing Jesus as the One Who Is, the community had moved a long distance from the convictions of Judaism.[21] Orthodox Jews could well tolerate their fellow Jews who believed in Jesus as Messiah, even as a Messiah who rose from the dead. But Jewish Christians who opposed the Temple, Jewish Christians who admitted the Samaritans into their company, and most problematically, Jewish Christians who affirmed that Jesus was preexistent, equal to God, stood in profound opposition to their treasured Jewish heritage which maintained as its most basic tenet of orthodoxy that God is One and One alone.[22] Both sides would have been deeply defensive with regard to the other.[23] Excommunication from the synagogue would only heighten hostility and defensiveness, tones which permeate the Gospel from the fourth chapter onward.

Gentile Christians
Separated definitively from any possibility of co-existence with the Jewish community, the Johannine Christians easily welcomed a fourth group, a company of Gentiles into its embrace (12:20-23).[24] The Gospel gives several indications of the admission of this cohort. In the third chapter, the author records Jesus telling Nicodemus: "God so-loved the world that he sent his only Son that all who believe might not perish but might have eternal life" (3:16), thereby

affirming openness to the inclusion of the Gentiles. Further on, the Samaritan woman, an accepted disciple, confesses faith in Jesus, acknowledging him to be "Savior of the world" (4:42), thereby indicating that disciples, too, are open to this latest company of converts. Further still, the images of Jesus as "Son of God" and "the One Who Is" are readily intelligible to this group. The portrait of the Johannine Jesus is so designed that it easily draws Gentiles into its embrace.

The picture of Jesus of the fourth Gospel, then, is drawn as it is for several purposes. On the one hand, it is crafted so as to facilitate the incorporation of diverse groups of converts, each bringing with them different religious identities and convictions. In this vein it seeks to interpret Jesus in light of the multiple traditions of these persons, striving to illustrate that Jesus bears in deeper measure the saving power which they had hoped to find in and through the religious themes and practices of their former life. On the other hand, the portrait of the Johannine Jesus is designed to fortify these same Christians in their appreciation of Jesus as they, their understanding of Jesus, and their relationship with the Lord became challenged more and more fiercely with equally convinced religious adversaries. The image of and insight into Jesus was both source of life and source of conflict for this community.

Thus, the community of the "Beloved Disciple" necessarily came to describe Jesus as the One from above, ranking before all others; the true Light who has come into the world, shielding all from death-dealing darkness; the One who, having existed eternally in God's presence, has seen God and speaks of God with intimate divine knowledge. The community of the fourth Gospel necessarily confessed Jesus as the One in whom alone true worship is given to God, the One who has replaced all former feasts, indeed has replaced the Temple itself in his own body, uplifted and glorified. The Johannine Christians necessarily reverenced Jesus as Bread of Life, Resurrection and Life, Savior of the world. For each of its members, whether they were disciples of John, Samaritan converts, anti-temple Jews, or Gentile neophytes, contributed to the faith and progression of the beliefs of this community. Having sought Jesus and God's saving love through him in the light of their own religious heritages and their own historical needs, they fashioned a portrait of Jesus by means of images and themes familiar to them. Thus it was together that each group, fashioning one community, came to know Jesus deeply as Lord and God, the One Who Is.

THE JOHANNINE JESUS AND THE WAY OF DISCIPLESHIP

In each of the Synoptic Gospels, Jesus teaches the disciples a way of life by counseling specific behaviors, be it a life of self-denial and humble service under the shadow of the cross (Mark), a life of faithfulness to the New Law articulated by Jesus and advanced by church authority (Matthew), or a life of journeying with Jesus in advocacy for the poor, in mediating God's abundant mercy, in prayer, repentance and continued fidelity to the teaching of the Apostles and the Spirit of Jesus (Luke). For the Johannine community, Jesus also offers a clear statement of the way of discipleship. But for this Jesus, that way is far less detailed than it is for the Christ addressing any of the other Gospel communities. Jesus tells the Johannine disciples simply, "I am the way.... No one comes to the Father except through me!" (14:8) No need to search further for precepts or a series of moral norms. For the community of the Beloved Disciple, Jesus is so central, so radically and completely one with the Father, that he himself is the fullness of life for them; he is the way of discipleship.[25]

The Heart of the Way:
Personal Relationship with Jesus

Though lacking in detail and in the clarity which concrete norms can offer, this depiction of the way of discipleship has its own power and beauty. It focuses the attention of the disciple, not on imitation of Jesus, nor merely on following him obediently in a series of specific behaviors, but on developing and enjoying a deeply personal and life-giving relationship with Jesus himself. "This is eternal life," says the Lord in prayer to his Father, "that they should know you, the only true God, and the one whom you sent, Jesus Christ" (17:3), where "know" implies intimate personal experience of one another in mutual love.[26]

The Johannine Jesus speaks of this deeply interpersonal way of discipleship often. He presents himself as the model shepherd who knows his sheep and whose sheep know him, the shepherd calling each by name (10:1-3, 14). He "no longer calls (his followers) slaves,... but friends"; indeed, slaves do not know what the master is about but these are truly friends, intimates, because, as Jesus states, "I have told you everything I have heard from my father" (15:15). The closeness of this relationship and its personal significance for Jesus shines forth as he informs them that it is not they who have chosen him, but he who has chosen them (15:16). Indeed, as the previous verse indicates, he chooses them out of personal, and freely given, love. Interpersonal communion with Jesus is the way of discipleship.

Jesus fosters this relationship with his disciples through the Eucharist.[27] The synoptic Gospels recall that Jesus instituted the Eucharist with the instruction to celebrate it *in remembrance* of him (Luke 22:19). The celebration, therefore, *looked to the past*. The fourth Gospel presents Jesus, telling his followers "Whoever eats my flesh and drinks my blood lives in me and I in him" for "my flesh is real food and my blood, real drink" (6:55-56). The Eucharist, in the fourth Gospel, *looks to the present*. Hence, the Johannine Christian, in partaking of this real food and real drink, is being fed by the living Jesus so as to deepen his or her life in the Lord. Christ is personally present nourishing the believer with his own life which he received from the Father (6:57).

The description of the intimacy of the personal relationship of Jesus to each believer reaches an apex as Jesus depicts himself as the true vine, the disciples being the branches (15:1-5). In this image, Jesus assures the disciples that he and they share one indivisible life; the follower of Jesus, walking the way of Johannine discipleship is alive in Jesus own being which the Lord has received from the Father. As a result, Jesus can pledge that "whoever remains (lives) in me will bear much fruit" (15:5b), for the disciple who shares the very life of the Lord must be life-giving as Jesus is. Union with Jesus fills the disciple with the potential for profound spiritual generativity.

The One Commandment
This exalted way of discipleship advocated by the Johannine Christ,

the pursuit of a living, intimate, generative and personal relationship with him who alone is the way, constitutes the single, overriding perspective governing all else that concerns discipleship in the community of the fourth Gospel. For example, while this way does not find expression in a series of concrete norms which would give it "flesh and blood," so to speak, it does overflow into one commandment: the Johannine Christians must love one-another as Jesus has loved them (13:34). Such love proves the truth of the interpersonal relationship which Jesus promotes with each disciple. It demonstrates the genuineness of the life which the disciples share with him. And it does so most clearly as it calls the disciples to give the ultimate gift, their own lives, for the other (15:12f). Thus Jesus affirms "By this all will know that you are my disciples, that you have love one for another" (13:35). While the way of Johannine discipleship is not spelled out in distinct and concrete moral formulas, it does touch on concrete behavior in one singular norm: the commandment of deep fraternal love which extends Christ's love and presence into the concrete history of the developing Johannine community.

The One Prerequisite

Further, the overriding perspective of Jesus' alone being the way, gives rise to the Lord's proclamation of the singular *prerequisite* for discipleship: belief in Jesus, precisely as the one who has come forth from the Father and has life from the Father. Such belief is the divinely ordained prerequisite for salvation itself, almost to the extent that nothing else is necessary. Thus we read that God sent his Son so that "everyone who believes in him may not perish but may have eternal life" (3:16)[28]. Anyone who believes in Jesus will never thirst (6:35), and even were that disciple to die, she or he will live (11:25) and be raised up on the last day (6:40). On the contrary, whoever fails to believe in Jesus as the One Who Is, the preexistent Son of the Father, will die in his or her sins (8:24b).

But not only does Jesus proclaim this singular prerequisite for discipleship and life, he also explains the reason for its absolute significance: Ultimately whoever believes in Jesus believes, not only in Jesus, but in the one who sent him; and whoever sees Jesus, sees the one who sent him (12:44f; see 8:18f). Hence, Philip is gently rebuked because he has inadequate understanding of Jesus, inadequate belief: "Philip, how long have I been with you and you still do not know me? Anyone who sees me sees the Father" (14:9). But Thomas ultimately professes adequate belief, identifying the risen Lord with the exclamation: "My Lord and my God" (20:27f). Such belief is the model for all Johannine disciples, even those who have not seen the Lord (20:29f). It is the singular prerequisite for sharing Jesus' life on the way of discipleship.

The One Challenge and the Singular Support
Finally, the way of discipleship knows one singular challenge: persecution for belief in Jesus as the One Who Is. Thus Jesus has warned that, "if they persecuted me, they will also persecute you" (15:20). "They will expel you from the synagogues; in fact the hour is coming when everyone who kills you will think that he is offering worship to God" (16:2). In such instances, the disciple's chief task is to testify in Jesus' behalf (15:27).

As trying as the singular challenge may be, however, the disciple is not left without a powerful resource. In these moments, he or she will also know the profound support and the encouragement of "another Advocate," the "Spirit of Truth' (14:14-17, 26).[29] As the name Advocate implies, the Spirit's role is directly ordered to having a voice in controversy and in a trial, in a manner analogous to the role of a lawyer, an Advocate who stands at one's side in a courtroom trial.[30] The Spirit, then, will guide the disciples in their witnessing to the Truth; he will teach them what to say and remind them of all that Jesus has told them (14:26; 16:13-15). He will do this in absolute fidelity to Jesus, speaking only what he hears from the Lord (16:13).

The one challenge for the Johannine disciple and the support he or she receives are clearly related. The Spirit of Truth will enable the disciple to stand firm in witnessing to the divine and eternal origin of Jesus. Further, through the Spirit the disciple stands united with Jesus, who remains the overriding expression of the way of discipleship. Through the personal presence of the Spirit, the intimate, life-giving, personal relationship with Jesus, which is all that really matters, is sustained and deepened.[31] Thus, the unfolding of the way of disciple comes full circle. By loving one another as Jesus has loved them, by believing firmly that he truly is the One Who Is, eternally begotten of the Father, and by witnessing to him faithfully in persecution, the Johannine Christian effectively will pursue the one way of discipleship: Jesus, in whom one sees and comes to the Father; Jesus, who alone remains the way, the truth and the life (14:6).

Living in the Presence of Christ Already Here[32]

Each of the evangelists had to deal with their readers' expectations regarding Jesus' return, a return which, for the communities of Matthew and Luke, seemed to be a disappointing delay. At the time of the writing of the fourth Gospel, that delay had already spanned another generation. Yet the image of the Johannine Jesus provided the community with its own unique way of bridging the time between Jesus "having gone to the Father" and his return. Jesus, God's eternal Word made flesh, the One who is with the Father, remains personally present to each believer in the Johannine community. There is no need to wait; Jesus is with each person now.

The presence of Jesus now drives into the present many themes which other evangelists attach to the final coming of Jesus. Thus, Jesus has already revealed his glory at Cana (2:11) through the first of his signs.[33] Similarly, the author had claimed, in the prologue to the Gospel, that "we have seen his glory" (1:14); there is no need to wait for the Son of Man to come on the clouds of glory at some future time. Further, Jesus has already executed judgement, for, as he states: "The judgement is this: the Light has come into the world but people preferred darkness to the Light" (3:19). Those who refused to believe have already been condemned, while those who do believe will not be condemned (3:18). And finally, Jesus has already conferred eternal life upon those who believe, for he assures his audience that "the one who hears my words and has faith in him who sent me possesses eternal life; he has passed from death to life" (5:24). For the Johannine Jesus and his community, the final days are already here.

Yet, in spite of this emphasis on what theologians call *realized eschatology*, the Christ of the fourth Gospel also indicates that *something more is to come* in the future, for he goes to prepare a place for the disciples that where he is, they may also come to be (14:2-3). As a matter of fact, he assures the disciples that he will come back to take them to himself. There is more to being with Jesus than the disciple can experience in this life. Further, this Jesus affirms the reality of the "last days"; he speaks in terms of a *final eschatology*; history will reach its conclusion. In this light, Jesus speaks of raising up the believer, even if he (she) die, on the last day (5:28f; 6:39f, 44, 54). Though he does not speak of the coming of the Son of Man with great power and glory (Mk. 13:26), he does affirm a fuller future for the disciple and the final culmination of history.

Granting this promise of future transformation, the Johannine Jesus, nevertheless, emphasizes the present realization of what are generally regarded as ultimate realities: Jesus' presence, his execution of judgement, and his gift of eternal life. The difference between this perspective and that of the other Gospels, then, is striking. The Marcan community is exhorted to be vigilant and to pray for strength to remain faithful until the Son of man returns (13:23, 32-37). Matthew's community must wait for the Son of Man to return in glory for the moment of judgement (25:31-46). The Lucan community also must wait; it must wait until the age of the Gentiles be fulfilled before the Lord returns (21:24). The Johannine community, however, knows Jesus' presence, experiences judgement, and possesses eternal life with its ever-lasting outcome even now. Such is the power and depth of the way of discipleship in the community of the "Beloved Disciple." In union with Jesus, the One Who Is, one possesses eternal life and knows the presence of the glorified Lord though the last days are yet to come.

The way of discipleship counseled by the Johannine Jesus, like the portrait of Jesus crafted by the fourth evangelist, is well designed to nourish, guide, strengthen, and support the community of the "Beloved Disciple" in its unique history of controversy, challenge, and quest for salvation in and through Jesus, the One Who Is. Jesus himself is Light, Life, Shepherd, Vine, Savior of the

World. He is Bread of Life, Resurrection and Life, Wisdom and Truth, the sole Way to the Father. He is present in power and glory, source and example of true love, the heart of the way of discipleship. He sends the Paraclete who speaks in his name and, in his personal glorified presence, brings judgement, condemnation, salvation, and life even now. The Jesus who is so controversial is also the Jesus who, one with the Father, enables the community to stand strong in his truth and love, fully alive in his name.[34]

Dimensions of the Four Gospel Communities and the Dynamics of Christology

At the end of the second chapter, we noted that the images of Jesus presented by each evangelist served as statements of belief, capturing genuine elements of the personal faith-experience of the individual Christian. Having traced the manner in which the life-setting, specific needs and particular concrete struggles of the communities of the four Gospels have prompted the evangelists to craft portraits of Jesus tailored to the communities they served, however, we can see that the totality of the Gospel portraits of Jesus include lines and tones which reflect a number of the dimensions of the communities which generated them. Thus, the portraits of Jesus, shaped in the traditions of the Gospel communities reveal, not only the personal dimension of their members' faith-experiences vis-à-vis Jesus in himself, but also the contextual/historical, the existential/moral,[35] and the ecclesial dimensions of these faith-experiences as well. We will conclude this chapter with several observations concerning each of these aspects of the faith-life of these Gospel communities, aspects which form an integral part of their nature and therefore necessarily affected their personal and communal experience of Jesus, their images of Jesus, and the shape of the traditions which these churches produced.

TRANSHISTORICAL CHRIST - HISTORICALLY SHAPED BELIEFS
The main thesis of this and the previous chapters has been that the evangelists wrote for persons in a variety of life contexts and that those historical contexts determined in large measure the ways the evangelists crafted their portraits of Jesus. The images, responses

and challenges of Jesus, as each writer depicted him, facilitated their communities' ongoing experiences of Jesus, who then gave them light and strength to meet their struggles and to move through them. Historical context occasioned and conditioned both the believers' seeking Jesus and also the particular images through which they encountered him. Thus, context entered into the very dynamic of faith-experience and the development of images and statements of belief. So vital is this relationship between the concrete historical situation and the dynamics of faith-development that it will be useful to consider this relationship from several vantage points.

First, in terms of the relationship of *the disciple toward Jesus*, it should be clear that the concrete life-setting of the different Gospel communities effectively led the disciples to seek ever deeper meaning within their overall experience of and belief in Jesus. Thus, disciples under the threat of persecution came better to appreciate that the shadow of the cross impacted Jesus and his life-experience as well as their lives, and that the way of the cross truly is the way to life. Christians seeking to be free from Pharisaical domination came better to appreciate Jesus' own integrity and courage in articulating the New Law as well as the gift of Godly freedom which that New Law had brought them. Churches experiencing themselves as "late-comers" in God's design, came better to understand the expansiveness of Jesus' person and role in his being the center of history, and more deeply knew his capacities of uniting them, who arrived after him, with others who had lived before him. Believers willing to extend a welcome to disciples of John the Baptist, to Samaritans and to anti-temple Jews grew, in and through their ability to extend such welcome, to appreciate the full meaning of Jesus as Light of the world and Wisdom Incarnate, a Light and Wisdom so expansive, freeing, and profound that it could only come from One who came from above, God's eternally preexistent Son. Thus the historical situations of these communities, with their struggles and conflicts, acted as stimuli for believers to put renewed faith and trust in Jesus and also *occasioned their discovering fuller insight and meaning* in the experience of his ongoing saving presence.

Second, in terms of the relationship of *Jesus toward the*

disciples, the concrete historical context occasioned, and in some manner shaped, Jesus' self-revelation. It enabled Jesus once again to show his face as suffering Servant/Son of God and to strengthen his disciples to walk valiantly under the shadow of the cross. It enabled Jesus once again to act as the New Moses leading his disciples courageously to opt for ever greater freedom from the Pharisees, willing to accept the consequences of such separation. It enabled the Lord to stand ever more powerfully before them as the center of history and to move them to greater and more generous love of the poor and forgiveness of the wayward. It enabled the risen Christ to inspire his disciples with his light, wisdom and ongoing personal love, as he empowered them to defend his unity with God before disbelievers. The concrete historical context occasioned Jesus' ongoing self-revelation and also conditioned the way in which Jesus more fully revealed himself. Hence, the concrete historical context of each community influenced the relationship of Jesus and his disciples in two directions. First, it became the prism through which the disciples actively reached out toward Jesus, seeking the life only he could give. And, secondly, it was the channel through which Jesus, also actively, reached out toward the disciples, drawing them to himself in ever richer ways as he deepened his relationship with them.

The variety of ways and moments in which Jesus revealed himself, and the fact that he did so in an ongoing manner as the one and same Savior of all humankind can lead us to appreciate more fully Jesus and his relationship to human history. Once again, we must view this relationship from two perspectives. On the one hand, the ongoing dimension of Jesus' self-revelation illustrates the fact that Jesus, the risen One, stands above and beyond history, for he is able to enter history, offering saving wisdom, strength, healing and love in a multiplicity of concrete historical situations. He is not restricted to any particular moment of time or to one historical setting. He is transhistorical. On the other hand, the diversity of his self-revelation demonstrates that Jesus continues to have effective concern for history in its actual and concrete unfolding, for the many human events that make up history, and for real people who must still journey through it. The diversity of Jesus' self-revelation shows that Jesus actually does have the power to transform people's lives concretely. Thus Jesus, living beyond history but with the capacity and the desire to enter history is rightly called "Lord of history." He is able to bring all historical persons to the climax of their own lives and to guide history itself to its conclusion. Like the God he names Father, this Jesus is transcultural and transhistorical. He is the Savior of the world.

Having made these observations, we are now in a position better to appreciate the nature of *christological beliefs* and the process of doing Christology. With regard to the nature of beliefs, it has become clear that the Gospel images of Jesus are portraits which capture, or seek to capture, both the transcendental and also the historical/concrete elements found within the early experiences of the saving Lord. And so, on the one hand, these images or beliefs express the conviction that the believer has experienced transcendent wisdom, strength, courage, hope, and love in these historical moments. They proclaim that the believer, in moments of "this worldly" experience, has been lifted up with gifts for life which no mere human being, no finite reality, could supply, gifts of salvation and deliverance that lead beyond the very history in which the believer is immersed. On the other hand, they convey the conviction that the believer has encountered God and the risen Jesus in the texture of their own human lives. These beliefs seek to express the fact the true God and the saving Lord are real for them. They express something of the human, something of their own transformation, something incarnational. They express the believer's conviction that God continues "to become enfleshed" in them and in their lives. But, given the fact that beliefs reflect God's action in human experience and human lives, these beliefs remain limited in their ability to describe the wonder of the God who acts on behalf of humankind. Beliefs remain human and limited expressions of faith-experience even though they "capture" something of the experience of God.

This fuller appreciation of the nature of christological beliefs, as well as our fuller understanding of the interrelationship of the concrete historical life-setting of the gospel communities with their experience of Jesus' transhistorical saving presence, can, in turn, shed further light upon our understanding of the process of doing

Christology. For, in light of this fuller appreciation, we must affirm that today as well as yesterday the only way we can meet God and God's Christ is in the concreteness of history, through the medium of dealing with our deeply personal struggle and need. Meeting Christ and his saving love in the concreteness of one's struggle is the very foundation for coming to understand Jesus and the saving God whom Jesus reveals. It was the foundation for doing Christology within the context of the New Testament churches which we have examined; it is the foundation for doing Christology today.

In doing Christology, therefore, we must always bring our own history and our own personal struggle to the task. It is from these dimensions of life that one will come to know Jesus and the God made present through him. Rather than abandon our own particularity and needs (whether they be personal, familial, national, or global, whether they be social, political, ethnic or religious), we can employ them as the necessary contexts in which we will come to know Jesus and his Father personally as God for us. True, this will lead us to see God in ways that may be limited, tied to our own time-conditioned circumstances, perhaps constricted by our culture and our historical world-view. But further struggles and changing circumstances will occasion further opportunities to seek the love and guidance of Jesus again, enabling us to come to know him more fully. They will serve to purify former ways of thinking about Jesus and will provide newer ways of conceiving him. For the process of doing Christology is ongoing. It takes place in and through the concreteness and the movements of history and the persons who fashion that history: the original disciples, the communities of the Gospels, the church through twenty centuries, and Christians who stand at the threshold of the third millennium.

IMAGES OF CHRIST - THE WAY OF DISCIPLESHIP
But these reflections do not exhaust the manner in which the interrelationships of God's transcendent loving action, Christ's transhistorical guiding presence, and the struggles of an historical community affect its experience of God in Jesus. The experience of God's and Jesus' saving love has an existential/moral dimension. For the experience of God's saving love in and through Jesus

always involves one in an experience of God's having "a claim" on one's life. When God (in and through Jesus) answers a believer's cry in the midst of struggle, God reveals a "way out," a path which promises salvation, a path which one experiences as deeply compelling. In God's and Jesus' response to one's call, one experiences in return the call to discipleship. And, just as the experience of Jesus' saving action takes shape in concrete, historical form, so the call to discipleship is experienced and takes shape in concrete describable norms, *a way* of discipleship.

Thus, as we have seen in detail, the community's portrait of Jesus always involves the evangelists' depicting Jesus as addressing his disciples with a call to follow him, a call always accompanied by distinct perspectives regarding Christian life, specific paths which the disciple is to walk. Thus, if the Son of Man had to suffer many things, the disciple also had to take up the cross. If the New Moses came, not to abolish, but to fulfill the Law, then the disciple, too, needed to live by that New Law. If Jesus engaged the disciples by way of his prophetic embrace of the poor and the sinner, then the disciple also had to exhibit generous concern for the poor and a readiness to welcome the returning sinner. And if Jesus spoke only what he was given by the Father to say, then the disciple too needed to journey through life, with Jesus, in unconditional attentiveness to the Father. The way we see Jesus has an immediate effect upon the way we view our own concrete life. We cannot hear Jesus without perceiving his call to a new vision of life together with the challenge to embrace the kind of behavior which this perspective demands.

And so, as the Gospel communities witness, the experience of transcendent light, healing, strength, and love in the midst of their deepest needs is not an experience of deliverance from life in this world, but an experience of a deeper presence which leads one more thoroughly into life in this world. The disciples, in interpreting their experience of Jesus, come to understand Jesus as one who calls them to live transformed lives in the very setting which had become burdensome. Their experience of Jesus includes within its very center the sense of a compelling call to conversion and transformation in the concreteness of their historical lives.

This perception of the unity of the disciples' experience of Jesus, on the one hand, and of their experience of the call to a specific way of discipleship, on the other, provides still further insight into the nature of beliefs and doing Christology. Having recognized the fact that the experience of God, in and through Jesus, is always an experience of a God who calls the community and shapes the way the community lives and acts, we can see that an adequate and accurate interpretation of the experience of this God and of Jesus will always include some formulations describing the way in which God and Jesus call the believers to live. Hence belief statements which express the community's faith-experience include 1) statements *about Jesus in himself* and in his relationship to the God he calls Father, 2) statements which describe *how he acts* toward and relates to people, both disciples and non-disciples, and 3) within that latter group, statements which reflect the community's convictions about *how Jesus calls his disciples* and guides their moral behavior.

Genuine and life-giving understanding Jesus, therefore, is never a purely speculative or morally irrelevant endeavor. True understanding of Christ always arises out of experiences of the Lord which touch and change our personal sense of meaning and our personal direction in life. Life-giving understanding of who Jesus is and what he says always involves us in the process of adopting deeper and more Christlike moral convictions and moral standards, the particularities of the way of discipleship. In experiencing Jesus, one always experiences the call to and the strength for fuller conversion, a call to walk the way of ongoing transformation in Christ and in the Godliness which Jesus mediates.[36]

For this reason it becomes clear that no one can "do Christology" without experiencing the call to walk more deeply and faithfully with Jesus. In doing Christology we must also be willing to walk the way of discipleship and be ready to enunciate a deeper moral standard as the necessary corollaries to our belief in who Jesus is. Processing our faith-experience of God, alive in Jesus, today as well as in the past, leads to statements about Jesus and statements about the way of discipleship in one and the same motion. The latter unfold, moreover, not merely by way of logical deduction, as if one reasoned: "Jesus is model; therefore all must live as he lived." They are that, but at a deeper level both the image of Jesus and the call to a particular way of life flow from one experience of God in Christ. The experience of transcendent light and love in the concrete, leads the believer, at once, to make statements about Jesus and to enunciate statements about fidelity and about a particular way of life expressing that fidelity.

The formal study of Christology, then, includes an existential and moral impetus. In doing Christology individual believers and the Church as a whole must be ready and open to have their life challenged, changed, and transformed as their understanding of Jesus draws them more fully into walking in Jesus' likeness on the way of discipleship. The precise way that that will happen cannot be defined beforehand. But the fact that it will happen is as certain as the Gospel itself.

CHRISTOLOGY - PERSONAL FAITH - ECCLESIAL BELIEFS
The final dimension of the faith-experience of the disciples of the synoptic communities affecting the shaping of the images of Jesus and the traditions which these communities have generated can be described as the ecclesial dimension. In one sense, to speak of community is already to say ecclesial; for the word "ecclesial" itself is the adjectival form of the noun "ecclesia" meaning "gathering" or "assembly." But the nature and living structure of that assembly are not always apparent. Hence, it is necessary to consider explicitly the nature and import of the ecclesial dimension of the experience of God in and through Jesus and to note its significance for the nature and development of beliefs and for the doing of Christology.

The ecclesial dimension of Christian faith-experience is itself many-faceted. It most obviously includes the communal aspect of faith-experience, underscoring the fact that *personal* experience of Jesus in faith does not mean *private* or *unqualifiedly individual* experience. Rather, it is always shared experience. The disciples of the Gospel communities, and even less the first witnesses of Jesus, quite clearly did not encounter Jesus by themselves alone; rather, their experiences of understanding, hope, joy or fear, sorrow, and even obtuseness in the presence of Jesus were experiences which they had together. What meaning, strength and challenge they found, they discovered in communion with one another.

Thus the Marcan Jesus addresses the group of disciples regarding the cross, humility and the need to be servants of all (8:33f; 9:35; 10:42-45). When they were disturbed by Jesus' remarks, all failed to understand and all feared to question him (9:32). The Matthean Jesus delivers his teaching, the word of God, in his "Sermon on the Mount," not to one or two, but to a group of disciples who came to him (5:1). And, in the interest of preserving unity in the community, Jesus offers the followers rules for helping the church bring wandering individuals back precisely into the community's embrace (18:15-20). Luke describes the early disciples as one family, held together by its dedication to the teaching of the apostles, prayer and the breaking of the bread (Acts 2:42). The fourth evangelist, even in underscoring the intimacy of Jesus' personal relationship with each disciple, speaks of the disciples as one flock with one shepherd (10:14-16) and as branches of one vine (15:1-5). And all the evangelists present Jesus as sharing his last meal with a community of chosen followers, when, in different ways he communicates to them his convictions regarding the in-breaking of the kingdom of God through his approaching death.[37] The disciples experienced Jesus together. Their understanding and experience of God's saving love in and through Jesus was an ecclesial experience.

The corporate nature of that experience of Jesus necessarily affected the experience itself. The fact that it was a shared experience enabled the disciples to support one another in interpreting it. Their common witness enabled them to offer corrective observations in their remembering and in their processing the original experience. Bonded together by the original event, they could strengthen one another in fidelity to its implications, finding courage through one another to withstand threats to their and the community's survival. The ecclesial nature of the experience of Jesus' saving presence affected the preservation, the authenticity of interpretation, and the deepening of the experience itself.

But the implications of the ecclesial dimension of the faith-experience of Jesus are not exhausted simply by noting its communal aspects and their effects. For the community of disciples, at least as it is reflected in the synoptic Gospels, is not a monolithic community; rather, it is a differentiated community. All are truly personal believers in Jesus, but all do not share the same role vis-à-vis one another. Individual disciples are entrusted with a variety of specific ministries for the sake of the community and its fidelity to Jesus, ministries which other members do not share.

Thus, the Marcan community personally knew both Peter and Paul who had lived in Rome, as leaders who played irreplaceable roles in the fashioning of the community. Mark holds Peter in prominence for the community to remember in spite of his weaknesses, while the community itself preserved an instructive letter which Paul had written for its benefit prior to his arrival in the Eternal City. Further, Paul, by letter, had counseled them explicitly with regard to the diversity of roles within the church given "according to the measure of faith that God has appointed" for the building up of the body, the church (Rom. 12:3-8; see I Cor. 12:1-31). Matthew underscored the role of Peter as "keeper of the keys of the kingdom," the final arbiter within the community in questions of Christian beliefs (16:17-19). That community also knew the significant assistance of other leaders upon whom Jesus conferred the powers of "binding and loosing" (18:18). The Lucan communities depended upon "witnesses of all that Jesus said and did from the time of his Baptism..." (24:46-48; Acts 1:8, 21-22), remained dedicated to the teaching of the Apostles (Acts 2:42) and relied on "presbyters" appointed in various churches (Acts 14:23; 20:17, 28). The synoptic communities were differentiated communities enjoying the ministry and service of some whom Jesus appointed to lead, to guide, and to discern the authenticity and truth of the beliefs of its members.[38] All believers enjoyed the same faith; not all enjoyed the same ministry. The communal reception of the saving gift of God in Christ also begot a multiplicity of ministries for the preservation and the deepening of that gift.

The ecclesial dimension of the disciples' experience of Jesus, like the other dimensions of that experience, provides further insight into the specifically Christian nature of beliefs. From one point of view, the ecclesial aspect of faith-experience enables us to establish some helpful criteria for judging true from false beliefs. Since faith-experience and the beliefs flowing from it are, from their origin, intended by Jesus to be shared experiences and beliefs, true beliefs must be communicable to others, understandable by others, and valuable for others. Beliefs which would be confusing in their articulation, unintelligible in their meaning, or divisive or valueless in their implementation would be suspect. True beliefs, by their nature, are intended to unite the community, to preserve the authentic experience of faith in Jesus within the community, and to foster Jesus' saving love and life in its midst. The inherent communal, ecclesial nature of Christian faith-experience provides useful criteria for ascertaining the genuineness of the beliefs of any and all members of the community.

Further, the communities' recognition of differing ministries within the churches, and the treasuring of their respective roles, are themselves beliefs of those churches. They are expressions of the disciples' personal faith-experiences of God's action in and through Jesus. Throughout these Gospel accounts, the authors articulate the faith-conviction that Jesus, and/or the Holy Spirit, had appointed these ministers, had given them their respective tasks, and stood by them in the execution of their roles in service of the church. The disciples' faith-experience of God, alive in and through Jesus, included the conviction that Jesus fashioned a diversified group of followers gifted with specific ministries designed to build up and to preserve the community in his name. Belief in Jesus and belief in a structured group of faithful disciples who live in his presence were two facets of the one belief, the latter intended to preserve, to authenticate, and to foster the development of the former. Both originate in the one faith-experience of God alive and acting in and through Jesus the Christ.

This ecclesial dimension of the disciples' faith-experience of God, alive in and through Jesus, like the historical and the moral-existential dimensions of that experience, has implications for doing Christology today. For today, too, individuals must come to interpret their faith-experience of God and Jesus in communion with other believers who will be able to foster insight and to serve as correctives for one another. And, since, within the community of believers, there will continue to be official and final arbiters of the community's efforts in interpreting the individual's and the group's faith-experience of God and of Jesus, believers who seek to do Christology will necessarily recognize the call to attend to the voices of official Christian leadership. How one exercises such attentiveness and what form such leadership takes, are themselves complicated ecclesiological questions, questions beyond the scope of this book.[39] But the necessity of exercising some manner of attentiveness to the voices of official leadership and the indispensability of embracing some form of leadership to serve the process of doing Christology are undeniable convictions of the faith-experience. They are intrinsic elements of doing Christology in any age.

The shaping of the portraits of Jesus and of the traditions of the Christian believers of the Gospel communities, emerging from the faith-experience of the disciples within those communities, reflects the many-faceted nature of the communities themselves. Each community is historical and concrete, existentially and morally committed, and bonded together, most often within a diversified structure. Each characteristic affects the shaping of the images of Jesus and the tradition which the community generates and embraces as vehicles of Christian life and fidelity.

Yet, the images of Jesus and of his way of forming his disciples, fashioned within each community, never appear to be generated solely out of these communities' contemporary historical experiences. While believing Jesus to be alive and to be guiding the church in the historical present, each evangelist and each community sought to remember and to preserve the historic words and deeds of Jesus. Living fidelity existed only in faithfulness to Jesus who taught specific truths, advanced concrete religious perspectives, presented concrete challenges to conversion, worked tangible healings, and ministered to a variety of very recognizable persons. Faith experience of the risen Lord, faith experience of the "Christ of faith," flourished in each community as it remembered and recognized Jesus of Nazareth, the "Jesus of history," in the power and presence which it knew came from the risen One. It knew the Jesus of history in its experience of the Christ of faith[40]

In doing Christology today, no less than in the New Testament era, the disciple must meet the Jesus of history in his or her experiences of the risen Lord. For, as the historical Jesus was the measure of the authenticity of the faith-experience and the beliefs of the Gospel communities, so that same Jesus is the measure of the faith and beliefs of disciples today. Hence, persons who seek Jesus and who desire to interpret their experiences of Jesus today, rightly ask: "What was Jesus of Nazareth like?" "What was he concerned about?" "What actually did this Jesus preach, teach and do for others?" "What did Jesus expect to achieve through his ministry?" What was it that led to Jesus' death?" "How understand his death...and his resurrection?" It is questions such as these, questions concerning the historical Jesus, the origin of the Gospel traditions, that we will address in the next section of this book. But before doing so, we invite the reader to reflect upon the following questions.

Questions for Reflection

1. What aspect of the fourth Evangelist's portrait of Jesus appears to you to be most apt to strengthen the Johannine community in its particular struggles? What aspect of his description of the way of discipleship appears to you to be most capable of strengthening the community in its greatest needs? Explain your response to each question.

2. In what ways would you see the Johannine community's experience and image of Jesus a healthy complement to the synoptic communities' experiences and portraits of the Lord? In what ways would you see the former as needing the complement of the synoptic tradition?

3. In what concrete contemporary situations would you judge the Johannine way of discipleship to be especially helpful (to yourself, to other individuals, to your local community and/or church, to your nation)?

4. What aspects of Jesus' person and of his way of relating to the church and world can you single out as indicative of his transcultural and transhistorical nature?

5. How have you come more fully to understand the unity between belief in Jesus and belief in his having a moral claim on the disciples' lives and behaviors? What aspects of this claim strike you as most relevant for the culture in which you live?

6. What aspects of the ecclesial dimension of a disciple's faith-experience of Jesus have you been most aware of in you own journey of faith? What manifestations of the ecclesial dimension of Christian faith and tradition have been most helpful to you?

PART III

Christology and the First Disciples

The Experience and Understanding of the Historical Jesus

CHAPTER 5

Experiencing Christ: Preaching the Reign of God

Having seen the intentions of each Gospel community and each evangelist to be faithful to a tradition already in place, and having noted their convictions that their present faith experience of Jesus rested upon and was measured by the record of "eye witnesses" who knew, saw and heard the historical Jesus, we too must find in our experiences of Christ the living presence of the Jesus of history. Indeed, it was in the historical Jesus that God first gave full expression to God's Self-revelation and saving action in our history. Hence, the Gospel communities before us, and we too, depend upon the memory of the historical Jesus to clarify the meaning and intent of God's revelatory action in our behalf. And we too, like the Gospel communities, must look to the historical Jesus, to understand accurately the true way of discipleship, the paths of life in which we will surely embrace God's and Jesus' life within ourselves. In a word, our present experience and interpretation of the risen Lord, who engages us today on the way to salvation, needs to be measured by the words and deeds, the death and resurrection of the historical Jesus.

Coming accurately to know the historical Jesus, however, has its own problems. How separate the sayings and deeds of the Jesus of history from the interpretation of those sayings and deeds reflected in each of the Gospels? Is it possible to do so? Is it even of much importance? Some scholars would not think it possible, valuable, or necessary.[1] They would argue that our belief is measured by

Jesus simply as he is reflected in the Gospel communities. The beliefs of those communities are normative for us; Jesus is normative for them. We meet the historical Jesus through them and that is sufficient.

Others, like John P. Meier and Raymond E. Brown, would be convinced that the "discovery" of the historical Jesus[2] is a genuine possibility. Such scholars articulate criteria[3] for discerning the historicity of particular sayings, deeds, intentions, and events of Jesus' earthly life, and remain strongly convinced of the value of seeking to ascertain with accuracy, the teachings, works, and events of Jesus' history. They, and we with them, judge that the task of determining the historical Jesus has decided value, for several reasons: First, the knowledge of the Jesus of history assures us that the Jesus we know and meet in faith has truly walked through our history having lived a genuine human life and human journey. Secondly, the precise work of clarifying the words, deeds, events of Jesus' historical life protect us from pure subjectivism in our efforts to interpret what Jesus was about, what God intended through him, and what he and God intend for us today. Thirdly, knowledge of the historical Jesus also helps us avoid partiality in interpreting our experience of Jesus today; that is, it keeps us from attending only to those aspects of his words and deeds which support our ideology or our personal view of what Jesus was about two thousand years ago and what we think he would want today. Recognition of the full concerns of the historical Jesus can help us to be humble in our assertion of his desires for our present world and culture, and to appreciate that God is interested in more than simply unfolding an ideology.[4]

In our view the effort to seek and to grasp the historical Jesus, the Jesus who grounds even the early New Testament interpretation, is worth the labor. Together with a recognition of the legitimacy of the New Testament interpretation of his presence, intentions, and self-disclosure in its own life-situation, the recognition of the truth of the "historical Jesus" reinforces the Christian belief that God truly entered history, became one with us, and saves us by leading us in a genuinely human life. It helps us to understand that we have, as the author of Hebrew states, one who is like us in all things but sin (Heb. 4:14-16). It enables us to avoid both the excesses and the laxity which have at times colored Christian understanding of the Lord. And so, it enables us better to hear the true challenges which Jesus continues to offer us today.

In this chapter the first of several which will present the Jesus of history, we will seek to unfold Jesus' primary intentions in living among us, his fundamental concerns. These intentions and concerns are summed up in his proclamation "The reign of God is here; repent and believe in the Good News" (Mk. 1:15). This chapter will seek to unfold the meaning of this proclamation of Jesus, and the meaning of the "reign of God," as Jesus understood it.

The chapter will unfold as follows: in the first section we will seek to uncover the origins of Jesus' vision of the kingdom of God from within his own life experience. This will necessarily include his experience both of God and also of the people of Israel whose own struggle and religious expectations shaped Jesus' understanding of God's intentions in Israel's behalf, in the past and in the present. At the core of this life experience of Jesus, we can detect Jesus' sense of his "divine mission," his "vocation story." In the second section we will describe Jesus' own understanding of the kingdom as is revealed in the many facets of his personal response to God and God's call within the context of his history. In this section we will attend not only to what Jesus said but also to how he ministered to others in need, and to how he himself lived. In the third section, we will seek to underscore three significant dimensions of the kingdom as Jesus proclaimed it: its God-centered character, its relationship to salvation, and its radical newness and finality. In sum, in our reflections upon Jesus' proclamation of the reign of God, it will become clear that in Jesus' mind, the presence of the reign of God most effectively describes the fact that, in the day of Jesus, God and Jesus (whom God has sent) engage people with a power never before witnessed by human beings. In Jesus' view, this new and deeper presence of God necessarily calls forth a dedicated response of commitment to Jesus and of walking the way of discipleship, so that people may live, even now, under the reign of God.

The Reign of God:
the Origins of Jesus' Vision

Each of the synoptic Gospels describes Jesus, at the outset of his public ministry, as proclaiming "The kingdom of God is here; repent and believe the Good News" (Mk. 1:15; see Mt. 4:17; Lk. 4:18-21). The authors, in recording these incidents, intend not only to recount Jesus' inaugural act of public ministry, but also to capture the major themes which pervaded Jesus' entire public life of teaching, healing, challenging, and forgiving others in God's name. Though these evangelists record Jesus' proclamation with colors particular to their respective portraits of Jesus, the basic lines of their sketches match one another and clearly reflect the life and preaching of the historical Jesus. In them, we can detect elements of Jesus' experience of God, his sense of Israel's calling and expectations as God's People, and his appreciation of their weaknesses, their oppression, and their needs. These elements lie at the origin both of Jesus' grasp of his mission and also of his vision of God's reign, the central goal of his calling. We will look at each of these elements in detail.

JESUS' EXPERIENCE OF GOD AND JESUS' VOCATION

One of the distinctive sources of Jesus' vision of the reign of God was Jesus' personal experience of God and the calling which flowed from that experience.[5] Indeed, Jesus' experience of God constituted the principal root both of the newness of Jesus' vision and also of the unshakable conviction which he manifested in his unfolding that vision in word and in deed. For, though in many ways, Jesus' experience of God can be likened to our experience of the Transcendent in the depths of our own consciousness and freedom, there is a depth and a fullness to Jesus' experience of God which accounts for the manner in which Jesus speaks of God and for the striking uniqueness of the kingdom reflected in Jesus' preaching and ministry.

The Gospels are replete with descriptions of Jesus immersed in a variety of experiences of God. Luke, in particular, emphasizes Jesus' frequent movements into prayer, where Jesus opened himself to the inspiration of God's Spirit and found light and strength for his life and ministry. As noted above,[6] Jesus enters prayer, seeking communion with God, prior to his Baptism (4:21), before choosing the Twelve (6:12), at the time of his Transfiguration (9:28f), and before his last trial and crucifixion (22:39-42).[7] The author of the fourth Gospel also underscores Jesus' prayer, often referring to Jesus' total concern for "doing the will of his Father" (4:34).[8] Equally significantly, the fourth evangelist depicts Jesus in profound prayer in chapter seventeen of his Gospel, offering what amounts to a summary of the attitudes and aspirations which Jesus had brought to prayer on many occasions. The Matthean account, while less intent on giving explicit reference to this dimension of Jesus' life, clearly presumes it in recording, among other events, Jesus' baptism, his sojourn into the desert prior to his entry into his public ministry, and his celebrating his final meal with the disciples. That same author offers explicit reference to Jesus' reliance upon God's will and initiative as he in records Jesus' prayer of praise of God for revealing God's Self to Jesus and for handing all things over to the Son (11:25-27). There can be no doubt that the historical Jesus found the source of his life and ministry in his prayerful communion with God.

Jesus' meeting with God at the moment of his baptism by John has decided significance among these encounters with God. All four Gospels indicate that Jesus enjoyed a singular experience of God at his baptism. Each of these texts describes the Spirit hovering over Jesus in the form of a dove. Readers would recall the testimony of the book of Genesis (1:1f) where the author refers to God's Spirit[9] as having "hovered over the waters," mediating God's creative energy and will to bring about life and order in the world. They would readily understand that the Spirit overshadowed Jesus, in the midst of the waters of baptism, to recreate life and order, to effect God's new creation in a world largely devoid of God's breath of life. Hence, the intent of the evangelists is to express the fact, on the one hand, that God personally engaged Jesus with God's own energy (God's breath of life, God's Spirit) at that moment, and, on the other hand, that Jesus, conscious of God's special presence to him, recognized and began to interpret the meaning of God's intimate presence to him for his historical life and ministry which Jesus was about to unfold.

On this occasion of Jesus' baptism, the synoptic accounts also record a voice "from heaven": "You are my beloved Son; in you I am well pleased."[10] The voice echoes the prophetic text of Isaiah (42:1-4) which refers to Israel as God's beloved, destined to bring forth justice for all nations.[11] Though this text should not be understood as an *explicit* affirmation of Jesus' divinity *as defined in the fourth and fifth centuries*,[12] the text does suggest that at that moment Jesus knew himself to be deeply and specially loved and chosen by God. It suggests that, as Jesus entered the ritual of baptism and embraced the meaning of that ritual (namely, surrender to God and rejection of sin), Jesus experienced a more profound intimacy with God and a fuller sense of his call to respond to God in faithful service. Jesus heard deep within himself the voice of God designating him as God's intimate servant and son,[13] called to bring about a "new creation." Moreover, if we allow the theology of the infancy narratives[14] of Matthew and Luke to add fuller context to this reading, we can affirm that the evangelists wish to assert that Jesus, already brought up as a dedicated, observant, and God-centered Jewish person,[15] encountered God in a more profoundly engaging way at this moment of his baptism. They understood that Jesus' experience of God at this moment stood at the origin of his public ministry and of the proclamation of the kingdom which provided the dominant theme of that ministry. It was such an understanding which these writers wished to portray in Gospel form.

A second event, having substantially equal significance for the unfolding of Jesus' experience of God and for his discernment of his ministry immediately follows the account of his baptism. Each of the synoptic Gospels relates that Jesus, subsequent to his baptism, was led into the wilderness by the Spirit (Mk. 1:12; Lk. 4:1; Mt. 4:1). There, engaged in reflection and prayer, Jesus struggled with Satan several times, each time opting for fidelity to God, each time choosing renewed and deeper trust in God's ways. Once again, the evangelists wish to underscore the fact that Jesus found himself drawn into deeper communion with God. And, once again, they wish to show that this encounter with God provided Jesus with the light and strength which he needed to defeat the challenges of Satan.

Moreover, in this setting, Matthew and Luke cast Jesus in the image of Israel, but with an important difference. The Israelites wandered for forty years in the desert, complaining about food and succumbing to the temptation to build an idol in the form of a golden calf (Ex. 32:1-6). Jesus, however, spends forty days in the desert, fasts from food, and resists the temptation to enlist the powers of Satan. While Israel sought manna to nourish itself (Ex. 16:1-8), Jesus, faithful to the stipulations of the Deuteronomist (8:3), states: "Not by bread alone does one live, but by every word which comes from the mouth of God" (Mt. 4:4; Lk. 4:4). Israel abandoned God to worship an idol, but Jesus rebukes his tempter's seductions with the resolve: "The Lord your God shall you worship and him alone shall you serve" (Mt. 4:10; Lk. 4:8). Unlike Israel, Jesus emerges from the desert untainted. The authors clearly intend to picture Jesus as succeeding where Israel failed; Jesus is faithful servant/son whereas Israel so often was unfaithful.[16] In the minds of the authors, Jesus, in the midst of his prayerful experience of God, is given fuller insight and courage to be the New Israel in word and life. In the struggle in the desert, Jesus chose to surrender to the God he would later describe as *Abba,* committing himself to following the movements of God in the unfolding of his life and ministry before humankind. In the desert, alone with God, Jesus perceives his divine mission with fuller clarity.

Finally, Jesus emerges from these powerful experiences of God to engage in ministry. With his own theological insight, Luke describes the outcome quite clearly: Jesus reads a text from Isaiah and identifies himself with it:

> The Spirit of the Lord is upon me, because he has anointed me to bring glad tidings to the poor. He has sent me to proclaim liberty to captives and recovery of sight to the blind, to let the oppressed go free, and to proclaim a year acceptable to the Lord. (4:18f.)

In substance, Luke gives fuller expression to what both Mark and Matthew record: Jesus begins to proclaim the advent of the reign of God. Hence, Jesus' public ministry flows from Jesus' experience of God and from the vocational discernment which this experience fostered, an experience and discernment especially heightened during the moments surrounding Jesus' baptism. And that ministry, itself expressive of Jesus' sense of God's life within him, was captured in Jesus' proclamation: "The reign of God is here; repent and believe the Good News."

JESUS' RECOGNITION OF THE STRUGGLES OF ISRAEL

Jesus, however, did not experience God or God's call in a cultural vacuum. Rather, he perceived God's compelling presence in the context of his own concrete historicity. His own human life, together with his human freedom and potential for mediating life and love, were enmeshed in the struggles of the very people to whom he belonged. This was a people dominated by Roman occupation, a situation which many regarded as oppression and an offense against the God-given autonomy they had long believed in. His people were governed internally by an aristocratic minority, the priests and elders, a conservative minority who, because of their status, judged that keeping peace with Roman officials was necessary at all costs. This same minority looked down on a significant segment of their own population: the physically disabled (the blind, the lame, the lepers, the deaf and the mute); the morally suspect and known sinners (herdsmen, tax collectors, prostitutes and persons deemed possessed by evil spirits); the uneducated and socially powerless (widows and orphans). Prophets had repeatedly challenged Israel to attend to these persons, known as "the poor," persons we might more readily refer to as "the marginalized" or "the outcasts" (Amos 8:4-12). However, past generations in Israel as well as the society of Jesus' day turned a deaf ear toward the cries of prophets and poor alike.

The plight of these "marginalized" persons was quite complex. Clearly, they suffered physical and/or spiritual pain. But further, they suffered a profound social pain: they had to endure oppression even at the hands of their fellow Israelites. They were forced to live as "second class citizens," having little or no status in Israel, and having no way of attaining status. Widows and orphans were helpless; for only through a husband or a father could one attain access to power in this patriarchal society.[17] Public sinners, fraudulent persons, unscrupulous herdsmen were powerless; they could not redeem themselves or make restitution because all their earnings were regarded as tainted (whether this were factual or not).[18] Persons suffering any form of disease or physical disability were looked upon as carrying "God's punishment" for sin and therefore were to keep their distance lest they "contaminate" others.[19] Physical and/or moral disability, real or suspected, placed the sufferers in social isolation. Rather than visit these persons with care, the more powerful and well-established within the Israelite society neglected them, belittled them, excluded them, and presumptuously affirmed God's supposed "displeasure" toward them. The prestigious and aristocratic segment of Israel had relegated its "poor" to a place of profound personal, social and religious misery.[20] Israel was far from a nation of one people, united in one covenant of love.

Jesus experienced God and God's call to action within this segregating context of life within Israel. This context necessarily appeared to Jesus as ungodly, quite contrary to the God whom Jesus knew welling up from within himself. Jesus clearly perceived that this God most certainly wished to transform this society and the people within it. Jesus' profound experience of God offered light and energy for God's decisive and salvific action in Jesus' world. And Jesus knew that he was called to be its mediator.

JESUS' AWARENESS OF THE EXPECTATIONS OF ISRAEL
Yet Jesus' conviction regarding God's desire to transform Israel did not develop within Jesus' consciousness from an entirely new and unique experience of God. There is still one further "source" or element which gave rise to Jesus sense of his mission. For Israel itself, through the centuries, had longed for a "new age," an age of "justice, love and peace," an age in which God would bring about "peace within individuals, peace with one's neighbor, peace between nations and peace with all creation."[21] Israel believed in the coming of a kingdom of "universal justice, love and peace," a kingdom which would embrace Israel itself and reach out from it to every other nation; it believed in the coming of "the kingdom of God."

Like Israel itself, Israel's belief in the advent of this kingdom developed over time.[22] The roots of this conviction rested on Nathan's prophecy to David (II Sam. 7:11-16). God's promise to David centered upon God's will to preserve the Davidic dynasty, securing for Israel a line of kings who would govern with justice, extend special love toward the poor and needy, and protect Israel from outside oppression. Israel therefore pictured the throne of David, as the mediator of God's benevolent care; the dynasty would serve as God's way of bringing about salvation, harmony and peace for God's People. It would be God's way of saving Israel both from external oppression and also from internal segregation and injustice. With this interpretation, we can understand the sacred author's record of the Lord's pledge to David through Nathan: "Your house and your kingdom shall endure forever before me; your throne shall stand firm forever" (2 Sam. 7:11). And in the same light, we can appreciate the prayer of the Israelites on the occasion of the enthronement of the king:

> Oh God, give your judgement to the king...that he may govern your people with justice, your oppressed with right judgement...that he might defend the oppressed among the peoples, save the poor and crush the oppressor.... May he rule from sea to sea... and his foes kneel before him, his enemies lick the dust (Ps. 72:1-4, 8-9).[23]

The advent of wicked kings from the eighth century B.C. to the Babylonian exile, however, brought about a concomitant refinement in Israel's expectation. The Davidic line did not serve God's ways faithfully; the throne did not stand firm in God's ways but succumbed to selfish greed and oppressive ambition. Israel lamented this contradiction to God's pledge to David (Ps. 89), and prophets renewed Israel's hope by focusing their expectation upon an individual monarch. Israel hoped that God would raise up a reputable king, one gifted with judgement, concerned for justice, and skilled in bringing about peace. And so we read:

> A child is born to us, a son given to us and upon his shoulder dominion rests. They name him wonder-

counselor, God-hero, Father forever, Prince of Peace. His dominion is vast and forever peaceful, from David's throne and over his kingdom, which he confirms and sustains by judgement and justice, both now and forever (Is. 9:5-6).[24]

And even after the exile, the prophet sustains similar hope:

A shoot shall sprout from the stump of Jesse and from his roots a bud shall blossom. The Spirit of the Lord shall rest upon him: a spirit of wisdom and understanding.... Not by appearance shall he judge, not by heresy shall he decide, but he shall judge the poor with justice and decide a right for the land's afflicted.... There shall be no harm or ruin on all my holy mountain; for the earth shall be filled with knowledge of the Lord, as water covers the sea (Is. 11-1-9).

From confidence in the permanence of a faithful dynasty, a line of kings, which would sustain justice and peace, Israel came to hope for the advent of a just and peaceful individual king. It would be this singular ruler who would, under God's design, signal the coming of the kingdom of God.

Jesus met and experienced God while bearing within himself these hopes and expectations of God's People. Deeply aware of Israel's plight and suffering in his own day, Jesus, nonetheless, remained convinced of the validity of Israel's hope-filled expectations. In the context of that dual awareness, he discovered within himself the same saving God whom his ancestors knew and hoped in. He experienced God directing him in his own life with even greater intensity and conviction than God had done with Jesus' ancestors. Thus, he confidently proclaimed that what had been at best a distant expectation within Israel was, at this new moment of its history - the day of Jesus - about to become reality: The reign of the God of justice, love and peace had come. Jesus interpreted his experience of God and of God's compelling movements within him in terms of Israel's hope in God and God's reign.[25] The plight of

Israel and its oppression was about to end. "The kingdom of God is here."

Jesus' Understanding of God' Kingdom

Jesus' proclamation of the presence of God's reign, however, did not echo within Israel without causing controversy and contradiction. For the failures of Israel during the five and one half centuries subsequent to the Babylonian exile left this people in a quandary not only with regard to whether and when God would establish God's reign, but also with regard to how God would accomplish this design. This latter question evoked a variety of responses and fostered significantly diverse ideologies within Israel. Pharisees focused upon faithfulness to the Torah. Zealots believed in a revolutionary overthrow of Roman rule. Essenes put their confidence in a life of asceticism. Sadducees, most of whom were members of the wealthy aristocracy, the chief priests and elders, maintained that the blessings of this life were the blessings God intended, and therefore argued for cooperation with the Romans for the *status quo*. Israel did not want for theories and/or efforts about how it could bring about God's reign.

In terms of bringing about a kingdom of justice, love and peace, a kingdom constituted of persons enjoying peace within themselves, peace with one another, peace between nations, and peace with the entire created world itself, however, each of these paths was doomed to failure. For each path relied on the native abilities of human beings to fashion that peace, abilities which had shown themselves powerless for hundreds of years. And it was precisely these all-too-human abilities, marked by human weakness, human sinfulness, and the forces of evil, that resisted the ideal of the kingdom and impeded its realization. What Israel really longed for, what it believed God had promised, was impossible for human beings to achieve. To paraphrase Walter Kasper,[26] what was needed was a fresh start, a new power which human beings could not produce, a power which only God could give, a transcendent power for justice, love and peace which would create a new world and a new way of being. This power, in essence, needed to be God's gift

-135-

of God's Self, in unsurpassable Self-communication to humankind.

In this context Jesus proclaimed that the longed-for reign of God is here. In contrast to all his contemporaries, he understood well and intended to call attention to the fact, that this wonderful event was truly God's doing, God's initiative, God's intervention in history. It was the reign of God. Truly, that is Good News: Good News for all who suffer human weakness, Good News for the oppressed, who had been helpless; for God's benevolent love and deliverance was theirs. And it was also Good News for the oppressor, who in his or her narrowness and selfishness, found him or herself prone to victimize others, even to the point of being enslaved in his or her own selfishness, for God willed to empower these persons to reform, to live more constructive lives. This was Good News for all, for God's power and presence had come to free all persons to live differently. All that was necessary was that people believe the Good News, repent, and act appropriately. Such was the astounding vision and proclamation of the historical Jesus as he began his public ministry.

THE IMAGE OF THE KINGDOM REFLECTED IN JESUS' TEACHING

Jesus clarified this vision in many ways: preaching, teaching, healing, mediating God's forgiveness, living in communion with all the marginalized, seeking and responding to God and God's will at every turn of his life. His teaching and his sayings - expressions of his unique and practical wisdom - occupy a central place in his efforts to unfold his understanding of the kingdom. Thus, as we have already seen in detail,[27] Jesus painted pictures of the kingdom by challenging his followers to walk specific paths of fidelity to him, the ways of discipleship. Although each Gospel account manifests the mind of its respective evangelist and of the community for which he wrote, the substantial teaching of the Jesus of history clearly lies behind this collection of sayings, exhortations and pronouncements. Each reflects that, in essence, the coming of the reign of God meant for Jesus that each individual who would accept God's Self-Gift would find the power and strength to live a transformed life. For the kingdom of God is nothing other than real persons alive with the transforming and energizing love which is God.

-136-

For the historical Jesus, then, the way persons live in faithfulness to God will express what God's reign looks like concretely. His injunctions and exhortations actually describe the way he understood the kingdom which emanated from the transcendent One. Thus he states that persons embracing the reign of God must seek a holiness beyond that called for by the Scribes and Pharisees (Mt. 5:20). They must live and pray for, not only friends, but even those who do them harm (Mt. 5:43-48). They must strive to integrate sexual strivings into genuine affection, reverence and respect for one another (Mt. 5:27-30). They must allow God so to calm their fears and mistrust of one another, that they can be simple and straightforward in their speech and in all their dealings with one another (Mt. 5:33-37). People living in the reign of God truly can be integral (perfect) as God is integral, for they know within themselves the power of God's presence in Godly love, justice, reverence, and truth. The presence of God within their minds and hearts will enable them to live differently.

In the same way, persons engaged by the reign of God experience God's strength and courage in time of persecution (Mt. 5:10). Seeking life in God, they know a Godly disposition of love, are enabled to serve one another humbly and selflessly, and can come to perceive and to foster the sacred in one another (Mt. 5:5, 9). They readily see the blossoming presence of God in the repentant sinner, and therefore, are themselves blessed when they extend mercy toward their returning neighbor (Mt. 5:7). They recognize that creation, God's gift to all, belongs to all; therefore, they take steps to share from their own possessions with all, especially those who have less (Mk. 10:17-27; see Mt. 5:45). All the specific stipulations of the Gospel accounts substantially reflect the vision of the Jesus of history. They clarify the nature of that kingdom which God fashions, the reign of God precisely as Jesus understood it.

THE KINGDOM IMAGED IN PARABLES
Jesus fostered the same vision and conviction through parables. Parables are story-images of the kingdom; in them, too, Jesus describes what life under the reign of God is like. Thus, in describing the kingdom in terms of a farmer sowing seed, the historical Jesus underscores God's (the farmer's) initiative and

generosity, graciously spreading God's creative power through God's Word far and wide. Jesus stresses that that Word shall bear fruit in good soil even though some falls by the wayside. His challenge is simply to listen and to hear (Mt. 13:1-9).[28]

Further, in describing the kingdom as a grain of mustard seed, Jesus emphasizes that God's reign is at first almost inconspicuous, but that this energizing presence is so powerful that it inevitably spreads and gathers many different persons into its ambit (Mt. 13:31-32). Jesus expands this same theme, picturing the kingdom as a great banquet in which all persons, especially the poor, the crippled, the blind, and the lame join with one another in fellowship with God, who is imaged as the Master (Lk. 14:15-24). And Jesus completes this theme by describing God as unconditionally merciful in the parables of the wayward son and the forgiving father (Lk. 15:11-32; see Mt. 18:21-35), thereby abolishing all bases for exclusion within the community which lives by God's love.

Through parables, too, Jesus not only proclaims the presence of the reign of God, but also describes its nature for all to hear. The kingdom of God consists in the presence of God's saving power among human beings which so empowers them that they come to live in an unsurpassed Godlike way.

THE KINGDOM ILLUSTRATED IN JESUS' SAVING DEEDS
A further description of Jesus' understanding of the reign of God, together with clear evidence of its presence in power, emerges not from what Jesus said, but from what he did: Jesus' miraculous deeds both reveal and make present God's reign (Mt. 12:28; Lk. 11:20). His acts of restoring sight to the blind, hearing and speech to the deaf and the mute, mobility to the lame and paralyzed, speak of the wholeness of life which human beings enjoy in the reign of God. Jesus' deeds of exorcising those possessed by evil spirits speak of God's power to restore and enhance human freedom for fuller human life and love under God's reign. His efficacious efforts to raise persons from the dead manifest the fact that God's intention, as well as life in the kingdom, cannot be stifled by physical death, but rather lasts beyond death for all eternity. Jesus' capacity to calm turbulent seas illustrates the fact that life under

God's reign produces harmony and peace with all elements of creation. Jesus' deeds of power further unfold the meaning of the reign of God while also giving evidence of its presence in power now.

THE KINGDOM REVEALED IN JESUS' LIFE AND PERSON

Finally, Jesus unveils the meaning, and illustrates the presence, of God's reign by the way he himself lives. For Jesus shows himself to be empowered by, indeed to be the principal manifestation of, the reign of God in his very person. Jesus is the foremost practitioner of what he preaches. And so, Jesus has the readiness and courage to forgive others in God's name (Mk. 2:5, 16f; 3:28), even to the extent of forgiving his own persecutors from the cross (Lk. 23:34). He is able to embrace all with reverence, particularly the "marginalized." He willingly associates with women, and, rather than use them for sexual gratification, he leads them to discipleship and to the kingdom (Jn. 8:1-11; Lk. 7:36-50). He manifests simplicity and directness in his speech, in teaching the crowds (Mt. 5-7), in challenging the Pharisees (Mt. 12:1-13), in approving and disapproving Peter's groping efforts to understand him (Mk. 8:27-31), and in standing firm in the struggle of his final trial (Mk. 14:43-25:15 and parallels). Thus, in his way of living, Jesus himself is the prime example of the presence of the reign of God. He is its foremost embodiment. As such, he enables all onlookers (who observe him with openness) to understand what it is like to live under the saving power of God, what it is like to live by God's power and love, on behalf of God and one's fellow human beings.

And so, through word and deed, through parables and actions, through his very way of life, Jesus proclaims the presence of God's reign - all the while unfolding the meaning of the reign for human life and human history. In essence, he illustrates that the reign of God means that God, in God's very Self, is present for human beings to welcome and to embrace. God in God's Self is given to human beings as New Power for life, abolishing the reign of sin and establishing the reign of love, justice, and peace for all. Such is Jesus' understanding of the kingdom of God; such is the mystery which Jesus unfolded; such is the overture of love which he called all to embrace.

Three Significant Aspects of God's Kingdom

Having described the kingdom of God as Jesus proclaimed, understood, lived, and mediated it, we can single out three dimensions of that kingdom which deserve further reflection: "the God-centeredness of the kingdom," "the salvific fullness of the kingdom," and "the newness and finality of the kingdom." We will treat each in turn.[29]

THE "GOD-CENTEREDNESS" OF THE KINGDOM

To underscore the "God centeredness" of the kingdom may seem redundant, particularly because we have already noted clearly that the reign of God comes about precisely because of God's initiative and through God's Self-Gift to human beings. As we have said, the reign of God is rooted in God's Self-communicating presence to humankind bearing the power of God's love. This central dimension of the kingdom, however, has several significant implications for a fuller Christian understanding of God and of Christ.

First, because the reign of God flows from God's profound self communicating presence, that kingdom necessarily reveals precisely who God is, what God is like. And since it is, as we shall see below, God's definitive action in our behalf, it expresses the whole of what God wishes to do, the fullness of who God is. The reign of God constitutes God's definitive Self-revelation. In the coming of the kingdom, and in Jesus who embodies that kingdom, we see clearly the Transcendent; we come to appreciate the integrity and power of transcendent love; we receive the light enabling us more adequately to name our God. Though that kingdom is yet to be completed, in living the life promoted by Jesus, in experiencing God's forgiveness through Jesus, in knowing the healing offered by Jesus, we are already given a clear insight into God and into the dynamics of Godly love.

Secondly, it becomes clear that Jesus was able to bring about the reign of God precisely because of his experience of and communion with this God, however we further define that relationship. Jesus is a powerful mediator because Jesus, in deep and steadfast surrender to God, experiences the insatiable love of the One he names Father. He is able to speak accurately of God and can act effectively in God's name because of his prayerful presence to God and because of God's Self-communication to him. Such is the faith interpretation of all the Gospels, whether we describe that communication as accomplished by way of the Spirit (as do all the synoptics in recounting Jesus' baptism and temptations, and more especially as do Luke and Matthew in their infancy narratives) or as accomplished by way of the incarnation of the preexistent Word and wisdom of God (as does the author of the fourth Gospel).

Jesus' God:
The Immanent God of Intimate Compassion
What is most striking in Jesus' experience of God and in the mutual relationship between God and Jesus is the way Jesus addresses and names God: Jesus calls God "Abba" (Father). In doing so, Jesus interprets his experience of God; he is doing theology. The name Abba is Jesus' preferred manner of expressing that experience. Of course, as we hear Jesus call God *Abba*, and as we observe him teaching disciples to name God in a similar way, we need to be careful not to misinterpret Jesus. We need to be careful to avoid imposing every aspect of our images of our fathers on Jesus' God. Rather, we need to examine Jesus' understanding of this term and the images he uses to clarify it.

In this light, it is important to note, as biblical scholars point out, that in the Aramaic language the word *Abba* conveys, not just the basic relationship of parent-child, but also feelings of warmth, affection and intimacy. Hence, Jesus, in using this term, would be seeking to convey his sense of God's being intimately close, his experiencing God in a profoundly personal and wholly loving manner.

Because of this experience of God, Jesus develops images of an unconditionally loving God in parables. In particular, we note the image of the father longing for the return of the wayward son, the father holding no grudge but eager to forgive, the father filled with joy as at his son's return (Lk. 15:11-32). Jesus presents this parable to express his experience of the one he named *Abba*. Further, we recall Jesus' description of God as provident: God cares for the "birds of the air" and the "lilies of the field." And so, Jesus confidently counsels his disciples to "seek first God's reign and God's way of holiness." God will take care of every other need the disciple may have (Mt. 6:25-34; Lk. 12:22-32). Jesus' experience of *Abba* leads him to know God was wisely caring and provident.

Jesus' God:
The Transcendent God of Unlimited Compassion
While stressing the immanence of God among God's People - God's deeply personal, warm, caring presence - Jesus, nevertheless, is cautious to affirm God's utter transcendence: God is our father in heaven (Mt. 5:9, 16, 45, 48); no one sees God except the One who is from above (Jn. 3:3; 1:18). Hence, the disciple must recognize that God's name (God's person) is holy and must pray that God's sovereign will be done (Mt. 6:10; Lk. 11:1-4). Because of God's transcendence, all things are possible for God (Mk. 10:27; 14:36; Mt. 19:26); because of God's transcendence, God's love and mercy, God's life among God's people, are inexhaustible.[30] Thus, while speaking of God's deeply personal care, Jesus also affirms God's utter transcendence. In the words of Walter Kasper:

> The dignity, sovereignty and glory of God are...preserved, but they are imaged in a different way: God's Lordship is Lordship in Love. God's Lordship shows itself in his sovereign freedom to love and to forgive. That is what shows that he is God and not man (cf. Hos. 11:9).[31]

In addressing God as *Abba*, then, Jesus sums up his experience of God, the God whom he reveals progressively in his own words and his own gestures of healing and love. This is the God who stands above and before him. This is the God whom Jesus reveals and makes present in proclaiming the presence of the reign of God. Jesus' proclamation of the kingdom of God flows from his experience of the "Father who is in Heaven," the Father who is unlimited compassionate love.[32]

THE REIGN OF GOD AND SALVATION

As persons heard Jesus' proclamation of the reign of God and opened themselves to the forgiveness, the healing, the integrity of life, and the transformation which he brought, they knew deliverance from human weakness, sin and powerlessness. They experienced salvation. Salvation is the deliverance from all the evils which burden human life and block the achievement of the deepest of human longings. The coming of the reign of God in human history is the advent of salvation.

Given that fact, we can now better understand salvation itself. First, it is clear that salvation, like the reign of God, consists in human participation in the very life and power of God, the human sharing in God's own sovereignly free life of love, justice and peace. Salvation is "being alive in God as Jesus is alive in God." Ultimately then, to see Jesus is to see salvation; to live in Jesus is to experience salvation; to be open and surrendered to the God who gives God's Self to us as abiding and life-giving love, is to be open to salvation. Salvation is the human participation in the being, life, freedom, and love which is God.

Secondly, salvation, like the reign of God, touches human beings in every dimension of human existence. God's gift of God's Self permeates every aspect of human life: human understanding, human freedom, human action, human love. All these dimensions of human life become vivified with the presence and power of the Transcendent. Persons who struggle with their world, persons in conflict with one another, persons facing human weaknesses, sickness, loss and death, persons searching for global justice and peace, persons seeking to foster environmental progress and care for the world find new vision, new strength and hope, new courage, more integral selflessness and generosity. Such persons become empowered so as to live by faith, hope and charity in the concrete world which is theirs. As a result, not only they, but the very society in which they live find transformation; in them and through them, the whole world is changed for the better.

The reign of God and salvation brought by Jesus, as we have mentioned in an earlier context, is not deliverance *from the world* but fuller, more Godly life *in the world*. It touches every aspect of life as human persons experience it. Hence, life enhanced by God's powerful and loving saving presence is not purely spiritual, but spiritual-physical, affecting human bodily being. It is not simply religious or God-oriented, but, affecting human persons in their human relationships, it is humanly interpersonally oriented. It is not merely future, but changes life now; and yet it is not just for today, for, as it transforms life through Godly living, it brings about the transformation of history itself. The reign of God and salvation touch every aspect of human life. Everything human - knowledge, freedom and love; religion, society, politics; the environment, culture, and history - becomes transformed as God gives God's Self to human beings. Salvation is "being alive in God as Jesus is alive," and life in God transforms the world creating a new age.

Discussion of salvation, reflection upon persons "being alive in God," brings us, in a full turn, back to Jesus' proclamation itself in its fuller statement; for Jesus' proclamation concluded in the summary challenge: "Repent and believe the Good News." What is required of human beings, therefore, in order that God's reign be present in power is repentance and faith. How shall we understand these fundamental dispositions of the human mind and heart, these fundamental dispositions by which God effectively enters the human?

Repentance calls persons to "let go" of the past and to begin a new way of life. Such is the attitude of the wayward son returning to his father's home (Lk. 15:17-201); such is the basic disposition which Jesus asks of the rich young man (Mk. 10:21); such is the mind and heart of the Matthean Christ as he announces each of the antitheses early in Matthew's Gospel (5:17-48; see also 6:24-33). Paul speaks of himself as an example of this repentance, stating that he counts even his fidelity to the Law as loss in face of knowing and following Jesus (Philip. 3:4b-11). And Jesus, in each of the synoptic accounts calls all his hearers to this "letting go of former ways of life" in order to live in God when he counsels disciples that they must "lose their very selves in order to find themselves," their true selves, in following him (Mk. 8:35 and parallels). Repentance is turning one's mind and heart from one's less life-giving ways and practices to the in-breaking of God's sovereign, free, empowering love in cooperative efforts of concrete love, work for justice, and labor for peace.

This understanding of repentance, therefore, is far from rigorism, far from embracing harsh practices which only serve to make one miserable and/or proudly self-reliant. Rather, it has as its most basic quality, a genuine disposition of surrender of the self, a surrender of the self to the omnipotent, sovereign, all-loving God, the God whom Jesus reveals. In this way it is one with what Jesus and the Gospels name as faith. For faith really is a fundamental and personal openness to God, an attitude of surrender to God, a disposition of trust in and commitment to God, wherever, whenever, and however God chooses to communicate God's Self. The essence of this faith, as Walter Kasper points out,[33] is to cease relying on one's own powers and to entrust oneself to the power of God. Such faith recognizes that, in trusting oneself, one can do nothing (Mt. 17: 19-20a), but that, when trusting in God, one can do everything (Mk. 9:23; see Jn. 15:5); one can act with new and deeper, transcendent strength. Faith, therefore, is actually a participation in the omnipotence of God (Mt. 17:20b-c), the God who, in God's very person, is sovereignly free, unlimited love.

Such faith, therefore, is the most fundamental disposition of the human mind and heart which makes participation in the reign of God possible. Faith, in this sense, is the absolutely necessary condition for human beings to receive salvation, that is, to "be alive in God." With such faith, and with the repentance which expresses it, human beings can be made whole. They begin to enjoy the fullness of salvation (Mk. 5:34). They are empowered to mediate salvation even beyond their individual selves. They become, in God, saving light, healing love, forces of transformation for the entire world and its history.

THE REIGN OF GOD - ALREADY HERE AND YET TO COME
Jesus' proclamation, his parables, his wonderful deeds of healing and mercy, all indicate that the reign of God is here, now. And yet, even though that kingdom is here, Jesus recognizes that it is still incomplete; something is yet to come. Hence, he speaks in parables

of the mix of weeds with the wheat and urges patience until the final harvest (Mt. 13:24-30). Obviously, it is not always easy to distinguish weeds from wheat. Therefore he cautions against rooting out the weeds; such efforts may, in fact, damage rather than preserve the wheat. Further, he urges that disciples pray for the coming of the kingdom (Mt. 6:10; Lk. 11:2), clearly indicating that the reign of God is yet to unfold. And he calls attention to the return of the Son of Man at some future date; only then will those who have walked the way of discipleship in this life enter the everlasting kingdom prepared for them (Mt. 25:31-46). The reign of God is a future as well as a present reality.

Jesus' forthrightness in underscoring the incompleteness of the reign of God - even though he proclaims it to be a present reality - raises several questions. Why is it that God does not bring about the kingdom completely now? Why is it that persons must wait for the full realization of this gift? In what sense is it true to say that the reign of God is here, when, in fact, much of the world, many persons of Jesus and of our day, know more suffering, oppression, and sin than they know joy, freedom, selflessness, and love? In response to these questions, we offer the following observations.

First, the truth of the presence of God to human beings in saving love on the one hand, and the incompleteness of God's kingdom on the other, underscore the fact that the reign of God is constituted, not simply by God, and certainly not simply by humankind, but by *God coming into deeper relationship with human beings in and through their freedom.* The only way God can transform human beings, their lives, and the world in which they live, is by empowering and permeating human understanding and freedom. But human consciousness and freedom exist in time. Persons, even those enjoying profound insight and inspiration, need time to process these gifts, time to allow God's Self-Gift to transform their behavior. Hence, the creation of an untainted kingdom of love, justice and peace, the integral healing of the human in all relationships (within the self, with others, between nations, and with the world and creation as a whole) cannot come about overnight. It takes time.

The fact that the reign of God requires time to unfold only serves once again to underscore the fact that the reign of God is God's Self-Gift abiding in and through human beings. The reign of God is not elsewhere. It is here in human life. That truth is "Good News" because it indicates that real human beings are actually transformed with new life which is theirs. But it is also "tough news" because it underscores the fact that human beings have the responsibility to surrender themselves to God, to God's inspiration, and to God's energy for Christlike love, or the reign of God will be slow to come to full realization. The fact that God's kingdom is already here yet not complete reveals an inbuilt dynamic tension within the kingdom. Though we speak of God's reign, that reign exists, not outside of but within the conscious aspirations, the freedom, and the love of human beings. It must engage real persons in human knowing, human freedom and human history or it will not exist at all.

The same insight into the relational character between the Self-giving God and the freedom of human beings in establishing the reign of God, and the reciprocal responsibilities that the Transcendent and the human partners have for its full realization, makes clear why Jesus and the evangelists speak of the "delay" regarding the future coming of Jesus. Human beings in their freedom have the power to hasten or to hinder the advent of God and the growing expression of Godly love, justice and peace within humankind. Holy persons, saints, hasten the coming of the kingdom in full splendor; they enable it to be more fully present even now. Selfish persons, persons of limited love, persons who allow injustice to creep into their lives, persons who so busy themselves with the finite that they refuse to allow the Transcendent to enter their human lives, prevent God's powerful Self-Gift from breaking into their love and, through them, into their world. Human beings graced by God's offer of new life have the power to receive that life or to reject it; they can hasten or delay the coming of the kingdom in its fullness.

Recognizing the continued presence of both good and evil in the world, indeed, noting that Jesus himself called attention to that mixture, and having called attention to the centrality of human freedom in bringing about the kingdom, we can now return to the heart of Jesus' proclamation itself. Jesus announced a new age, the age of God's reign. In face of this mixed reality, we may be inclined to ask: What is new about this age, the age of Jesus and of the post-resurrection communities living in Christ?

What is new is that God has poured forth God's life and love upon human beings as God had never done before. What is new is the fact that human beings have a possibility, a capacity, for living in truth, love, justice, and peace which they never had before. Jesus introduces a genuinely new age, an age qualitatively different from days of a previous era.

Because people are presented with new opportunities and new capabilities (in God), it is time for new decisions. When the ground thaws, it is time for planting; when a new child is born, it is time for rejoicing. When day breaks, it is time for rising; so, because Jesus has come, it is the time to decide for God's way of love, justice and peace.[34] It is the time to walk through life as Jesus walked, the time for acceding to Jesus' call and challenge to discipleship. The opportunity for living more fully in God is here. As Paul writes to the disciples in Corinth:

> We appeal to you not to receive the grace of God in vain. For God says: "In an acceptable time I heard you; on the day of salvation, I helped you." Behold, now is the acceptable time; behold, now is the day of salvation (II Cor. 6:1f).

Now is the time for believing this Good News, a time for repentance, a time for a change of heart, and a time for a change of one's way of life. It is such a time, because God is present to human beings as never before. Thus, it is the "final age" (the *eschaton,* the "last days"), because God having poured forth God's love and Self-Gift upon us can give no more. There is nothing more to give, nothing greater to be given. Once again Jesus exultingly proclaims the challenge: "The reign of God is here; repent and believe this Good News."

The Reign of God and Doing Christology

In a very real way, this entire chapter has been an exercise in "doing Christology," an exercise in processing our faith-experience of God alive in Jesus. In this regard, we have attempted to advance our own understanding of Jesus himself. Interwoven with our efforts to understand Jesus and the reign of God which he proclaimed, we have reflected upon Jesus' own personal experience of God and his progressive understanding of what God wished him to accomplish. In this section, we wish briefly to highlight and to reflect upon Jesus' personal experience in order to deepen our appreciation of the nature and dynamics of doing theology itself. We will consider three dimensions of God's Self-revelation to Jesus. These observations will provide us with several fundamental guidelines for our own efforts to do Christology.

First, it is most significant to remember that Jesus' proclamation of the reign of God rested on several aspects of his own personal experience. These include his experience of God, his grasp of the struggles and needs of his own age, and his awareness of his tradition, a history of beliefs reflecting his predecessors' faith-experience. From these three sources - the first clearly dependent upon God's personal initiative, the second reflective of the ever-present human need for salvation, and the third embracing the religious wisdom and insight a previous era - Jesus came to speak of God and God's intention for Jesus' contemporaries and for humankind well into the future. In this way Jesus engaged himself in the task of doing theology.

Jesus' way of interpreting his experience of God models for us the process of doing theology and Christology. It brings into full relief the necessity of being open to experience God, of being sensitive to our contemporary setting and to its vulnerabilities, and of being respectful and knowledgeable with regard to a tradition, in order to process our experience of God in a life-giving manner. For us, of course, Jesus himself, his words and deeds, are the most significant elements in our tradition. We believe God has become fully alive for us in and through Jesus. And so, Jesus both offers a model for doing theology and also stands at the center of our religious tradition, providing the specific content and shape of the experience of God to assist us in our own efforts to engage in this process. Doing Christology in our own day then is doing theology in the likeness of Jesus, within a tradition framed by Jesus, and at a moment of history about to be more fully transformed by Jesus.

Second, it is especially significant to appreciate the nature and relationship of the mission of Jesus to the very person of Jesus. Indeed, we cannot understand Jesus without fully appreciating the kingdom of God which he proclaimed. We cannot understand Jesus' death and resurrection without understanding the reign of God which these last events of Jesus' life brought to fullness. Nor can we understand the reasons behind Jesus' death without understanding the significance and meaning of the reign of God precisely as Jesus proclaimed and lived it. For it was this teaching and way of life which deeply divided Jesus from the authorities of Israel. It was controversy over the kingdom, as Jesus preached and embodied it, that led these authorities to plot against Jesus and led Jesus to be willing to forfeit his physical life. While our unfolding of the connections between the reign of God and Jesus' death and resurrection is yet to come, it is important here to underscore the fact that Jesus' proclamation of the reign of God stands at the center of his demise at the hands of the chief priests and elders, and likewise stands at the center of his glorification and resurrection at the hands, so to speak, of *Abba*.

Third, it is significant for one's understanding of God, the transcendent One, and of the nature of God expressed by the name *Abba* that we understand the kingdom proclaimed and mediated by Jesus. No other image, action or revelation of God so captures God's being as that of "Saving Love." Granting the fact that God's action in definitively establishing God's reign reaches its climax only in Jesus' death and resurrection, the death and resurrection on the one hand and Jesus' mediation of the reign of God on the other mutually clarify one another. The image and the reality of the reign of God are essential for understanding God's true intentions in our behalf, the intention which God definitively fulfilled in raising Jesus from the dead.

But our reflections upon the words, deeds, life and ministry of the Jesus of history and upon the tradition which he established have only begun. During the development of Jesus' public ministry, certain deeds stood out, evoking wonder and amazement, faith and praise. How shall we understand these deeds? What relationship do they have to the reign of God which Jesus proclaimed? What relationship do they have to Jesus himself and to the mystery of the presence of the transcendent God he named *Abba*? In what manner do they make possible, or at least facilitate, the disciples' belief in the Good News? These questions regarding the miracles of Jesus will require fuller investigation and reflection. They will, therefore, frame our inquiries in the next chapter. Before beginning that chapter, however, we suggest that the reader reflect upon the following questions, questions which will lead the inquirer more deeply into the process of doing Christology and enable him or her to profit more fully from the material of this chapter.

Questions for Reflection

1. How, in reading this chapter, have you come to understand more fully the experience of Jesus in, and the christological meaning of, Jesus' baptism and Jesus' temptations? If you have read a biblical commentary on these passages, what further light have you gained? In what way has your further reading enhanced and/or complemented what you have learned in this chapter?

2. What is the most striking dimension of the reign of God which you have come to appreciate in reading this chapter? What sayings and/or parables of the kingdom not mentioned here have been especially striking to you in the past? How would you understand those sayings and/or parables in the light of what you have read here? (You may also wish to consult a commentary on scripture to gain fuller insight into those sayings and parables).

3. How have you come better to understand the mission and ministry of Jesus through your reflection upon the nature and reality of the reign of God? How have you come to appreciate the person and the concerns of Jesus, as well as the nature of God, through your reflection upon the themes of this chapter?

4. Having read this chapter, how have you come to understand the nature of Christian salvation? How would you articulate the nature of Christian salvation to an inquiring friend?

5. What similarities do you see between the plight of Israel in Jesus' time and the plight of your community and/or your world today? In what way or ways do you perceive God's active presence in fostering the growth of God's kingdom in your life, your community, your world today?

6. In what ways have you found the image of Jesus, his proclamation of the kingdom, and/or his call to deeper faith and conversion stirring your own feelings in response to his call? In what concrete ways do you sense God, alive in Jesus, urging you to advance the reign of God in the world today?

CHAPTER 6

Experiencing Christ: Worker of Miracles

In the previous chapter we sought to understand Jesus' deepest concerns as he proclaimed the presence of the longed-awaited "reign of God." We noted that Jesus clarified his understanding of the kingdom of God both by word and also by deed. He described the kingdom verbally by using parables, by teaching a New Law, and by challenging persons to live in a more Godly manner in the context of their own world. He offered images of the reign of God through his actions by reaching out to the marginalized, among whom were persons dominated by evil spirits, persons suffering a variety of physical disabilities and persons known to be or regarded as sinners. He called sinners to conversion, forgiving them and eating with them. He welcomed women and children, those who were insignificant in society, into his company. He healed all those whose diseases consigned them to live lives burdened, not only with physical misery, but also with emotional shame and social disrepute, offering them compassion, rehabilitation, fuller participation in social life, and the restoration of their esteem and self-respect. Jesus went out of his way to include those who often found themselves excluded from the company and respect of the very people who constituted their religious brothers and sisters. He showed by his words, by his deeds, and by the way he lived that a new way of life, a new world, was not only possible but was here. The reign of God had come.

Within the context of Jesus' preaching, action, and very way of life, certain remarkable works, frequently named "wonders," stand out. They attracted the attention of his contemporaries, who often asked: "Who is this man?" "Where did he get such powers?" (See Mark 1:27; 6:1-3). They have also attracted believers ever since, persons who ask even more questions: "Did these events really happen?" "How can we recognize an event truly to be a miracle?" "What were the purposes of these wonders?" "Why don't we see such wonders today as persons saw them in the past?" The topic of Jesus' miracles has attracted attention of professionals and non-professionals, believers and nonbelievers throughout the centuries of Christian history. Theologians and lay persons, believers and nonbelieiver, have raised questions about their historicity, their nature, their relationship to Jesus' divinity and to Jesus' divine power, and their role with regard to faith and to the call to faith.

The history of humankind's understanding of, reaction to, and evaluation of Jesus' miracles, including each of the specific concerns just mentioned, could engage us for several chapters, obviously an enterprise too lengthy for an introduction to Christology.[1] Our aim in this chapter will be more restricted. We will seek merely to unfold the factual occurrence, the nature and purpose(s) of these wonders, worked by Jesus, in the light of his proclamation and mediation of God's reign. In doing so we will seek to distinguish inadequate from adequate understandings of miracles from three points of view: their historicity; their nature in relationship to God, to God's creation, to the Reign of God and to Jesus himself; and their relationship to faith and discipleship. Ultimately, our inquiry will seek to foster a fuller understanding of Jesus' miracles in themselves and a richer appreciation of how these deeds reveal and promote the reign of God which Jesus proclaimed and mediated.

Miracles:
Gospel Creations or Historical Events?

Believers and nonbelievers have questioned the historicity of miracles for numerous reasons, ranging from philosophical convictions which deny the very possibility of miracles to literary observations which question the accuracy of the miracle narratives as records of true history. Given the fact that we are attempting to "do Christology," that is, attempting to interpret faith-experience, we will presume the openness of faith in our inquiry and therefore will not delay our efforts by considering those positions which deny, *a priori*, that miracles as actions of God breaking into history are possible.[2] Rather, our concern in this section will focus upon questions entertained by scholars who believe that God can enter history in ways that are truly extraordinary. We will engage these questions in three stages. First, we will consider those literary and textual observations which prompt questions about the historicity of miracle stories as a whole. Secondly, in light of these same observations, we will consider the stories of Jesus' miracles in their particularity, noting the different weight which these observations have with regard to establishing the historicity of the various kinds of miracles attributed to Jesus. Finally, we will attempt to draw together several conclusions regarding the historicity and interpretation of Jesus' miracles before moving further in out efforts to understand their meaning and purpose. Throughout this section, we will attempt both to deepen our understanding of the beliefs of the early Church which surround and develop out of its memory of Jesus' miracles and also to establish with firmness the genuinely historical origins of those beliefs and the processes by which those beliefs developed. Ultimately, we hope to uncover a fuller understanding of the historical Jesus, the One in whom Christian faith is grounded.

THE HISTORICITY OF JESUS' MIRACLES: CONSIDERED GLOBALLY
One of the more compelling reasons for questioning the factual truth of Jesus' miracles arises from the findings of biblical research itself.[3] The presentations of Jesus' miracles in the Gospel accounts show clear signs that the Church had embellished, if not created, these narratives out of its post-resurrection experience of the nature and mission of Jesus. In this light, scholars point to the way these stories become intensified as accounts within an earlier Gospel are recast in the later Gospels. Thus one blind man in Mark's Gospel (10:46-52) becomes two blind men in Matthew (20:29-34); one possessed man in Mark's account (5:1-20) becomes two possessed men in Matthew's narrative (8:28-34); Jairus' sick daughter (Mk. 5:21-24 35-43) is later remembered as having died before Jesus heals her (Mt. 9:18-26). The Gospel miracle stories, giving some evidence of conflict in detail, cause one to wonder which aspect(s) of these narratives represent historical truth and which aspect(s)

flow from later faith-interpretations of the Church.

Further, some scholars observe that the miracle narratives often reflect an understanding of Jesus and of these events which the original witnesses would not have enjoyed. For example, prior to Jesus' raising of Lazarus, the Johannine Jesus claims: "I am the resurrection and the life...." (11:25). The text presents Jesus unfolding, with absolute clarity, his personal identity as the preexistent One as he proclaims "I am." In truth, Jesus is expressing his self-identity in terms which, as we have seen above,[4] derive from the interplay of the post-resurrection Johannine community and its post-resurrection converts. Further, this same text describes Jesus as envisioning himself in the present in terms which reflect the state of being which he had yet to accomplish. And he presents himself as having the capacity to be for others the source of that fullness of life which he himself did not as yet possess. He does not say that he will be raised; rather, he declares that he already is the embodiment of risen life, and that he is mediator of that life for others, even as he speaks. Thus, on the one hand, it is true that Martha and the witnesses of Jesus' action of restoring Lazarus to health - an action quite surprising in itself - would be struck with wonder as the historical Jesus worked this miracle in its original setting. On the other hand, however, it would be unlikely that they (or Jesus himself) would interpret (at that historical moment) this astounding event in terms of Jesus' resurrection and preexistence. Only after experiencing the fullness of God's action in raising Jesus from the dead and after absorbing the theological traditions of post-resurrection converts to the Johannine community would the witnesses arrived at such profound insight into the event. Only then would the Johannine community come to appreciate that Jesus, in this action, was manifesting not only power over the physical health of a human being, but also his own preexistent identity and his mission of leading his disciples to share his risen life of glory. Only then would the community recognize that Jesus is "the Resurrection and the Life," and that, in raising Lazarus, Jesus would have been working a sign to reveal the depth of his "glory" (11:4,40).

The fact that this narrative shows clear evidence of

embellishment and amplification by the post-resurrection Church makes it difficult at best to discern which aspect(s) of the narrative are traceable to the Jesus of history. Quite naturally, this difficulty has led some liberal theologians to question this historicity of the event itself. More moderate scholars, however, using the historical-critical method of interpreting the Scriptures, willingly undertake the task of distinguishing post-resurrection reflections from the pre-resurrection origins of the narratives. In light of that effort, they would maintain that this Gospel story rests upon an historical event of Jesus' ministry while also affirming that the original event is remembered and retold by the Church with post-resurrection insight. The post-resurrection insight which the Church included in its service of handing on its memory of the event enabled the believer to remember the miracle with a fuller recognition of its ultimate meaning, a recognition which would have been beyond the capabilities of the original witnesses.[5]

A second example of a miracle story reflecting post-resurrection embellishments centers upon the story of the multiplication of loaves and fishes, the only miracle recounted in all four Gospels. The narrative of this miracle reveals allusions, not to Jesus' resurrection itself, but to his institution of the Eucharist. The details of Jesus' actions of blessing, breaking, and distributing bread to feed the hungry pilgrims (Mk. 6:41 and parallels) recall Jesus' actions at his final meal (Mk. 14:22 and parallels). Likewise the care "to gather up the remaining fragments" (Mk. 6:43 and parallels), and the early Church's speaking of the Eucharist as "the breaking of the bread" (Acts 2:42) all indicate that the post-resurrection Church retold this story of the multiplication with the desire to portray the historical Jesus as anticipating his future action of nourishing worshiping believers with his own sacramental flesh and blood in the Eucharistic meal. The stories of the multiplication of the loaves and fishes were retold with insights and allusions which the original witnesses could not have imagined. Again, this fact has led some scholars to question which elements of the narrative truly reflect the event as it unfolded in the life of the historical Jesus and has caused others to question the historicity of the narrative as a whole.[6]

Despite these observations, however, contemporary scholars continue to maintain their conviction that the historical Jesus indeed worked wonders as the four Gospels narrate. While acknowledging the evidence that post-resurrection awareness and insights have been incorporated within Gospel miracle stories, and granting the fact that the recounting of the same miracle by different evangelists has produced discrepancies in details, many scholars, though differing among themselves with regard to the historical origins of each individual miracle story, decidedly reaffirm the historicity of Jesus' miracles *taken as a whole*.[7] As John P. Meier brings out, the tradition of Jesus' miracles is found in *every Gospel source* (Mark, Q, special Matthew, special Luke, and John) and also in *a wide variety of literary forms*.[8] With respect to the latter, the tradition is reflected not only in the form of miracle stories (narratives of exorcisms, of healings, of raising of the dead and of nature miracles), but also in a variety of other forms, for example: parables (Mk. 3:27), a dispute story (Mt. 12:27f and parallel), a mandate (Jesus' command, within the missionary discourse to his disciples, to heal and to exorcise [Mk. 6:7, 13; Lk. 10:9]), and general biographical statements (Mt. 11:5-6; Lk. 13:32) to name only some.[9] Thus, this tradition enjoys the support of broad multiple attestation, a singularly reliable criterion for ascertaining the historicity of any Gospel pericope.

Further, miracle stories and sayings cohere, stories from one source being explained by sayings from another source.[10] Coherence is another significant criterion for establishing the historicity of both narratives and sayings. Hence Meier firmly concludes that

> (T)he tradition of Jesus' miracles is more firmly supported by the criteria of historicity than are a number of other well-known and often readily accepted traditions about his life and ministry (e.g., his status as a carpenter, his use of "abba" in prayer, his own prayer in Gethsemane before his arrest). Put dramatically but with not too much exaggeration: if the miracle tradition from Jesus' public ministry were to be rejected in toto as

unhistorical, so should every other Gospel tradition about him.[11]

In light of this ample support for the historicity of Jesus' miracles taken globally, one question, nonetheless, still remains. How are we to evaluate and understand the evangelists' obvious inclusions of post-resurrection embellishments, and even the discrepancies in detail, which so many of these narratives clearly reveal? In response to this query, we wish to make the following observations.

First, with regard to the discrepancies in detail, we need recall that the Gospel narratives as a whole, and therefore, the miracle stories within them, are not equivalent to modern day scientific records or journalistic reports. They are more akin to "family stories," narratives through which one hands on one's family history. Just as in telling the story of one's own or of one's families' origins, so in the recounting of the history of Jesus, concrete detail is less important than the substance of the event which Jesus enacted. For it was the substance of the event, not the detail, which revealed the unique power and mission of Jesus; it was the substance of the event, not the detail, which grounded the salvific meaning which the narrator perceived in faith and subsequently wished to develop. As we have already indicated, the Gospels were written by a person of faith for people of faith. Their purpose was not to prove Jesus' divinity or his divine mission to anyone, but to strengthen the faith of persons already convinced of Jesus' divine mission. The same needs to be said of "miracle stories," a distinct form of Gospel narrative and a distinct element within the oral tradition of the early Church. Miracle stories were told and written down by believers for believers, to awaken and to strengthen their faith-filled memory of Jesus. Hence, though those stories truly reflect an event of the past, they also quite legitimately seek to convey the meaning of those events as perceived by the Church at the time in which the evangelists recorded them. The Church loved to retell the wonders of Jesus in light of the way it had come, after Christ's death and resurrection, to understand Jesus, his mission, and God's saving presence in its own day.[12]

Second, in retelling the miracles, the early Church remained absolutely convinced of the fact that Jesus was alive, inspiring and guiding its life and understanding years after Jesus' death and resurrection. And so that same Church readily placed its ever deepening understanding of Jesus' miracles in the mouth of Jesus himself. After all, it believed its present depth of understanding truly did come from him.[13] Such "freedom" in retelling the event of history could legitimately present a concern for the biblical theologian seeking to separate the original event from later interpretation;[14] but it was not the concern of the early Church.[15]

THE HISTORICITY OF JESUS' MIRACLES: IN THEIR PARTICULARITY
Having affirmed the historicity of Jesus' miracles as a whole, however, does not give us much more than a general picture of the historical Jesus. It enables us to affirm that Jesus of Nazareth was indeed a worker of wonders, but leaves open two interrelated questions: Which particular miracle stories originate with a wondrous event in the ministry of the Jesus of history? What kind of miracles did Jesus truly perform?

Giving answer to the prior question obviously would provide an answer to the second. But that path of investigation, while rewarding, is long and tedious, and, in a number of cases results in uncovering disagreement among scholars. For example, John P. Meier, in his most recent effort to research the historicity of each of the Gospel miracle stories, concludes with a clear affirmation of the historical foundations of most of the accounts of Jesus' works of exorcism and physical healings (including those reporting Jesus' acts of restoring life to those believed to be dead). But, with the exception of the narrative(s) concerning Jesus' multiplication of the loaves and fishes, he finds little convincing evidence in support for maintaining that the stories recounting the so-called nature miracles originate in an event of Jesus' public ministry.[16] René Latourelle, however, takes a more inclusive position. After careful analysis, he concludes that one can discern probable evidence that the origin of every miracle story rests in an event of Jesus' earthly life.[17] Walter Kasper, inclining in the opposite direction, judges it better to hold in question the historicity of the resurrection miracles as well as the nature miracles, although he regards "the core stock" of Jesus' exorcisms and physical healings as reflective of Jesus' historical ministry.[18]

The impressive solidity of Meier's reasoning and the thoroughness of his research incline us to concur with his conclusions. The fact of scholarly disagreement regarding the origins of some of the miracle stories, specifically those reporting the resurrection miracles and the so-called nature miracles, invites us to consider these types of miracles in particular.[19] Engaging in this reflection, we hope to discern more fully how Jesus actually did express himself in his public ministry and how or why the early Church may have amplified its stock of authentic narratives of Jesus' miracles by adding to them non-historical portraits of Jesus of Nazareth.

Raising questions concerning the historicity of specific kinds of miracles performed during the earthly life of Jesus, however, is also fraught with difficulties. Among these difficulties, we need to attend to three: contemporary bias against the possibility of the historical Jesus' actually having raised the dead; a similar bias against the possibility of Jesus' actually having controlled nature; and the difficulty of defining what constitutes a class or kind of miracle, particularly when one names a given miracle a nature miracle. The first two problems are largely questions of world-view and/or philosophy; the third is a question of literary analysis. Each, however, affects one's method of inquiry and its fruitfulness. Concerning these difficulties and/or questions, we offer the following remarks.

First, with regard to the contemporary hesitancy to entertain the possibility that Jesus raised dead persons to life. Some of this hesitancy flows from the modern world's frequent experience of natural healing and recovery contrasted with its equally frequent (to say the least) experience of the finality of death. People recover from illness; they do not recover from death. As a matter of fact, theologically, Christians understand death as a movement forward to a fuller life. Restoration to life in this world makes little sense if one has moved (definitively) into a richer life in the next.

In light of this hesitancy, several precisions are in order: First, the miracles of Jesus' raising the dead end in a result which, although fruitful, must be distinguished from his own resurrection. Lazarus (Jn.11:1-45), the widow's son (Lk. 7:11-17) and the daughter of Jairus (Mk. 5:21-43 and parallels) all return to this life and die again; Jesus rises to a new and fuller life, never to die again. Jesus, therefore, in raising persons from the dead, does not "call them back" from a definitive movement into a new and fuller life. Rather, he revives them so that they can actively continue their journey in and through this life, moving definitively into fuller life at some later time.

Second, these miracles may be understood to touch on an experience which the ancient world would have regarded as death, but which the modern world would know as coma. The ancient world did not embalm their dead, but buried them rather quickly. That world did not have the capacity to ascertain clinical death as the contemporary world does. Persons may have appeared to be dead to the ancient mind, when, in fact, they were not. Hence, in this light, the miracles of "raising the dead" would better be termed miracles of "restoration or revival of life."[20] For this reason, many exegetes classify Jesus' resurrection miracles as a sub-class of Jesus' healing miracles, and subject the narratives about these events to the same criteria which they use for ascertaining the historical origins of other miracle stories.[21]

Having addressed the reluctance regarding the historicity of Jesus' miracles of restoring life to the dead, however, we must still ask: Do these narratives find their origins in events in the public ministry of Jesus? In response, we note that these stories are found in no less than three of the five Gospel sources: John, Luke and Mark (and parallels). Further, the sayings tradition also provides a clear reference to Jesus' raising of the dead in Jesus' response to the disciples of John the Baptist:

> Go back and report to John what you hear and see:
> the blind recover their sight, cripples walk, lepers
> are cured, the deaf hear, dead men are raised to life,
> and the poor have the good news preached to them.

Blessed is the man who finds no stumbling block in
me (Mt. 11:4b-6).

Hence, the criterion of multiple attestation supports the tradition that
the stories of Jesus' raising the dead originate in events in the life of
the historical Jesus.

Further, elements of each of the narratives of resurrection
miracles incline one to affirm that the origin of each individual story
must be located in an event in the public ministry of Jesus. For
example, the story relating the raising of the daughter of Jairus (Mk.
5:21-43) includes numerous supports for claiming its origins with
Jesus of Nazareth, supports such as the preservation of the Aramaic
words of Jesus (*Talitha, koum*, which Mark translates for his
audience with the meaning "Little girl, get up" [5:41]), the mention
of the name of the petitioner (5:22) and the preservation of the fact
that the petitioner was a synagogue official (an unlikely fact if the
story were composed by the early Church).[22] Hence, we conclude
that the criteria of historical criticism clearly lead to the affirmation
that the historical Jesus performed miracles regarded as raising the
dead to life.[23]

*Second, with regard to the contemporary reluctance to entertain
questions concerning Jesus' performance of the so-called nature
miracles.* While it is imperative to consider each of these miracles
individually in order to evaluate evidence of their specific historical
origins, it is equally important to avoid prejudging their plausibility
on the basis of what we think Jesus could or could not do.
Recognizing the fact that whatever Jesus did was a manifestation of
the divine power flowing in and through him, we need to affirm that
that power, and, indeed, the God who is its source, stand above
nature as well as above human life. God is the Creator of both.
How God acts with respect to nature remains a legitimate question,
but that God may ultimately wish to bring the forces of nature into
harmony with each other and with human life must remain a
possibility. If God has truly sent Jesus, and if God truly expresses
God's Self through Jesus' actions, one must be open to investigating
whether or not God has, in fact, acted with respect to nature, in and
through Jesus. Hence, once again, it is imperative to sort out the

evidence of historicity with regard to each of these so-called "nature" miracles before deciding what Jesus of Nazareth may or may not have done.[24]

Third, with regard to the classification of the so-called nature miracles. The effort to sort out the evidence in support of the historicity of Jesus' so-called nature miracles, however, meets with a difficulty beyond that of the opposition of contemporary presumptions and biases: these miracle stories, being exceptionally diverse in themselves, are difficult to classify. The difficulty of classification occurs from two vantage points. First, with regard to the general classification, "Miracle Story"; and secondly, with regard to the specific category, "nature miracle." With respect to the generic classification, "Miracle Story," these narratives present a problem because they do not manifest the stylized pattern common to the other narratives which report Jesus' miracles. Other miracle stories follow a threefold structure of *setup* (presentation of a problem occasioning a request for help from a petitioner or an initiative to bring about relief on the part of Jesus); *a miraculous word or action of Jesus* which unexpectedly resolves the problem together with some confirmation of the reality of the miracle; and *a response from the audience*, be it amazement, wonder, further questioning or deepened faith (or disbelief). Some stories of "nature miracles," however, omit at least one of these elements. For example, some lack the setup; they do not originate in a dire problem (e.g., Jesus' cursing the fig tree; Jesus' walking on the water); some do not offer any explicit word or action of Jesus which directly brings about the miracle (e.g., the multiplication of the loaves; walking on the water); and some do not terminate with any manifestation of wonder, praise, query or belief (e.g., the multiplication of the loaves). On the other hand, the narrative of the calming of the sea has all three characteristics, further illustrating the lack of uniformity among the stories grouped together in this class. Hence, one may question whether or not it is appropriate to classify these narratives truly as miracle stories.

Second, the wisdom of uniting these diverse events under the category of nature miracles is itself tenuous, for it is unclear what one should regard as nature or natural.[25] Even human health and human life are natural. The concept nature seems to include everything, the whole of God's creation. It is not a class distinct from anything else, but a category which can include anything left out of another class. For this reason, John P. Meier (and others) reclassify these wonders, Meier electing four categories: *Gift miracles* (the multiplication of the loaves, the transformation of water into wine);[26] *Rescue miracles* (calming of the wind and sea); *Epiphany miracles*, miracles focused directly upon the manifestation of divinity rather than upon producing some fruitful benefit for others (Jesus' walking on the water); and *Curse miracles* (cursing of the fig tree).

The problem of classifying the so-called nature miracles, moreover, has a clear relationship to the effort toward ascertaining the historicity of these stories. Most of these stories are unique to their category; hence they can do no more than reflect one Gospel source. Nor are these miracles clearly reflected in other literary forms (parables, sayings, pronouncements, etc.). Therefore, they do not meet the all-important criterion for establishing antiquity: multiple attestation. The one exception is the miracle of the multiplication of the loaves and fishes. This miracle story is found in both the Johannine and the Marcan sources. Further, it is recounted two times in the Marcan source, manifesting an antiquity which, at the very least, resulted in its being retold prior to Mark's composition in two forms. Finally, it coheres with the historical activity of Jesus, his frequent celebration of joyful meals with his disciples throughout his public ministry and with his frequent use of the meal theme, the eschatological banquet, in his parables of the kingdom. Among the stories of Jesus' so-called nature miracles then, only the narratives of his multiplying the loaves survive the test of historical criticism.

As a result of this analysis, we would, on the one hand, feel safe in regarding the narratives of Jesus' raising of the dead, together with the stories of the multiplication of the loaves and the fishes, as originating in events during Jesus' public ministry. On the other hand, we would regard the other so-called nature miracles as stories originating in the early Church's faith-experience of the risen Lord.

HISTORICITY OF JESUS' MIRACLES: OVERALL CONCLUSION

While it is clear, then, that Jesus worked wonders, it is also clear that the task of establishing the historicity of individual miracles is by no means easy. Nevertheless, we find substantial evidence within the stories themselves and remarkable consensus among scholars affirming the historicity of Jesus' exorcisms and his works of healing all sorts of physical ills. Hence we can be secure in affirming that the historical Jesus did perform these types of wonders leading to amazement and joy among his followers in general and among those cured in particular. Further, we would judge that the weight of internal (literary) evidence leans toward some historical foundation of the resurrection miracles as well as the miracles of multiplication of loaves and fishes. We would regard these narratives, too, as reflecting the life, ministry, and concerns of the historical Jesus.

On the other hand, those miracles which are often grouped together as nature miracles, miracles which tend to focus more directly upon revealing Jesus' divine identity than upon his efforts of establishing the reign of God, seem, in their entirety, to be compositions of the early Church rather than post-resurrection interpretations of actual events in the life of the historical Jesus. We would be slow to use these narratives as vehicles for understanding Jesus of Nazareth in the context of his life and public ministry. At the same time, however, these narratives do offer us a valid interpretation of Jesus, precisely as perceived in and through the faith-experience of the early Church. We tend to think that these latter narratives were composed to convey that Church's beliefs concerning the power, not of the historical Jesus, but of the risen Christ, present to it in its unfolding history. They convey that Church's conviction that Jesus, risen in glory, is, like Yahweh, Lord of all creation, able to bring nature itself into harmony.[27] In that context, they also indicate that the post-resurrection Church recognized that Jesus of Nazareth was, from the beginning, one with God in this radical capacity, destined to bring nature and human life to a profoundly peaceful co-existence.

With regard to these latter accounts, then, we would conclude that these stories spoke more of what Jesus was doing at the time of their telling than of what Jesus had done historically. As we have stated above, present reality and the present meaning of these narratives was more important for the early Church, living in faith, than was the historical fact. These stories tell us what Jesus, crucified and risen is doing, not what he has done. They look more to the future rather than to the past. In this sense, the majority of the narratives of the so-called nature miracles fill out the implications contained in the accounts of those miraculous events which clearly originate from the historical Jesus. Understood in this manner, they are reliable interpretations of what God is doing in Jesus, interpretations of the Church's experience of God alive in Jesus, even though they offer little insight into the Jesus of history.

As we conclude this section on the historicity of Jesus' miracles, we can affirm two co-related but distinct convictions. First, the historical Jesus did work wonders, miraculous events which struck his disciples with amazement. These events included numerous exorcisms, a variety of physical healings, astounding events regarded as restoring the dead to life, and a marvelous work of feeding the multitude. These events had a profound relationship to what Jesus proclaimed, namely, the advent of the reign of God. They truly unveiled something of the nature, meaning and presence of that kingdom. Our efforts, then, to interpret the Christian faith experience of God, alive in and through Jesus the "worker of wonders" will continue to focus primarily upon the historical Jesus. For it is the historical Jesus, in his words and deeds, who revealed and clarified God's power, love, and intentions in the concreteness of our world. We will, in the next section, trace further, the nature, the meaning, and the purpose(s) of these works which truly flowed from the mind, heart and will, the vision, power and love of Jesus of Nazareth.

Second, the early Church, influenced by its experience of the risen Lord, reinterpreted these genuinely historical events. It did so both by embellishing those stories which originated in actual events worked by the Jesus of history and also by creating stories which set in dramatic relief its deepened insight into who Jesus is and what Jesus is doing. In this manner, it unfolded for itself and for us, a fuller understanding of Jesus. Its concern was to grasp and to proclaim at depth who Jesus truly is and what God's fullest intentions were and are in sending God's beloved among us. These post-resurrection interpretations are also significant for our fuller understanding of the miracles of the historical Jesus, for our understanding of who Jesus truly is, and for our ongoing effort to interpret what God intends to accomplish in and through the crucified and risen Lord. Hence, we will also keep these post-resurrection interpretations in mind as we move into the next sections dealing with the nature, the meaning and the purpose(s) of the miracles of Jesus.[28]

The Nature of Jesus' Miracles

The question of the nature of a miracle in general and the attempts to define that nature in a manner which is both clear and theologically useful, have seen some development in the fairly recent past. In order to illustrate that development and to glean fuller insight into the nature and meaning specifically of Jesus' miracles, we will evaluate two ways of understanding and of defining miracles: the classical and the contemporary.

THE CLASSICAL DEFINITION: AN EVENT BEYOND NATURE
Classical theology formulated a rather clear definition of a miracle: a miracle is a visible, tangible, extraordinary event, which cannot be explained by the laws of nature. Since the miraculous event does not flow from natural causes, that is, since it cannot be explained by way of a natural cause-effect relationship, it can only be explained by "divine intervention." By definition, then, a miracle is an event which must be caused by God; for only God, the Transcendent, is "beyond nature." Hence, miracles were understood as "super-natural" (beyond the natural) event.[29]

Because of the clarity of this definition, in its ability to maintain the distinction between transcendent (divine) causality and finite, natural causality, and because of its unquestioned implication that all observers would be able clearly to separate events (effects) attributable to finite causes from events (effects) which could not be attributed to such causes, the definition seemed quite workable and useful. In naming certain events as miraculous, anyone operating from the perspective of this definition or principle of interpretation would immediately be able to conclude that "God is here" in circumstances which would be otherwise inexplicable. Theologians interested in defending the divinity and/or the divine mission of Jesus had at hand a series of events as well as a principle which apparently would have offered incontrovertible testimony to Jesus' supernatural origin and mission.

THE CLASSICAL DEFINITION: INHERENTLY PROBLEMATIC

The classical definition of a miracle, however, leaves much to be desired. For as Walter Kasper has pointed out,[30] the definition rests on scientific and philosophical presumptions which must yield to two facts:

First, the classical definition of miracles presumes that we know all the laws of nature (all the finite causes and the effects which they alone and/or in combination can produce). But we do not have such knowledge. Medical science, physical sciences, the social sciences continue to do research and to make beneficial discoveries concerning the interrelationship of finite causes and their effects with a frequency which forces us to recognize that we have not yet observed all the laws of nature. We have not yet come to recognize all of the ways in which nature itself operates in fostering healing and growth, restoration and unity among all of the forces of this world.

Second, even with the knowledge we do have, it is tedious and difficult to determine whether or not a specific event truly falls beyond the laws of nature. The ecclesiastical process that determines the validity of miracles proposed as indications of the sanctity of a candidate for canonization is a good illustration. That process is a highly scientific and lengthy task. Certainly the events worked by Jesus were not put to this type of scrutiny. Even Jesus' adversaries accepted the extraordinary nature of the surprising events worked by Jesus, although they attributed these deeds to the powers of evil spirits (Mt.9:34; 12:24; Lk.11:15). In relationship to the wonders worked by the historical Jesus, therefore, such a definition is useless.

-169-

But further, this classical definition of a miracle is misleading. It focuses our attention on the predictability or non-predictability of the event rather than on its meaning. It puts us in the position of judges rather than in the position of blessed recipients of a gracious favor. In the context of Jesus' ministry, however, Jesus was not trying to startle persons with surprise events; he was not trying to give airtight proof of his mission. He simply wanted to manifest and to mediate the reign of God for the benefit of all who were open to the overtures of God's love. Hence, when the Pharisees protested that Jesus worked wonders, healings, and cures through an alliance with evil spirits, Jesus called attention to the fact that since he indeed drove out evil spirits, the only possible origin of the power of his deeds lay in the power of the Holy Spirit and the presence of the reign of God (Mt.12:28; Lk.11:20). Indeed, as he responded to the disciples sent by John, he pointed explicitly to his deeds of giving sight to the blind, mobility to the lame, hearing and speech to the deaf and mute, as illustrations of the fact that he truly was the one to come with Messianic blessings (Mt. 11:2-6). Rather than describe these wonders as events occurring beyond the laws of nature, Jesus describes them as signs of the kingdom of God, events characteristic of the coming of the final days of God's saving presence and reign.

The classical definition, then, in focusing our attention somewhat abstractly upon nature and super-nature, fails to shed light upon the rich dynamic inherent in the miraculous event as Jesus understands it. Rather, it raises the question of what is or is not "of nature." To the degree that it directs one's attention to an analysis of nature rather than the advent of God's reign, it removes Jesus' miracles from their revelatory context and is misleading.

Finally, as Walter Kasper has suggested,[31] we hold that the classical definition of a miracle is dangerous. It implies that God, the transcendent cause, enters history by substituting for and replacing finite causes. In effect, it states that finite causes cannot bring about healing, so God does. But such a presumption relegates God to the level of created finite causes themselves. It implies that God has become dissatisfied with the very nature or creation which God himself had already established and which God had affirmed as good.[32] The definition implies that, "in God's eyes," nature itself needs to be corrected. God must "re-do" more perfectly what God had done imperfectly in God's original creation of this world.

An examination of the miracles which Jesus wrought, however, does not indicate that God is in competition with or dissatisfied with nature. Rather such an examination of miracles reflects the fact that God supports nature and its very goals: The blind do see (as nature intends); the deaf do hear (their capacity for perceiving sound, a capacity which God in God's Self actually has created has been healed); the lame do walk, the lives of the dead are restored, people are nourished. God does not act beyond nature, but frees nature from obstacles so that it can attain its own original and God given destiny. When the reign of God arrives, God so sustains and supports creation that, in Walter Kasper's words "nature is made well again."[33] God embraces human beings and creation as whole with saving love. Jesus' miracles are signs of the power, presence, and destiny of that saving love. They are and must be defined as "signs of the presence and manifestation of life under God's reign." No other description or definition is adequate for understanding the miracles of Jesus.[34]

THE CONTEMPORARY DEFINITION: SIGNS OF THE KINGDOM
As has become apparent from the foregoing analysis, contemporary theologians, desiring to be faithful to the insight and tradition of the early Church, have come to understand and to define Jesus' miracles in the context of Jesus' proclamation of the reign of God. The Roman Catholic Church, in its solemn teaching formulated at the Second Vatican Council, has itself endorsed this perspective. Addressing the question of the interrelationship of God's word and God's action in its Dogmatic Constitution on Revelation (*Dei Verbum: "The Word of God"*) the Council stated:

> Through... revelation..., the invisible God..., out of
> the abundance of His love, speaks to men as
> friends... and lives among them so that He may
> invite and take them into fellowship with Himself.
> This plan of revelation is realized by deed and words
> having an inner unity: The *deeds* wrought by God in

the history of salvation *manifest* and *confirm* the *teaching* and the *realities* signified by the words, while the words proclaim the deeds and clarify the mystery contained in them. (*Dei Verbum*, paragraph 2; emphasis mine.)

The actions of God, and specifically, the wonders worked in and through Jesus, are best understood as works which manifest and confirm the preaching of Jesus They show forth (and advance) the reality of the reign of God which his teaching points to. Jesus' miracles are "signs of the kingdom."

THE CONTEMPORARY DEFINITION: THEOLOGICALLY ENLIGHTENING
The utility and fruitfulness of this definition, in contrast with the questionable value of the classical definition, can be illustrated in several ways.

First, this understanding of miracles is clearly a theological definition. It is grounded in and arises from the overall faith-experience of God which the Gospels seek to interpret. By way of contrast, the classical definition, with its apologetic intent, emerged from an attempt to stand apart from the experience and the evidence of faith. It emerged from an effort to describe a miracle in a manner which could appeal to a nonbeliever, to one who would be capable of interpreting reality only from the vantage point of reason. Only the believer, therefore, a person gifted with faith, can offer a truly theological (and positive) definition of the miraculous event. For a believer, a miracle is a manifestation of the in-breaking of God, revealing God's presence and God's reign in the last days. By contrast, the nonbeliever and/or the person who, to appeal to a nonbeliever, would prescind from the inspiration and the light which faith-experience provides, can offer a merely philosophical (and conditional) definition a miracle. They describe it as an event which (if it were to happen) stands outside what reason can predict, expect, and explain; it is an event beyond the laws of nature. When we limit our perspective to the light of reason alone, however, we cannot grasp the center of the miraculous event. We cannot perceive the event as an expression of God's personal love, breaking into our lives and history with transforming life and meaning. The active presence and appearance of the Transcendent must remain, at best, on the fringe of our understanding and consciousness. A truly Christian theological definition and interpretation of Jesus' miracles, therefore, demands and flows from the reliability of the experience of God in faith. We will develop this consideration further in the final section of this chapter.

Second, when Jesus miracles are defined, experienced, and interpreted fundamentally as "signs of the presence and unfolding of God's kingdom among human beings," one can understand how and why God empowers Jesus to work these signs and yet why these events occur neither everywhere nor on every day. For just as the kingdom is here already, but not yet complete, so the miraculous signs which God works through Jesus are meant to *indicate the beginning* of God's reign, *pointing toward the goal* of full communion, health, and harmony of life under God's reign. But they are not intended to *establish the full realization* of the kingdom. The fullness is yet to come. In this light, miracles give us a glimpse of what God's and humankind's future together can and will be like. They indicate that the power of God's reign is truly taking hold of the universe and is moving the universe toward a fuller future! But, by remaining extraordinary and infrequent, they also indicate that the appearance of God in Jesus' miracles marks only the beginning. Human cooperation with God's intention, human reception of and living in God's love through faith and Godly life in Jesus, must deepen if the wholeness manifested by Jesus' miracles is to become widespread. The factual unfolding of Jesus' miracles makes clear that Jesus' proclamation of the reign of God corresponds to historical truth. Their relative infrequency underscores the fact that the reign of God has only begun. Humankind must acknowledge the signs through belief in the kingdom and walk in Christ's likeness to facilitate the kingdom's further growth.

For these reasons, Jesus' miracles may, on the one hand, rightly be interpreted as signs of the presence of the reign of God which validate and in a human way giving flesh to Jesus' preaching. On the other hand, they may be equally understood as prognostic signs, offering humankind a glimpse of the future. In this latter perspective, it is important to remember that, in these events, God is not acting outside nature but is in fact leading creation to its divinely preordained fulfillment in God's very Self. One might look upon the miracles therefore as "anticipations" of the future. Even more precisely, they reveal the beginning of God's deliberate and irreversible action of making the wholeness and well being of all creation a reality. They are the true beginning of the definitive process of salvation, which will gradually unfold under the dynamic influence of God's saving love during this, the final age.

Third, since Jesus' miracles are basically signs of the presence of the salvific reign of God, these miracles shed light upon and define Jesus' mission and Jesus' power. Part of the intention of the classical definition, as it was formulated by believers, included the desire to affirm Jesus' divinity, particularly for those who would be lacking in faith. Apologetically-minded theologians of the Age of the Enlightenment hoped that the classical perspective would lead nonbelievers to acknowledge a transcendent presence because of the miracles and come to see that Jesus must be divine. The perspective of Jesus in performing these deeds, and the vision of the New Testament writers in recording them, however, did not center upon establishing Jesus' personal divinity. Rather, they focused upon Jesus' God-given mission; miracles proclaimed primarily what Jesus was about, and not who he was. They proclaimed what God's intentions were with regard to us, not simply what God's intentions were with regard to God's Son. Again, the focus is upon what God was (is) doing in and through Jesus, not who Jesus is.[35]

It is in this light, then, that Jesus' miracles actually serve to define and to clarify Jesus' mission and power. They reveal the purpose of that power: it is a power for salvation, a power to mediate effectively the transforming dynamic energy of God's saving love. Everything Jesus does, everything Jesus says, is focused on that goal and that goal alone. Within that context, Jesus' miracles also say something about the quality of Jesus' power. The power of Jesus (for the reign of God) is *conditioned* and *limited*. It depends upon human openness and receptivity for its efficacy. It can be refused, rejected, resisted, thwarted. Hence, Jesus could not work many signs in his hometown precisely because the people of his hometown lacked faith (Mk.6:5). By contrast, to persons who received his healing gift, Jesus proclaimed "your faith has saved you" (Mk. 5:34; see 9:23-27). Like God's own power and presence, Jesus' capacity for bringing about the kingdom, through word and deed, was a non-coercive power. Limited by the freedom of Jesus' hearers, it was effective only in the context of people's faith.[36]

Thus, the miracles of Jesus are best understood as "signs of the kingdom," not as events beyond the laws of nature. They confirm Jesus' preaching, illustrating its content; they advance the realization of the truth of Jesus' proclamation in these, the final days. They show that, under the reign of God, everything within creation, everything human, every human endeavor, becomes healthy in humankind's pursuit of harmony within the self, with all persons, all nations, and all creation. Everything becomes healthy through the establishment of that fourfold peace which the kingdom envisioned, a kingdom realized by humankind's living in a communion energized by God's life and love. But, like the reign of God itself, the miracles demand faith in anyone who would benefit from them if God's saving presence were to become a reality. So significant is this condition of faith, both in regard to Jesus' proclamation of the kingdom (as we indicated in the last chapter) and as a condition for the efficacy of his efforts to work wonders (as we have just seen) that we must now turn to a more focused consideration of this dimension of the disciple's response to Jesus. For living faith is the fundamental aspect of the life of any disciple and of any person who wishes to enjoy life under the reign of God.

The Reign of God
Miracles, Faith and Discipleship

When Jesus proclaimed the presence of the reign of God, the fundamental challenge he extended to his audience consisted in the twofold call to repent and to believe. Similarly, when Jesus reached out to persons with the offer of deliverance through miraculous healing love, he either asked if the person believed he had such power or he confirmed that the individual's faith had brought about healing already accomplished. As we have seen in the previous chapter, so we observe once again that faith blossoming in conversion is the appropriate response to the presence of God's reign. Faith is the proper response to God's presence whether God breaks into history in word or in deed. The unfolding of Jesus' miracles underscores this fact: in some way faith made the entrance of God's saving love and power into history possible. How shall we understand that faith?

JESUS' MIRACLES AND THE PRESUPPOSITION OF FAITH

The faith which the historical Jesus asked of persons as he mediated God's saving love in their behalf clearly was not a faith which fully understood him or a faith which fully grasped the meaning of his ministry. That level of faith, reflected in the explicit beliefs of the post-resurrection Church, could develop only after Jesus' disciples experienced the Lord, crucified and risen. Likewise, the faith which Jesus required was not necessarily a faith which understood and adhered to every facet of belief expressed in the Jewish Tradition. Jesus worked miracles in behalf of non-Jews also (Mt. 8:5-13 and parallels). On the contrary, the faith which Jesus demanded is best understood as a more generic faith, that type of faith which we described earlier as "a disposition of mind and heart by which one is open to, and ready to recognize, the presence of the transcendent," however and wherever the transcendent becomes manifest. Rather than being principally an acceptance of specific truths or beliefs, this faith is fundamentally a quality of mind and heart that enables one to turn toward the transcendent for a response to one's need, seeking and waiting for an answer. We might use Karl Rahner's term for this type of faith and name it "unthematic," "non-categorical" faith since it had not yet come to explicit expression in any formula or specific belief. The capacity to hear Jesus' words as divine truth, as well as the ability to benefit from Jesus' healing powers, presumes and requires at least this generic, unthematic, faith.[37]

JESUS' MIRACLES AND THE CALL TO FAITH

Jesus uttered his proclamations and worked his signs and wonders, however, primarily in the context of Israel with its expectations of the coming of God's kingdom. Israel's faith had already become thematized in specific beliefs concerning God (Yahweh), the law, and the covenant. While Jesus could and did work wonders in behalf of non-Jews, he professedly came primarily for the salvation of Israel. Thematically Jewish faith (as distinguished from thematically Christian faith) provided believers with fuller background for discerning God's active and engaging presence in and through Jesus. A fuller understanding of the Lord and a deeper healing and transformation by way of his deeds required faith already shaped by Israel's belief and expectations. It presumed the faith that had identified Yahweh as "always present to save" (Ex.3:14) and could recognize that God as present and saving now. Jesus' call to faith through word and deed invited the hearer to open his or her mind and heart to the advent of, not just an anonymous transcendent God, but of the transcendent recognized as the saving God of Israel, acting in new and deeper ways.

Hence, Jesus' words and deeds not only presupposed faith for their efficacy; they also intentionally led to a deepening of faith. The historical Jesus proclaimed the in-breaking of the reign of God in fuller power then and there. He invited disciples to follow him by embracing a richer life in God, then and there. For Jesus' miracles were meant to advance the presence of the kingdom and such an advancement required that persons give themselves to a deeper surrender of faith, to a fuller commitment to God's ways, to a life shaped explicitly by the words, actions and lifestyle of Jesus himself. Jesus' particular miracles, as acts of "making the world and those within it well again" were meant to release persons from all that hindered discipleship, to free persons for discipleship and for living that kind of faith which discipleship represented. The miracles of Jesus, therefore, not only presume faith but lead to a fuller, richer faith, a thematic faith expressed in very specific beliefs and behaviors which would come to be designated as specifically Christian. Jesus' miracles were intended to help people find the loving God by living a life of faith centered upon and mediated by Jesus himself.[38]

JESUS' MIRACLES AND THE LACK OF FAITH

Obviously not everyone in Jesus' audience had that faith which his power to work wonders required; not all had the faith necessary to perceive that God was truly alive, acting in and through Jesus. Faith takes profound openness to and trust in the transcendent One.

But the struggle and difficulties of living with this generic openness to God was not the only source of resistance on the part of Jesus' hearers. More clearly, the resistance of Jesus' audience also flowed from their own thematic faith, that is, from the way their faith had been shaped in specific beliefs. Thus the Pharisees, the chief priests, the elders, all seemed incapable of seeing God in Jesus precisely because their adherence to specific tenets of their tradition would not allow Jesus, and God acting in and through him, to speak and act precisely as Jesus did. They could not fathom that God would relativize the holy command of the Sabbath observance; violation of that command, for them, was a sign of the evil one.[39] Religious persons, desiring to live responsibly according to God's law, could not believe that God would want one to associate with sinners and grant them liberation from their debts; only the evil one would sponsor such association with evil.[40] Persons dedicated to the Jewish Law could never take upon themselves the prerogative of forgiving that sin; only God could do that. Anyone who attempted to forgive sin would be feigning the truth; he would deserve repudiation as a blasphemer.[41] Jewish thematic faith, a faith which led many persons to be ready to experience the fuller overtures of God, so shaped the minds and hearts of some Jewish leaders that they lost the capacity to perceive the presence of God in the fuller expansiveness of God's saving love manifested in Jesus. The thematic faith of these religious leaders limited the deepening of the very generic faith which had formerly stood at the origin of Israel's beliefs. The rigidity of their own system of beliefs led them to stifle the dynamism of faith; hardened beliefs made it nearly impossible for these persons to experience God in Jesus.

The contrast between the disciples of Jesus and those who became his persecutors enables us better to understand the relationship of faith to the effective realization of the reign of God and the capacity of Jesus to work miracles. The advance of the reign of God, and the possibility of moving along the path of transformation and healing in God's kingdom, presupposes a people open and ready to recognize the goodness and saving presence of the God who leads to life and truth, however unexpected and challenging that may be. The proclamation of the kingdom and the miracles of Jesus both presupposed this openness of faith and also were intended to deepen that faith. Sometimes, this meant challenging a hardened faith. At all times it meant advancing the kingdom by freeing persons for discipleship centered on Jesus who embodied the reign of God in himself.

Doing Christology in Light of Jesus' Preaching and Miracles

In light of the reflections of this and of the previous chapters, we can now move further in our understanding of the task of doing Christology. In some manner what we say here will merely reaffirm observations already made; in another way these observations will deepen the principles already stated, broaden them, and more securely anchor them in a fuller christological context. For these purposes, we offer four reflections.

First, having observed the interaction of the historical Jesus with would-be followers, we are given living examples of the fact that growth in faith requires openness to surprise, openness to the possibility of reformulation of beliefs, and a willingness to let go of images of God and of God's ways which one may have absolutized in the past. The challenge of Jesus' preaching and the challenge of his wonderful deeds call a person to allow the goodness and saving love of the Transcendent to flow into his or her consciousness unimpeded by past convictions or dreams of what God could or could not, would or would not do. Without such openness, God cannot be God for us. With such openness, God can work "wonders"; with such openness, God can break into our lives with such overtures of love that we can find ourselves, the concreteness of our lives, and even the physical shape of our lives (health, finances, relationships, losses, work opportunities) transformed. Only at that point, after having unconditionally surrendered to God and, subsequently having experienced anew God's saving love, can we safely and accurately understand and interpret our experience of God and more accurately name the Transcendent.

Second, since Jesus, in his words and deeds, Jesus in his personal and historical life and journey, mediates the fullness of

God's presence and God's designs, both the experience of God and the interpretation of who God is and what God is doing must find their truth and meaning in him. And so, once again it is necessary to affirm the conviction that, on the one hand, the capacity to experience the in-breaking of the personal God whom Jesus names *Abba*, and the ability rightly to understand that God and to interpret God's action, require openness and freedom from any images of God we may have absolutized. On the other hand, we who recognize the centrality of Jesus may not enter the process of doing theology or Christology outside of, or oblivious of, the God-revealing and God-defining person, life, and ministry of Christ. Openness to transcendent love and freedom to let God be God should lead us better to understand and to interpret the mystery of Jesus; while the mystery of Jesus should guide us in our efforts to understand God and our experience of God.

Third, the image of the reign of God, being the driving image of Jesus' proclamation and the contextualizing image of Jesus' miracles, must remain the governing image in doing Christology. It must govern every effort to understand and to interpret God's active presence manifested in and through Jesus as well as every effort to interpret and to understand our experiences and our Church's experiences of Jesus. No one aspect of the reign of God, no one saying of Jesus, no particular miracle, is adequate to define the kingdom, much less to describe and name the God who is Father of Jesus. Yet the totality of Jesus' preaching, of his action, and (as we shall see) of his suffering, death and resurrection, can and does give adequate expression to that kingdom and to the God who is its center. The reign of God as proclaimed and illustrated by Jesus in his life, ministry, death and resurrection, then, must always stand in the forefront of one's consciousness in every effort to interpret the experience of Christ and of God alive for us in and through Jesus.

Fourth, in striving to interpret our experience of God in accord with these three guidelines and/or reflections, we in actual fact will be doing Christology as did the early Church. We will be allowing God to unveil God's deeper Self in the immediacy of each moment, whether that be a moment of light or of healing, a moment of surprising transformation from sickness to health, a moment of conversion to a fuller life of discipleship, or a moment of darkness, lived and managed in communion with Christ before the cross. Further, we will allow that moment both to be indicative of the fact that the reign of God is genuinely here for us and also to be an anticipation of what we know God is doing for everyone in Jesus' death and resurrection. We will be capable of doing this because we, like the early Church, bring to our efforts two resources: a living and open faith in God alive for us now and always; and the conviction which we have (as Christians) that God has fully revealed God's love and intentions for us in Jesus, crucified and risen. Hence, we have every reason, as did the early Church, to interpret our contemporary experience of God's saving love for us now in the light of Christ's proclamation of the kingdom and in the light of its fulfillment in his death and resurrection. We have every reason to affirm that, in these experiences of God's saving love, God is leading us more deeply into that kingdom and incorporating us more fully into the crucified and risen Christ now. Like the post-resurrection church of the Gospels, our seeing Jesus crucified and risen in our own experience of the surprising in-breaking of God's saving love is not to "read into" the event. Rather, it is to see it in unity with the culmination of our life and our history which Jesus' proclamation of the kingdom announced, which Jesus' miracles illustrated, and which Jesus' death and resurrection accomplished.

But how is God revealed in Jesus' death and resurrection? Why is it that in these events more than in any others, the reign of God is established and the gift of salvation is forever poured forth upon humankind and human history? More specifically, what is the meaning of Jesus' death? Why did Jesus "have to" suffer and to die for us and for our sin? How did Jesus himself view and experience his trial and the cross? These questions beckon us to take the next step in doing Christology. But first, to aid my readers in summing up the insights of the present chapter and in relating these beliefs and the dynamics of doing Christology reflected there to their own experience, I offer the following questions.

Questions for Reflection

1. What miracle story has been the most striking and/or perplexing to you in your reading of Scripture or in your hearing the Scriptures proclaimed? How has your understanding of the distinction between miracle stories and the historical miraculous event helped you better understand that story? How has that story helped you better to understand the reign of God and Jesus' primary concern for the reign of God in his working deeds of wonder? (You may wish to further your understanding through reading a commentary on such a story or the reflections of a biblical scholar on such a story, such as J. P. Meier's commentary on the miracle stories in his book The Marginal Jew, Vol. 2.)

2. Often persons wonder why God does not work miracles more frequently or answer prayers as we would desire, or move forward the kingdom more rapidly. How do the reflections of this chapter concerning Jesus' power provide insight into possible responses to these questions?

3. How have you come, through the journey of this chapter, better to understand the nature of faith? How have you been helped to understand the priority of faith over beliefs, images of belief, and/or statements of belief? How would you understand and explain, nonetheless, why and how faith affirmations (beliefs) concerning Jesus and his role provide a necessary context and guide for the authentic interpretation of one's faith experience of God?

4. What events in your own life or in the lives of people you know personally, strike you as wonderful and surprising experiences of the in-breaking of God offering salvation, signs of God's reign? In what ways have you or people you know seen these events as foreshadowing God's ultimate gift of everlasting life? In what ways have you or others interpreted them as initial experiences of your share in Christ's kingdom now?

CHAPTER 7

Experiencing Christ: Crucified and Dying

The words and wonders of Jesus of Nazareth focused upon the presence of God's powerful saving love, the emergence of God's reign. Jesus centered his historical life upon *Abba*, upon what *Abba* intended and was accomplishing for human beings. God wished to give God's transcendent Self as abiding power and transforming presence to foster an unsurpassed wholesomeness and peace in the lives of all peoples. Jesus spoke of this transcendent Power, illustrated it with deeds, and exemplified it through his life. The reign of God had come; human life and human history were being gifted with the possibility of such profound transformation that the fourfold peace[1] which Israel had longed for for centuries had become clear opportunity. That transformation and peace, previously impossible for humans to achieve, was truly possible in God and in God's Self-Gift.

As we have seen in earlier chapters, Jesus' proclamation of the Good News of the reign of God, his unveiling of that presence and power in miraculous deeds, his manifestation of the character of that God through his personal life of unconditional service to others, brought him to the cross. The man who brought healing was hatefully wounded; the one who reconciled was treated as a sinner; he who brought life was brutally killed. Jesus' earthly life of compassionate love ended with death on the cross.

Christians throughout subsequent centuries, however, have viewed Jesus' death, not as final defeat, but as ultimate victory: the victory of life over death; the victory of love over selfishness; the victory of God over sin. Believers have come to reverence Jesus' death through the symbol of the crucifix and even to celebrate it joyfully in the liturgy of the Eucharist. To some degree, therefore, Christian tradition has given a definitive interpretation to Jesus' death.

Christian familiarity with and acceptance of Jesus' suffering and death, however, while very commendable, also can be detrimental with regard to the development of faith. These attitudes can lead one to take the cross for granted and, as a result, can blind one to the profound human and painful tragedy that it was. They can foster an unquestioned perception that Jesus had a vision of the cross before his mind from the very beginning of his ministry and that he moved rather easily to embrace it as his earthly life neared its conclusion. They can lead one to accept too readily, and perhaps for false reasons, the fact that Jesus "had to suffer these things so as to enter into his glory" (Luke 24:26). The passion and death of Jesus, therefore, still raise serious questions.

This chapter will focus upon Jesus' crucifixion and death in relationship to God's offer of salvation and God's establishing of God's kingdom. We will trace this theme through several stages. First, we will seek to uncover Jesus' own mind and heart as he anticipated, sought to understand, and actually experienced the cross. Second, we will gather together and reflect upon the biblical and the post-apostolic interpretations of the meaning and the necessity of Jesus' death on the cross, selectively attending to voices from the New Testament, through the classical period up to the present century. Finally, we will conclude with some further observations for doing Christology followed by the usual questions for reflection.

The Cross in Jesus' Own Experience

Questions regarding the historical Jesus' anticipation, under-standing, and experience of the cross are difficult to answer for reasons with which we are already familiar. The written Gospels are not primarily records of history, but rather are documents of faith composed in a post-resurrection Church. It is not surprising, therefore, that Jesus' *predictions* of his passion, death, and resurrection[2] as reflected in the Gospels offer explicit details which show them to be compositions after the fact. Nor is it surprising that Jesus' statements disclosing his *understanding of the salvific meaning of his death*, statements which the evangelists place within the context of his last meal with his disciples, not only differ one from the other, but are reflective of the language of the Eucharistic liturgies of the early Church.[3] For the Gospels as a whole, and the passion narratives in particular, flow toward the climax of the resurrection. Therefore they contain a variety of textual allusions which help the reader understand the cross in the light of the resurrection, of Jesus' victory over sin, and consequently in the light of God's definitive gift of salvation for all the world. While all these faith-filled reflections upon the historical event of the cross happily provide fuller theological insight into Jesus' passion and death, they make it somewhat more difficult to discern the historical Jesus' mind and heart, not to mention other dimensions of his human experience, as he anticipated and eventually endured his crucifixion and death.

Recognizing these difficulties, we will continue to draw upon the resources of historical-critical methodology as a reliable and fruitful way of gaining access to the historical Jesus, including some insight into his mind and heart as he faced the cross. To this purpose we will consider Jesus' anticipation and foreknowledge of the cross, his understanding of the meaning and significance of this event, and his truly human experience of suffering and dying, an experience within which his relationship to *Abba* continued to deepen and unfold.

JESUS' FOREKNOWLEDGE:
HIS DEATH AND RESURRECTION - AN INEVITABLE EVENT

The Gospel of Mark and the synoptic parallels, as we have seen above,[4] present Jesus predicting his passion, death, and resurrection. Scholars,[5] however, have questioned the historicity of these predictions as they are formulated for two reasons. First, these predictions manifest a number of details (the chief priests' and elders' condemnation of Jesus, their action of "handing him over" to the Gentiles, the Roman soldiers' mocking, spitting upon and scourging him) which, in their concreteness, would hardly have been known beforehand. Second, the clarity of Jesus' predictions seems to be counter-indicated by the fearful and despairing dispositions of the Apostles who ran from the scene and apparently returned to their earlier trade as fishermen. If Jesus had been so clear in his prediction of his passion, death and resurrection, why were these disciples so shaken at Jesus' death, so surprised and unsuspecting at his resurrection? Hence, from the scriptural report of Jesus' explicit statements alone, it would be difficult to establish with certainty that Jesus foresaw and spoke with clarity of the striking climax of his historical journey.

On the other hand, it would be difficult to understand how Jesus would not have foreseen, and talked with his disciples about, his eventual suffering and death at the hands of the Jewish religious leaders. He knew he was a source of consternation and provocation to the Pharisees, Sadducees, priestly class and elders in an ever growing fashion. In their estimation, he violated the holy Sabbath Law (Mk. 2:23-24; Lk. 13:14), ate with persons of disrepute (Mk. 2:15-17), and presumptuously forgave sin, presuming a prerogative belonging only to God (Mk. 2:5-7). The latter offense was, in their judgement, a blasphemous act, punishable by death.   Jesus obviously walked on a collision course with the leaders of his day and he could not help but know that.

Jesus also knew of the fate of many a prophet. Israel persecuted the prophets (Lk. 13:32f; Mt. 23:34-39); the death of John the Baptist was a glaringly case in point (Mk. 6:14-29). The dangerous consequences of taking a prophetic stance before Israel and its leaders would be apparent to anyone who knew anything of Israel's history. To seek to mediate God's transforming love was risky business and Jesus must have realized that. In that context, the perplexing question would not be whether or not Jesus would have foreseen his approaching death at his adversaries' hands. Rather the perplexing question would be why Jesus did not cease from his preaching, teaching, healing, and forgiving ministry so as to avoid such persecution.

The response to this latter question, however, is fairly clear. Jesus stayed the course because he believed that his way spoke more truly of the God he named *Abba* than did the way advocated by the chief priests, the elders, the Scribes, and the Pharisees. For Jesus, the truth about God consisted in God's fidelity to God's Self in being a God of abiding love, forgiveness, healing, and life for all persons. The truth about God consisted in God's decisive intent to empower human beings to live and to love God and neighbor without condition. For Jesus, living by that truth, stating it clearly, and showing it in wondrous deeds was worth the price he would eventually have to pay: rejection, persecution, and death on a cross. Jesus foresaw the human tragedy which was unfolding before him, if not in all its concrete terms, certainly in its basic movements. He accepted those movements in view of the greater good which he was convinced would flow from his words and deeds.

However, the establishment of evidence that Jesus would have surmised and even, with some apprehension, accepted his journey to the cross does not respond to the entire question. We also must ask whether he would have been able to foresee and speak of his resurrection. The risen body is so indescribable (even by those who later had come to experience the risen Lord, as we shall see in the next chapter) that we wonder how anyone, including Jesus, could humanly foresee, much less speak of, resurrection before experiencing it.

This difficulty, however, is not as overriding as it might seem. For, as a matter of fact, resurrection language did flow through the religious consciousness of Jewish society during Jesus' time.[6] Such language expressed, at the very least, the clear hope that God would bring *the whole person* to everlasting life at some future time as the ultimate gift of God's redemptive love. The historical Jesus would have been aware of this language and would have appreciated its meaning.

But Jesus was aware of more than this language and its meaning. As we have observed in our reflections upon his life and ministry, Jesus possessed an unshakable appreciation of *Abba's* loving and saving presence for human beings, especially for persons in the most desperate need. It is consonant with such an appreciation of God that Jesus would believe in, and affirm, God's life-giving love for Jesus himself even as he faced his death. In this light, what Jesus, in envisioning his future resurrection, would have experienced was unshakable confidence in God, including an unshakable trust that God would vindicate him. Without being able to describe concretely the nature of risen life, he would have been expressing his radical trust in God's life-giving power, a trust consonant with his driving convictions regarding the unrestricted healing love of the God he called *Abba*.

Finally, while granting the fact that Jesus foresaw, in a general manner, both his death and also his resurrection, we must also focus upon the question of whether or not Jesus actually spoke of these events to his disciples. As we mentioned above, the facts that the disciples ran from the cross, went back to their labor of fishing, and were obviously surprised when Jesus, the risen Lord, appeared to them, poses a question at least with regard to what Jesus actually had shared with them. In face of that question, we offer the following. It would be hard to imagine a person as dedicated to truth and honesty as Jesus was, not sharing such important aspects of his life with his followers. From his sense of the movement of his journey of pursuing faithfulness to *Abba* and loving service of Israel, he certainly could have shared the substance of his own convictions about his future without necessarily being able to offer concrete details concerning either his passion or the nature and time of his glorious resurrection. Even if he had, the impact of Christ's ruthless execution could understandably have caused the Apostles to run away from the scene and ultimately lose heart. The mere pledge of resurrection which the Apostles had heard would not have been adequate to make them believers or to provide them with the courage to stand firm with the Lord in this hour of darkness. Only the powerful experience of seeing the risen Jesus could instill in them such strength. And so the fact that the disciples did not understand, lacked courage and manifested surprise when Jesus finally manifested himself in risen glory does not disprove the likelihood that the historical Jesus spoke of his crucifixion to his chosen followers. Rather, it is most probable that Jesus not only anticipated his suffering, his death, and his resurrection himself, but also that he spoke about this openly, even if in only in a general manner, with his disciples.[7]

We can reasonably conclude, then, that the Jesus of history lived with and shared a growing awareness that suffering and death would beset him because of his preaching and ministry. Unshakable confidence in God and in God's will to vindicate God's beloved, however, sustained him on his mission. For Jesus lived and ministered out of his perception and experience of that God whom he knew unquestionably to be the God of unlimited mercy and love. Fidelity to that God and openness to that God's wisdom, life, and love, together with constancy in mediating that God's presence to God's people, was all that mattered for Jesus.

JESUS' UNDERSTANDING:
HIS DEATH AND RESURRECTION - A SALVIFIC EVENT

Jesus' vision of his forthcoming death and his understanding of this dreadful moment, however, were not limited simply to foreseeing its inevitability. Nor was his vision limited to understanding it as the unfortunate price which he would have to pay for his fidelity to *Abba* in the context of a world of faithlessness and sin. Rather, he also understood his death as a meaningful event in the context of the accomplishment of his God-given mission. His death constituted the definitive moment in which the reign of God and the salvation of humankind would be established forever.[8]

Like the question of Jesus' anticipation and foreknowledge of his death, however, the question of his understanding of his suffering and crucifixion is not easily discerned. The statements of Jesus, as recorded in the passion narratives show the influence of the final Isaian hymn in praise of Yahweh's "suffering servant" (Isaiah 52:13-53:12). It would be difficult to tell whether this hymn had stimulated Jesus' own intuition into the meaning of his death, or whether it first stimulated the consciousness of the early Church and evangelists, and from the latter alone made its way into the composition of the Gospels. What is clear, however, is that the notion of the suffering just man and of the expiatory power of such suffering had become widespread by the time of Jesus, as the books of the Maccabees witness.[9] Hence, the historical Jesus certainly would have been gifted with the religious background which would have enabled him to interpret his death positively and salvifically as the moment drew near.[10] It is reasonable, then, to draw on the material of the passion narratives as reliable indications of Jesus' own perception of the saving import of these moments. It is with that conviction that we will seek to gain fuller insight into Jesus' understanding of the cross as we consider several statements of the Lord recounted by the evangelists.

The first series of our reflections will center upon Jesus' words during his last meal with his specially chosen twelve disciples. There, as the synoptic Gospels record, Jesus claims: "I shall not drink of the fruit of the vine until I drink anew in the kingdom of God" (Mk. 14:25 and parallels).[11] Jesus recognized that the reign of God, which he had come to establish, would become full and definitive reality as he journeyed through death.

But the reign of God is the salvation of humankind. The definitive presence of God in powerful saving love establishes salvation for everyone and forever. This, too, Jesus understands. He recognizes that, in his death, in his final surrender to the in-breaking of God in his own life and through him into history, he brings the entire broken and sinful world forever into the presence of God's unbounded mercy and readiness to forgive. For this reason, at his final meal with his disciples, in blessing the bread, he speaks of his body given for us. Likewise, in blessing the cup, he speaks of his blood poured out for the forgiveness of sin.[12]

The Gospels, moreover, indicate the fact that the historical Jesus, even at moments outside of this final meal with the twelve, had envisioned his death as redemptive. The Marcan Community remembered Jesus as explicitly linking his life of service - a life dedicated to the eradication of sin in all its forms - with his death as he instructed his disciples: "The Son of man has come not to be served but to serve and to give his life as a ransom for many" (Mk. 10:45). So also, the Lucan tradition recalled Jesus as uttering words of forgiveness: "Father, forgive them for they know not what they do" (Lk. 23:34a) and also words of promise focused on the kingdom "This day you will be with me in paradise" (Lk. 23:43), even as he neared his death. Though not necessarily the exact words of Jesus, these passages do reflect Jesus' basic mind and heart[13] as he moved through life into death.

And so, we can conclude that Jesus understood and embraced his death as the necessary way of bringing about the definitive establishment of God's reign in the midst of a sinful world. Jesus saw his death as the vehicle providing humankind with God's abiding gift of salvation in the enduring act of mercy and selfless love for all.[14] For Jesus, the journey toward death was the journey toward life; the moment of ultimate self-emptying was the moment of embracing God's fullness; the final and climactic act of human rejection and sin would be the definitive and life-giving act of divine acceptance; the act by which humankind strove to destroy Christ's kingship would be incorporated into the act by which God would establish God's reign of love for all human beings forever.

JESUS' HUMAN EXPERIENCE:
HIS PASSION AND DEATH - A SELF-EMPTYING EVENT
To say that the historical Jesus, during his human journey on earth foresaw his approaching death and resurrection, or to say that he understood these events as filled with meaning and power for the establishment of God's reign, does not imply that Jesus entered upon or accepted his suffering and death easily. The Gospel accounts of Jesus' passion, again reflecting not only theological insight but also substantial historical truth, would tell us otherwise.

Thus, Mark writes that Jesus, taking Peter, James, and John with him to Gethsemane "began to be distressed and full of dread.[15] Then he said to them, 'My soul is sorrowful even unto death'" (Mk. 14:33-34). The words, as recorded by the evangelist, portray Jesus experiencing an overwhelming, almost crushing, sorrow,[16] profound apprehension, and deep inner turmoil.[17] Then, with full realization of what was breaking in upon him, he counsels his disciples: "Pray that you may not undergo (succumb to) the test (Mk. 14:38).[18] The motive of his warning, as stated, reveals that he anticipated that nothing less than the full force of evil was about to confront him and would, to some degree, also challenge his followers.[19] Most understandable then is Jesus' plea: "*Abba*, Father, all things are possible to you. Take this cup away from me" (Mk. 14:36). However deeply Jesus appreciated the meaningfulness of his death, his faith-filled convictions did not remove his desire to escape the pain, the ignominy, the darkness which his trial and crucifixion would impose upon him. As the author of the letter to the Hebrews asserts: "We do not have a high priest who is unable to sympathize with our weaknesses, but one who, like us, has been tested in every way" (Heb. 4:15).

It is true, nevertheless, that in the midst of his apprehension, fear and emotional strain, Jesus did preserve confidence in God's wisdom and saving presence. He prays: "Nevertheless, not my will but yours be done" (Mk. 14:36). Although faith could not overcome Jesus' apprehension, neither did his apprehension and fear conquer Jesus' trust in *Abba*. Both fear and trust, both profound apprehension and profound faith, touched Jesus deeply in this last hour of his earthly journey.

The conjunction of such profound competing feelings within Jesus deserves our fullest attention. What needs to be taken seriously is that while Jesus chose freely to surrender to *Abba* in the midst of calamity, he did not persevere in that trust without allowing the frightening and almost overwhelming pressures of anticipated suffering to permeate his mind and spirit. On the contrary, he met the pressures of that challenge with equally profound courage, a courage which became deeper and was made perfect as Jesus moved beyond fear and weakness to face his adversaries with even greater strength and selflessness.[20] Jesus' anticipation of the cross called forth and shaped Jesus' freedom so that it might reach its full depth of selflessness and courage. Only by appreciating the devastating power of the passion and the cross as they lay before Jesus, and only in appreciating the manner in which this unfolding event penetrated Jesus' entire being, can we appreciate the depth of Jesus' self-giving love and bravery.

Our recognition of these two dimensions of Jesus' experience is of singular importance in doing Christology. For if we do not do justice to Jesus' apprehension, we will not do justice to his courage either. And if, in our estimation, we mitigate either of these powerful human movements within Jesus, we risk seriously dehumanizing and completing misunderstanding him. Jesus was truly human as we are (Heb. 4:14-16); and he, knowing profound dread as he anticipated the cross, endured that moment of darkness with a courage all the more inspiring.[21]

But the greatest expression of Jesus' struggle and pain was yet to come. It is from the cross itself that Jesus reveals the deepest dimension of his suffering; for it is from the cross that Jesus, as depicted by two evangelists, cries out: "My God, my God, why have you forsaken me" (Mk. 15:34; Mt. 27:46). Abandoned by all his disciples (save his mother, several women and the disciple "whom he loved"), deserted by those who had acclaimed him as the "one who had come in the name of the Lord,"[22] ridiculed by so many who looked on, Jesus felt abandoned by the very God he had so valiantly served.

In some ways, the cry of Jesus constitutes an embarrassment to today's believers, not to mention those of the early Church.[23] How could the Son of God, the One whom the later Church confessed as divine, feel abandoned by God? How could *Abba* withdraw from the Chosen Servant? The cry of Jesus raises questions which challenge very fundamental beliefs of the Christian Tradition.

Respecting the validity of these questions, contemporary theologians[24] begin to respond by noting that Jesus' cry echoes the first verse of Psalm 22. For a pious Jew, the recitation of the beginning of a psalm implied his or her praying of the psalm in its entirety. Psalm 22, however, while opening with a cry of desolation, moves toward, and then concludes with, expressions of renewed confidence and trust in God. It is most likely, therefore, that the evangelists, in composing the passion narratives, intended to depict Jesus both as enduring the deepest feelings of God's absence and also as continuing to embrace the faith and convictions which the psalmist manifests as the prayer develops. They wished to convey a memory of Jesus which in no way softens the intensity of his personal suffering while also affirming that he endured this bleakest of moments with unwavering trust.

Understanding Jesus' prayer in this light, however, does not completely resolve all questions. At the very least, it still leaves us with the question of how Jesus, who had walked in such evident communion with *Abba* throughout his earthly life, could come to experience and to give voice to such a deep sense of being abandoned by God.[25] One avenue of response and insight focuses upon the nature of the experience of God itself. That experience, while often recognized by deeply felt gifts of comfort, strength, and peace, is, in itself, distinguishable from these gifts. God is also experienced simply in a confident longing for, and an abiding trust in, life and love beyond that which life in this world can provide. That longing and the trust which permeates it can remain constant in times of darkness as well as in times of light. The profound peace, comfort, healing, and strength which one often recognizes as signs of God's presence can evoke, support, and strengthen such longing and confidence, but God also reveals God's presence by sustaining us in longing and trust in moments of darkness. Such longing and trust are the purest signs of God's Self-giving presence.

From this point of view, then, Jesus' prayer leads us to recognize that Jesus, indeed, need not have lost his longing for and trust in *Abba*, even as he cried out in overwhelming anguish. But that cry also forces us to appreciate the full extent of Jesus' powerlessness and helplessness: Almost every dimension of Jesus' experience of the cross awakened within him a pervasive sense of the absence of God. The mockery of the soldiers, the condemnation of the elders, the cowardice of the disciples, the ridicule of the spectators, the weakness of his own body, everything which Jesus experienced seemed emptied of true life and of the Godlike love which brings about and nourishes life. Everything appeared to Jesus as Godless. And so, he cries out[26] "My God, my God, why have you forsaken me." Nothing surrounding him, little within him, offers Jesus a sense of the loving presence of God.[27]

The intensity and extent of Jesus' suffering as well as his enduring trust in and fidelity to *Abba* speak volumes. They call all who see or hear the crucified Lord to wonder and to question: Who is this man? How shall we understand him? The words which Mark puts in the mouth of the Roman centurion attempt to give an answer to this question: "Truly, this man was the Son (that is, the most singularly faithful servant and most beloved child) of God" (Mk. 15:39).[28] And, in that light the Church continues to answer: Jesus is human, fully human. Jesus is also unique among humans: Jesus has within himself an unprecedented gift, empowering him to be faithful in the midst of the darkest and most desolate hour a human being would be called upon to face. Jesus lives and Jesus dies in the power of Godliness. And in so doing, he shows that Godliness, and its expression in his life in the form of love and trust, lie deeper than even the darkest experiences which humans must face. He is, in every moment of his humanness, born of God, alive in God. He is the Son of God finding the fullness of God's saving love in his greatest act of self-emptying. Jesus is the revelation of the enduring power and presence of God in a human being, the revelation of the true reward of self-emptying fidelity for all ages.

The Cross: its Significance and Power for Salvation[29]

It is one thing to affirm and to seek to appreciate Jesus' experience and understanding of the cross, including his conviction that it would definitively bring about God's reign and the enduring gift of salvation for all people. It is quite another thing to understand how the cross has actually brought about the kingdom of God and human salvation. The former affirmation touches the mind, heart, freedom, and convictions of the historical Jesus himself. The latter seeks to make fuller sense of the paradoxical event which he willingly endured.

To clarify the question being addressed here it will be helpful to recall the manner in which we have previously[30] defined salvation. Salvation is a human being's "being alive in God as Jesus was (and is) alive in God." That life empowers the recipient to live with a deeper sense of unity, wholeness, and purpose within the self; to live in love, justice, and peace with friend and foe; to live in harmony, respect, and gratitude within the world. The transformation of life within one's self, with others and with one's world, flows from and necessarily expresses the truth of God's presence in the abiding power of God's Self-gift to each individual.

To clarify the question even further, we should note and delineate two elements of the gift and the experience of salvation. The first element, the origin, the principal cause, and the core of salvation is God in God's Self-communicating presence and love. God is the absolutely necessary, transcendent element within the experience of salvation. Later theology, reflecting upon the biblical witness and upon its own experience, will further distinguish several dimensions within God's transcendent Self-Gift by speaking of God's active Self-giving, the divine initiative of transcendent love, by speaking of God's indwelling, God's abiding presence and power within each person, and by speaking of God's fullest Self-expression, the historical appearance of transcendent love in the life of Jesus. God so gives God's Self that God becomes an immanent source of divine and Christlike love within each believer, just as God reveals and communicates God's Self through the Word made flesh.[31] The origin, cause, and very core of salvation, then, is the God who is inexhaustible love, the God who effectively communicates God's Self by uniting that Self with each believer at the deepest center of his or her personal existence.

Where God is, however, God acts; and where God acts, things change. When God communicates God's Self and dwells deeply within human beings, they are necessarily transformed. They are necessarily rejuvenated with the power of Godly love. They participate in God's way of being toward the world and toward people. Hence, we rightly speak of a second element, a human, participatory element of salvation, the element which later theology named (created) grace and described as the human "sharing in divine life." The sign and the effect of this "sharing in divine life," itself rooted in God's new and saving presence, is the transformation of human consciousness and freedom in Christlike love; the willing expression of this love in human actions of love, justice and peace; and the communion of life among people with one another and the world which such actions help to create.

Salvation, therefore, has several dimensions: It has a God-centered, transcendent, dimension and it has a human, participatory, dimension. God and human beings, in effect, become partners in the journey of life and the achievement of salvation. Persons become "alive in God as Jesus was and is alive in God." Our precise question, therefore, is: How does Christ's death and resurrection effectively bring about (or mediate) God's presence and Self-Gift to human beings? How does that death bring about a transformation and participation of human consciousness, freedom and love so that they become expressive of God's life?

Before moving to respond to this question, however, we need to reflect upon another way of understanding salvation: salvation involves the eradication of sin. The New Testament and subsequent Christian Tradition have always understood salvation in relationship to sin. As Jesus' name implies, he has come "to save his people from their sins" (Mt. 1:21b). The question at hand, therefore, also demands some clarification of the nature and meaning of sin.

Sin, though definable in many ways, essentially is "being dead to God," the very opposite of salvation. The core and ultimate cause of sin is best described as an "emptiness." Sin, at root, consists in "the absence of God in the lives of human beings," or "the human incapacity and the human failure to live with the power and in the likeness of Christlike love." Sin, therefore, has a dimension parallel to the transcendent dimension of salvation. Sin consists in "isolation from the Transcendent," a condition which leaves human beings desperately weak..

But sin, like salvation, also has a human, participatory dimension, a dimension which is both sign and effect of this "isolation from or absence of God." This human participatory dimension of sin brings the "lack of God's presence and power" to a more obvious level of human experience. At this level, sin refers to acts of selfishness, injustice, violence, and oppression. It speaks of actions which flow from and express people's fragmented, vulnerable, and self-enclosed powers of freedom in conflict with other uncentered and uninspired powers of freedom in the world. Without a profound, God-invigorated center, the best persons can do is make temporary agreements and compromises to avoid total destruction of one another.

The Christian experience of salvation involves an experience of *being rescued* from the powerlessness and the plight which people know and lament in their experience of sin (whether that be their own sin or the sin that surrounds them). Salvation consists in deliverance from both aspects of the human sinful condition: the emptiness and helplessness of the human spirit deprived of the power and presence of God's personal life and love, and the wounded Godless ways of living which separate people from their true selves, divide them from one-another, create chaos in society, and enslave humankind as a whole. Salvation is "being made alive in God's life and love as Jesus was and is alive in God's love"; as such, it is also the healing of sin, both at its root and in its every expression.

Recognizing the interrelated elements of both salvation and sin should help us clarify the question which stands before us. The question seeks a twofold insight: an insight into the relationship of Jesus' death on the cross to God's definitive Self-gift, the gift which ultimately works the interior renewal of all persons and the eradication of sin; and also an insight into the relationship of the cross to the transformation of human life, human freedom, and human history in human expressions of Godliness through human acts of love, justice and peace. We ask: How does Jesus' death affect (influence) and effect (decisively bring about) the salvation of humankind in its God-centered core, and in its human participation? We will offer our response in two parts. First we will consider the witness of the New Testament; then second, we will present a summary of what we consider the most significant post-apostolic perspectives which can help move the question at hand.

The Saving Power of Jesus' Death: New Testament Witness

The New Testament uses a multiplicity of concepts and images to express the Christian believers' convictions concerning the salvific efficacy of Jesus' death. The dominant concept and image is that of "redemption." Allied to it, we also find the image of "sacrifice."

Both become specified by explicit reference to Jesus' being an "expiation" for our sin and to his having redeemed us "by his blood." In that fashion, Paul writes to the Church of Rome:

> All have sinned and are deprived of the glory of God. They are justified freely by his grace through the redemption in Christ Jesus, whom God set forth as an expiation, through faith, by his blood, to prove his (God's) righteousness because of (by) the forgiveness of sins.... (3:23-25).

Similarly, the author of the letter to the Hebrews, speaking of the supremacy of Christ in relationship to the priests of the Old Law, and of the superiority of Christ's death over the sacrifices of the Old Law, writes:

> But when Christ came as High Priest of the good things that have come to be..., he entered once for all into the sanctuary, not with the blood of goats and calves but with his own blood, thus obtaining eternal redemption. For if the blood of goats and bulls and the sprinkling of a heifer's ashes can sanctify those who are defiled..., how much more will the blood of Christ... cleanse our consciences from dead works to worship the living God. (9:11-14).

And in the next chapter, he continues:

> Every priest stands daily at his ministry, offering frequently these same sacrifices that can never take away sins. But the One offered one sacrifice for sins, and took his seat forever at the right hand of God...., for by one offering he has made perfect forever those who have been consecrated (sanctified, made holy). (10:11-14)

It is through a mosaic of interrelated images that the New Testament sought to express the truth and the reality of its faith experience of salvation through Christ. So central and pivotal are these concepts and images for expressing and conveying the Christian experience of salvation that each deserves some comment and clarification.

The Cross as Redemptive[32]

Redemption is a concept quite similar to salvation. Literally, it means a "buying back," a "deliverance." It evokes the image of landowners' buying and selling slaves, of "redeeming" them for a price. This meaning, however, raises as many questions as it answers. If God has redeemed us, from whom have we been bought back? From what, or from whose servitude, have we been delivered? The exact meaning of this term, as applied to God's work of effecting salvation in Christ, is not immediately clear.

We can gain some insight into the meaning of the word, and to some degree the implied dynamics of redemption, by recalling its original use in the writings of early Israel. The Israelites knew deliverance and redemption in their experience of the Exodus, their escape from slavery among the Egyptians through the intervention of Yahweh (Ex. 6:6f; 15:1-13).[33] Clearly, they recognized that Yahweh had not "paid a ransom" to their oppressors to bring about their freedom. Nevertheless, the Israelites likened their experience of deliverance to the freedom which a former slave knew when some benefactor redeemed him, securing his release from his former master (at some cost to his beneficiary). Obviously they employed the term redemption metaphorically. By using this term, they intended to express what their experience was like rather than to give a literal explanation of the nature of their deliverance or of how God had actually accomplished it.

The early Church used the image of "redemption" in a similar manner as it sought to convey its exhilarating experience of having been saved, freed, lifted up by God, through the death and resurrection of Jesus (Col 1:12-14; Eph. 1:7-8). In employing this image the Christians basically meant, like their Jewish ancestors, to describe an experience: the experience of unexpected deliverance, a release from bondage and hopelessness culminating in a new found freedom. Unlike the redemption of Israel in the Exodus, however, Christian redemption was primarily interior. For the

Christian, redemption denoted the experience of a deliverance from the oppression one knows when one's deepest longings meet frustration again and again, a deliverance from Godlessness and spiritual powerlessness. Like the Israelites, however, they used the word redemption metaphorically to create, as powerfully as possible, a feeling-laden image of the wonder of *what* God had worked in their behalf and in behalf of all people. Christians did not intend the term to explain literally *how* Christ's death and resurrection actually brought this deliverance about.

Through the image of redemption, then, the early Christian communities intended to convey their experience of salvation as we have defined it.[34] There are, however, two differences between these two expressions. First, as an image, redemption has the power to evoke a fuller, felt, personal experience of what salvation is truly like: Salvation is "like the freedom, joy and ecstasy a former slave knows when he is released from bondage and given a new life." Secondly, the image of redemption has the potential of more fully underscoring the deep sense that the gift of salvation is a truly unmerited, graciously bestowed gift. In reference to this new life, humankind previously had been as helpless, as thoroughly without recourse, as a slave before an oppressive master. Salvation has come as a most generous and free gift of a God who is transcendent Love, bringing humankind back to a life it no longer had any claim to whatsoever.

SALVATION BY WAY OF EXPIATION

Another term used to describe the meaning and power of the cross is "expiation." The notion of expiation is derived from the Hebrew *kippur* (atonement). Its basic meaning is "to make pleasing to God." In the context of Israel's religious heritage, this action was primarily God's own work. It consisted in God's cleansing God's people from sin and imparting righteousness to them.[35] We should note especially that the word expiate was not meant to convey the notion of appeasing an angry God.

The intent of Paul (Rom. 3:25) and of the author of Hebrews (2:17) coheres with this meaning. As they write of God's expiating sin through Christ's crucifixion, they wish to focus upon Jesus' and their being (made) pleasing to God. In doing so, they wish to underscore another significant aspect of their experience of salvation. Just as Christ, enduring the cross in trusting love of *Abba*, was wonderfully pleasing to God, so also, his ultimate Self-gift has become the vehicle by which God has made Christ's disciples pleasing to God. By it, God has, in effect, imparted to us a share in Christ's (and God's) holiness; God has removed, "cleansed us from," our sin. The Christian believers, knowing the gift of salvation, humbly (for they experience this standing under the power of God's love as gift) rejoice in the experience of being, with Christ, truly pleasing in God's eyes.[36]

JESUS' DEATH AS SACRIFICE
The image of sacrifice offers a third figure which Christians used to describe Christ's saving death. In some ways it constitutes an overriding image. It makes explicit the ritual context within which the desire for expiation is expressed. It likewise fills out the ritual context in which the image of pouring forth a victim's blood and sprinkling people with it, finds its meaning. How shall we understand this image of sacrifice?

Often both religious and secular society today use this word in the sense of "giving up" something (e.g., time, money, pleasure, status, friends...) for the sake of something else (family, further education, security, health, spiritual growth...). In keeping with this mindset, we frequently focus upon what we give up, the sacrifices we make; and we dwell upon how much we have foregone and/or "how difficult" the sacrifice is. The notion of sacrifice carries with it a sense of deprivation and suffering (at least interiorly), a sense that has a negative, sometimes even masochistic, quality to it. Etymologically, however, the word sacrifice means "to make holy." The focus is not on deprivation, giving up, but on the goal of one's action, what one hopes to achieve, holiness.

This analysis sheds light on the meaning of the ritual sacrifices of Israel, and by that very fact, illuminates the basic meaning of the term as the New Testament churches and writers used it to describe the death of Jesus. Let us note its use in Israel first.

Within Israel, the offering of a ritual sacrifice expressed that people's desire to be sanctified, to acquire a share in God's holiness. The entire ritual action was highly symbolic,[37] unfolding in three stages: First, the priest and people offered a victim. In this action, the victim symbolized the people so that, in the action of offering the victim, the priest and people were figuratively expressing their offering of themselves to God. Secondly, the altar symbolized God. Placing the victim upon the altar, therefore, expressed both Israel's giving of itself (in the figure of the victim) to God and also God's (in the "guise" of the altar's) accepting Israel for God's Self. This latter action included the understanding that, when God accepted and took the victim to God's Self, the victim began to share God's life. Since the victim symbolized Israel, however, this under-standing also was transferred to God's People: They (figuratively) began to share God's Life. Finally, the victim, symbolically "alive in God," would be eaten. In symbolic gesture, the priest and people shared a meal with God, a sign of being in communion with God. And more deeply, they ate food symbolically filled with God's life; they came to share divine life. God was making God's People holy, sharing with them the one life which is God's Self.

With this background, it is easy to see why the early Christians, in general, and the author of the letter to the Hebrews in particular, looked at Jesus' death through the imagery of sacrifice. Jesus offered himself to God, a victim because of the sin of humankind. Through his death, God filled Jesus with holiness and poured forth that holiness in a manner far more effectively than God had accomplished through Israel's sacrifices. Jesus, and those who followed him in similar trust and faithfulness, had been made holy indeed. As part of this figure, the early Church also underscored both the perfect nature of Christ's self-offering (expressed through his death on the cross) and also the fullness of his acceptance by God and entrance into God's life (realized in his resurrection and ascension to God's right hand). Jesus offered the perfect sacrifice; there was no longer need for any other.

It was with great assurance, then, that the first disciples believed that, by offering themselves with Christ, they too would come to share in the holiness imparted to Christ. With that mindset, they celebrated the Eucharist, not only in memory of Jesus, but as the sacrificial meal of the New Law, a sacrificial meal in which they entered into deeper communion with their God, shared life with Christ, and became more fully enlivened with his holiness.

SALVATION BY THE POURING FORTH OF CHRIST'S BLOOD[38]

A final image puts vividly before our minds the full extent of Christ's physical sufferings. "We have redemption by his blood" (Eph. 1:7); "God set (Christ) forth as an expiation...by his blood" (Rom. 3:25); "God was pleased...to reconcile all things for him, making peace by the blood of his cross" (Col. 1:19-20). In each of these passages, the writers deliberately call attention to the manner of Christ's death: his pouring forth of his blood.[39] Without doubt, this emphasis underscores the finality and even the brutality of Jesus' death. But the frequency of the use of this figure should make us suspect that the desire to underscore the reality of Christ's death was not the only reason because of which Christians stressed the fact that redemption had been accomplished through Jesus' "having poured forth his blood."

Once again, the Jewish mindset, and particularly Jewish ritual, offer illuminating background for our understanding of this image. The Semitic mind understood blood to be the "seat of life." Hence, in ritual sacrifice, when God, in effect, was thought to have taken the victim into God's own realm of existence, and therefore to have made it a participant in God's own life, the blood of the victim was thought (symbolically) to have become the bearer of divine life. To be sprinkled with that blood in a ritual effecting expiation, therefore, symbolized one's being given a share in God's life, one's having been made pleasing to God, and one's having been reunited with God. God and God's people were being made "blood brothers and sisters" so to speak. So strong is this symbolism that sprinkling the people with the blood of a sacrificed animal ritually sealed the covenant[40] of the Old Law (Ex. 24:3-5).

The early Christians, rejoicing in the fact that they had become pleasing to God and one with God through Christ's death and resurrection,[41] quickly perceived a parallel between the blood of sacrificed animals and the blood of Christ. So, they employed the image of Christ's pouring forth his blood to underscore their full appreciation of what Jesus had accomplished for them. God had established a new covenant, a new and deeper pledge of mutual fidelity and communion, with them. God had sealed that union, not with the blood of an animal, but with the blood of Christ. So powerful was this figure that it dominated ongoing Christian ritual. Christians celebrated the Eucharist in memory of Jesus, sharing the blood which he had poured out for the forgiveness (expiation) of their sins (Mt. 26:28 and parallels). For Christ, himself filled with God's life, continued to be the Gift by which God united all persons with God's Self. Sharing in Christ's (flesh and) blood, symbolized, nourished, and sealed that union.

Through a series of rich images, then, many of them taken from the ritual patterns within Israel, the early Christian communities powerfully conveyed their sense of God's having definitively and superlatively saved them from inner bondage and widespread hostility through Christ's death on the cross. It should be noted, however, that each of these images, statements of belief, are in themselves just that, no more and no less. They are images or metaphors *expressing faith experience*; they are not explanations, given in critical terms, of reflected understanding of precisely how Jesus' death on the cross brings about human salvation. Each detail therefore is not meant to be taken literally, as if the believer, the author of the letters, or the Gospel writers, were attempting to provide a blueprint of the dynamic interrelationship of Jesus' death, Jesus' resurrection, and Jesus' effective establishment and communication of God's saving love within the world. The experience itself of the outpouring of salvation so powerfully grasped the disciples' imagination that such questions did not arise. As a matter of fact, within the Semitic culture not given to this type of analysis, such questions may never have arisen. It would be Christians of a later age and of a different culture who would press the question of precisely how Jesus' death, an event which seemed to be defeat and failure, actively in God's wisdom and love accomplished and communicated God's salvific presence and power. For that reason, we now turn to the post-New Testament tradition, past and present, offering a brief summary of its responses to this question.

THE SAVING POWER OF JESUS' DEATH:
CHRISTIAN TRADITION

To attempt to offer a synthesis of the reflections of the post-apostolic Church with regard to the saving efficacy of the cross would shackle us with a voluminous task. There are as many ways of understanding this event as there are theologians who have sought to interpret it. Our efforts here, therefore, must be quite modest. We will limit our considerations in two ways: First, we will confine ourselves to efforts to respond to the precise question as stated above. How does the cross influence and bring about life in God for all? How does Jesus' death enter into the dynamic process by which God communicated God's Self to the whole of humankind. Then we will limit ourselves to formulating a brief summary of the major perspectives within medieval tradition,[42] to which we will add, in a slightly fuller form, a consideration of some of the insights of Karl Rahner.

CLASSICAL THEOLOGY: A SUMMARY
In response to the question of how Jesus' passion and death have brought about salvation, certain theories or models run through classical theology. We can distinguish four.[43]

The Reparation Theory[44]
The earliest perspective focuses upon the fact that Jesus' suffering and death on the cross exemplified supreme love and supreme fidelity. That love and fidelity repaired a broken order. Where humankind had been weak, unfaithful, unable to live in sinlessness and love, Jesus succeeded. Because of his success and the example he has forever given us, the course of history has been forever changed. History boasts of a new dynamic within itself, namely, the figure of Jesus, with the power of drawing others to admire, imitate, and live like him.

The notion of Jesus' having presented an example, a perfect example, of human love and fidelity to all people is clearly the core of this perspective. Jesus, in his passion and death, has offered the absolute model of human love and fidelity. The truth, the beauty, the fruitful outcome of his way of living and dying strike responsive chords in the minds and hearts of all. His example has a compelling attractiveness which can draw persons to emulate Jesus and provide them with a new way of understanding and journeying through human life.

What this perspective does not in itself explain, however, is how people are *enabled to accept* Jesus' example and how they are *empowered to undertake* its challenge. The gift and communication of God's Spirit is necessary if the reparation of the broken order and Jesus' example are to have an overriding effect upon humankind. The theory does not tell us how Jesus' death relates to the bestowal of God's Spirit upon those who (wish to) follow him.

The Satisfaction Theory[45]

Another perspective, known as the satisfaction theory, originated with St. Anselm. This model puts fuller emphasis upon the relationship of Jesus' suffering and death to God rather than to history. According to Anselm, Jesus' death, a perfect gift of love, freely given,[46] makes infinite satisfaction for sin; it restores honor to God who had been otherwise irreparably dishonored by sin.[47]

Recent research[48] has revealed that Anselm, in speaking of the restoration of divine honor, did not intend to imply that God was desirous or greedy for God's honor. Rather, Anselm saw that where true honor is given to God, the community of humankind is necessarily helped. For just as respect for any legitimate human authority provides an atmosphere which facilitates peace among people within any given community, so respect for God creates a disposition among people prompting them to live in mutual harmony and peace. Jesus restored God's honor and paved the way for people to live in harmony when they would follow his example. In this latter respect, the theory is very similar to the reparation theory and stands or falls under the same critique.

The Penal Substitution Theory[49]

A third model for understanding the manner in which the cross of Christ is efficacious for salvation focuses on sin and the punishment which sin engendered. Theologians spoke of Jesus' suffering and death as "paying the debt" which human beings had incurred through their sin. They offered diverse opinions with regard to the recipient of that payment: the devil, God, the order of justice. Later theologians developed this perspective, unfolding what is known as the *penal substitution theory*, proposing that *Jesus was punished in our place*. In pressing the model in this direction, they created a picture of an angry God, a God whose primary interest seemed to lie in weighing and monitoring the execution of a penalty for human wrongdoing. Such a portrait of God is quite different from the image of a loving, forgiving God presented in the New Testament. Because of this conflict with the New Testament, the theory creates more darkness than light not only with regard to the manner in which Jesus' death constituted the means by which God communicated salvation to all persons, but also, and more radically, with regard to the manner in which it imaged and understood the very God whom Jesus revealed as genuinely a God of love. The penal substitution theory represents the nadir of the theology of the cross.

The Representation Theory[50]
A fourth theory lays emphasis upon Christ's relationship to humankind as a whole and to the Church in particular. Jesus is the New Adam, the Head of his Body, the Church (Col. 1:18). Irenaeus deepened this perspective, gleaned from Pauline theology, by speaking of Christ's "having summed up" or "recapitulated" human history in his life. Given the fact that Jesus is perfectly human, and given the fact that he was sent by God to save us from sin, Jesus can and does stand before God in solidarity with all people as their representative. What God has given to our representative, God has also given to us.

In order to partake of what our head has gained, however, each individual must personally receive the gift of the Spirit as the source of strength for living a Christlike life. Further, each individual must personally and freely ratify what the Lord has accomplished in walking the paths of discipleship. This theory, however, does not explain how Jesus' death relates to our personal reception of the gift he has received (even in our behalf). Neither does it explain how the cross works to empower us to ratify the way he lived through our own journeys of fidelity and service. Nor does it make clear why Jesus had to die in order to represent us. Thus why Jesus' death was necessary, and it was effective, for salvation still remains at issue.

In the context of the vast, nearly two thousand year old tradition concerning this question, Karl Rahner, the German Jesuit 20th century theologian, has provided still another perspective regarding the manner in which Christ's death has effected universal salvation. Rahner focused on the nature of death in general in order to provide fuller understanding of the meaningfulness and necessity of Christ's death.[51] We will summarize Rahner's thought in three stages: death as a natural event; death as a personal event; and death as a penalty for sin.

Death as a Natural Event[52]
Death flows from human nature itself as the necessary point of culminating human historical life so that the person can move into transhistorical existence. Rahner argues from the composite nature of human being (humans are a composite of matter and spirit), pointing out that it is natural for every composite being to break apart. We witness this in the decomposition of material reality all around us, be it food digested by plant or animal life, leaves fallen from trees fertilizing the soil, or simply iron rusting or fuel burning. We also note the gradual decomposition of the human organism, beginning in sickness, moving through aging, and completed after a period of time in the grave. The pivotal moment within this gradual process is centered in the decomposition of the unity of soul and body (or spirit and embodiment) which we speak of as death. One dies as the body becomes incapable of responding to the organizing and vivifying action of the spirit. The soul (the human spirit) therefore separates itself from the body and the body no longer manifests life.

The nature of human spirit, however, is different from an angelic spirit; it is not pure spirit, but spirit necessarily (intrinsically) related to matter. Since, by its nature, it is related to matter it cannot and does not lose that relationship in the moment of death. Rather, in death, it is freed from the space-time limits of matter and assumes a relationship to the world as a whole. The soul, in Rahner's terms, becomes, not "a-cosmic" but "all-cosmic." Death, therefore, is not entirely negative. As one dies, one's soul, one's personal center, becomes present to the entire cosmos, able to act upon that entire world. Death marks, not the end of life, but a transition to a more inclusive life, a more expansive life, even in relationship to the universe.

This perspective enlightens the Christian faith-experience of Jesus. In dying, Jesus, in his humanity, became free of the limits of space and time; he became present to the world as a whole, present to all persons at all times.[53] Thus Christians can experience Jesus as saving Lord, present in faith-filled prayer, in the proclamation of the Word, in the celebration of the Eucharist, in the active life of the Church which as a visible, tangible people has become his body. Death has enabled Jesus, in his humanity, to become all-cosmic. Only by dying, by becoming free of the material limits of space and time, could Jesus become universally present to all with saving love.

Death as a Personal Event[54]
In many ways death strikes at the heart of the person, the heart of consciousness and freedom. Death is fraught with darkness; it is a point of "no return"; it comes as an imposition upon one's freedom and autonomy. We must surrender to death, for death will not surrender to us.

Yet death is also the moment of expressing in fullness, the moment of "summing-up," one's freedom. It is the moment in which we finally bring together the entire movement of our whole life, in effect making an everlasting statement of who we really are and have come to be. How we die expresses and sums up how we have lived.

A brief reflection will make this clear. In every act of freedom we choose one value (study, marriage, a particular job, forgiveness, generosity) and reject another (play, single life, a previously possible partner for marriage, a different job, the harboring of an injury, personal convenience). As we move on in life, we reinforce these choices and reaffirm them, often at personal cost. We gradually let go of ("die to") possibilities that do not fit in with these choices. The movement is costly, for the possibilities we die to will never return. In the process, however, our consciousness and freedom become more centered; the values which govern our choices become more unified, more mutually supportive. Death is the moment in which one unifies and sums up freedom once and for all; it is the moment of absolute trust and love, or the moment of absolute despair and self-enclosure.

In dying, Jesus summed up his freedom, his life.[55] Indeed he lived in the process of expressing his freedom in a series of progressively more profound acts of faithful trust in *Abba* and of selfless and forgiving love of all persons. In approaching death and in dying, he expressed that fidelity, trust, love, and forgiveness definitively. Because he loves and trusts unto death, the point of no return, his love and trust can never be retracted. He has affirmed his choices, his selflessness in love, his unshakable trust in *Abba*, forever. Hence, he lives eternally saying to his followers: "This, my body, is given up for you," and to his God: "Father, into your hands I entrust my spirit."

For Jesus, then, as for all persons, death constituted the moment in which he summed up his freedom for all eternity. Only in dying could Jesus attain finality and fullness as the person who is truly the embodiment of faithful trust and merciful love for all ages. Death, though it is fraught with darkness, is also the event by which Jesus, in his humanity, becomes fully himself, faithful Son of God, the embodiment of God's compassionate love for us, the most acceptable gift pleasing to *Abba*, forever.

Death as Penalty for Sin[56]

If death is natural, in what sense does it flow from the "sin of Adam" as Scripture (Gn. 3:3, 22-24) and Tradition affirm? One way of responding to this question is as follows: because of sin, faith and trust are weak; decisions for embracing love are very tenuous. We cannot be sure that we will persevere in faithfulness or that our lives of repentance will be received by God. Death can be an event of damnation or an event of salvation; at best, the outcome of death is dark and ambiguous.

This darkness of death must be understood as the *consequence of sin*. Had Adam not sinned, had he remained alive in sharing God's life, he and his posterity would have moved smoothly and confidently through the consummation of life in this world into a personally fulfilled life in communion with God and with the universe as a whole. Having lost this relationship with God, having lost communion with the Source of all life, Adam and his posterity became powerless to negotiate the transition of death successfully. As a consequence of sin, death has taken on the character of darkness; it confronts human beings with the threat of marking the end of everything one desires and longs for.

The darkness which enshrouds death, however, though it be the consequence of sin, is not the full realization, nor the full meaning, of death as *penalty for sin*. The penalty, the punishment, for sin consists in the experience of dying without the strengthening power of the Spirit of God, and in the achievement of the final consummation of one's personal life devoid of communion with God, the only Source of truly life-giving love. The true penalty which we may incur because of sin is not death itself but rather the kind of death which we die. The penalty of sin lies in ending this life eternally dead to God and to all that can be possessed only through radical surrender to God. And so, darkness is the consequence of sin; final isolation from the Spirit of life is the ultimate penalty for sin.

Jesus, human as we are in all things but sin, suffered death in itself (which was not sin) and endured the darkness which surrounds death, the consequence of his humanly being of Adam's race.[57] But because of the way in which Jesus embraced death and because of the way God accepted Jesus' death, the death of Jesus has transformed the human reality of death for all time. The dark event which could be the moment of final loss and damnation has become the event of final victory and redemption. In completing his human journey on earth, by enduring death's all-enveloping darkness in an act of confident surrender to *Abba*, Jesus has enabled the act of dying and the darkness which surrounds it to become the moment of being filled with the fullness of light and life. The event which seems to close in upon freedom and to annihilate personal life and love becomes for him, and for all who will follow him, the event in which freedom opens up into an eternity of communion with all in everlasting life and love.[58] What could have been the ultimate penalty for sin and damnation has become the door for ultimate life and redemption. Jesus, always alive in God, transformed death itself by enduring it in full reverence, obedience, and trust in God.

In sum, in the perspective of Karl Rahner, Jesus' death stands as the final and deepest act of his human freedom, fidelity, and love. In his death, Jesus chooses and assumes the personal disposition of unconditional faithfulness and merciful love for all eternity. Jesus' death stands as the necessary and only way through which he could enter the transhistorical world and assume a transhistorical relationship with the world as a whole. Death prepares him, makes him able to be, the savior of the world.

To accomplish this mission, however, Jesus must, in his humanity, be accepted by *Abba*, receiving in fullness the life which is truly God's life; AND he must become one with *Abba* in pouring forth God's Spirit upon all. Further, in order for each follower to experience salvation, it must become clear to each disciple, that Jesus is fully alive in God and that, through and with him, God's Spirit of love has been given to each. As pivotal as Jesus' death is, it needs completion in his resurrection and exaltation at God's right hand and in their Self-communication in the Spirit. As Daniel Helminiak has pointed out,[59] redemption requires, not one, but three elements: Jesus' absolute fidelity and love (Jesus' death); God's full, life-giving acceptance of God's Son (Jesus' resurrection and ascension); and God's pouring forth of God's presence to us in the empowering gift of the Spirit (Pentecost). Before reflecting upon these further dimensions of the one saving mystery, however, we must pause to gather together some implications of the foregoing for the doing of Christology.

The Cross of Jesus and Doing Christology

As with all the moments of God's appearance and Self-communication in and through Jesus, so God's presence in Jesus' passion and death on the cross draws the believer both to encounter God and also to seek fuller understanding of the God whom that believer encounters. Given the fact, however, that the cross represents the culmination of the historical Jesus' redemptive mission, it has the capacity (together with Jesus' resurrection, ascension and pouring forth of the Spirit) to reveal God and God's true nature, to express Jesus' full identity, and to define the way of discipleship, as no other manifestation of God can. Hence, the cross of Jesus and the disciple's experience of it are foundational for understanding God and Jesus; they are foundational for the doing of Christology. Their centrality to this task and the way they impact our understanding of God and Jesus, our interpretation of Christian experience, and our appreciation of the way of discipleship can be illustrated as follows.

First, the mystery of Jesus' passion and death reveals to us something of the true nature of God. It reveals to us, albeit in light of the experience of the resurrection, that there is no depth of darkness, no moment of human abandonment, no experience of human brokenness that God cannot and will not embrace. No one stands so destitute, so rejected, so despised by humankind as Jesus on the cross. And no one is so embraced, so deeply loved, so filled with divine life as Jesus on the cross. It is true that our perception and experience of this powerful embrace of divine love and life rest also, necessarily, upon the first disciples' experience of the risen Lord; but our perception of the cross enables us to appreciate how far and how deep that love extends. It enables us to grasp how unconquerable that love is. In witnessing and/or remembering the cross, each believer's limited vision of Godly love is broken open. He or she stands in the presence of God's boundless longing and compassion for human beings. The cross reveals the true nature and power of the God of Jesus: God IS unconditional and inclusive outreaching love.

Second, Jesus' entry into his passion and death holds before us the fundamental pattern of how one comes genuinely to experience the God of Jesus. It is in surrendering ourselves to God that God reveals the fullness of who God is and what God wishes to be for us. It is in abandoning ourselves to God and God's wisdom, that God's light, wisdom, and love break into our lives. It is in accepting the passing nature of every dimension of this life that a new and richer life, God's life within us, comes to be. It is in self-emptying love that lasting life is born. It is in dying with and like Christ, that one comes to know the undying presence and life of the saving God.

Hence, every moment of life, in which we move forward in self-emptying love for others and reliance upon God in our weakness, becomes a moment in which we gradually but surely share in the full mystery of Christ's self-gift to God and to humankind in self-surrendering love. Such moments have the potential of revealing the blossoming of Christ's fidelity in us and the sustaining power of God's saving presence for us. They have the power of leading us to know and experience the heart of Jesus' life. They have the capacity to unite us more fully with Jesus' life-giving death and so to offer us a glimpse of his resurrection to fuller life. And so, understood as opportunities to participate in Christ's own passion and death, these moments provide us with personal foundational experiences for doing genuine Christology. They enable us to personalize the Christian Tradition which we have received and offer us occasions for further explicating our faith.

Third, the experience of God and of Christ, perceived in the light of the cross, opens the door for the Christian's search for God in the midst of the brokenness of the world, the shabbiness of life, the dereliction of the wayward, the powerless of the poor. The experience of God's embrace of Jesus, broken on the cross, tells us that God wills to embrace and to give life to all persons in all such situations. That experience invites us to look for Christ in the face of the poor (cf. Mt. 25:31-40), never to discard the downtrodden, and never to lose hope for what only God can save. It tells us that what is impossible for us is not impossible for God, even though God's saving love may work its victory only in "the last hour."

The cross of Jesus and the doing of Christology in its light, therefore, inspire an active love for the poor no matter how broken the poor are. The cross of Jesus and God's ready embrace of God's Christ, the paradigm of all who suffer human rejection, challenge us to a moral life which excludes no one from the ambit of our own compassion and love. God's response to Jesus on the cross defines the fundamental principle of a truly Christian ethic. The way Christians must live in order to share and to mediate fully the life and the holiness of God even now is to walk in God extending the embrace of God's accepting and empowering love to all, especially the most rejected.

But each of these insights into the process of doing Christology, each of these insights which are in fact the fruit of doing Christology, while focused on the passion and death of Jesus, presume the resurrection of Jesus. For each observation, in fact, interprets Christ's passion and death in light of the fact that in the resurrection we know and perceive that Jesus has come to be fully alive revealing the fullness of God and communicating God's life, power and saving love which establishes God's reign for us. As Paul has said: "If Christ be not risen, your faith is in vain" (I Cor. 15:17).

But what has enabled us to know the risen Lord, alive for us now? What was the experience of the privileged disciples which so firmly grounds this belief within the Church? How did they and how shall we understand what happened to Jesus in the resurrection? What does the resurrection reveal of God, God's reign and God's action in history? The meaning of the cross of Jesus stands or falls in relationship to the experience and meaning of Christ's resurrection. This series of reflections, which we will attempt to unfold in the next chapter, then, may be the most significant of all. But before moving to these considerations, we invite the reader to reflect upon and to gather together his or her experiences of the cross of Jesus and of the material presented in the present chapter by working through the following questions.

Questions for Reflection

1. How has the unfolding of Jesus' anticipation of his passion, death, and resurrection affected your previous understanding and/or images of Jesus in his movement to, his willing acceptance of, and his experience of his passion and death? How would you explain Jesus' motives for accepting the cross and the "freedom" of his decision in regard to his passion and death in light of what you have learned?

2. How had you understood the necessity of the cross and the manner in which it has influenced human salvation prior to your reading of this chapter? With what "theory" had you identified? How do you understand the necessity and saving efficacy of Christ's passion and death now?

3. In what ways can you find in your experience of trust in God and of self-emptying love, glimpses of Christ's experience of the cross and of the in-breaking of the power and life-giving love of Abba? In what experiences of persons you know and/or in what experiences of your community have you seen the dynamic of Christ's self-emptying love providing occasion for the in breaking of God with fuller life?

4. How does the image of God's love and acceptance of Jesus, broken on the cross, as well as the life and love of Jesus directed toward the marginalized of the world, concretely affect your understanding of the way Christians need to frame their life and freedom before God in Christ today?

CHAPTER 8

Experiencing Christ:
Risen in Glory

With his death, Jesus brought his life on earth to its definitive conclusion. He expressed, without any conditions or reservations, his absolute fidelity to *Abba* and his abiding love for all persons. Thus, he summed up his freedom and stands forever as the embodiment of fidelity, God's faithful Son and Servant par excellence for all eternity. He, likewise, became free of the limits of space and time, capable – from within the depth and center of the universe – of unifying the world and of communicating his deepest self to the world. Jesus died as he lived, and lives now and forever as he died.

But what enables us to affirm that Jesus is fully alive? What enables us to believe with assurance that the reign of God is, in fact, definitively established? What has prompted Christians to proclaim with absolute conviction that God, in and through Jesus, is present and active, pouring out God's powerful, healing love, not only for Jesus, not only for the disciples of Jesus' own era, but assuredly for people of all ages, even for us? Each of these questions forces us to explore the significance and the impact of Jesus' resurrection, not only for Jesus and for his everlasting life of glory and blessedness with *Abba*, but also for all Christians, indeed for all persons, seeking salvation in communion with God and God's transcendent life. For each question calls us to seek a fuller understanding of the nature of Jesus' risen life both in itself and in its relationship to the salvation of all persons.

Jesus' resurrection, his emergence as a human being into the fullness of the life of the age to come, is the reverse side of his death. In Johannine terms, Jesus is glorified in his death, the hour of the cross being the hour of his glorification. In Lucan terms, Jesus' resurrection is the fulfillment of the cross, the event which Jesus had to suffer so as to enter into his glory. Thus, death and resurrection speak of two sides of the same event: a transition within a human being's life with God from its historical and progressively developing phase to its final form, its full maturity, in the form of a person surrendered to God and overflowing with the presence and life of God forever.

In this chapter we will ask two basic questions. First, we will inquire: how did the early Church, expressing its belief largely through Paul and the four evangelists, experience and then come to understand the resurrection of Jesus? The question itself is clearly twofold, inviting us both to inquire into what the first disciples actually experienced and also to ask what the experience meant to them. Secondly, following upon this inquiry, we will ask: how shall we understand Jesus' resurrection, the Apostles' experiences of the risen Christ, and the saving significance of this event today? In addressing these questions from a contemporary perspective, we will also be advancing our efforts to engage the reader, him or herself, in the task of doing Christology, a Christology centered upon and grounded in the Christian experience of the crucified and risen Lord.

Experience and Initial Understanding of the Resurrection in the New Testament Churches[1]

As we begin to review the New Testament accounts which serve to stimulate faith in Jesus' resurrection, we quickly notice that no letter of Paul or any other author, no account of any evangelist, nor any passage in the Acts of the Apostles, describes Jesus in the act of emerging from the tomb. Rather, the New Testament offers us stories of the risen Lord's *appearances* to his disciples *after* he was raised from the dead; narratives of the disciples' *visits to the tomb*, only to find it empty; and accounts of the apostles' *testimony to the fact* that God raised Jesus to new life. All of these accounts originate in the disciples' experiences of the risen Jesus' appearances to one or to many, transformed in "glory." No account, however, describes the resurrection itself.

Any effort therefore to picture Jesus' resurrection must be highly subjective. Visualizing Jesus as "stretching his arms as he awakens from death," portraying the Lord as "getting up and moving aside the stone which blocked the entrance to the tomb," describing Christ as "walking about and searching out the disciples so as to show himself alive" are efforts of pure imagination. As such, they are not reported, nor are they grounded, in the New Testament. As a matter of fact, such descriptions of the resurrection, or of the risen Lord himself, mislead us in our efforts to understand the experience and the belief of the early church. They do so because they tend to cast the nature of the risen Lord and his risen life in images which picture Jesus as *resuming life in this world* rather than as having been *transformed and as having taken up a life beyond this world.* What the New Testament Church proclaims in the Gospels, Acts of the Apostles, and letters of various authors, is its profound experience of the already risen Lord. For Jesus to have arrived at that state, however, required that he be transformed, be "raised up." Resurrection simply refers to the first moment of Jesus' attainment of this new, transformed, life; it refers to the action by which *Abba* glorified this faithful Servant. It designates the divine action upon Jesus, and the experience of Jesus' himself, which made possible his actual but subsequent appearances to his disciples in his glory.

What is this "new life" like? What precisely did the disciples see, hear, and experience in the risen Lord? How did they relate the self-revelation of the risen Lord to God's establishing God's kingdom and to their own reception of the gift of salvation? Such are the questions which will frame our inquiry through the remainder of this section.

THE RESURRECTION:
GOD'S FINAL WORD AND DEED IN HUMAN HISTORY
The earliest statements of the Church's belief in the resurrection of Jesus are found, not in the Gospels, but in the letters of Paul and the Acts of the Apostles. These passages are very direct and quite

simple. They do not give us a description of the risen Christ or of his appearances. Rather, they offer us a record of the early Church's bold testimony to the fact that Jesus was raised by God and focus upon that Church's understanding of the import of this event for all who would become believers. In a word, the earliest written records witnessing to Christ's resurrection are not stories (narratives) but proclamations.

The most primitive record of these proclamations of Christ's resurrection occurs in Paul's first letter to the people at Thessalonica: "You turned to God from idols to serve the living and true God and to await his Son from heaven, whom he (God) raised from the dead...." (1:10).[2] The author repeats the same proclamation, with some fuller interpretation in his letter to Christians in Rome: "Justice will also be credited to us who believe in the one who raised Jesus our Lord from the dead, (Jesus) who was handed over for our transgressions and was raised for our justification" (4:24f).[3] The texts underscore the central element of Christian belief. God responded to Christ's fidelity and to humankind's obstinacy with an unprecedented manifestation of life-giving power and love; God raised Christ from the dead. The resurrection is God's act, God's response to Christ's love.

Still recounting the Church's beliefs in the form of records of early proclamation and dogmatic statements, Luke, in the Acts of the Apostles, preserves the substance of Peter's proclamation of the resurrection on the day of Pentecost. In this account, too, we find the belief of Peter, representing what became the established creed of the Church, expressed in a simple formula:

> God raised this Jesus; of this we are his witnesses....
> Exalted at the right hand of God, he (Jesus) received
> the promise of the Holy Spirit from his Father and
> poured it forth, as you see and hear .... Therefore, let
> the whole house of Israel know for certain that God
> has made him both Lord and Messiah, this Jesus
> whom you crucified (2:32f, 36).

This text, confirmed by many others, expresses a most fundamental conviction, a primary element in the Apostles' experience: Jesus' resurrection was at root *an action of God*, not an action of Jesus himself; God raised his beloved and faithful servant. Jesus' resurrection, therefore, stands as a sign of God's abiding love for and God's enduring presence to Jesus, a presence and love which has filled Jesus, even in his humanity, with the transcendent life and love of *Abba*.[4] The witnesses, in encountering the risen Lord and in experiencing the outpouring of the Spirit which he received from the Father, experienced a manifestation of the transcendent One which exceeded all prior moments of God's revealing God's Self. They experienced the full Self-communication of God in God's life and love to the risen Christ. In giving God's profound answer to Jesus' life and his death on the cross, the resurrection shows forth that God is truly transcendent, merciful, and life-giving love beyond measure, beyond sin and death themselves. Hence the resurrection is an *act of divine power*; it is God's own Self-revelation, an action by which God expresses God's truest and deepest Self.[5]

Further, the text unfolds the *salvific meaning* of God's action: God has made Jesus "Lord and Messiah." We will consider both titles briefly.

"Lord" is the name given to Yahweh, the God who is "always present to save." To give that name to Jesus is to say that Jesus, in his humanness, is constituted one with Yahweh, the transhistorical God whom Israel had come to know as the dependable source of saving love. In the words of the christological hymn cited by Paul in his letter to the Christians at Philippi, Jesus,

> humbled himself, becoming obedient unto death, even death on a cross. Therefore, God exalted him and bestowed upon him the name that is above every name, that at the name of Jesus, every knee should bend, of those in heaven and on earth and under the earth, and every tongue confess "Jesus Christ is Lord" (2:7-11; see also Heb. 5:7-10).

The witnesses, encountering the risen Christ, immediately recognize that he bears forever the fullness of God's saving power and love:

"Jesus is Lord!"

Similarly, God has made (and confirmed) Jesus as Messiah. The title Messiah means "Anointed One." In Israel's history, as we have seen in Chapter 5, it was the king who was constituted God's anointed, anointed to be God's representative in preserving and fostering the life of God's people. The Apostles, in the post-resurrection Church, named Jesus Messiah. They perceived that Jesus, in his resurrection, had brought about God's reign definitively, even to the extent of embodying that reign fully in his own person. Hence, in proclaiming Jesus' resurrection, they wished to affirm that *Abba* had made Jesus Messiah in an absolute and superlative sense: Jesus had ushered in the reign of God forever.[6]

A third aspect of the Apostles' experience of and explicit belief about the glorified Christ as reflected in these texts touches upon the identity of the risen Lord: The risen Christ is truly the crucified One:

> This man...you killed, using lawless men to crucify him. But God raised him up, releasing him from the throes of death.... God has made both Lord and Messiah, this Jesus whom you crucified (Acts. 2:23f, 36).

The risen One and the crucified One are one and the same person. In effect, the text is making clear that it is not an angel who has appeared to these witnesses; rather, it is a human being recognized as the historical Jesus, the one who had been nailed to the cross for his fidelity to God, who has appeared before them. Their ecstatic joy stems, not from the message of an angel, but from the vision of Jesus whom they knew well, Jesus who had died and was buried, Jesus alive and transformed. The text underscores the fact that the Apostles wished to affirm the continuity of the transhistorical glorified Jesus with the historical Jesus who walked, talked, lived, and died in their midst. It is the one who had walked with them in their own history who truly lives on.

Finally, the text, also underscores the Apostles' conviction concerning God's judgement. God's verdict on Jesus and on Jesus' life is exactly opposite to the verdict and judgement of the chief priests and elders: "God has made Lord and Messiah, this Jesus whom you crucified." Human judgement regarded Jesus as a blasphemer, as a criminal, as one who had infringed the holy law of God. God's judgement, however, declared that Jesus was the true prophet of God's love, God's most faithful servant, the Just One, the trustworthy Advocate of God's Law. God's verdict and Israel's judgement upon Jesus were total opposites. Israel condemned Jesus' way of life, crucified Christ and sought to disgrace him forever; God affirmed Jesus' way of life, raised him up and presented him to people of all ages as worthy of the highest honor.

The most primitive and most significant affirmations of belief concerning the resurrection in the early church, then, come to us in the form of proclamation and statements of conviction. They do not focus on *descriptions* of the glorified Jesus, but on the *fact* of the resurrection and on its *significance* for us. In this fashion, they present the resurrection primarily in the context of the first disciples' own history and ongoing experience, not only of Jesus, but of God. Hence, they understand this astounding event primarily as a word and action of God, holding up for us their belief that the transcendent God, *Abba*, in raising Jesus from the dead, had not only definitively given God's Self to Jesus but also had poured forth that divine Self upon all persons in and through him. Jesus' resurrection is the indomitable act of God's saving presence and love, erasing Israel's judgement on Jesus. In the resurrection, God has put God's seal on Jesus' way of life, telling all witnesses and all future generations that Jesus' way of life is the way all must live. In Christ's resurrection, God has constituted Jesus "Lord and Messiah," filling him with divine life and thereby with the power to mediate that life to all. In the resurrection, God has shown God's Self to be the God of unending life and insatiable love. In Jesus' resurrection, God constitutes God's reign forever, calling all persons to seek life in God's kingdom with and through Jesus, the Lord.

The Resurrection: The Transformation of
Jesus, Body and Soul, with Divine Life
The resurrection is not only God's ultimate Word, a gesture by which *Abba* has fully revealed the nature and extent of divine

power, indeed the nature of God's truest Self, but it is also God's final gesture of love in behalf of Jesus, an act which truly transforms Christ in every aspect of his humanity. The disciples came better to understand *Abba* only because they saw what *Abba* had done for God's faithful Son. Hence, it is necessary to explore the nature of the risen Christ in himself. As always, it is he in his humanity, who reveals the truth of God and of God's intent. In the last analysis, our knowledge of God rests upon what we experience in and through Jesus.

The focal question of this section concerns the physical, bodily, nature of the risen Lord. We will seek fuller insight into the biblical testimony concerning the bodily resurrection of Jesus. Surrounding this focal question, however, we discover several others. We will need to ask: what enables us to claim that Jesus' resurrection was truly a bodily resurrection? Can we imagine his (or any) risen body? If not, how shall we understand the nature of a risen body? What actually did the witnesses of the risen Christ experience in Jesus? To pursue answers to these questions, we will look at the letters of Paul, and then the testimony of the Gospels, treating the stories of Christ's appearances and the narratives focusing upon the empty tomb separately.

The Testimony of the Pauline Letters[7]
Paul has written of the risen Christ, reflecting upon his personal experience, in several of his letters. When referring to the resurrection and the risen Lord, however, Paul at times focuses more directly upon God's action in Jesus' behalf rather than upon the physical, bodily, character of the risen One. This difference in the focus within the writings of the same author has provided a ground for some scholars to regard Paul as ambiguous and/or to claim that the New Testament does not clearly affirm that Jesus was raised bodily.[8] In the opinion of these scholars, we can be sure only that the New Testament, in proclaiming the resurrection of Jesus, wishes to affirm merely an interior revelation to the Apostles, a spiritual presence of Jesus, providing them who are so gifted, with the conviction and understanding that Jesus lives.

In support of this opinion, these scholars offer many citations.

For example, they recall Paul's letter to the people of Galatia: "The gospel preached by me is not of human origin.... It came through a revelation of Jesus Christ" (1:11f). "God...was pleased to reveal his Son to me" (1:15f). Elsewhere Paul writes that God "exalted Jesus" (Phil. 2:9)[9] or simply that "Jesus lives" (Rom. 14:9; II Cor. 13:4), both being manners of speaking which bypass resurrection terminology.[10]

While respecting the observations of these scholars, other theologians firmly hold that the New Testament in general, and Paul in particular, clearly attest to Jesus' bodily resurrection. They make two observations in support of this position. First, they point out that when Paul, writing in the year 57 to the Christians of Corinth, addressed the question of Jesus' resurrection at length, he unambiguously affirmed Jesus' bodily resurrection. Thus he recalls:

> I handed on to you as of first importance what I also received: that Christ died for our sins in accordance with the Scriptures; that he was buried; that he was raised on the third day in accordance with the Scriptures; that he appeared to Kephas, then to the Twelve. After that, he appeared to more than five hundred brothers at once, most of whom are still living, though some have fallen asleep. After that he appeared to James, then to all the apostles. Last of all, as to one born abnormally, he appeared to me (I Cor. 15:3-8).[11]

Second, this second group of theologians note, as Raymond Brown[12] points out, that there were other ways available to the New Testament authors to express continuation of an individual into the next life, ways of understanding and of expressing an "after-life" other than by affirming and/or using the term "resurrection."[13] Therefore, when writers such as Luke, recounting Peter's speeches (Acts 2:24, 31; 3:15, 26), or Paul, writing numerous letters, deliberately chose "resurrection" terminology to express their convictions, we must conclude that they intended to proclaim not only that Jesus stands victorious over death. Rather, they also intended to affirm Jesus' bodily resurrection and the physical nature of their experience of him. And so, the real and most challenging question which lies before us does not concern whether or not Jesus was raised bodily. Rather it concerns the nature of Jesus' risen body and the nature of the Apostles' experience of the risen Christ.

The question of the nature of the risen body, however, is very tantalizing. It prompts us to try to envision, to imagine, the bodily appearance of the risen Lord. But, at the same time, the question of the nature of the risen body can lead us to skepticism. For, in our experience, material bodies are by nature corruptible; bodies which we experience do not last forever. It would seem to be impossible for a bodily being to live in a bodily way forever.

Paul seeks to move this question by addressing it in two steps (I Cor.15:35-49). First, honoring the question, "What kind of body did Jesus have?" he states that the question is largely unanswerable. His reason for taking this position is most important. Jesus' body, is, in Paul's experience, so utterly different from any body which we have encountered that he (Paul) has nothing to compare it with. There are no terms or words which he can glean from common experience that could describe Jesus' body. Hence, the best Paul can do, from his experience of Jesus, is to tell us, on the one hand, that Jesus' body is incorruptible (negating the corruptibility we experience in our bodies) and on the other hand, that it is spiritual and glorified (stating positively that Jesus' body fully participates in, reflects, and mediates God's spirit and God's glory [divine presence]).[14]

Second, while affirming that the question of the nature of Jesus' risen body is largely unanswerable, Paul seeks to relieve his readers' insecurity and doubt over the resurrection by focusing upon the creative power and wisdom of God. To do this Paul calls attention to his readers' experience of the diversity of bodies within the material world. That experience should incline them to be open to the possibility that there may be still another type[15] of body which is beyond their present experience. Thus, Paul calls attention to the fact that there exist different bodies in our universe, (seeds, plants, fish, stars, sun, moon, etc.), and that God gives to each the body suitable to itself. In making this observation, Paul wishes to lead his audience to affirm as a self- evident principle the truth that God, in creating and sustaining the (evolving) universe, fashions a suitable and appropriate body for each kind of being.[16] In effect, Paul implies that God acts in this way so that each being can operate and express itself adequately within the whole of creation. The body enables each being to be true to itself and to contribute some of its own giftedness to the world. Paul wishes the reader to draw the conclusion that God also wills to give Jesus a body suitable to his glorified way of being. He wishes the reader to recognize that God can and does transform Jesus in the entirety of his humanity. God, in raising Jesus to fuller life, can and does bring Jesus' inner life of love and fidelity to fullness. Concurrently, God transforms Jesus' corporeality that it may continue to be an appropriate expression of Jesus' transformed and risen Self. Hence the force of Paul's fundamental conviction: "God gives to each a body which is suitable for itself"; in glorifying Jesus, God glorifies the body of Christ.

Paul's testimony regarding the bodily resurrection of Jesus, then, is firm, but far from imaginative. Having experienced the risen Lord, he seems, nevertheless, largely at a loss to describe Jesus' risen body. He simply states that the risen body surpasses in its splendor any body which his readers have experienced. Nevertheless, he unambiguously affirms that Jesus' body reflects the fully transformed and divinized life Jesus now lives. Jesus possesses a bodily form appropriate to his personal glorified state with the God who wondrously creates all things. For Paul, it is the same Jesus, the crucified one, who lives, who appeared to those chosen witnesses, and who was present to the Church mediating salvation. His bodily resurrection underscores the continuity of the crucified Jesus with the risen Christ, the reality of his full human transformation in divine life, and the certainty of the fullness of God's saving presence for all who believe in him. In Paul's mind, there is no need for any further description of the risen body.

The Witness of the Appearance Narratives of the Gospels
The record of the Christian community's experience of the risen Christ and its understanding of Jesus' resurrection, however, is not exhausted by the reflections of Paul. The four Gospels offer us similar, even further insight. Precisely what that insight consists in,

however, may not be so easy to determine as the Gospel form of "appearance narrative" may lead us to think.

At first reading, it may seem that the deepened insight of the Gospel stories consists in their providing us with a clear description of Jesus' bodilyness, a description which Paul thought impossible to offer. Thus, Luke describes Jesus walking and conversing with two despondent disciples (24:13-27), while both Luke and John, in different ways, describe the risen Lord revealing himself to his disciples in the context of a meal (Lk.24:29-31, 41-43; Jn.21:10-14). Again, in slightly different presentations, the same two evangelists recount incidents during which Jesus called attention to his hands and feet, pointing out the place of the nails, the evidence of his crucifixion (Lk. 24:39f; Jn. 20:20,25-27). And all four Gospels record the risen Christ's giving explicit instructions to his disciples prior to or during his final appearance.[17] A first reading could easily lead us to believe that the Gospels offer us a clearer description of the "bodily-being" of the risen Lord than Paul does. Further, it would seem that these narratives, beyond the Pauline writings, provide us with exact expressions of Jesus' mandates to the disciples. Indeed, the story form of Gospel teaching offers much food for the imagination.

The same story form, however, while being a medium by which the evangelists effectively engage their respective audiences, can also be a means which leads the reader to misconstrue reality. The story form can mislead the readers who, in their desire to picture resurrection-reality, may fail to notice the subtle ways in which the authors indicate that the appearances of the risen Lord defy the powers of imagination. For example, a careful reading of the Gospel narratives shows that each evangelist deliberately portrays the risen Christ as confusingly different and unrecognized. At first glance, Mary Magdalene thinks Jesus is the gardener; she does not recognize him (Jn. 20:15). Peter and several other disciples, having gone fishing, spot Jesus on the shore, but do not realize who he is (Jn. 21:4). The disciples, journeying to Emmaus, converse with Jesus along the way without knowing who he is, coming to recognize him only in "the breaking of the bread" (Lk. 24:16, 30f). On another occasion, the disciples see Jesus but think that they are seeing a ghost (Lk. 24:37). Each story, in its own way, confirms what Mark, the earliest of the Gospel writers, expressly stated in a more generic, yet more exact, way: Jesus appeared *"in another form"* to two disciples "walking along the way to the country" (Mk. 16:12). However manifest and tangible Jesus bodily form is, these writers clearly attest to the fact that it is quite different; so much so that Jesus is not immediately recognizable.

A further, somewhat mystifying, aspect of Jesus' bodily appearance consists in his capacity simply *to come and to go at will*. He appears in the upper room "though the doors were locked" (Jn. 20:19). In breaking the bread, he simply vanishes from the disciples' sight at the moment in which they recognize him (Lk. 24:30f). He appears apparently from nowhere while the Eleven were at table, only to rebuke them for their unbelief and hardness of heart (Mk. 16:14). Clearly, each of the evangelists attempts to affirm that Jesus' bodilyness had substantive qualities very different from the bodies which we possess. These qualities made Jesus unrecognizable in the first moments of his appearances and allowed him the freedom to move easily through, in, and out of space and time without restriction.

Nevertheless, each evangelist affirms that the disciples do come to recognize the risen Lord in these appearances but only *as Jesus addresses them* in some manner. The fourth evangelist presents a bewildered Mary Magdalene coming to recognize Jesus precisely as he calls her by name (Jn. 20:15-18). He describes the apostle Thomas moving from doubt to faith as Jesus speaks to him, inviting Thomas to recognize him as the crucified One by observing the place of the nails and the wound in his side (Jn. 20:24-28). And that same evangelist notes that Peter and the disciples come to identify Jesus only after the Lord tells them to lower the nets once again in order to meet success after a frustrating night of fishing (Jn. 21:4-7).

Luke, too, underscores the significance of Jesus' personal address to the disciples as the prelude to their recognizing him. In recounting the story of two disciples journeying to Emmaus, Luke emphasizes the fact that they came to recognize Jesus only as the Lord personally led them through the Scriptures and "broke bread" with them (24:13-35). And each of the Gospels unites the disciples' recognition of the risen Lord to his "giving them a commission," again a very personal word touching upon their responsibilities of continuing his ministry.[18] The Gospel stories illustrate that the disciples' abilities to identify the risen Lord depends not only upon Jesus' *appearance* before them, but also upon *his speaking a personal word* to them.[19]

The Gospel narratives, furthermore, carefully underscore the final effect of the risen Christ's appearing and word: Jesus' Self-manifestation leads the disciples to a richer and deeper faith in his personal identity. The disciples express this deeper faith in Jesus by giving Jesus, still recognized as the crucified One, a new name. Thus, singly and together, they enthusiastically rejoice: "I (we) have seen the Lord" (Jn. 20:18, 25; see 21:7), while Thomas even more explicitly confesses: "My Lord and my God" (Jn. 20:28). Like Paul, in writing to Philippi, the evangelists seek to underscore the fact that the disciples, as they see and hear the risen Christ give Jesus the "name that is above every other name" (Phil. 2:9): Jesus is One with Yahweh; he is filled with divine life; "Jesus is Lord."

The Gospels, then, do not actually describe Jesus' bodilyness any more thoroughly or concretely than Paul does.[20] What the Gospel narratives do elucidate for us, however, is 1) that however one might describe Jesus' bodily appearance, it was such that, on the one hand, he was able to be present to and communicate with his disciples, while, on the other hand, he was able to enjoy a freedom from space/time limits; 2) that the recognition of the risen Lord arose, not just from Jesus' appearances, but from his personal address, as he verbally engaged the disciples; and 3) that the recognition of Jesus immediately evoked from the disciples a response of deepened faith in the person, life, and mission of Jesus. Seeing and hearing the risen Jesus led the disciples to experience and affirm him as Lord and God.

The Empty Tomb Narratives
Before concluding our reflections upon the Gospel witness to the risen Jesus, we must pause briefly at the so called "Empty Tomb" narratives. These narratives are, in themselves, quite complex.

They are compositions which, in a manner similar to the miracle stories, reflect both historical reality and post-resurrection-appearance insight. In this light, as we shall see below, these narratives recount not only the surprise and confusion (historical truth) on the part of the women who first discover the tomb to be empty,[21] but also firmness of faith and clarity of understanding (post-appearance insight) of the angels who proclaim that Jesus is risen.[22]

In analyzing these stories, historical-critical exegetes bring out the fact that the emptiness of the tomb, in itself, would be inadequate to lead one to faith in Jesus' resurrection, for the empty tomb, in itself, is ambiguous. While calling forth the question of what happened to Jesus' body, the vacant grave gives little answer to that question. Someone could have stolen the body and hidden it elsewhere.[23] Hence, contemporary scholars point out that some factor in addition to the empty tomb would have been necessary to lead the witnesses to faith in the risen Christ. They point out that only the appearances of the risen Lord to the disciples could reveal and confirm in a convincing manner the truth of Jesus' resurrection and, therefore, the reason why the tomb was empty. Only after the disciples had experienced the appearance of the risen Christ did the reason why the tomb was found empty become absolutely clear to them. God had raised God's faithful servant, glorifying him with fuller life. God had transformed Jesus' earthly body itself, enabling it to participate in this fuller life. It is Jesus' appearances themselves which explain the emptiness of his grave.

Further, recognizing the centrality of Jesus' appearances in the process both of the disciples' coming to believe in Jesus' resurrection and also of their coming to understand the reason why his grave was found empty, some historical-critical exegetes regard *the inclusion of angels*[24] and their *clear and firm proclamation of Jesus' having been raised*, to be later additions to the empty tomb narratives. These exegetes judge that the early Church, after witnessing the appearances of the risen Christ, wished to tell the story of the discovery of the empty tomb as a proclamation of Easter faith. In this interpretation, the angels would be seen primarily as "messengers," "the revealing presence," of God.[25] The angels would have been included so as to clarify the meaning of the empty tomb, thereby raising these narratives to the level of resurrection stories.[26] In accord with this interpretation, we would see this revelation of God, portrayed as mediated by angels, as representative of a more vague and tentative historical experience of divine inspiration: The "clear and firm proclamation of the angels" may actually reflect the disciples' experiencing a "glimmer of light and hope," an initial suggestion of Jesus' resurrection, in the midst of their confusion and wonderment at the tomb. In this sense, the "clear and firm words of the angels" could reflect a less clear but genuine beginning of the process by which God led the disciples to fully formed Easter faith. After these same disciples came to see the risen Lord, they realized that what they had experienced merely as the stirrings of a faint hope was truly God's action gradually leading them to know that Jesus had actually been raised and that they would see him as he had told them (Mk. 16:6-8). The introduction of the clear voice of the angels would simply strengthen the reader's recognition of this gradual in-breaking of faith beginning with the discovery of the empty tomb.

While the empty tomb narratives depend on Christ's post-resurrection appearances for their clarity, they also serve to enhance at least one dimension of post-resurrection faith. In recalling the emptiness of the tomb, these stories accentuate the bodily reality of the risen Christ together with his personal identity with the crucified Jesus. Surely if Jesus' dead body had been found, the disciples would have remained in a quandary with regard to the identity of the person appearing to them, for one's body is the necessary means by which the human person manifests and reveals him or herself. The continuity of Jesus' body, therefore, underscores the continuity of his person. The empty tomb enables the witnesses to grasp that the Christ who had been raised is truly the Jesus who died and was buried. It is Jesus of Nazareth, Jesus born of Mary, and no other, who enjoys life forever. For Jesus, who remains wholly human, life has not ended; it has dramatically and wondrously changed.

The Resurrection: Transformation of Jesus: Conclusion
The letters of Paul and the Gospel post-resurrection narratives, then, affirm the Church's profound faith in the glorification and transcendent transformation of Jesus' fully human life, a transformation

which, as Jesus manifests himself, engages the disciples themselves in personally transforming ways. The Pauline letters and the Gospel narratives repeatedly affirm and teach first, that in experiencing the risen Christ, the Apostles came to perceive in him the presence of the transcendent, everlasting, saving God. Second they affirm that the Apostles' encounter with the risen Lord was a matter, not only of seeing, but of hearing; the presence of the risen Christ was such that he could only be recognized through the hearing of a personal word, a word which reached into their minds and hearts, a word which called forth faith and, at the same time, deepened that faith. Therefore, third, the risen Lord himself, in his fully human presence, tangible yet elusive, shares bodily the very same transformation which he knows personally. He is alive in God and present to the world *as God is present*. He is unrestricted by space and time, incorruptible, able to come and to go, to energize, to heal, and to love *as God is capable of doing*. That is to say quite directly and simply: Jesus is God in the flesh; Jesus loves powerfully as God loves. In his risen presence, rescued from death, alive in everlasting responsiveness and fidelity to *Abba*, Jesus manifests how fully salvific the life, love, and power of *Abba* are for human life and human history. All this the disciples affirm when, in seeing and hearing Jesus, they cry out: "It is the Lord!". All this the New Testament affirms as its records the Christian Easter proclamation: "Jesus is Lord!"

THE RESURRECTION AND THE GIFT OF SALVATION:
AN OUTPOURING OF GOD'S SPIRIT FOR ALL AGES
The appearances of the risen Lord brought great joy to the disciples who encountered him. The one whom they loved did not remain subject to death, but found a renewal in both life and love far beyond what he had enjoyed during his historical journey. The vision of the transformed Jesus, the evidence of the presence of God "shining on the face of Jesus" (II Cor. 4:6), caused the disciples to appreciate more fully than ever before what God's life-giving power could accomplish for humankind and how deeply God willed to be wedded with human beings and human history.

This joy in experiencing the risen Jesus, however, did not arise solely out of love and appreciation for him and his glory. It also arose out of the disciples' immediate experience of their own renewal, their own being lifted up with Jesus, their own finding a deeper energy of God's life flowing in them and through them. In a word, in the revelation and experience of the risen Lord, the disciples themselves were transformed. They experienced God bestowing upon them personally the gift of salvation.

Paul affirmed this dimension of the experience of the risen Lord quite directly in writing to the Christians of Rome: Jesus "was handed over to death for our sins and was raised up for our justification" (Rom. 4:25). Paul's assertion reflects his joyful recognition of the fact that his experience of the risen Lord radically changed his life. He experienced God's saving love, not by way of his strict observance of the Law, but because of his ongoing faith in and his continued fidelity to the way of Jesus (Phil.3:7-11).

Each of the synoptic Gospels also reports a process of the transformation of the disciples as flowing from the risen Christ's Self-revelation to them. In experiencing the risen Lord, the Marcan disciples understood that they must "go to the whole world and proclaim the Good News to every creature" (Mk. 16:15). So certain and appealing was his presence that they unhesitatingly "preached everywhere while the Lord worked with them and confirmed the word through accompanying signs" (16:20). Likewise, the Matthean community understood that the Lord had full authority, and that they were to make disciples of all nations, teaching all that Jesus had commanded. In doing so, they knew the strength and effectiveness of Christ with them at every moment (Mt. 28:18-20). And in a more elaborate description, Luke recalls the risen Lord in an action of leading the disciples (once again) to understand the Scriptures and his Messianic mission. The author recounts their experiencing this new life more deeply as they perceive the Lord's commission to carry his word of mercy and repentance to all people and as they hear his promise to give them a share in his Spirit (24:36, 44-49). In his Acts of the Apostles, Luke recounts the fulfillment of that promise as the Eleven become imbued with Christ's Spirit, a powerful gift which so transforms them that they cannot but proclaim the Good News of salvation both by word and by deed (Acts. 2:1-36).

The fourth evangelist, too, relates the Easter appearances of the risen Christ to the Apostles' transformation in their becoming enlivened by God's saving love. In revealing himself to the Apostles, the risen Lord breathed his (holy) Spirit upon them that they might experience God's forgiving presence and subsequently share that forgiving love with others (Jn. 20:19-23). And the same evangelist describes Peter's encounter with the risen Lord, not only as an event in which Peter declares his love for Christ, but also as a moment in which Peter hears the Lord's command to serve him by ministerially caring for others in Jesus' name (Jn. 21:15ff).

Each New Testament author, then, affirms the fact that to experience the risen Lord is to experience personally the gift of salvation, the saving power of God effectively transforming one's freedom and life and love. To experience the risen Lord is to know the invigorating power of Jesus' Spirit so that one finally lives as Jesus lived (Gal. 2:19-20; Rom. 8:11, 14-17; I Cor. 12:1-3). This gift and indwelling of the Spirit must be understood as the necessary outcome and abiding fruit of Jesus' resurrection, of his engaging and personal appearances to his disciples as risen Lord, and of his ongoing presence to the Church. We have already called attention to the fact that the disciples' recognition of Jesus, and their naming him "Lord," manifested the fact, not only that Jesus was raised up but also that they, in seeing him, were simultaneously "lifted up." They were enlivened in this event so as to perceive Christ and God's active saving presence in him in a new way. Their pre-resurrection faith was deepened, transformed into post-resurrection Easter faith, a source of renewal and of discipleship lived at a more profound level.

The disciples' encounter with the risen Lord, then, carried with it two interrelated, yet distinct, dimensions. On the one hand, that experience consisted in the appearance of Jesus truly glorified and transformed in himself. He manifested himself physically and engaged the disciples verbally. On the other hand, the disciples themselves were transformed. As they met Jesus standing before them, *outside of them*, they also experienced an inner, gentle, elevating grace, the movement of Jesus' Spirit *within them*. In the encounter with the risen Lord, they knew a fuller infusion of divine life which lifted them beyond the human weakness which they had experienced at Jesus' trial and crucifixion. Jesus' very presence, as God's living word in glory, breathed forth the Spirit. Jesus' glorified presence communicated salvation.[27]

The Apostles' and early witnesses' experiences of the appearances of the risen Lord generated a profoundly transformed life of faith and belief within the early Church: The Jesus of history, having expressed God's truth and love in word and deed, lives forever with *Abba* and in the midst of God's people. The Apostles and all who gathered around them in shared faith saw Jesus' resurrection as the definitive transforming event of history - their history as a people and their history with Yahweh, the saving God. They expressed this experience as being at once a revelation of the one loving God who is *Abba*, Word and Spirit.

Thus, the resurrection is primarily *God's Action, God's Word*. The resurrection of the crucified Jesus stands forever as *Abba's* loving response to Jesus and *Abba's* final word to humankind. God has shown himself to be a God of enduring life and love, raising up the rejected Servant and making him Lord and Messiah, the powerful bearer of salvation for all.

Further, the resurrection speaks of the *full transformation and divinization of Jesus*. Jesus, in his integral humanity, standing beyond space and time, lives body and soul, filled with the Spirit of God's life and love. Jesus, in communion with the Father, is forever present to the Church, able to share this Spirit, this power for life and love, with all who approach him in humble faith and self-emptying love. The Jesus of history is glorified in body and soul, in mind and heart, in freedom and love. By the power of the resurrection, he establishes and embodies God's reign in fullness. By the power of the resurrection Jesus, deeply endowed with God's life, is constituted in his humanity as Lord and God, the messianic Savior of the world.

Finally, the resurrection is the event through which *God pours forth the earth-shaking force of God's Spirit upon people of faith*. In the presence of the risen Lord, disciples hear a transforming word, see Jesus in a new way, feel their hearts burning with hope and love, and find themselves transformed by the Spirit of life. In and through Jesus' resurrection, God gives himself as the enduring power of saving life and love to all who believe. The resurrection, and the risen Lord who reveals the resurrection, are the Word by which *Abba* forever breathes forth the Holy Spirit of everlasting life and love.

Thus, the experience of the risen Christ radically transformed the faith and beliefs of the Apostles and of the other early witnesses. God who is *Abba* raised God's crucified Son from the dead. Jesus, who had walked among them, truly glorified, is the Lord of history; and the Spirit of God, empowering Jesus, dwells within them, filling the earth. In the risen Lord, *Abba* has given people of faith the Spirit of God's love, the Spirit who is the sure pledge and in-dwelling source of everlasting salvation. All this the early Church, having experienced the risen Christ, sought to communicate as it proclaimed "Jesus is Lord" -- forever!

Interpreting the Experience of the Risen Lord Today: Doing Christology in Light of Jesus' Resurrection

Our efforts in the previous section of this chapter have focused upon the experiences of the original witnesses of the risen Lord and upon the beliefs of these first Christians precisely as recorded in the texts of the New Testament. So powerful was their experience of the risen Lord that the proclamation of the crucified and risen One became the center of the Christian understanding of life before God and of life in the historical world in every age. Christians under-stood that the transcendent loving God had fully expressed and communicated God's own Self as enduring life and love for them through Jesus' crucifixion and resurrection. They perceived clearly that Jesus' crucifixion and resurrection must be understood if human life, human love, human existence, and the human destiny itself be understood.

It will be our purpose, in this section of our work, to seek more fully to understand the nature, meaning and impact of Christ's resurrection, particularly in light of contemporary theology. In doing so, we will leap over many centuries of theological reflection.[28] Having benefited from the lengthy tradition which this thought has established, however, we will attempt to offer some fruitful avenues of thought particularly adapted to contemporary interest and understanding.[29] We will focus our reflections upon four areas. First, we will seek further insight into the nature of Jesus' resurrection and his post-resurrection appearances, both in themselves and, more particularly, in their relationship to the full realization of God's reign. Second, we will inquire into the present-day Christians' experiences of the risen Lord, comparing and contrasting them with the Apostles' privileged experiences of that same Christ. Third, we will strive to clarify further the nature and the meaning of the "resurrection of the body" and of the risen body itself. Finally, we will underscore the importance of attending to the resurrection in every effort to do Christology today.

JESUS' RESURRECTION AS ESCHATOLOGICAL EVENT: THE COMING OF GOD'S REIGN IN FULLNESS

Jesus began his historical ministry with the proclamation "The reign of God is here! Repent and believe this Good News." The Good News focused upon the presence of God who wished to offer healing and forgiveness to all persons without exception. Jesus illustrated this wonderful Good News by curing diseases, healing physical impairments, exorcising evil spirits, and forgiving sins. He made that Good News a reality by welcoming widows, orphans, tax collectors, repentant sinners, and all the marginalized Israelites into his company and that of his disciples. He himself lived what he preached as he served God and neighbor with unsurpassed love, compassion, and faithfulness. Certainly, in and through him, things were different; a new era had begun.

But the New Age had more than begun. The Gospels also recount Jesus' vision of a fuller unfolding of God's presence and power when, at his final meal with the disciples, he affirmed: "I will not drink of the fruit of the vine until it be accomplished in the kingdom of God." Jesus believed that his death would usher in the reign of God with greater fullness. In his resurrection, Jesus' vision became reality. In his humanity, Jesus was glorified; he came personally to participate in the fullness of God's life and was empowered actively and personally to communicate that life to all persons of all time. And in Jesus, history itself had reached a splendid conclusion as God's benevolent rule of life and love reached its full realization and final expression. The New Age has not only begun; it is already here in fullness in the risen Christ. What was and is forever accomplished fully in Jesus, need only be further unfolded and accomplished in us.

The Coming of God's Reign:
An Experience of the Transcendent

In an effort better to understand what happened to Jesus in his resurrection and to appreciate more clearly the reality and significance of the expression "new" or "eschatological" age "established in its fullness," it is important to recall that we are speaking fundamentally of the full and enduring Self-communication of transcendent reality. Such reality cannot be detected merely by the senses; much less can it be adequately described in empirical, concrete terms. Rather, this reality can be known only by faith. Further, as we have underscored in the first chapter and have illustrated thereafter, the human encounter with the transcendent One always energizes and transforms the believer with an energy and life which finite reality can never offer: When one stands openly and receptively before the Transcendent, one experiences and attains new life.

In essence, then, the suffering, dying, and rising Jesus - as well as the Apostles in their "seeing the Lord" - found themselves engaged primarily in a profound experience of transcendent reality. Jesus and the Apostles, though manifestly in differing degrees, found themselves encountering and drawn by transcendent reality, fully alive and powerfully present. They recognized that reality in the surrender of trusting faith; and in that surrender of faith, they experienced the deepening and expansion of their lives (again manifestly in different measures). They were energized and transformed with fuller divine life.

This effort to interpret and to seek fuller understanding of Jesus' resurrection and of the Apostles' experience of the risen Lord clearly changes the focus of ordinary inquiry, even of theological inquiry, into these experiences. It situates our inquiry within the context of what is primarily religious experience. Rather than centering attention on the nature of Jesus' risen body, or on the physical dimensions of the Apostles' encounter with the risen Lord, it focuses our attention on Jesus' and the Apostles' awareness of and communion with the Transcendent. In order to clarify and to develop further the import of this perspective, we will illustrate it more fully, both with regard to Jesus and also with regard to the privileged experiences of those who witnessed Jesus' post-resurrection appearances. In doing so, we will underscore the differences as well as the similarities within the experiences of each.

Jesus' Resurrection:
Transforming Encounter With *Abba*
Jesus' historical life itself consisted of a series of religious experiences. As we have seen, the historical Jesus developed his human life in general, and his mission to Israel in particular, in a continued prayerful search for, and an active self-giving response to, the transcendent One. In his openness and trust of *Abba*, Jesus had found an ongoing source of wisdom and courage, of truthfulness and mercy. That source was so engaging and so fruitful that, in the words of the fourth evangelist, the will of *Abba* was the nourishment of Jesus' earthly life (Jn. 4:34). Thus, in Jesus' everyday encounters with *Abba*, the historical Jesus found a depth of renewal and transformation that in a very real way, enabled him to precede and to surpass his fellow men and women in unshakable love and service.

In his passion and death, this same Jesus encountered the transcendent One as never before. As in every one of his previous experiences of transcendent Presence and Love, this final encounter with *Abba* called forth from Jesus a self-abandoning trust and also carried with it God's energy for the transformation of Jesus' human life. The uniqueness of this moment in Jesus' experience of *Abba*, and the consequent uniqueness of Jesus' transformation in this moment, however, consisted in the *totality of Jesus' self-gift, the totality of Abba's response* to Jesus, and therefore the *totality of Jesus' participation* in the transforming life and reign of the transcendent One. It is this total faith-filled experience of *Abba*, an experience in which Jesus was totally renewed and transformed in the depth and very center of his humanity, that most accurately describes what is meant by Jesus' resurrection. The resurrection speaks of the total transformation of Jesus' humanity with the transcendent life and love of *Abba*. As a result, though Jesus remains truly human, his entire human being is suffused with transcendent life and love. To perceive his risen presence is to perceive the presence of the Transcendent. He is "raised up" to new and fuller life.

The uniqueness of this moment of Jesus' resurrection and glorification, therefore, consisted both in the unreserved manner in which Jesus finally surrendered the whole of himself in faith-filled trust to God and, also in the manner in which, within Jesus' total surrender, transcendent life and love totally communicated the transcendent Self, thereby affecting every aspect of Jesus' human nature.[30] This transcendent transformation of every aspect of Jesus' humanity is what we attempt to describe when we say "Christ is risen bodily."[31] We cannot, therefore, give an adequate description of Jesus bodilyness in "this-worldly" terms. The best that we can do is to state that Jesus is fully transformed in and because of his profound experience of *Abba*. In his humanity, he is fully divinized. Hence Paul could say nothing more accurate than: "We saw the glory of God shining on the face of Jesus" (II Cor. 4:6). In Jesus, the fullness of God's reign, the final age of God's Self-communicating love has come to completion.

The Apostles' Vision of the Risen Lord: "Seeing" in Faith

This perspective regarding the nature of Jesus' resurrection sheds light upon the nature of the Apostles' "seeing" and "conversing with" the risen Lord as he appeared to them. Since the risen Christ necessarily manifested the human *fully infused with transcendent life and love*, one can understand that the disciples' "seeing" and "conversing with" the Lord would be an experience primarily of faith rather than one of physical sight and sound. It is precisely for this reason, as we have already noted (see pages 228-231), that Mary Magdalene did not immediately recognize Jesus at the tomb (Jn. 20:14). Neither did the disciples grasp immediately who he was while they encountered him on the shore of the Sea of Galilee (Jn. 21:1-4). Seeing and conversing with the risen Lord, even for these privileged witnesses, was more a matter of faith than of sound and sight. In the words of contemporary scholars, it was a "believing-seeing"[32]; it was more a matter of insight rather than sight[33].

Therefore, faith in and commitment to the risen Lord was not easy or automatic for those who saw and spoke with him. It required, as all experiences of transcendent reality require, an openness, a surrender of faith, a willingness to be transformed, and a desire to live one's life with deeper and more overriding trust in God than ever before.

This emphasis on the primacy of faith in the Apostles' experience of the risen Christ, however, does not mean that there was no physical, bodily, dimension to that encounter. For human beings, the manifestation of the presence, love, and saving power of the Transcendent has always taken place in the midst of some concrete word and/or event. Moses perceived God and God's voice in the midst of a "fiery bush" (Ex. 3:14). The Israelites came to know Yahweh and Yahweh's election of them as God's people through their phenomenal escape from Egypt, their passage through the Sea of Reeds, and their ultimate entrance into the promised land.[34] The disciples of the historical Jesus came to see him as God's emissary and began to follow him because they perceived the presence and power of *Abba* in Jesus' exorcisms and healings, signs and wonders[35] leading them to believe that "God had visited God's People."[36] In each case, it was a "this worldly," concrete experience of seeing and hearing which drew the beneficiaries and all who witnessed these events to wonder and praise the transcendent God. The elements involved in the Apostles' experience of the risen Lord are similar. In the appearances of the risen Lord, a concrete experience of seeing and hearing moved the Apostles to open their minds and hearts in faith.

Nevertheless it was faith itself which enabled them to perceive the full nature of whom and what they were experiencing. As with the miracles of Jesus, so in Jesus' appearing to the Apostles, it was "faith which saved" them. In that faith, they perceived clearly that the historical Jesus was wholly alive, fully transformed, bodily risen. For this reason, the best description of what they perceived lay, not in phrases describing Christ's physical body, but in an exclamation of profound faith, the proclamation "Jesus is Lord!"

Further, the effects of the Apostles' seeing and conversing with the risen Jesus are also best understood in light of the more generic pattern of religious experience. They find themselves transformed from weak, fearful followers (who scattered at Jesus' trial, who disowned him before an inquiring servant of the high priest, who went back to fishing), to courageous, dedicated, and faith-filled disciples (who proclaimed Jesus crucified and risen, who knew joy in suffering in his name, who grew in self-emptying love as they shared life together, and who willingly faced death themselves rather than denounce Jesus). Having met the transcendent One, *Abba*, in this fullest disclosure of Godly life in the glorified Christ, they themselves were alive with new vigor and life. They too were "raised up" in the risen Christ. Their only task was to live in the power of his love in this world and to await the fullness of the embrace of *Abba* as they too would pass through death and be raised up to everlasting life in the next.[37]

With the death and resurrection of Jesus and his appearances to his Apostles, the reign of God has been definitively established, the final days of salvation are fully here, and history is forever changed. In affirming that these events establish God's kingdom with finality, the Church and its theologians wish to underscore their conviction in faith that the transcendent One has given the divine Self to humankind fully and forever. They wish to affirm that, in the event of Jesus' death and resurrection, God has *communicated with Jesus more deeply and fully than ever before*, in fact, in the fullest way possible. And they wish to state that, in Jesus' appearing to the Apostles, God also has *communicated with humankind more profoundly and fully than ever before*. The eschatological age becomes reality when and where human beings open themselves to, experience, and come to participate in the Self-Gift of the

Transcendent in God's all-embracing promise and gift of life and love. When, in such openness and trust before God we experience God's pledge of unending love, we necessarily find renewal in life and love; we find ourselves invigorated and transformed in God's love. If the faith-experience of the Transcendent is always a transforming experience, then the experience of God in the fullness of God's Self-giving must involve human beings in a total transformation of life never known before. The whole of our humanity is transformed with the enduring, never ending, life and love of God. We can truly experience this reality, but it is an experience of faith, not empirically demonstrable. It is an experience known only in the faithful and committed surrender to the in-breaking of the transcendent God.

Thus the eschatological age speaks of the full and decisive in-breaking of the Transcendent into time, an in-breaking which includes 1) the transformation of the humanity of the historical Jesus in his experience of *Abba* as he offered himself in unreserved trust; 2) a fuller and decisive, though not yet complete, experience of the transcendent God of Jesus, on the part of the witnesses; and 3) the transformation of the witnesses in their coming to share more deeply in the life of the Transcendent, as Jesus has revealed that God.

THE EXPERIENCE OF THE RISEN LORD:
CONTEMPORARY CHRISTIANS-ORIGINAL WITNESSES
Given the fact that Jesus' resurrection and his appearances to the Apostles marked the in-breaking into time of the reign of God in its fullness, we can better understand the role of these original witnesses of the risen Christ: They stood at the most decisive moment of human history, the moment at which humankind's most ruthless rejection of God's invitation to life became the moment of God's most gracious act of love for humankind. As a result, having been gifted with a vision of the breadth and depth of God's saving power in the person of the risen Jesus, it became their privilege and their God-given responsibility to be the historical witnesses through whom *Abba*, with Christ, in their Holy Spirit, would make this central saving deed of the transcendent One known to all generations.

And yet, one must ask: what enables the contemporary believer to accept the testimony of these relatively few witnesses? What enables the contemporary Christian to share the conviction, the wonder and certainty of this new, fuller life expressed in the proclamation: "Jesus is Lord!?" Contemporary believers must have personal reasons to unite themselves with the Apostolic confession of faith or that proclamation of faith will hardly influence the development of their deepest selves at life's critical moments. Today's Christians need not "see" the risen Lord, but they need to experience Jesus alive, communicating to them even now the power of life in his likeness. As the risen Lord, in appearing to the apostles, lifted them up in his Spirit, so every Christian must know the presence and power of Christ revealing himself to them now, lifting them up with the life and the love of his Spirit. Disciples will be made, today as well as yesterday, only through a personal and transforming experience, in faith, of the risen Lord. So we must ask: "What enables the today's Christian to know with certainty that the testimony of the original witnesses is true?"

The New Testament itself provides some initial insight into this question. It respects the fact that the majority of the early, even first generation, Christians experienced the risen Jesus without seeing him. Rather, they knew the power of his Spirit, his hidden Presence, as they listened to believing disciples give personal witness to Jesus' death and resurrection. In faith, they experienced the transcendent God, disclosing God's life and love to them through the Church. In the surrender of faith, they embraced the transforming effects of God's Self-disclosing presence as they accepted conversion to Christ and his way of life. The proclamation, not the appearance, of the risen Lord became the vehicle through which they, like the Apostles, experienced the presence of *Abba*, now revealed fully in the risen Christ and his Spirit.[38]

In the Acts of the Apostles, Luke offers a paradigmatic record of this experience. In this account of the first Pentecost, as Peter proclaims the saving love of God culminating in Christ's resurrection, the members of Peter's audience begin to experience the presence of Christ and the movement of the Spirit as a feeling of being "cut to the heart." Hence they ask Peter anxiously: "What shall we do?" (Acts 2:38). To foster their fuller encounter with Christ in personal conversion, Peter urges them: "Repent and be baptized in the name of Jesus for the forgiveness of your sins; and you will receive the gift of the Holy Spirit" (Acts 2:38). His listeners heed Peter's advice, turn from their former way of life and embrace lives of sustained faith, prayer, and selfless generosity (Acts 2:42-47). They experience the power of Jesus' Spirit in the movement to full conversion. In that experience, these new Christians came to know the power and presence of the risen Lord. Without seeing him, they came to believe.[39]

The same evangelist, in the Gospel bearing his name, focuses upon the unfolding of the Word of God and the prayerful celebration of the Eucharist as central ways in which every believer will experience the comforting and strengthening presence of the risen One. In this account of the disciples' encounter with Jesus while journeying to Emmaus, Luke seeks to illustrate this point in a singularly artistic way. While recounting the fact that these disciples saw and conversed with the risen Lord along the road, the author seeks to underscore the reality of Jesus' presence at every moment when the Church proclaimed God's Word and on every occasion when the Community joined together in the "breaking of the bread" of the Eucharist. In recording the disciples' questioning exclamation: "Were not our hearts burning within us while he spoke with us... and opened the Scriptures to us?" (Lk. 24:32), the writer attempts to lead later disciples to realize that they experience that same risen Lord in their hearts as they listen to, ponder, and find themselves renewed in their hearing of God's Word.[40] And further, in recalling that these privileged disciples recognized the (presence of the) risen Lord in the "breaking of the bread" (Lk. 24:30, 31, 35), Luke intends to draw all Christians to an explicit awareness of the fact that, as they remember the journey of Christ and find personal encouragement to follow him in every Eucharistic celebration, they are experiencing the life-giving presence and power of the very same risen Lord.[41] And so, in this passage, Luke wishes to affirm that the experience of the risen Christ is as real for those who have not seen the Lord as it was for Jesus' privileged witnesses. The experience of Christ, enjoyed by every believer in moments of conversion to Christ and to following the Gospel, and in moments of listening faithfully to God's Word and celebrating God's saving deeds in the Eucharist, gives its own testimony. Every believer, as the privileged Apostles, experiences the same Jesus, the same risen Lord mediating the same powerful, saving love of God.

Nevertheless, these experiences of the power and love of the risen Lord are not enough to explain why one would take the initial steps of listening to the Word, of embracing conversion or of ritually celebrating Jesus' memory. What leads us to be open even to the possibility of Jesus' resurrection? In response to this question, Karl Rahner[42] has noted still another similarity between the Apostles and later generations in their experience of the risen Christ. He observes that in the longing of every human heart one can detect what he names as a "transcendental hope" in the resurrection, in one's own resurrection. By the term "transcendental hope," Rahner seeks to underscore the fact that this hope or longing is present within every human person who wonders about his or her life and its meaning. No one relishes the prospect of death which, in its darkness, seems like a passage into oblivion. Everyone desires to live on, albeit in a better, more peaceful, and more integral way. In that desire, everyone wishes to continue to live on bodily; for the only way we understand ourselves as persons is as embodied spiritual persons.

The Apostles, the early Church, and all future generations share this transcendental hope in the resurrection together with ever deeper experiences of God's gift of Christ's Spirit of transcendent love. And all are left with the question: how will God answer this longing, this gnawing hope deeply imbedded in every human heart? Glimpses of God's goodness may offer some level of response to this question. They may in some measure lead us to hope more fervently. But they do not give us God's clear or final response.

The experience of the Apostles, who saw the risen Lord, however, assures them and us that God has given God's ultimate answer to this hope with a definitive and total acceptance of all that is truly human, with an action by which God wonderfully embraces and communicates an expansion of life for human beings. The Apostles' unique witness touches a readiness, and offers a compelling reason, to believe within us. Our own transcendental hope for the resurrection, together with our own experiences of the in-breaking of God's saving love in the Spirit of Christ, enable us to hear in the apostolic witness the firmness of a genuine Word of God.

Hence, the longing in every heart for risen life invites us to cry out to God and to search for God's answer to our hope. The experience of the in-breaking of God in God's love leads us to an ever greater willingness to trust that God will indeed answer our every true and noble desire. The witness of the Apostles provides us with testimony that the answer has been given. Our further experiences of living in accord with this belief proves it true. Christian life even now becomes ever richer in love when lived in communion with Christ the risen Lord! Our *transcendental hope in the resurrection* has received, through the Apostles' testimony and our own surrender to Christ's presence in his Spirit, an unshakeable confirmation in the experience of faith. What we hope for has become in Christ, and is becoming in us, an *accomplished fact.*

These reflections help us to understand the similarities and the differences between the contemporary Christian's and the original witnesses' experiences of the risen Lord. On the one hand, these experiences are quite similar: All Christians, whether they be the Apostles themselves, members of the early Church, or twenty-first century believers, must experience and come to recognize the presence and power of the risen Christ in the experience of ongoing conversion/transformation of their lives in Jesus' likeness. All must recognize God, alive for them in saving love, in the crucified and risen Christ, who himself remains active and alive in the world of the disciple. All must meet Christ through the gift of the post-resurrection faith, finding him revealed in both everyday events as well as specifically religious celebrations. Even for the Apostles, the enduring experience of the risen Lord consisted, not in seeing him as he appeared to them in his glorified body, but rather in discerning his power in the unfolding of their lives, as they strove to walk in his likeness.

On the other hand, the experiences of the Apostles and those of later Christians are quite distinct: The Apostles witnessed the historical Jesus in the flesh of his earthly body. They heard his historical words and marveled at the wonders worked by his hands. They experienced the tragedy of the cross in its historical concreteness; they came to recognize his life in *Abba* in his glorious appearances among them. All this marked their encounters with the crucified and risen Lord as something unique.

For these reasons, the Apostles play a distinct and irreplaceable role for all future generations in the genesis of Christian faith and in the transmission of Christian beliefs. First, they provide the means by which all generations can come to identify and to name the saving presence and power which beckons them in their transcendental hope in the resurrection. The Apostles provide the means by which all can identify this presence and power as alive for them in word and sacrament, in the call to ongoing conversion and to deeper selfless love, and in the pledge of unending life. For clearly, only the original witnesses knew the Jesus of history, and only they saw the full revelation of the presence and power of the risen Christ. Hence, only they could affirm that the transcendent love which all can experience in faith and conversion as the love mediated by the crucified and risen Christ.

Second, the Apostles provide all future disciples with a Christian understanding of the final destiny of humankind and the fullness of life to which ongoing conversion to Jesus will lead. For only the witnesses saw Jesus in his glorified state; therefore, only they could give full testimony to the enduring fruitful outcome to which conversion to the way of Jesus would lead. Only they who saw the risen Lord could describe what the presence and power of the transcendent One looks like and leads to when fully embraced by human beings in their own history unto their own death.

Thus, all future generations of Christians depend upon the Apostles who have seen the risen Lord. It is their witness alone which tells us concretely what to expect and how to foster the very life of the risen Christ. Yet like that of the Apostles, every Christian's experience of the risen Lord is essentially a religious experience. It is an experience of the transcendent One in faith.

Only the moment of history, the setting of one's concrete life, the concrete circumstances which call one to faith are different. In word and sacrament, in crisis and in success, in ongoing conversion and in steadfast fidelity, the Christian has the capacity to encounter the saving presence of the crucified and risen Lord, and in a faith-filled surrender to God, to know the transforming presence of the One Jesus calls *Abba*.

THE RESURRECTION OF THE BODY:
FULLNESS OF SALVATION - THE DEFINITIVE REIGN OF GOD

To speak of the Apostles' having seen the risen Lord in eschatological fullness of life has led us to note that their vision of Jesus consisted in what was primarily an intense experience of faith. They saw Jesus personally and bodily transformed with transcendent life. Jesus appeared visibly "in another form"; his body was real, yet different. Further, to speak of all persons' transcendental hope in their own resurrection as a fundamental desire of every human heart led us to focus our attention upon our own expectations for life. We look forward to unending life as transformed and integral human beings, persons who remain both body and spirit. Our continued bodily existence remains a significant dimension of our hope; a purely "spiritual" life, lived forever, seems inadequate, disappointing, even frightening. Why? Why is bodily resurrection so important to us as we envision our future life in the eternal kingdom of God? What are we striving to express when we speak of the resurrection of the body?

We have already attempted to provide insight into the nature and meaning of the risen body, as well as into the disciples' experience of the risen Lord in his glorified state, by using the interpretative paradigm of the transforming character of the human encounter with transcendent Love as one surrenders oneself to God in trusting faith. Contemporary theologians, however, offer some further perspectives for understanding the nature and meaning of the risen body, perspectives which can enrich our appreciation of this Christian belief. They underscore the fact that our bodies are the exterior expression of our inner and personal selves. Through smiles and frowns, tones of voice, words and gestures, we express and communicate to others our innermost thoughts, feelings, intentions, and love. In doing so, we actually express, our true inner selves in ever more profound ways. Through our bodies we extend our unique selves to others, thereby influencing and enriching our world and our history as a whole.

Our bodies are also the vehicles by which we receive the gifts others bring to us. We need to see with our eyes, to hear with our ears, to touch, to taste, and to smell in order to perceive and to recognize the presence of other persons. At a more profound level, we need our senses to understand and to appreciate the intentions and love of others. Only by first seeing, listening and perhaps feeling the touch of other people, only by experiencing with open eyes and ears the world around us, do we become capable of discovering the deepest meanings of life, including the value of our communion of life with one another. And so, our bodies are the vehicles by which we meet others, receive their love, perceive meaning, and extend our insight, care, love, our very selves to others in return.

Similarly, it is through our bodies that we also encounter our God. God reveals and communicates God's Self, God's life, and God's love in the concrete events of history, in the conscious and free actions of persons, in the words and deeds of men and women gifted with insight and wisdom. As we have indicated above,[43] it is in the midst of our world of persons and events that people of faith detect the hidden presence and overtures of transcendent saving love. And it is also through human bodily expressions, by human words of understanding and human acts of love, that we, having been transformed and enlivened by God's Spirit, extend God's life and love to others. We experience God and share Godly life with others precisely as bodily beings. As Walter Kasper phrased it, our bodies become the "meeting place" for ourselves and God, the "meeting place" in and through which we encounter others and share God's life with one another.[44]

Recognizing the intimate connection, indeed the unity, between our bodies and five senses on the one hand, and our inner, most personal selves on the other, we can better understand the meaning of the "resurrection of the body," the meaning of a "spiritualized" or "glorified" body, as the sacred authors have proclaimed it. As we all are at times painfully aware, in this world we often fall short of loving others as Christ loved us. We mediate God's life and love to others imperfectly at best. To speak of the resurrection of the body or of a spiritualized body (in the Pauline sense) is to affirm the fact that, in our life beyond death, our bodies will have become fully capable of mediating to others the Godly life and love which transforms our minds and hearts. The belief in the resurrection of the body seeks to express the fact that, after we die in Jesus' likeness, having given ourselves to God in the total surrender of our lives, God, in a return of love for us, fills our whole being, our bodily being, with the resilience, the depth, the power of God's own spiritual energy, life and love.

Thus, the resurrection of the body seeks to express the Christian conviction that our bodies need to be and will be transformed so that they will be capable of being the means by which we, deeply imbued with transcendent life, can and will express that life. We who, like Jesus, become finalized in Godly love and trusting fidelity, we who will have become alive in God and present to God in our deepest selves, will also become capable of expressing and communicating that life and love to one another in an everlasting communion of life referred to as heaven. Our whole selves, body and soul, physical visibility and inner depth, will be fully transformed in God's Spirit. Our present transparency before one another, our present capacity to share faith and to give ourselves in love to one another, is but a glimpse of the dynamic communion and all-embracing experience of life and love which will constitute our full participation in God's reign. The resurrection of the body speaks of this final, full transformation of our integral human selves in the power of Godly life and love.

One further helpful reflection: One may ask, "Will we rise in the very body which our friends buried at our death?" The question underscores our natural tendency to focus upon our corporeality as the source of our personal identity. Yet science forces us to recognize that the material of our bodies changes over the years. We do not have the same physical matter at two years of age, at twenty-five years of age, and at seventy-five years of age. Still, we remain the same persons and speak as if we had the same body.

What we sense and seek to express when we ask this question is our sense of *personal identity*, our sense of *personal and historical continuity*, a sense of the *unity within our personal existence* in our presence to God and to others in the world.[45] In this sense, our firm hope of enjoying the resurrection of the body expresses our desire for and our firm conviction that we will preserve personal, conscious, never-ending continuity with our historical existence as we move beyond this world. In proclaiming the resurrection of the body, we affirm that we will remain, in the fullness of God's life, the persons we have become in this world. The resurrection of the body expresses our confidence in our remaining our true and unique selves in a continuous life of being present to God, to ourselves, and to others whom we knew in the world.

The resurrection of the body, then, as our belief in the risen Lord seeks to express it, underscores the fact that God's gift of saving love not only draws persons beyond death to fuller life. It also transforms the whole person, body and soul, to participate in that life. The reality of the resurrection of the body, first accomplished in the risen Jesus, stands as the firm and final Word of God. It proclaims to all generations with the certitude of God's Truth, that not only the individual person and his or her spiritual center will continue to exist beyond the grave, but also that everything about that person will continue to exist, transformed with the fullness of God's life and love. Having met *Abba* in faith-filled trust as we join with Christ in the total gift of ourselves, we too will be totally transformed in the glory of God. Our entire being, our life and history, our bodies and our souls, will be accepted, embraced, loved, and taken up by *Abba* so that all that we have labored for, lived through, endured, and achieved will find place in God's reign. Our whole being and life will participate in the glory of God. We will then know the full meaning of the proclamations "Jesus is Risen!" and "Jesus is Lord!" for "when he is revealed, we shall be like him, for we shall see him as he truly is" (I Jn. 3:2). Such is the meaning of the resurrection of the body. Such is the gift of salvation, given us in the crucified and risen Lord.

THE RESURRECTION:
FOUNDATION FOR DOING CHRISTOLOGY TODAY

We have defined Christology as the process of interpreting one's experience of God alive for us in and through Jesus. The Apostles' vision of the risen Lord provided them with the capacity to name the Christ whose presence they perceived in prayer, word, and sacrament, in community and in ministry. Their understanding of the very nature and being of the saving God, the very Self of God, became irrevocably shaped by God's Self-revelation in God's raising Jesus from the dead. Their vision of the risen Lord forever determined the shape of their lives and the development of the lives of all disciples of Christ. Hence, their experience of the risen Lord and their testimony to the reality of his resurrection, must forever be the foremost experience and interpretation of God's love which grounds every effort of doing Christology and of doing Christian theology as a whole. It must influence every aspect of Christian life, Christian faith and hope, Christian action, Christian theological reflection today.

Some examples of how this experience and belief must permeate Christian theology will help to clarify this point. First, with regard to the nature of God and human suffering, we must steadfastly affirm that it is the resurrection, not the cross, which finally defines who God is and what God is about in our world and with us. Therefore although suffering does exist, and although God does not destroy the forces which perpetuate suffering, the Christian experience of the risen Lord and the belief in God's supreme act of raising Jesus from the dead clearly show that God does not leave persons to remain in pain and misery, much less desire or inflict the suffering itself. Rather, God supports persons in their suffering. God helps persons find the inner strength to trust, to hope in God, to forgive and to love. And ultimately God leads them, as God led God's faithful Servant Jesus, through their suffering to a richer and fuller life. Always and everywhere, God is supremely the giver of life. Suffering may still evoke confusion and darkness, but a Christian understanding of suffering, *in light of Jesus' resurrection*, must interpret it ultimately as an occasion in which one is not abandoned by God. Indeed, Christians will interpret that suffering as an occasion in which one comes to encounter the God of Jesus and *Abba's* transforming love in everlasting power and depth.

Second, with regard to Christian spirituality and asceticism, we must affirm that God does not will harshness, self-punishment or negativity toward ourselves or our life as a way of spiritual growth. What God does desire and bless are continued efforts to remain faithfully trusting in God and to manifest generous, even forgiving, love of others through all the circumstances of our life. The resurrection illustrates with finality that *Abba*, and *Abba's* Son Jesus, do not desire to punish, but to forgive and to lift persons up to fuller life. Self-discipline and self-denial are necessary, but not for their own sake. Rather, all discipline needs to be employed in the service of Godly, Christlike love. Anything less makes punishment rather than the resurrection and God's Self-communication in love the goal of life and the intention of the God of Jesus.

Third, with regard to the cross itself, Christians do and should proclaim the death of Jesus, death on the cross. They do and should reverence the cross and place crucifixes in their homes and churches. They do so, at least in part, to remember and to honor the inspiring depth of Jesus' fidelity to God and the steadfastness of his love for us. But the cross of Jesus, *in the light of the resurrection*, speaks much more. What this Cross tells us is that love and life are greater than all suffering and even death itself; that the expansiveness of living Godly life and love can deepen even when one suffers profound injustice and acts of sinful vengeance; and that the love and life-giving power of God can, and indeed does, embrace God's children no matter how wounded, broken, or despicable they may seem. The cross, in light of the resurrection, tells us that the saving love of God has no limits.

Finally, with regard to salvation, we can affirm that the resurrection, not the cross, constitutes the definitive action of God by which God brings about salvation. For it is in the resurrection that *Abba* accomplishes and expresses the ultimate and total transformation of Jesus' humanity with divine life as Jesus, in the total surrender of his life and history into the hands of *Abba*, encounters *Abba's* love in its fullness. And it is in the resurrection of Jesus that *Abba* signifies what this transcendent God is actually doing for and within each Christian who, in his or her ongoing surrender to God in faith, encounters the transcendent One ever more deeply. Christ's resurrection signifies and expresses the desire and action of *Abba* to enable all who encounter God with Jesus to be raised up, to be alive in God as Jesus was and is alive in God. The resurrection constitutes the action of God, by which God gives God's Self to all in everlasting life and love, in the gift of salvation.

This chapter concludes Part III of this work, the first major portion of our efforts to do Christology. We have attempted to complete our reflection upon the New Testament communities' and the first disciples' experience of and reflection upon God alive in and through Christ. In the Jesus of history, the disciples perceived God's saving love, a saving love so powerful that it enabled Jesus to endure the cross rather than stifle or compromise that love. In the Christ of faith, they also perceived God's saving love, the love of a faithful God so powerful that that God brought God's Chosen One to fullness of life forever.

But what does this mystery, the mystery of God alive in Jesus, imply about the very being and person of Jesus? What does this entire mystery disclose about God's life and communion with us? What does it mean with regard to Jesus' own personal identity: the Son of God and the Son of Mary? The Christian community of the second century and beyond continued to struggle to understand the mystery of Christ as well as to meet new questions and challenges to its beliefs in Christ within its own history. How the experience of God in and through Jesus, crucified and risen, continued to enliven the Church and how the Church continued in the process of interpreting that experience, particularly in the period of the Great Councils, defines the goal of the next portion of our endeavor.

Before we enter upon that period and seek insight from its christological reflections, the reader is invited to reflect upon, and give personal answer to, the following questions.

Questions for Reflection

1. What were the most significant aspects of your understanding of Jesus' resurrection which you held prior to reading this chapter? What would you regard as the most important aspects of your understanding of this event now? Explain.

2. Which appearance narrative from among those recounted in the Gospels do you personally find the most engaging? What aspects of that narrative engage you the most? Explain.

3. How have you come to understand the interrelationship of Jesus' resurrection and the nature of the reign of God? The interrelationship of Jesus' resurrection and God's effectively establishing that reign?

4. How had you understood the bodily dimension of Jesus' resurrection before reading this chapter? What aspects of your reading and reflection have led you to modify your previous understanding? Explain.

5. In what ways have you experienced the presence and power of the risen Lord in your own life? Where do you see these experiences also reflected in the New Testament, and, therefore, in the experience of the early Church? In what ways are these experiences also experiences of the power of Christ's resurrection and even glimpses of one's own resurrection?

6. From your own reading of the New Testament, in what way(s) have you noticed that the disciples' experience of the risen Lord has influenced the reporting of events and/or sayings of the historical Jesus? Do you think that the influence of these experiences has falsified or has led to the perception of a deeper meaning within these events and/or sayings? Why?

PART
IV

Christology Unfolded
In Classical Form

The Experience and Understanding
in the Post-Apostolic Church

CHAPTER 9

Understanding Jesus: Human and Divine

Our investigation of the Jesus of history and our efforts to understand him and his mission in light of the faith-experience of the first disciples have led us to proclaim in mind and heart a most powerful affirmation: Jesus is Lord! We have come to understand and, hopefully, more deeply to identify with, the faith-experience of the New Testament churches -- knowing and experiencing God, alive in Jesus crucified and risen. Clearly, "God was at work in Christ, reconciling the world to himself!"(2 Cor. 5:21). The reign of God, embracing the conversion and faith-filled transformation of all people, expected in Israel and shown forth in the historical Jesus, had reached its irreversible accomplishment in the risen One. In Jesus, the reign of God -- everlasting life and communion in the mutuality of Godly love -- has arrived for all people!

But what does Christian belief in the definitive establishment of God's reign in the raising of Jesus say of Jesus himself? What is required of Jesus that he be mediator and revelation of that reign, the definitive sign and symbol of God's transforming life in and for the world? Indeed, we have underscored a number of characteristics of Jesus' inner life and human transformation which his death and resurrection show forth. We have noted his utter fidelity before *Abba*; the utter selflessness of his love for all persons; the transformation of his humanity, his divinization, his full participation, humanly, in the divine life of *Abba* whom he experienced totally in his complete and trusting surrender of his life to God on the cross; his transhistorical presence with *Abba* to persons of all times and all places, offering a like transformation in the abiding power of Godly love. We have underscored many characteristics of Jesus, crucified and risen, so that we have been able truly to affirm: Jesus is Lord, the first-born of many brothers and sisters (Col. 1:15-20).

But has our effort to underscore these many characteristics of Jesus given us an understanding of him that is adequate for every age and culture? For example, have we perceived and articulated well enough the precise nature of the divine power in Jesus? Have we understood clearly enough that power which energized his openness to *Abba*, his surrender to his mission, the depth of his teaching, the attractiveness of his presence, the transforming efficacy of his wondrous deeds? The New Testament communities would have responded to these questions with a resounding "Yes." But the post-apostolic churches, the churches expanding into a pre-dominantly Hellenistic world during the second through the fifth centuries would offer an emphatic "No." For, while affirming that Jesus clearly is the one Mediator between God and humanity, while experiencing Jesus' saving presence in celebrating his memory in liturgical worship, these later churches would have stated that we have not yet entertained in clear enough fashion what the precise nature of the divine power in Jesus consisted of. Among Christians of the post-apostolic churches, the crucial question became: "What is required of Jesus himself that he be Mediator of the reign of God and of the fullness of salvation?"[1] In a word: "Is Jesus Divine?" "Shall we call Jesus, God?" "What truly is the nature of the divine power in Jesus?"

We may wonder why, after all that the New Testament churches had affirmed, would this question (and all the interconnected questions[2] which flow with and after it) would emerge so urgently, indeed so controversially. A moment's reflection, however, will yield some significant insights which will alleviate that wonder: First, the New Testament itself does not respond decisively to this question. Rather, it presents a variety of ways of understanding the nature of the divine power in Jesus. For example, it names him God's prophet; it calls him God's Chosen Son/Servant (retaining a title formerly applied to the faithful kings of Israel); it presents him as anointed and led forward by God's Spirit. The New Testament speaks of him as God's Wisdom, and the first-born of all creation. Only within this context of a diversity of ways of speaking of Jesus' divine power, does it also call Jesus "God."[3] As a matter of fact, the New Testament often presents Jesus as "less than God" as it calls attention to Jesus' prayerful custom of seeking light from *Abba* and of his submitting himself to *Abba's* will time and time again. Even in the fourth Gospel in which Jesus is named "God's Word become flesh," the Gospel in which Thomas confesses Jesus as "my Lord and my God," Jesus himself claims to be less than the Father who is greater than he (Jn. 14:28).[4] The variety of ways in which the New Testament speaks of Jesus, especially of his divine power and his relationship to *Abba*, caused some Christians to misinterpret the sacred writings and to foster serious controversy within the Church.

Second, the new and different historical situation, the "foreign" Hellenic culture, into which the post-apostolic Church found itself expanding, also evoked this question and demanded its resolution. The most significant elements of this new situation, this new culture, which led the Church to focus intensely upon this issue of the nature of the divine power in Jesus deserve a moment's attention.

A primary factor which urged the Church to address this issue lay in the diverse ways of thinking that distinguished the Semitic from the Hellenic culture. The mode of reflection characteristic of the Israelites focused on the historical, on concrete events and experiences, from which they inferred what they regarded as truth. Thus, from their experience of God, they developed an understanding of God. God's saving deeds showed God to be eminently merciful. God's allowing Israel to suffer at the hands of its enemies, showed God to be just, ready to chastise God's people, and desirous of leading them to repentance for their frequent infidelity. This way of thinking left Israel open to integrate ever new data into its understanding of God, of itself, and of its relationship with God. The Israelites could fairly easily refashion their understanding of God and of God's ways, integrating the new while preserving the old. The development and the refinement of Israel's understanding of the nature of God's reign would be a clear example of this historical, developmental and inclusive way of thinking. Historical reality was the test of the truth.

The Hellenic way of thinking, on the other hand, tended to focus upon the transhistorical, the abstract and universal, as the criterion of the truth. Historical reality was merely an imperfect reflection of what was perfect, stable, and universal in a world known primarily by the mind or reason. Thus, Plato had contemplated the world of ideas and universal essences of which created realities were mere shadows. The Stoics prized order and freedom from passion, both of which could only be approximated in the created world. What was new in the world could not influence the Greek understanding of "Eternal Truth," for the latter was unchanging and absolutely stable. What was new in the world, what was surprising, needed to be incorporated into a highly abstract speculative schema, or remain as a troublesome and unresolved question.[5] Thus, for the Greek mind, previously affirmed *truths* became the criteria of *what could be* whereas for the Semitic mind, *unfolding reality* became the criterion of *what is really true*.[6]

A second aspect of the diversity of cultures which forced the discussion and resolution of the question of the nature of the divine power in Jesus was centered in the radical differences within the religious traditions of these cultures, especially the differences in their ways of understanding God.[7] Thus, for the Semite, the appearance of Jesus, his prophetic mission, his healing works, and his resurrection to the fullness of life constituted the climatic moments of *a lengthy history of God's loving kindness toward the Israelites*. Israel had enjoyed two thousand years of *dialogue with Yahweh*; it knew God's presence and personal involvement in its own life. It even named God by using dynamic, interrelational terms: Yahweh is One who is always present to save (Ex. 3:14). For the Greek, however, the appearance of Jesus could not be so easily understood within a context of divine-human interaction. For Hellenic philosophers had understood God *as distant and uninvolved* rather than as close to human beings and deeply concerned for their welfare. Hence, the proclamation of the Good News of salvation, the ultimate overture of a God of love, had little context in Hellenic religious thought to foster its correct understanding. As a matter of fact, Hellenic thought so framed its understanding of God that its religious tradition in some ways presented a serious challenge, if not an obstacle, to the correct understanding of God's work and presence in Jesus, as we shall see.[8]

In many ways, therefore, the proclamation of Jesus crucified and risen in the context of Hellenism, required a profound *theological* conversion before it could embrace *christological* insight and genuinely Christ-centered transformation. While the presenting question may have been "What is the nature of the divine power in Jesus?" the unarticulated question (with a presupposed answer) – causing an undercurrent of turmoil in the divergent interpretations of the crucified and risen Savior – remained, "What is the nature of God and of God's divine power in itself?" Clearly the God of Abraham, Isaac and Jacob, the God of Moses and Aaron, the God of David and Solomon was quite different from the God of Socrates, Plato, and Aristotle, the God of Plotinus and the breadth of Greek philosophers. Differences in their approaches to understanding God made it very difficult to understand Jesus and God alive for us in and through him.

The movement of the Church, therefore, into the Hellenic culture of the second century onward, clearly marks the Church's entrance into a new stage of doing Christology. In a manner which may be likened to the efforts of the four Gospel communities, the churches of the second to the fifth centuries and beyond found that they needed to interpret anew their experience of God alive for them in and through Christ Jesus. Like the first-century churches of each of the evangelists, they found themselves confronted with unique challenges inherent to a new historical situation. But, unlike their ancestors of the first century, they could not rely upon a common tradition to provide an interpretive key for communicating and deepening their understanding of God, alive in Christ. In a real way, therefore, the challenges of the second through the fifth centuries, the challenges of developing an authentic understanding of Jesus in the classical milieu, may have been more difficult and more treacherous than the challenges of the New Testament era. Not only were the questions different, not only were the religious traditions different, but the very style of thinking itself was different, foreign to the thought patterns of the Sacred Writers who crafted Christian Tradition at its outset.

Chapters 9 and 10, the two chapters discussing the tradition of classical Christology, will deal not only with new perspectives concerning Jesus and the salvation event. They will also be dealing with a new way of thinking, and therefore with a radically different idiom for interpreting the Christian experience of God alive in Jesus. Classical Christology is clearly Christology in a new and different key. The present chapter will be divided into three sections: The first will deal with the question of the divinity of Christ, or more accurately, the divinity of the eternal Word, the *Logos,* who became flesh in Jesus of Nazareth. The second will deal with the humanity of Christ, a question which became all the more vital as the divinity of Jesus captured the central position in the Church's understanding of the nature(s) of Jesus. The third section will offer some reflections drawn from the foregoing material concerning the doing of Christology.

The Divinity of Jesus:
Its Affirmation and Meaning

The struggle to understand Jesus and to express clearly the authentic experience of salvation had its beginning even within the apostolic churches themselves as those churches strove to communicate the import of the experience of Christ's death and resurrection for all believers. The expansion of Christianity into the Hellenic culture, however, brought this struggle to a new pitch of intensity, largely because the Hellenic religious tradition and the abstract ways of Greek thinking prompted questions and called for a precision which the Semitic culture had not dreamed of. The missionary Church proclaiming the Gospel and the converts who recently embraced the Gospel quickly became one Church within the Greek world. They were joined together in a common effort to make the import of God's revelation in Jesus, the gift of universal salvation, known and appreciated. The endeavor centered upon Jesus, the one Mediator of salvation. The underlying concern, however, was to safeguard the authentic experience of salvation itself, the salvation which these churches experienced again and again in worship and life as they encountered the healing presence of God in and through the crucified and risen One.

The first section of this chapter will present the Church's journey toward its solemn affirmation of the divinity of Jesus, or more precisely, the divinity of the *Logos*. We will do so in three stages. First we will unfold the parameters of the journey, which will themselves serve to situate and clarify the definitive statement of the Church at the Council of Nicea (325). Second, we will present, and contextualize the terminology of the definition of the divinity of the *Logos* crafted at Nicea. Third, we will offer some reflections on the meaning of the Church's definition, highlighting its intentions and positive content as well as its limits.

THE INITIAL STRUGGLE REGARDING CHRIST'S DIVINITY
Early post-apostolic Church leaders themselves offered diverse ways of expressing and understanding the divine power in Jesus. The so-called *Shepherd of Hermas* wrote that

> The Holy Spirit, who exists beforehand and created
> the whole of creation, God, settled in the flesh which
> he willed (*Similitudes* 5:6:5).

The Holy Spirit, in the mind of Hermas, is the same as the Son of God, clearly God's Self, not just a lesser being of the divine order.[9]

Similarly, Ignatius of Antioch (110) wrote:

> There is one physician, fleshly and spiritual,
> generate and ungenerate, God in human being, true
> life in death, both from Mary and from God, first
> subject to suffering and then incapable of suffering,
> Jesus Christ, our Lord (*Letter to Ephesians*, 7:2)[10]

Yet, as clear as these affirmations may be, they do not even approach the question of how the divine and the human can be and are related (much less united) in Jesus. Their silence in this regard left fertile ground for controversy as the second century unfolded and the Greek mind hungered for some answers.

Justin Martyr, writing in defense of the Christian faith (135), stands among the first theologians to press the question, drawing upon the perspectives of Greek philosophy. For Justin, Jesus was truly the Word (*Logos*) become flesh (Jn. 1:14). But what is the nature of the *Logos?* Employing Platonic and Stoic thought, Justin understands the *Logos* as Reason, as a principle of order, intrinsic to the universe. The Stoic notion of a "first principle of order, intrinsic to the universe" makes good sense. We too might readily observe: The flowers "know" exactly when to bloom, how to produce seed, how to find nourishment. How do they "know?" We might respond: "It is their nature," meaning "They have an inner source of direction prompting meaningful movement, a principle of order within them." Further, we might observe that bees "know" how to find flowers, how to extract nectar, how to find their way back to their hive, how to produce honey. How do they "know?" Finally, we might recognize that planets "know" how to revolve around the sun without colliding with one another or collapsing in upon the sun. The earth "knows" to remain tilted so as to create predictable seasons. How does it know to do this? And, putting all this together, how do plants, bees, earth and its seasons understand one another, know how to work in harmony, in good order, together. How does the universe know how to create this good order? The Stoic response was: There is an "intrinsic principle," a governing mechanism, within the center of the universe, a principle which orders (organizes) the entire universe so that all its members act in harmony. This principle was established, created, at the very beginning of creation. The Greek name for this principle was *Logos,* Reason.

We should note two things which become apparent from this analysis: First, it makes eminent sense in itself. There is an observable order in the universe, reflecting an overriding principle of unity resting at its center. Second, the term which the Stoics used to express this ultimate of created principles was the same term which the fourth Evangelist used to denote a very different reality. For, in speaking of the *Logos,* the author of the fourth Gospel wished to build upon Semitic thought and to refer to God's eternal Wisdom.

Thus, for the Johannine author, *Logos* means God's creative Wisdom, an aspect of God's creative action in the world, a Wisdom remaining within God's very Self. Because of the divergent ways in which Justin and the fourth Evangelist understood this term, Justin's writing set in motion a lengthy and at times a bitter controversy. And the fact that the New Testament itself, taken as a whole, offered diverse ways of understanding the nature of the divine power in Jesus, provided freedom for such controversy to flourish.

In a similar vein, but in the earlier quarter of the third century, Origen, head of the catechetical school in Alexandria (Egypt), offered his understanding of the nature of the *Logos*. Devoted to Scripture and imbued with the traditions of Greek philosophy, this theologian taught that God truly begot the *Logos,* God's own Wisdom, eternally and that this Wisdom is the complete expression of God's own being. Yet, for Origen, the *Logos* was not God's own Self, but God's image, subordinate to the Father, a "second level God."[11] The soul of Jesus, contemplating and embracing this Wisdom, became one with it and hence became capable of mediating God's saving Wisdom to the world.

The Christian understanding of the *Logos,* during the second and third centuries, however, cannot be reduced to the viewpoints of Justin and Origen. Irenaeus, bishop of Lyon, found himself uncomfortable with the teaching of Justin (which teaching he knew), largely because he felt that God did not need an intermediary between God's Self and the world in order to accomplish redemption. Toward the year 185, Irenaeus explicitly defended the "fullness of the divinity of the *Logos,*" maintaining that the *Logos* becomes Mediator in the very action of its assuming a human nature in Jesus of Nazareth, rather than by being a "distinct middle reality" between God and humankind. Of course, this teaching posited some level of distinction within God, a distinction which Greek philosophy in general, and both Justin and Origen, in particular, could not accept.[12]

Another theologian, a Latin-speaking North African following the Roman legal tradition, lent further support to the perspectives of Irenaeus. Writing at the outset of the third century, Tertullian was able to maintain that the *Logos* was fully divine without dividing God into separate beings. Tertullian insisted that God is absolutely one and indivisible in nature, but that this one God is threefold in the way in which God expresses God's Self. Hence, for Tertullian, the *Logos* could be both distinct from the Father and yet truly one with the Father, God remaining one indivisible (though not indistinguishable) reality.

This brief survey, then, describing the movements within the controversy concerning the nature of the divine power within Jesus indicates that much more than a discussion of Jesus was at stake. On the one hand, theologians were deeply concerned to understand and to explain the depths of the reality of the salvation experience accomplished for us in and through Jesus. Hence they sought to avoid any minimalization of the nature of the divine power in Christ. On the other hand, theologians wished to protect the transcendence, the absolute unity and the uniqueness of the one true God. And so, they avoided any semblance of introducing multiplicity into the realm of the divine Being. In the last analysis, what becomes apparent is that neither human understanding nor human language, neither that of the Semite nor that of the Greek, had reached the point of maturity and refinement that would enable Christians adequately to express the profundity of the saving reality which God had revealed and communicated in Jesus. Only through controversy and struggle, through conciliar decision and further linguistic refinement, were theologians able to craft adequate terminology and fuller understanding of the mystery of salvation in Christ. The Church took its first decisive step in this long journey early in the fourth century at the Council of Nicea.

THE DEFINITION OF NICEA (325): ITS CONTEXT AND THE TERMS
The controversy over the divinity of the *Logos* reached a head in the fourth century with the teaching of Arius, a presbyter of Alexandria. Convinced of the validity of Greek philosophy as the way of interpreting Christian faith and beliefs, Arius held firm to the Hellenic postulate concerning divine transcendence: God's being must be absolutely one; God's transcendence renders it impossible for God to have any contact or relationship with the created world. Therefore, the *Logos* cannot be God in the proper sense of the term;

the *Logos* can be mediator only in the sense of being a "secondary"[13] or "subordinate" member of the divine realm. He is *first in the order of creation*, the *firstborn of creation*,[14] superior to everything created, God's agent in creation, but not God. He is divine, but only in a secondary sense. The implication was that this *Logos* had assumed flesh in Jesus, making Jesus "Son of God" in an exalted (but not fully divine) sense.

While Arius' reserve might be understandable, his teaching had serious consequences, not only with regard to the Christian beliefs concerning Christ, but also with regard to beliefs concerning salvation. If Arius were correct, then we would have to acknowledge that in Jesus, we would not truly encounter God, nor would we experience unconditional salvation in the Lord. For, in Arius' view, the *Logos,* and therefore the Christ assumed by the *Logos,* would not make present, or mediate, God's Self. Humankind might receive good example through him, but it would not receive the energy of God's own life, nor would it be reconciled with God in God's Self. It is this profound soteriological concern, stemming from its deep faith-experience, which moved the majority of Church leaders to oppose Arius' teaching.

Imbued with these soteriological concerns, a deacon (later to be bishop) of Alexandria, Athanasius, opposed Arius. Athanasius believed that if Christ were not truly God, we would not be redeemed, for only the immortal God could redeem us from our subjection to death, only the God of limitless love could heal us from our inclinations to selfishness and sin, only the eternal God could give us a share in everlasting life. Christians, in and through Jesus, experience salvation precisely in this form. Therefore the *Logos,* in taking flesh in Jesus, necessarily both reveals and communicates God's very Self to humankind.

In order to secure this perspective, the Church leaders gathered at Nicea (located in modern Turkey), condemned the teaching of Arius, and affirmed their conviction that the *Logos* was "one in being with the Father," a statement of belief which later was incorporated into the Eucharistic Liturgy. The formula, of course, was articulated in Greek and the decisive word, here translated by the words "one in being" was *homoousios.* Several literal translations of this word could be forged: "same fundamental nature," "same substance," "same being," "same basic reality."[15] In its literal meaning and abstractness, it unequivocally indicated that whatever the Father is, the Son is; they are absolutely equal, one God. In the background stood the conviction that the *Logos* took flesh in Jesus; in Jesus, therefore, one encountered God.

THE TEACHING OF NICEA: FURTHER IMPLICATIONS AND LIMITS
The most obvious, and the central, focus of the solemn creedal definition of Nicea concerning the *Logos,* then, is no more nor less than stated above: The *Logos* is fully divine, equal to the Father, the same true God as the Father is God. The *Logos* and the Father are "one in being," or "of the same substance," with the necessary result that, in Jesus, one meets God's very Self. Put negatively, the Council formally refused to accept any suggestion that the *Logos* was created, no matter how exalted a creature the *Logos* might be. Thus, it settled the question of the nature of the divine power in Jesus. Jesus expressed and mediated the power, life, and love of God's very Self.

But how shall we understand "divinity," "the divine nature?" How describe this divine Being whom Jesus makes present and mediates? And more pointedly, what does it mean to say that Jesus is divine? The Council, in its carefully crafted statement, did not define, or describe, the divine nature. Neither did it engage in a discussion of precisely how that nature, how the *Logos,* related to Jesus of Nazareth. It answered neither of these questions.

In the background of the discussion, however, lay the breadth of the Hellenistic thought about God. Greek philosophy, as we noted above, understood God to be infinite (non-finite, not limited in anyway), changeless (immutable) and eternal (meaning non-temporal), uninvolved and unrelated to the world, unbegotten and without origin in God's very Self. This philosophy captured the utter difference between God and creatures, first, by mentally negating change and movement (and therefore relationship to time) and then, by attributing the resultant abstract concepts to God, a process known as theology *by way of negation.*

The Council did not endorse this perspective. What the Council did do, however, through its use to the word *homoousios,* was formally to introduce non-biblical, Hellenistic, terminology into official Christian theology and into solemn Christian statements of belief. Thereby, it gave a least indirect recognition to a Hellenic (metaphysical) way of thinking and left a door open for the Greek philosophical understanding of God to enter Christian theology.

How did the Council understand the nature of God? Its understanding is best captured by the context of its solemn use of the Greek term *homoousios,* a context which consists of a series of biblically and ecclesiastically grounded phrases bringing forward its tradition of beliefs in God principally as author of salvation history.[16] The context is one, not of Greek thinking, but of an historical biblical way of thinking about God. God is understood as One who is "always present to save" (Ex. 3:14), merciful, benevolent, just, and forgiving; ultimately, "God is Love" (I John 4:8). The difference between God and humankind is captured, not by way of a theology of negation, but by predicating *positive and dynamic qualities* of God, qualities found in a limited manner among human beings, but predicated of God superlatively. Thus, while humans love sometimes, or even most of the time, God is always and supremely loving. While humans forgive some persons and some misdeeds, but at least occasionally withhold forgiveness, God forgives all persons, again and again, no matter what the sin (Mk. 3:28; Lk. 12:10) for "God's mercy endures forever" (Ps. 136). While people make promises, even contracts, but at times fail to follow through, God is always faithful to his Word, to his promises, to his covenant with God's people. The eternity of God does not consist in a static, non-involved changelessness, but rather in a never-failing fidelity, an everlasting disposition of active mercy and forgiveness, an abiding and unconquerable attitude of love for all people of every age.[17] Christian faith, the biblical understanding of God, the mind of the Council itself, remained antithetical to much of the Greek philosophical way of thinking about God. The Council's definition meant that the *Logos* was God in the sense that Old and New Testaments describe God: the ever-active and dependable transcendent God who saves from every evil because that God is enduring love.

It should be noted that only the latter, the biblical way of thinking about God is compatible with the Christian belief that the Word became flesh in Jesus. For the divinity of the *Logos* emerges in Jesus, not in leading Jesus to be changeless, manifesting a type of "non-involved, static perfection." Rather, the divinity of the *Logos* provides Jesus with a depth and centeredness rendering him capable of unsurpassed faithfulness, mercy, and love, so that his love, his human love, like God's love, never fails. The Council fully recognizes the depth of Jesus' capacities to walk his human journey and to fulfill his God-given mission by defining that the divine power within him, the *Logos,* is truly God in God's truest, most faithful, and most loving Self.

The Council of Nicea, then, clarified and advanced the Christian understanding of the *Logos,* of the nature of the divine power in Jesus, and of the transcendent depth of salvation mediated by the crucified and risen Lord. Even in the midst of the diversity of New Testament perspectives concerning the nature of this divine power in Jesus, Christians had come to affirm that, in encountering Jesus of Nazareth they encountered none less than the transcendent, ever-active, saving, and loving God. The struggle with Hellenistic thinking and questioning had yielded undeniable fruit.

On the other hand, the Council did not resolve all questions about Jesus, nor about the *Logos.* It did not give answer to how the *Logos* could and actually did relate to Jesus of Nazareth. Nor did it explain how the *Logos* could be "one in being" or "the same substance" with the Father and yet be distinct from the Father, as Christian Tradition also affirmed. Rather, it took a first step toward clarifying and further processing the Christian faith experience of God, and more particularly of God alive in and through Jesus. As a result, it required further reflection and fuller precision. And so the door remained open for further struggle and continued controversy, as the Christian community continued its efforts to be faithful to God's saving gift in Jesus in new culture and a new age.

Jesus' Integral Humanity:
Its Affirmation and Salvific Import

Surprising as it may be, the post-apostolic Christian Community struggled, not only with regard to understanding the nature of the divine power in Jesus, but also with regard to its appreciation of the integrity of his humanity, his being "one who has similarly been tested in every way, yet without sin" (Heb. 4:15). Distance from the historical Jesus, together with a focus upon the living presence of the glorified risen Lord, served to cloud the believer's sense of Jesus' full humanity. Further, the heretical perspectives of a number of Gnostic sects which regarded all matter as evil, prompted some to question the reality of Jesus' flesh,[18] for how could God immerse the divine Self in evil? This position, like that which denied the full divinity of the *Logos,* imperilled the truth of the Church's experience of salvation in and through Jesus. Hence, the integrity of Christ's humanity needed careful clarification and exposition.

This section of our inquiry will trace this second aspect of the Church's struggle to understand fully and accurately, in a Hellenic context, the nature of Jesus, Mediator of universal salvation. In doing so, we will first note the various strains of controversy concerning the fullness of Jesus' humanity prior to its emergence as an issue warranting a conciliar decision. Next, we will present the terms of the controversy and its definitive resolution at the first Council of Constantinople in 381. Finally, we will offer several reflections concerning the saving import of the Church's recognition of Jesus' integral humanity.

Jesus' Humanity: Early Confusion and Doubts
Clearly, for the original disciples, the humanity of Jesus was never a question. People regarded Jesus as "the carpenter's son," "the man born of Mary." The perplexing question was rather: "Where does he get his Wisdom?" "How does he work such wonders?"

For early post-apostolic writers, Jesus' humanity was not a question either. Clement of Rome, writing in approximately the year 96, spoke of Jesus in his humanness as descendant of Jacob (1 Clem. 32:2), while Ignatius of Antioch easily referred to Christ as one of David's lineage, son of Mary, one who had eaten, drunk and suffered before God raised him from the dead.[19]

A number of later second century leaders, however, espousing heretical Gnostic principles, thought that the suggestion that God took on flesh implied that God had united God's Self with evil. Thus Marcion of Pontus, and others categorized as "Docetists,"[20] regarded Jesus' humanity as mere appearance, not real. For them, redemption and the role of Jesus consisted in extricating the spiritual, non-material, dimension of men and women from the material world in which it was supposedly trapped. It was in this context that Irenaeus of Lyons wrote his work known by the generic title *Adversus Haereses (Against Heresies)*, in which he strongly defended the full humanity of Jesus.[21] And shortly thereafter, Tertullian also rebuffed Marcion and the Gnostics in general, insisting that the flesh is an object of God's love.[22]

The question of the integral humanity of Jesus, however, soon became threatened from another direction, particularly in the Eastern Church. Eastern theologians began denying, not the flesh or body of Christ, but the reality of Christ's human soul. And, once again, it was culture and terminology which paved the way for misunderstanding.

The Greek word *sarx* (literally: "flesh"), *as it was used in the New Testament* denoted "the whole person," "body and soul," "mind, heart, flesh and bone." Such was the understanding of the fourth Evangelist when he wrote that the Word (*Logos)* became flesh (*sarx)*. Such also was Paul's understanding when he used the antithesis, "flesh-spirit," not to denote a distinction between body and soul, but to distinguish between the whole person, first as unredeemed (weak, "in the flesh") but now redeemed (strong, "in the spirit").[23] For the Greek mind, however, *sarx* meant *body* (materiality), precisely distinguished from *psyche* (soul) or *nous* (mind), the non-material, spiritual dimension(s) of each human. Hence, for the Greek mind, the affirmation that the Word genuinely had become flesh left open the question of whether or not that Word had assumed a human soul. And so, for these thinkers, the reality of Jesus' human soul was not certain.

Arius himself was one of the thinkers who had denied that Jesus had a human soul, having maintained that the *Logos* itself had taken the place of Christ's human soul. This element of his teaching, however, had remained in the background at the Council of Nicea, for both the Council fathers as a whole, and Athanasius in particular, had focused principally upon Arius' denial of the divinity of the *Logos*. Thus, they left Arius' perspective concerning the humanity of Jesus free to flourish. Such was the case until Apollinaris of Laodicea, a disciple and friend of Athanasius, advanced this teaching, making it a focal point of dispute within the wider Church.

Constantinople I (381): Debate and Decision

Apollinaris took seriously the teaching of Nicea and the work of Athanasius. Yet he wished to address the unanswered question: How is the *Logos* related to Jesus of Nazareth? If the relationship were merely extrinsic, leaving the *Logos* and Jesus to be two distinct beings, Jesus would be merely human as we are, and our salvation would not be assured. Apollinaris, therefore, sought to discover a way in which he could demonstrate that the *Logos* and Jesus were intrinsically united. The Greek philosophical distinction between the human soul and body and the unchallenged teaching of Arius with regard to Christ's humanity opened the way for Apollinaris. In his way of thinking, the *Logos* took the place of the soul of Jesus. Thus, Apollinaris sponsored what has become know as a *Logos-sarx* Christology, a Christology already suggested in the writings of Athanasius and supported by the theologians of Alexandria.

But Apollinaris, wishing to uphold Jesus' likeness to us as fully as possible, made a further distinction. Borrowing from Platonic philosophy, he envisioned human being not merely composed of the dichotomy of body-soul, but rather of a trichotomy of material body, sensual soul *(psyche)* and mind soul *(nous)*. The *Logos,* in Apollinaris' later teaching, replaced only the mind soul of Jesus. With this understanding, the theologian judged, not only that he had explained the union of the divine *Logos* with Jesus of Nazareth, but also that he had secured the sinlessness of Jesus. The *Logos,* being God's Wisdom itself, perfectly attuned with *Abba* as transcendent love, became the sole principle of understanding, judging, choosing, and acting in Jesus. Thus, Jesus necessarily acted in accord with God's will; he could not sin.

The Christian churches of the East, however, also knew a contrasting view of Jesus' humanity. The theologians of the Church at Antioch taught that the eternal Word had assumed an entire human nature, body and soul, sensual and intellectual, in Christ. This view later theologians classified as a *Logos-Anthropos* (Word-Human or Word-Man) Christology. The champion of this position, Theodore, a monk in Antioch and later bishop of Mopsuetia in Cilicia, taught clearly that are two distinct natures in Christ: Jesus lived among us as fully human and fully divine.

The Antiochene theologian described the union of the two natures in terms of a divine indwelling, much as God had dwelt with the prophets, apostles, and saints, and continues to dwell in all good-living Christians.[24] To underscore the uniqueness of Jesus, he maintained that the indwelling of the *Logos* in Christ was a special kind of indwelling. In Jesus, God dwells "as in a Son." By indwelling "as in a Son," Theodore means that the *Logos* united himself to the humanity of Jesus "as a whole...and equipped him to share with himself in all the honor which he, being Son by nature, participates so as to be counted one person in virtue of the union with him and to share with him all his dominion, and in this way to accomplish everything in him...."[25]

In speaking in this manner, Theodore clearly affirmed the integral humanity of Jesus as well as the fullness of the divinity of the *Logos*. He did not, however, so tightly secure the union between the two natures in Jesus as Apollinaris and the school of Alexandria might have wished. Some of his contemporaries, therefore, would have interpreted Theodore as implying that there were two distinct subjects in Jesus.

With the distinctive positions of Apollinaris, on the one hand, and Theodore, on the other, the terms of the christological struggle were clear. The fact that Apollinaris found himself teaching in Antioch during the last quarter of the fourth century, in the midst of the opposing school, fanned the dispute into open conflict. The turmoil necessitated the convocation of another universal council, the first at Constantinople, in 381.

The focus of the theologians gathered in Constantinople, how-ever, did not center upon the two diverse ways in which Apollinaris and Theodore had understood and explained the relationship of the *Logos* to Jesus of Nazareth. Rather, the leading figures at the Council, like their predecessors at Nicea, remained principally concerned with upholding the truth and reality of Christian salvation. They firmly believed, from their and the Church's faith-experience, that in Christ, God had granted to human beings the gift of divine life. But, if Christ were not fully human, then the gift established by the Incarnation of the *Logos* and fulfilled through Christ's journey through death to the resurrection, would not have been given truly to them, to human beings. Rather, that gift would have been given to a creature radically different from them, one who would not have known the struggles which confront the human mind and human will. However one might wish to describe Jesus, and however he may have been sanctified by his union with the *Logos*, he would not be a sign, a true expression, of the fact that God wished to fill humans with God's life-giving presence. And whatever the Church experienced in faith in its worship and in its life, it would not be the definitive gift of God's Self precisely as given to humankind. In short, the human community would not have been redeemed.

To underscore their logic, and to solidify their conviction, the fathers of the Council adopted a principle which Gregory of Nazian-zen had formulated earlier in his effort to refute Apollinaris: "*What is not assumed, is not redeemed; what is united with God is also saved.*"[26] The principle reflected an earlier axiom, crafted by Ori-gen: "*The whole man would not have been saved if HE (the Logos) had not assumed the whole man.*"[27] If the *Logos* had not assumed a human mind and human will, God would not have embraced these human powers; they would not be healed of darkness, weakness, sinful inclination. Thus, for the fathers, it was necessary to affirm that the *Logos did assume* an integral human nature. Therefore, in Christ, the fullness of what is human has been united with God. It is we, in all that we are, who have been truly and fully redeemed. To secure this understanding, however, the Council crafted no new formula. Rather, in addition to condemning the teaching of Apollinaris, it corrected an ambiguity in the Nicene creedal formula, dropping the troublesome phrase "born from the being of the Father,"[28] a phrase which could not but have opened the door to doubt, or even denial, concerning the fullness of Jesus humanity.[29]

THE CONCILIAR DECISION: SALVIFIC VALUE AND LIMITS

The salvific importance of the affirmation of Christ's full humanity, endorsed by the fathers at Constantinople I, should not be underestimated. Just as the integral humanity of Jesus had been questioned prior to the Council, so also, Christian Communities in subsequent ages have ignored or disregarded Jesus' humanity in practical piety, if not also denying aspects of his humanity in formal teaching. Walter Kasper clearly brings out the fact that forgetfulness of Jesus' humanity has led Christians to place Christ on a pedestal in such a way that he no longer could serve persons as a true model and leader. Ignoring the fullness of Jesus' humanity, these Christians could not find in him a genuine companion, one who could show them the possibility of successfully negotiating the temptations and pitfalls which challenge Christians in their own struggle to embrace God's reign.[30]

While not answering every question concerning Jesus, the first Council of Constantinople assures us that we, in the entirety of our humanity, like Jesus, in the entirety of his humanity, have been embraced by God. Hence, we can find God in the depth of whatever is human, in the breadth of our every human experience. Nothing of our life's experience escapes the possibility of redemption; God's saving presence and saving love touch every facet of our being and our lives.

Reflection upon the journey of the historical Jesus will serve to illustrate concretely the truth and the significance of these statements. First, as all the evangelists remember, Jesus moved through life *seeking* God and God's designs. God's ways were not always immediately evident to him. Thus, he prays, he searches for God's will, he makes decisions, and he revises them. The temptation accounts of Matthew and Luke serve as one moment, a paradigmatic moment, of Jesus' life which, like ours, was characterized by frequent struggle with ungodly suggestions and desires which threatened his perseverance in the way of Godly love. It was through genuine human search and struggle that God's light and love "took flesh" in Jesus. So, we can be assured that God's light and love can and will visit us in similar struggles as we walk through our lives with him.

Second, Jesus' human efforts to establish and maintain healthy and fruitful relationships with men and women also show that he knew and negotiated difficult human trials. Jesus was hardly a man devoid of human feelings -- joyful and sorrowful, promising and disappointing -- as he sought to build life-giving relationships with very real, sometimes complex, people. His relationship with Peter stands as a prime example. As he called, counseled, and entrusted himself to Peter, he found Peter to be a man of mixed responses. Though basically loyal, Peter also was, at times, obtuse (at the lakeside in Caesarea Philippi [Mk. 8:27-31]), fearfully weak (before the maid-servant at Jesus' trial [Mk. 14:66-72]), yet repentantly loving. Jesus met Peter in all these circumstances, knowing in himself the many human urgings of hurt, anger, disappointment, renewed hope, and, ultimately, joy.

Other examples also run through the Gospels. Jesus found surprise and joy at the faith of the Roman centurion (Mt. 8:10); he knew disappointment as the so-called "rich young man," a man whom Mark tells us Jesus looked on with love, turned away (Mk. 10:17-27). He felt an oppressive darkness, impenetrable as a brick wall, close in on him as Judas resolutely moved to betray him (Mt. 26:20-25, 47-50; Jn. 13:21-30); yet he enjoyed, and even found him-self nourished by, the reciprocal love and affection he shared with Mary, Martha, and their brother Lazarus (Lk. 10:38-42; Jn. 11:1-5).

Through all these examples, it becomes clear that Jesus knew the wonder and joy of human love. But with that, he also knew the pain which that love can bring. He wept at the tomb of Lazarus, and shed tears while looking over Jerusalem, the city representing the people whom he loved. Jesus knew fear and anxiety, struggle and

darkness, as he approached and then experienced the cross –
humiliated, abandoned, his dignity and his life stolen from him. No
one could be more human than Jesus; no one faced the challenges
and complexities of the human journey, no one negotiated the
struggle to be faithful to the call of human love more than Jesus.

In each moment of that historical, fully human journey, however, Jesus found light, wisdom, constant fidelity and saving love from
Abba given to him. In no circumstance of life did Jesus, in his
human striving, not have life-giving access to *Abba*. God embraced
him in the entirety of his humanity. Absolutely no dimension of his
human life remained outside of the touch of God. What contem-
plation upon the humanity of Jesus, in all its concreteness, teaches
us, then, is that there is no circumstance, no moment of exhilaration
or joy, no struggle, hurt or experience of pain, no hour of darkness
or moment of human weakness, in which God cannot be found.

The leaders at the First Council of Constantinople clearly wished to reaffirm and to support this fundamental truth of salvation.
Their decision in favor of the integrity of Jesus' humanity proved
vital in this effort. Even further, their affirmation of Jesus' "mind-
soul" served as a pivotal element with this overall effort. For the
character and the intensity both of human feeling and also of human
responsiveness flow from an individual's *concrete perceptions* of
the persons and events which he or she encounters, as well as from
the *system of meanings and images* by which that individual
interprets these perceptions. And so the Church's refusal to accept
the views of Apollinaris safeguards the very heart of a human
being's capacity to receive the gift of salvation. For the transformation of human life and action comes about only through an expansion, a deepening and alteration, of the system of meanings and
images by which an individual interprets his or her experiences. It
is through fuller understanding, deeper insight, more balanced and
more far-reaching appreciation, that feelings change, doors open,
capacities for a fuller and more mature response awaken, and a
deeper spiritual vision and richer active way of life take hold of a
person. But such understanding, insight and appreciation take place
in, and constitute the work of, the human mind. Thus, the human
"mind-soul" is the gateway for the transformation of the whole of

the human person. It is the gateway for God's breaking into the life of human beings, imparting divine light, wisdom and the energy of divine love to the whole man or women. If Jesus did not have a human "mind-soul," then God and God's *Logos* would not have been able to affect, transform and divinize Jesus at all. His conscious freedom, his human way of life before God and others, would have been untouched by God. Clearly, he would not have been truly human, and human beings would not have been redeemed with him or through him.[31]

The import of these reflections for the life and salvation of each Christian, then, is clear. The affirmation that Jesus possessed a genuinely human "mind-soul" immediately implies that all human beings can grow to understand and to appreciate life, human life, God's life for and within them, in ever more profound ways. As a consequence, they can respond to their concrete historical lives with a love which is both human and God-given. Further, there is no dimension of any Christian's life, no situation or circumstance that any human being does or will face that God cannot or will not visit with truly redeeming and life-giving wisdom and love. For, Jesus' life shows us that we can and will meet the saving love of *Abba* precisely by being open to and by seeking that love with Christ. Like Jesus, we are human and for us, as for Jesus, the fullness of what is possible for us human beings, in God, will open up and become a new, fulfilling way of life.[32] Jesus reveals, not only who and what the true God is; Jesus reveals what it is to be truly human, persons remaining their authentic selves as they are lifted up by God's redeeming love.

Thus, the first Council at Constantinople provided a second milestone in the Church's journey toward a fuller and more adequate understanding both of Christ and also of Christian salvation as it expanded in a Hellenic culture. Just as the *Logos* had been affirmed (at Nicea) as consubstantial, one in nature, with the Father, so Jesus was affirmed as consubstantial, one in nature, with us. Nevertheless, the Council did not clarify, nor even address, other questions lingering in the wake of Nicea. It did not entertain the questions of how the *Logos* was actually related to the humanity of Jesus, to him who was born of Mary. Both Apollinaris and

Theodore, both the Alexandrian and the Antiochene schools, had broached the question. But the need to affirm the integral humanity of Jesus had so occupied the Council and was so clearly a priority, that it absorbed all of the Council's attention. The question of the unity of Christ, the relationship of the two natures, the relationship of the *Logos* to the humanity of Jesus, remained undefined for decades to come. The next chapter will trace the resolution of this question and others which followed. But before moving into that discussion, we will pause to make a few observations concerning the implications which the Church's expanded understanding of Christ and especially its expanded statements of belief have for doing Christology.

Doing of Christology and the Earliest Councils

Our efforts to appreciate Christology during the early stages of the classical period have led us to ask questions concerning salvation which have had a different "flavor" from the questions asked during the apostolic period. The former are more abstract, more precisely defined, more analytical, though they are less likely to inspire, at least in their immediate resolution.

Our efforts in this chapter, however, can and should offer us more than simply a deeper understanding of Jesus. These efforts also should enable us to appreciate even more fully the nature and the task of doing Christology itself. For, what we have traced in this chapter, surveying the Church's struggle rightly to understand and to proclaim Jesus over a period of nearly three hundred years, is in fact the tracing of the Church-in-process, in the process of living, expressing, and coming more fully to possess its own experience of faith in the saving God and in God's Christ. We have observed the Church grappling with its understanding of Jesus and of the salvation which it experienced in and through him, *precisely as it struggled to be faithful*, both to that foundational experience of the in-breaking of God, alive for it in and through the crucified and risen One, and also to itself as a human community with its own language, culture, needs, and struggles.

And so the development of classical Christology clearly illustrates that all Christology is in fact, and must be by its very nature, historically situated and historically conditioned. Christology is a living process through which the Church, always an historical community of historical persons, seeks to meet the saving God in Jesus once again, in the particularity and the concrete demands of its own setting. Without engaging in this task, the Church, its faith, and its beliefs would die. The advent of classical Christology, perhaps even more than the development of the diversity within the Christologies of the four Gospel Communities, shows how fully the life of faith, communion in grace with the crucified and risen Jesus, must permeate the human, including the human diversity of varied cultures and ages. To do so, it will always challenge the believer with new questions and invite him or her, together with the entire Christian community and its leaders, to search for and to find new ways of expressing its beliefs. These new ways will remain continuous with the past but must be formulated differently so as clearly to respond to the manner in which persons of faith experience God, in Christ, in the midst of challenges not foreseen in a previous era.

The study of the development of the Church's Tradition as reflected upon in this chapter also has relevance for the doing of Christology from another point of view. The Tradition established in the first centuries of the post-apostolic Church constitutes a significant dimension of every believer's understanding of Christ, even as he or she seeks and discovers God today. But in the contemporary Church, the teaching of the early post-apostolic Community needs also to be rightly understood. It is important that the development be appreciated as much for what the fathers did not wish to affirm as it is to appreciate what they did in fact affirm. Failure to understand and appreciate this has led many to falsify the Tradition, claiming the Councils included in their definitions further unarticulated positions and understandings which, in fact, the Councils deliberately avoided. Such a failure only makes it more difficult for uninformed Christians to recognize the God and the Christ, whom they do know in their hearts, in the Christian beliefs so inaccurately but nevertheless so forcefully stated.

A final benefit flowing from the study of the Christology of the classical period (as articulated both in the present and in the following chapters), emerges from the fact that often the very questions asked by a previous generation, indeed by a previous era, are present-day questions also. For every age shares the common element of one humanity, bearing with it similar radical needs, questions, and struggles. All ages wish to understand God and to make sense of God's mysterious but elusive presence. Every age wishes to locate and to identify what is truly of God in the human experience of the divine. And every age seeks to appreciate how God and human beings can be genuine partners in the human journey, how they can be truly one, and yet remain distinct. The questions of the divine power in Jesus, of the divinity of God's *Logos*, of the truth and the integrity of Jesus' humanity are our questions, too. We may not have come to the final answer to these questions, but we must ask them. We may not find the answers of the second-through the fourth-century Church easy to grasp ourselves, but by understanding the language, the process, the contexts and concerns, ultimately the historical intent behind these responses, we can at least avoid the pitfalls which that Church negotiated as we ourselves pursue a fuller understanding. Indeed, the doing of Christology in the classical idiom is necessary and fruitful for any believer who wishes to have a relevant understanding and an energizing appreciation of the God who remains alive for us in and through Christ Jesus, the crucified and risen Lord, leading Christian people to fuller life in the struggles of today.

But how shall we speak of Jesus, not only crucified and risen, not only divine and human, but as a living glorified person, eternally begotten yet fashioned through interaction with a this-worldly history? What did his divinity mean for his human becoming? How did his divinity affect his understanding of reality, his consciousness of his very self, his freedom and his genuinely human love? In short, how are the divinity (the divine *Logos*) and the humanity of Jesus related? And what does that relationship mean for Christ's work of being Mediator of salvation, indeed for the very salvation and the reign of God which we experience? It is to these questions which we must finally turn.

Before doing so, we invite the reader to reflect upon and, hopefully to discuss with other believers, the following questions.

Questions for Reflection

1. Having read this chapter, how have you come better to understand the differences (as well as the similarities) between classical Christology and biblical Christology? How would you express these differences and similarities?

2. How has the unfolding of the historical context leading up to each conciliar statement enabled you better to appreciate precisely what each Council intended to affirm and what it did not affirm? What other historical circumstances surrounding the Councils would you be aware of which would further illuminate the precise teaching of these Councils? Explain.

3. Having read this chapter, how would you express your understanding of the nature of the "divine power" in Jesus? the nature of the Logos? the nature of God and of transcendent divinity Itself?

4. How would you explain why Christ's divinity, and the affirmation of the Council of Nicea, is absolutely necessary for our salvation? Have you, or anyone you have known in the past, found it difficult to affirm the fullness of Christ's divinity? Why has that been so? Has the discussion of the Counciliar teaching at Nicea alleviated this difficulty in any manner?

5. What historical perspectives and/or concerns have led believers of the second through the fourth centuries to question the full humanity of Jesus? What presuppositions and/or prior (erroneous) convictions lay behind those concerns? In what way(s) has this presentation of these concerns and presuppositions helped you come better to understand God, Christ and Christian salvation? Explain.

6. Having read this chapter, how would you understand the importance of the full humanity of Jesus for our salvation? Have you, or anyone you have known found it difficult to affirm that Jesus was human as we are? What would have led you or persons whom you have known to question the fullness of Jesus' humanity? Does the material treated in this chapter clarify this question?

CHAPTER 10

Understanding Jesus: One Person Uniting Eternity and Time

The Christian Community, in its quest for a more exact understanding of Jesus and a more precise appreciation of the salvation experienced in and through him, weathered a series of considerable storms from the second through the fourth centuries. Nevertheless, the turmoil it experienced served to deepen its understanding of the Lord whom it knew as its crucified and risen Savior. As a result of wrestling with controversy, Christian believers clearly recognized that God had communicated God's very Self to Jesus and to them in God's *Logos*, and therefore, that Jesus made present to his followers no One less than the living God in the fullness of God's being and love. They also recognized that Jesus, empowered by the *Logos*, was no less human than his disciples themselves, human beings consisting of body and soul, of mind, heart, feeling and will. Hence all believers could be assured that in Jesus they encountered God's Self and that in Jesus they had a companion who walked the human journey just as they walked it. In and through Jesus, the wonder of God's life was forever given to all, penetrating and transforming human life with God's own powerful presence and love.

And yet, this deepened understanding which the Church had achieved was not deep enough. Questions and confusion continued to plague the most earnest believer, the most brilliant Church leader. How describe this union of God and human being in Jesus? Does the *Logos* stand next to Jesus, acting upon him as we might act upon one-another? Does the *Logos* "dwell" in Christ as in a person who already had an independent existence? Or is the *Logos* so deeply one with the child of Mary that that *Logos* becomes the very center of the living historical Jesus, the undivided source of Jesus' entire human life and human activity? But if the latter be true, could it really be said (as the Church already had said) that Jesus is human as we are, that his understanding is truly a human understanding, and that his loving is truly human loving?

Thus, in spite of the progress which Christians had made in understanding Christ and salvation, the issues faced by the Church of the fifth century and beyond were no less perplexing than those which the second-through the fourth-century Church had faced. As a matter of fact, the questions became more refined and more difficult to resolve as time advanced. For it is one thing to affirm, at separate moments, both the divinity and the humanity of Jesus, but quite another thing to attempt to understand and to explain precisely how the divinity and the humanity of Jesus (what became known as the "two natures") are interrelated.[1]

This final chapter will seek to describe the efforts of the Church to answer the question of the relationship of the divine and the human in Jesus. It will do so in two stages. First, it will trace the development of the Church's appreciation of the unity of the two natures in one person in Jesus, giving due attention to the precise meaning of those terms and the intention of the Councils which crafted them. Second, it will seek to explore and to give an intelligent account of the manner in which this unity affected Jesus' understanding and freedom, his "historical becoming" so to speak, as he journeyed through his earthly life. Both stages of reflection should serve to make clear that Jesus truly is one Person uniting eternity and time, one Person who, having so united eternity and time, stands before us as the model, the prime example, of what God destines each believer to become and in fact, is empowering us to be. For, as always, the reflections of the Church upon Jesus found their origin in the Church's experience of the salvation it has received in and through him. And so, such reflections gave firmness and fuller appreciation to what she had already received in the new life which Jesus manifested and mediated to all. In this light, the chapter will include a third and final section, a series of reflections upon the relevance of this material for the overall task of doing Christology.

Jesus: One Person in Two Natures

The struggle of the Christian Community in seeking to understand the interrelationship of the divine and the human in Jesus has a history as lengthy as Christian Tradition itself. New Testament questions such as "Where did he get such Wisdom?" uttered by so many of the witnesses of Jesus and the Lucan motif "The Spirit of the Lord is upon me; to preach Good News to the poor he has sent me!" (4:18), placed on the lips of the historical Jesus himself reflect some of the early interest in and efforts toward the resolution of this issue. In the classical period, after the Church had defined the divinity of the *Logos* and the humanity of Jesus in precise Hellenistic philosophical categories, the issue became more clearly and explicitly formulated. Given the two natures within Jesus, can and should he be understood to be one person (one acting subject) who exists and acts in accord with the two natures? Or, is Jesus, in fact, constituted of two independent but interrelated persons (two interrelated acting subjects)?

For the contemporary Christian, the statement: "one Person in two natures" carries with it an air of confusion if not contradiction. It appears to make Jesus in some sense "stand behind" each nature, faced with a decision regarding which nature he should use. This seeming contradiction, this schizophrenic image of Jesus, arises for today's Christian (and in some manner had arisen for the fourth-fifth century Christians) because the terms "person" and "nature" are not well defined or distinguished from one another in everyday language.[2] The fifth-century Christians who crafted the formula, "one Person in two natures," however, would not have selected these terms, if they were not useful to them in furthering clarity and precision concerning the *Logos*, Jesus, and their faith-experience of God alive in him.

Nevertheless, fourth-and fifth-century Christians in general, and their theologians in particular, also had to work to arrive at that precision and clarity. For even in the context of fourth-and fifth-century Hellenism, the intended theological meaning of these terms was not immediately clear or universally agreed upon. Hence, much of the effort *to clarify the relationship between the divinity and the humanity in Jesus* involved an effort to craft and to agree upon *revisions of terminology* adequate to express the uniqueness of Jesus.[3] The development of the *classical concept of person* and the continuing *evolution of its meaning*, therefore, form a pivotal dimension of the Church's growth in understanding and in expressing its understanding of the reality of Christ.

This section of our final chapter will focus on the unity of Jesus, understood as Son of God and Son of Mary, one Person who is fully divine and fully human. It will seek to foster an understanding of the relationship of the divinity and humanity in Jesus and ultimately to offer insight into the profound way in which the child of Mary is and was deeply rooted in God while remaining fully human. The vehicle for unfolding this understanding of Jesus will center upon the classical concept of person and Christian theology's ongoing efforts to shed light on the meaning of that concept and the reality behind it. We will strive to capture the progression of the Church's understanding in four stages. First, we will consider the fourth-century Church's use of the Hellenistic terms for person. Second, we will present the fifth-century controversies concerning the relationship of the *Logos* to Jesus together with their resolution at the Councils of Ephesus (431) and Chalcedon (451), controversies and resolutions which required a careful use of the term person as applied to Jesus. Third, we will seek to unfold the meaning and salvific import of the formulae crafted by these Councils. And fourth, we will trace the Christian Community's further inquiry into the meaning of the term and the reality of personhood, during the later classical period into the early seventeenth century, underscoring the fruitfulness of that inquiry for the Christian appreciation of the unique character of the Son of Mary who is the Eternal *Logos*, alive in our own history.

THE CONCEPT "PERSON": EARLY DEVELOPMENT AND USE[4]
Hellenistic philosophy during the early post-apostolic period of the

Church offered the word *prosopon* (translated by the Latin *persona* and the English *person*) to designate an individual human being, a person. This word originally meant either the human "face" or the "mask" worn by an actor during a theatrical performance. Both of these original meanings have significance. The human face constitutes the clearest *identifiable difference* which distinguishes many concrete individuals of the same (human) nature. One recognizes which *one of many* men or women one is encountering by looking at the individual's face.

Similarly, the theatrical mask provided the actor with a means of indicating the role which he wished to assume in a performance. Here, too, the need for a mask rested on the accepted fact that human beings, on stage or in real life, played differing roles. The mask of an actor, or one's face, in real life, provided an observer with a sense of which concrete individual he or she was encountering as well as what concrete set of human qualities or what specific role one might expect an individual to play. The notions of face and mask, therefore, implied an active interrelationship between people. Actors and people in general actively manifested and expressed themselves in relationship to others by means of their mask or face.[5]

The inadequacy of this term, however, began to arise in the midst of the theological debates of the fourth century. Its inadequacy emerged, not in respect to its value in speaking about human beings, but in its appropriateness in understanding the divine. As we mentioned in the previous chapter, after the Council of Nicea had declared that the *Logos* was fully divine, "one in Being with the Father," the Christian Community naturally asked: "How, then, is the *Logos* distinguished from the Father?" The word *prosopon* (person), the reality it reflected, and the image it evoked, were inappropriate, for the word *prosopon* denoted a *concrete autonomous individual* and, if applied to the Father and to the *Logos*, would imply that they were two concrete individuals, two separate beings, two "Gods." But both Semite and Greek held firmly that there can be only one God. Transcendent reality is one Being. Two divine *prosopa* (two divine Persons, in this concrete sense of the word) contradicted the very nature of God's being God.

Greek philosophical language of this same period, however, had another term, *hypostasis,* which theologians introduced into the debate. Literally, the term *hypostasis* means "standing under," "underlying reality," the "deepest dimension of a being." Up to the fourth century, this term was synonymous with the words *ousia* ("being") and *physis* ("nature").[6] Both *ousia* and *physis,* however, implied concreteness and individuality; *ousia* meaning "concrete reality" of a thing or individual, *physis* meaning "concrete nature" which undergirds the growth of a thing or reality. Hence, prior to the Council of Nicea, one could not speak of two (or three) *hypostaseis* in God any more than one could speak of two (or three) divine beings or natures in God.

Nevertheless, this period also saw the beginnings of some linguistic developments: Both Stoic and Neo-Platonic philosophies began distinguishing the term *hypostasis* from the term *ousia.* By *hypostasis* they meant "active realization" or "manifestation," distinguished from *ousia,* by which they meant "established reality." Using this distinction, Neo-Platonists sought to resolve the question of "the One and the Many." The former term, *hypostasis,* denoted "dynamic activity," "a movement of profound self-expression," whereas the latter term, *ousia,* denoted the final concrete being resulting from this self-expression.

Athanasius was the first to utilize this distinction in the service of Christian thought. At the Synod of Alexandria (362), this champion of Nicea suggested that the Father, the Son (*Logos*), and the Spirit constituted three *hypostaseis* (three dynamic Self-expressions) in the one *ousia* (Being, Reality), the one God. Each *hypostasis* could be understood as a distinct and dynamic way in which conscious and free divine love expressed and manifested itself. Athanasius' suggestion paved the way for both the East, in the persons of the Cappadocian Fathers (Sts. Basil, Gregory of Nyssa and Gregory of Nazianzen), and also in the West, in the person of St. Augustine, to understand the Father, Son and Spirit as the distinct and perfect expressions of God's Self-understanding and Self-giving.[7] As a result, through the clarification of Athanasius and the work of Basil and Gregory of Nazianzen, the First Council of Constantinople sanctioned the term *hypostasis* as suitable to express the distinction between the Father and the *Logos*, always understanding that the Father and the Son are one in Being, consubstantial, equally divine, one God.

This development in terminology, as abstract and refined as it is, was extremely important for the Christian appreciation, not only of the Trinity, but also for an accurate understanding of the relationship of the *Logos* to Jesus. What is especially noteworthy is the fact that the word of choice to designate the distinctness of the *Logos* from the Father was the word *hypostasis*, not the word *prosopon*. Though both Greek words were translated by the one Latin word *persona* and its English equivalent *person*, they clearly did not carry the same meaning. *Hypostasis* meant "deepest underlying dimension" of a reality, "underlying dynamism toward self-expression and self-realization"; *prosopon* meant "concrete individual of a given nature," "concrete individual actively relating to others." Thus *hypostasis* denotes a dynamic dimension within a concrete reality, not the whole of the concrete reality itself. As such, it offered new insight and new opportunity to understand and to speak intelligibly of the *Logos*' relationship to Jesus, preserving both the full humanity of Jesus and the full divinity of the *Logos* as the fourth century drew to a close.

The Conciliar Affirmation of the Unity of Jesus: One "Person" in the Logos

The Church of the fifth century had inherited a well-refined intellectual legacy accurately expressing its deep and transforming experience of God, communicating God's saving love to it in and through Jesus. It also had moved a long way in appreciating the distinctness of the *Logos* from the Father. One might have expected a rather facile and rapid resolution to the question of the relationship of the *Logos* to Jesus. The resolution of difficult issues, however, especially for persons passionately concerned with the proper understanding and expression of their experience of salvation, could never move forward with ease. The struggle to advance this specific question, moreover, confronted the Church with exceptional distress. Advancing the question required considerable intellectual dexterity. But it also demanded that the Church endure the stress of political rivalry between the sees of Constantinople and Alexandria as well as between their bishops who led the christological debates during the second quarter of the fifth century.

The bishop of Constantinople, formerly an Antiochene monk named Nestorius, fanned the fires of the debate in the year 428. In direct opposition to the views of Alexandria, he insisted and preached that Mary, the mother of Jesus, could not be called "mother of God" (*Theotokos)* but rather, must be referred to as "recipient of God" (*Theodochos)* or "mother of Christ" (*Christotokos).* Underlying his convictions stood Nestorius' understanding of Jesus: Jesus always was and remained solely (not only fully) a human being; the *Logos* merely dwelt in Jesus. The ultimate subject, the initiator, of Jesus' activity, the one who acts, is purely human. Thus, for Nestorius – thinking concretely and continuing the *Logos-Anthropos* emphasis of the Antiochene school,[8] – Jesus is a wholly human person (*prosopon)* in whom the person of the *Logos* dwelt. In Jesus there were two active and independent subjects. Mary gave birth to the human subject.

Nestorius' sermon, not without intention, inflamed his brother bishop, Cyril of Alexandria, who followed that Church's leaning which emphasized the divinity of Jesus as well as the unity of God and the human in Christ, a modified *Logos-sarx* Christology. Cyril, responding by letter, begged Nestorius to reconsider his position. At the same time, Cyril continued to press his own view of Jesus using the phrase "the one incarnate nature of the divine *Logos*."

The phrase "one incarnate nature," in turn, angered Nestorius, since it appeared to deny the human nature of Jesus (even though, taken in context, it became clear that Cyril did not deny Jesus' humanity).[9] Rather, by this phrase, Cyril wished to affirm that the *Logos* took to himself a true human nature in becoming flesh, and thereby became the ultimate active subject of the human life and activities of Jesus. In Cyril's mind, this was the intent of Nicea and the meaning of the fourth evangelist when the latter wrote: "the Word became flesh and dwelt among us" (1:14). Consistent with this view, Cyril affirmed that the union of the *Logos* and the humanity of Jesus consisted of a "union in *hypostasis"* or "*hypostatic* union." Thus the bishop of Alexandria understood the

Logos to constitute the deepest dynamic dimension, the underlying initiating dynamism, which enlivened the entire humanity of Jesus, born of Mary.

The struggle reached its peak at the Council of Ephesus (431). Both parties met separately and excommunicated one another, causing both civil and ecclesial division. As a result, imperial authorities responded by recognizing only the session over which Cyril presided, the session which not only affirmed Cyril's position and condemned that of Nestorius but which also asserted that "the Eternal Son of the Father and the Son of the Virgin Mary, born in time after the flesh, are one and the same."

The universal Church, however, particularly the churches of Antioch and Alexandria, continued to suffer division until, two years later, John of Antioch wrote a profession of faith which Cyril also affirmed. The profession employed the more Antiochene phrases "one *prosopon*" and "union of two natures," omitting Cyril's formula "union in *hypostasis*" and "one incarnate nature of the *Logos*." Finally, at the Council of Chalcedon (451) the two positions were united in one formula and one profession of faith as the fathers solemnly declared:

> We affirm that one and the same Lord Jesus Christ, the only-begotten Son, must be acknowledged in two natures, without confusion or change, without division or separation. The distinction between the natures was never abolished by their union but rather the character proper to each of the two natures was preserved as they came together in one person (*prosopon)* and one *hypostasis*. He is not split or divided into two persons, but He is one and the same only-begotten, God the Word, the Lord Jesus Christ.[10]

Thus, the Church had come to understand and to affirm with profound insight, the unity of God and humanity in Jesus, the manner in which the *Logos* actually was and is related to the child of Mary. The *Logos* forms one concrete being, one *prosopon,* with the humanity of Christ; the *Logos* constitutes the deepest underlying dynamism, the one *hypostasis*, which enlivens the man Jesus. In both senses, Jesus is one Person, one integral active subject, our God, fully alive in the world with us.

THE CONCILIAR FORMULAE:
CHRISTOLOGICAL AND SALVIFIC IMPORT

The affirmations of Ephesus and the solemn definition of Chalcedon, in so far as they distinguish the Person of the *Logos* from, and yet unite that Person with, Jesus' human nature may, at first reading, appear to be terribly abstruse, "hair-splitting," and quite foreign to our human experience, even faith-experience. For that reason, we would do well to pause for a moment of reflection upon our own self-experience as a way of gaining fuller access to the insights of these fifth century councils and theologians.

In contemporary speech, each of us readily distinguishes *who* we are from *what* we are. *What I am*, I share in common with others; *who I am*, I hold as my very own. *What I am* refers to the humanness which makes me like all other persons of the human race. *Who I am* refers to the center of my being which distinguishes me from all others, making me a relatively independent self. I can define what I am by stating that I am a "human being," a man or woman, a creature endowed with the capacities for knowledge of all things, for self-consciousness, for free decision, and for freedom in action in the world. These capacities of mind and will, oriented toward life in the material world, define me specifically as a human being and comprise what we mean by *human nature*.

Who I am is more difficult to define. Certainly I am a unique, independent individual among many who possess a human nature, but I clearly am much more than these terms, in themselves, call attention to. Sometimes I may answer the question "Who are you?" by responding "I am an American, a Christian, a teacher, a home-maker; I am the mayor of a certain city, the manager of the local supermarket...(and so on)." But, although these facts in some manner begin to distinguish me more and more from others, they basically represent characteristics and roles which I have, more or less, freely chosen to assume. They do not express adequately who

I am; they do not capture my individual, personal, identity. In this line of thought, I can best define and express who I am simply by stating my individual name.

We can shed light upon the question of "who I am" more fully, however, by noticing dimensions of our self-awareness which we often ignore. Each of us can recognize the transcendent and profound depth of our personhood, our deepest self, when we tell the story of our lives. We recognize that we are the same person who went to grade school, to a different high school, and to a college, perhaps at some distance from our former home. In telling the story, we become aware of a self which transcends time and the multiplicity of events we experience. Similarly, in recalling our present state of life, we recognize that we are the same person who holds a job, perhaps has married and is raising a family, and has given him or herself to a number of friends through life, having kept some but forgotten many. We are the same person who has dealt with a series of problems, resolving some, meeting frustration in others, and hopefully learning from them all. Each of us is a *transcendent center of unity* holding together many experiences, integrating them into our selves; and each of us is a *transcendent center of activity*, initiating innumerable acts which express who we are and who we wish to be.

Thus, each of us is conscious of a time-transcending personal center, deep within ourselves, the "I," the "self" which endures all that happens to us and which initiates all that we do. Each of us acts through our human nature, through our capacities to know, to reflect, to decide, to act; but each of us is more than that human nature, more than those capacities. Each of us is a dynamic and (relatively) independent center of existence, fashioning ourselves as unique individuals through the journey of time until we completely express ourselves and hand our earthly life back to our God at the end of our earthly history.

Classical theology sought to capture this awareness, and to denote the depth dimension of the person by utilizing the word *hypostasis*. In so-doing, the fifth-century fathers called to consciousness the underlying dynamism, the transcendent unifying center of the concrete individual, the unique "I" which, even more than one's nature, flowed from the creative hand of God. They recognized that within each individual lay a center of energy which expresses itself in each and every decision and act which the person exercises. They pointed to a dimension of ourselves which we too become aware of when we reflect upon our consciousness of our selves and/or when we use the pronoun "I." What we are aware of when we say "I" is the underlying depth dimension (*hypostasis*) of our very being, the stable and permanent center of our singular lives underlying all that we experience and all that we do.

The insight of the Councils of Ephesus and Chalcedon, then, consisted precisely in this: the underlying dynamism, the Self, which expresses itself in all Jesus did, was and is no other than the *Logos*. The personal center which unified all the human experiences of Jesus' earthly journey; the underlying subject and the deepest dimension of Jesus' concrete being, initiating Jesus' human consciousness, free decisions and personal actions was none other than the eternal Word of God, itself.[11]

The implication of the conciliar formula and the insight which it bears drew Christian belief concerning Jesus to the very center of what constitutes the Christian faith-experience. For, in affirming that the personal dynamic center of Jesus of Nazareth is none other than the Eternal *Logos*, the eternal Son of God, Christians confessed their conviction that when Jesus teaches, God teaches; when Jesus speaks words of encouragement, God speaks words of encouragement; when Jesus heals, God heals; when Jesus forgives, God forgives; and when Jesus rejoices, God rejoices. Likewise, when Jesus struggles, God struggles; when Jesus suffers, God suffers; and when Jesus empties himself in love, God pours God's Self out in love. The deepest dynamism in the child of Mary is the Son of God. It is God, in God's self-emptying love, who lives among us and relates personally with us in the human journey of Jesus, crucified and risen.[12]

In unfolding these implications of the achievements of Ephesus and Chalcedon, we also must note that these formulae emerge from more than merely logical reasoning and deduction. If mere logic established their truth, they would be hardly more than interesting speculative conclusions. Such, however, is not the case. The insights and the formulae of Ephesus and Chalcedon, like previous conciliar statements, emerged out of the Church's concerted effort to understand and to express what it already knew intuitively in its ongoing, life-giving experience of Jesus. For in its prayer and worship, it recognized that Jesus, in giving himself to believers, actively communicated nothing less than the fullness of the saving life and love of the transcendent God. Jesus was not only the mediator through whom the loving God gave God's Self to them; but further, in Jesus' own acts of human forgiveness and human love, God, the *Logos*, loved them and embraced them with God's life. Therefore, in response, believers knew intuitively that Jesus, truly as human as they, deserved the thanks and praise, the worship due to God. The believer grasped intuitively that Jesus was worthy of their complete dependence, the gift of their total surrender and trust, the offering of their adoration. For Jesus, Son of Mary, truly was and is God, the eternal Son, the *Logos*, alive and present to them, emptying himself for them in pouring out upon them the transforming dynamism of his life-giving love.

ESSENTIAL CHARACTERISTICS OF JESUS' PERSONAL CENTER
JESUS: SON OF GOD IN ETERNITY AND TIME
The clarity of the fifth-century insight into the unity of Jesus, one Person, the incarnate Son of God, a clarity captured and made definitive by the formal statements of Ephesus and Chalcedon, did not, however, keep the Church, particularly those skilled in "doing theology," from seeking fuller understanding of what, in reality, constitutes a "person." How can one define what it is to be a person? How can one describe the uniqueness of each person, distinct from another? Without doubt, these questions continued to tantalize the minds of believers because of their desire to understand better the three Persons, the three *Hypostaseis*, within the one God, as much as because of their hope to attain fuller appreciation of Jesus. In this section we will attempt to present the highlights of what became, particularly in the medieval period, an intricate and highly technical discussion.

Already in the fifth century, the Cappadocians sought to give fuller description of the nature and effect of the dynamism which they had designated by the term *hypostasis*. For them, each *hypostasis* in God carried with it a unique set of identifying characteristics, a unique manner in which God, Absolute Love, expressed God's Self eternally. Since all three Persons (*hypostaseis*) are one God and are expressions of the one divine Love, the distinctness of the Three rests simply in the distinctness of the ways the one divine Love expresses itself.[13] They are ways, therefore, in which God's expressing God's Self in Self-consciousness and love are related to one another.[14] The deepest dynamic center of Jesus, then, would not be simply divine love, but divine love in the Person of the *Logos*, divine love as *Abba* expresses it and manifests it to himself. The deepest center of Jesus is not "divine love begetting," but "divine love eternally begotten."

In spite of this insight, consciousness of the relational dimension of the person seems to have receded into the background of philosophical and theological reflection during the next century. For example, the influential sixth-century lay philosopher and theologian, Boethius, chose to emphasize individuality, uniqueness, autonomy, and independence in defining person as an "individual substance of a rational nature."[15] And, during the same period, Leontius of Byzantium, in a more descriptive way, wrote that "to be a person" is "to be for oneself," to "exist in oneself."[16] Thus, these definitions served to underscore the autonomy, self-possession, and relative independence of a person, but did not do justice to the dynamic dimension of a person, the dimension which constituted the core of the original insight conveyed by the term *hypostasis*.

Only in the twelfth century did another theologian, Richard of St. Victor, shed fuller and complementary light on the question. Richard defined a person as an "incommunicable existence of an intellectual nature."[17] Not only did the theologian perceive that personhood meant individuality, uniqueness, a certain autonomy and centeredness in the self (*incommunicable* existence), but it also denoted a dynamic "going out of" oneself (*ex-istence*), a dynamic "being in relationship" to another.[18] To be a person was to hold one's existence, as a conscious and free being (a being of an intellectual nature) "from and for another."[19] The implications of

Richard's understanding deserve fuller attention.[20]

Each of us, as human beings, holds our existence from God as Creator and from our human parents (who are often called "procreators," God's partners, so to speak, in creating us). Our distinctness as one of many human beings, precisely who we are, is most clearly designated by naming our parents, and if we have brothers and/or sisters, the order in which we were born. Less clearly, but none the less truly, who we are in our distinctness is determined by the way in which we proceed from the creative hand of God, who communicates to us the dynamism of our own created existence. Our individual and personal life-projects consist in carrying forward what we have received from God and from our parents, fashioning those gifts and ourselves ever anew as we come to express ourselves ever more fully in relationship to our world. In thus becoming and expressing ourselves, in achieving our personhood, we never cease to be related to God and to our parents. Our independence itself is relative and is directly proportioned to what we have been given: The more we have received (the more dependent we are), the more independently we also stand.

The critical reflections of Richard of St. Victor open the way for fuller insight into the Person of Jesus of Nazareth, the Word made flesh. For, if to be a person is to hold one's existence from and for another, Jesus is person in a way like, but far superior to, ourselves. For Jesus of Nazareth receives his existence, not simply by way of God's creative hand, as we do, being born of a human mother, a human parent, as we are. Though his human nature is truly created by God, Jesus, in his humanity, receives the existence of the uncreated eternal Word, the divine existence which the Word possesses from the Father from all eternity. Thus Jesus of Nazareth is related, in his very being, not just to God as Creator, but to *Abba*, to God as Father, from whom he eternally receives all that he is, the fullness of God's life of love.

Thus, when the Word becomes flesh in time, he nevertheless remains the same person who he has been in eternity. The underlying dynamism which motivates the child of Mary, the depth and center of all that Jesus is and does, is the Person of the Word, eternally begotten of the Father. But the distinct character, the distinct personality, of the eternal Word consists in being the perfect expression and perfect manifestation of who the Father knows himself to be. Therefore, being precisely this eternally begotten Word of God in the flesh, constitutes the distinctive character of the personhood of Jesus. Thus, when the Word made flesh journeys through time, he, being authentic to himself, most faithfully expresses who he is by seeking the Father's will, by learning from the Father all he comes to understand, by listening to and being obedient to *Abba*. Christ's fidelity and obedience not only fulfill his humanity in search of God and everlasting life; they express in time who Jesus is from all eternity. Jesus obedience unto death, his giving of the whole of his life to *Abba*, constitutes the fullest expression of the personal and distinctive character of the *Logos*. And, in that act, in what we have named earlier[21] Jesus' most profound religious experience, he becomes most fully receptive of *Abba's* life. In his humanity he becomes fully divinized, completing the divinization begun in the incarnation. The Word becomes in time most completely the distinctive Person that he is in eternity.[22]

Fidelity to love and obedience in loving just as the Father loves, then, constitute the distinctive *hypostatic* character of the Son. In time, as in eternity, Jesus is none other than the Son of God. Jesus' human nature, that is, his capacity to grow in self-understanding, to discover his role in the world, to make decisions regarding his future and to act in behalf of other real people, remains thoroughly human. The "I" of Jesus takes on a nature just like our own. But the one who is born of Mary, the one who sees, hears, learns, decides and acts in the world is the *Logos*, the Son of God, begotten fully of the Father in eternity.

The Christian reflection upon the personal identity of Jesus of Nazareth, then, manifests a lengthy and ever-deepening history. From the fourth to fifth centuries into the early seventeenth century, classical theology recognized that in Jesus, there was only one acting subject, one person who lived among us and walked the human journey with us. It also recognized that that person, the one born of Mary, is none other than the Word (*Logos*) of God, and that, therefore, each human word and deed of Jesus is truly God's Word and deed, or more precisely, the human speech and action of the eternal Son of God. Jesus of Nazareth, Son of Mary, is the eternally begotten Son of the Father. That is who he is. Further, the Church also came to recognize that the divine life of God's Son constituted the unifying center and fundamental dynamism of Jesus' human life, gifting this man, our brother, with an unsurpassed desire and energy for making God's love real in our world. Finally, it recognized that, true to himself as the Word of God (not the Father), Jesus of Nazareth exemplified the *unique personal character* of the Eternal Son in all he said and did in this world. Jesus lived with an unconditional openness to and trust in *Abba* from whom he received in time the fullness of life he receives from *Abba* in eternity. The Word made flesh is the eternally begotten Son of God, expressing his personal identity, expressing who he is, in time.

But if Jesus is truly the eternal Son of God, if he is truly God's eternally begotten Word in the flesh, if the center of Jesus' life-giving humanity is the personal existence, the *hypostasis*, of the *Logos*, can he genuinely be said to be "like us in all things but sin?" Can it truly be said that he *had to search* for the will of God, that he *could be tempted* as we are, that he *struggled* before his passion, that he *exercised* genuine *human freedom* in his acts of fidelity and love? Affirming the divine personhood of Jesus has led many, from the fifth century up to and including the present to think of Jesus in his human journey as very much unlike us. It has brought some, once again, to question the truth of Jesus' humanity. And it has led others to argue against the value and usefulness of speaking of Jesus as a Divine Person. The former, in the aftermath of Ephesus, and periodically in the course of subsequent centuries (as we shall see in the next section) began to return, in some manner or other, to a "one nature" (solely divine) understanding of Jesus. The latter, seeking to defend Jesus' humanity, have wondered if the classical formulae of Ephesus and Chalcedon, and even those of Nicea and Constantinople, should not be abandoned because they tend to be misleading in a contemporary language and culture. These issues, subsequent to the affirmation of the divine personhood of Jesus cannot be ignored. The next section of this chapter, therefore, will concern itself once again with the true humanity of Jesus of Nazareth, focusing upon the integrity of that humanity in Jesus' earthly life and activity, while giving faithful recognition to the fact that it is the humanity of the Son of God.

Human Life and Activity of Jesus, Son of God

In the wake of the Council of Nicea, which defined the divinity of the *Logos* (as we saw in the previous chapter), the Christian Community struggled, in its explicit understanding and teaching, to uphold the integrity of Jesus' humanity. Similarly, in the fifth century, after the Council of Ephesus (431) and the confession of faith jointly accepted by John of Antioch and Cyril of Alexandria (433), the Church once again found itself embattled in a dispute concern-ing the humanity of Christ.[23] The success of the Alexandrian position and the deposition of Nestorius so focused attention on the divinity of Jesus in the person of the *Logos*, that an Alexandrian monk named Eutyches, a notably unintelligent man, began teaching that Jesus was not only one Person, but that he existed in only one nature, the divine nature.

Eutyches' position, which acquired the technical name *Monophysitism*,[24] quickly prompted discord in the wider Church, especially since the "symbol of union," the formula which John and Cyril had agreed to, explicitly stated that the one person, Jesus, existed in two natures. A synod at Constantinople, over which its bishop, Flavian, presided, condemned Eutyches and *Monophysitism* in the year 448. This action provoked Dioscorus, the bishop of Alexandria, who then presided over his own council in Ephesus in August of 449. With imperial support, Dioscorus countered Con-stantinople by restoring Eutyches and deposing Flavian. Once again, the church suffered the throes of division over its way of understanding and speaking about Jesus.

The intensity and significance of the dispute, however, could not be contained within the Eastern Church. Leo I, bishop of Rome, had recognized the seriousness of the discord even before Dioscorus deposed Flavian. In June of 449, Leo had sent a letter to Flavian condemning Eutyches' doctrine and approving the action taken by the Synod of Constantinople. In the same letter, Leo set forth the formula of the Western Church concerning Jesus, using the terms "one person in two natures," and underscored the conviction that each nature remained the source of its own proper activity. Papal legates then carried the letter to Alexandria. Dioscorus, however, refused to accept both the letter and the legates who brought it. Leo, therefore, demanded still another council which finally met in Chalcedon in 451.

We have already cited the definition of Chalcedon, noting that it affirmed the singleness of the person of Jesus and that it brought together, for the first time, the two Greek terms, *hypostasis* and *prosopon*, to articulate the center of unity in Jesus. What needs to be emphasized here is that this same formula also defined the *two natures* (two sources of activity) of Jesus and, perhaps even more significantly, insisted upon their *unaltered integrity and clear distinction from one another even after their union in the person of the Logos*. In this regard, the definition stated explicitly that the two natures remain "unconfused (unmixed) and unchanged" in their being united, that "the distinction between the natures was never abolished by their union, but rather the character proper to each of the two natures was preserved as they came together in one person...."[25]

We have returned to this brief but important period of the history of the Christian Community to underscore two facts. First, the achievement of a correct and balanced understanding and expression of faith-experience is far from an easy task; rather it requires great care in both thinking and in speaking. Second, the affirmation of Jesus' divinity alone or of his humanity alone inevitably misrepresents genuine Christian faith-experience. Rather the correct understanding and fruitful articulation of faith which experiences God alive in Christ must account for both Jesus' divinity and his humanity. Further, it must show how his divinity and his humanity maintain their proper distinctness and integrity in the life's journey of Jesus of Nazareth.

This section of the chapter, then, will focus on the integrity of Jesus' humanity specifically as the humanity of the Word made flesh. It will attempt to show that the union of two natures in one

Person results in a unity of the divine and the human in the life and activity of Jesus. It will seek to answer the questions: "What happens to humanity when the Word becomes flesh?" and "How is Jesus' human life truly like ours, save sin?" We will ask these questions in face of three areas of Jesus' lived experience: the area of his human knowledge and self-understanding; the area of his human freedom; and the area of his sinlessness. We will then bring this section to a close with several observations intended to shed light on the fact that it is precisely because Jesus is the Word made flesh that he can be the mediator of salvation for all people.

JESUS' HUMAN KNOWLEDGE AND SELF-AWARENESS

One of the most significant dimensions of human life in which devoted Christians have thought and, in some quarters, continue to think that Jesus of Nazareth is singularly different from us, centers upon his human knowledge. This singular difference would regard both his knowledge of events and persons *outside of himself* and also his consciousness *of his own true self*, his personal identity. In the thirteenth century, Thomas Aquinas taught that Jesus possessed three "types" of human knowledge:[26] knowledge by way of experience (knowledge of a language, of customs, of the location of towns and villages, of the names of people, and so forth), knowledge infused by God, and beatific knowledge (knowledge of God such as the saints in heaven enjoyed). Thomas argued that Jesus needed experiential knowledge in order to journey in the concrete world. Because it was appropriate that he who was the Word of God be perfect in knowledge and know all things, Thomas contended that Jesus required knowledge directly infused by God. And in order to lead humankind to know God and ultimately to "see God face to face," Thomas believed that Jesus would have had to have known God fully and to "see God face to face"; he would have had to enjoy the beatific vision.[27] Thomas' reasoning remained unchallenged for centuries in theological discussions concerning Jesus' humanity, thereby leaving many Christians with at least a felt distance between Jesus and themselves. Only in the twentieth century, largely through the work of biblical scholars such as Raymond E. Brown[28] and systematic theologians such as Karl Rahner[29] and Bernard Lonergan[30] have Christians begun to question the validity of the Thomistic position. The considerations which follow will in great measure manifest dependence on their efforts.

The Biblical Witness to Christ's Human Knowledge
The New Testament not only clearly reflects the Christian conviction that Jesus was truly human, it regards his way of knowing to be hardly different from our own. Luke writes early in the Gospel bearing his name that Jesus grew in wisdom as he journeyed through time (2:52). Mark presents Jesus as lacking the knowledge of who it was who touched him, when a woman suffering from a flow of blood grasped at the hem of his garment (5:30). Even toward the end of his earthly life, the Gospels present Jesus attesting to his own lack of knowledge, as he tells his disciples that neither the angels in heaven, nor the Son, know the day or the hour when the end of time will finally come (Mk. 13:32).

It is true that the Gospels also portray Jesus as possessing superior insight from time to time. Thus, Jesus perceives the hidden thoughts of the Pharisees who object to his forgiving the sins of the paralytic (Mk. 2:6-8). Similarly, Jesus recognizes that Simon the Pharisee inwardly questioned Jesus identity as a prophet when the penitent woman ministered to Jesus with deep affection (Lk. 7:39f). And the Lord knew that Peter, weak as he was, would deny him at the moment of his trial (Mk. 14:27-30). But none of these instances required "supra-human" knowledge. Rather these and similar instances could merely illustrate that Jesus was a man of keen perception, capable of knowing persons and their inclinations well, and therefore able to detect their true feelings and the paths that they would most likely take when confronted with actual danger.[31]

We would draw similar conclusions from Jesus' apparent foreknowledge and predictions of his passion, death, and resurrection. As mentioned above,[32] the concrete details of these predictions most likely found entrance into the Gospel through the embellishing done by the post-resurrection Church and the evangelist. Jesus more likely had a less detailed, but nevertheless substantially accurate, foreknowledge of his forthcoming death and resurrection. This foreknowledge could understandably have grown out of his attentiveness to the hostility of his opponents, his awareness of the measures which Israel had taken in the past to "rid itself" of challenging prophets, his own firm resolve to continue his mission at all costs, and his abiding confidence in *Abba* and the life *Abba* offered him throughout his earthy journey. Thus Jesus would not have required infused knowledge to arrive at an awareness or to predict the final outcome of his earthly life. He needed only to be openly perceptive of the real effects his life and teaching had on others and to be firmly trusting of the life which he received from *Abba*, the life which constituted his personal center.

A further question concerning Jesus' knowledge, however, touches, not on his knowledge of others and/or of events outside of himself, but on *his consciousness of his own self*, his awareness of his own personal identity. Did Jesus see himself as "Messiah," "Son of Man" and/or "Son of God?" In regard to these questions, the various portraits painted by the four evangelists would undoubtedly lead the reader to respond with a resounding "Yes." Clearly, the fourth evangelist imaged Jesus as identifying himself unambiguously as God's "only Son,"[33] the One who alone among others has truly seen God.[34] The Johannine literature, however, offers such a refined and richly developed post-resurrection reflection upon the Church's experience of the Lord, that it is difficult to ascertain how accurately the texts reflect the explicit claims and consciousness of the historical Jesus. As with so many issues witnessed to even within the New Testament, the answer is not quite so simple.

The Synoptic literature, however, provides a broader and perhaps more likely reflection of the original claims of Jesus. Both Matthew (11:27) and Luke (10:22), utilizing the Q Tradition, support a memory of Jesus affirming his status as "Son of God" in recalling his teaching that "No one knows the Son except the Father, and no one knows the Father except the Son and anyone the Son chooses to reveal Him." Similarly, both Mark (12:6) and Luke (20:13) record Jesus describing himself in the parable of the tenants and the vineyard, as the "uniquely beloved" Son, culminating the line of rejected and martyred prophets. And, in another Marcan passage, Jesus refers to himself as Son, though limited, stating: "Of that day or hour no one knows, not even...the Son, but only the Father" (13:32). In light of these passages from the Synoptic

Gospels, Brown concludes that it is "likely that Jesus spoke and thought of himself as 'the Son', implying a very special relationship to God that is part of his identity and status. Yet he never indisputably uses of himself the title 'the Son of God'"[35]

More difficult is Jesus' apparent reference to himself as "Son of Man."[36] Though the title appears some eighty times in the Gospels, largely as a self-designation by Jesus, it does not appear to have been a widely circulated title in Judaism during Jesus' earthly lifetime. Nevertheless, one does find background for New Testament usage in Ezekiel (where it means "human being," underscoring the prophet's mortality in contrast with the divine character of the message which he is given to communicate) and in Daniel 7:13, where it describes a "heavenly figure" who would bring about God's final victory and who would be God's emissary in judging all peoples. Jesus may have spoken of himself in this light at his trial before the high priest (Mk. 14:61f) where, having been asked whether or not he were the Messiah, Jesus chooses to refer to himself as "Son of Man" whom one will see "seated at the right hand of the Power and coming on the clouds of heaven." The question is not whether Jesus was conscious of having a central role in bringing about God's reign and God's judgement; rather the question concerns whether or not Jesus used this explicit title to articulate that consciousness, and if so, how early during his earthly life Jesus would have enlisted the aid of this title. It is possible that Jesus, aware of his role in bringing about God's final victory, enlisted the use of this title, taken from Daniel 7, to express his convictions at the end of his life. Taking the lead from Jesus, the early church may then have applied the title to him at much earlier stages of his life.[37] In any event, the titles which Jesus may have used to express his self-awareness would likely have been late developments in his ministry. His explicit understanding of himself as "Son of God" and "Son of Man" probably evolved only after he had already engaged repeatedly in ministerial experiences, responding to the ever more challenging call of *Abba*.

An analysis of texts which present Jesus speaking of himself, however, do not exhaust the New Testament evidence of how Jesus understood his own self-identity. For, in addition to these at best probable *explicit claims*, the Gospels also offer evidence of Jesus awareness of himself in their record of *how he acted*. From this perspective, data indicative of Jesus' self-consciousness as well as his consciousness of his relationship to *Abba* and to Israel is vast and quite certain. Thus, the historical Jesus clearly took initiative to speak in his own name with divine authority. He unhesitatingly forgave sins, an action which he, the Pharisees, and all observers recognized as the prerogative of God alone. He freed persons from demonic oppression by his own word and worked wonders, miraculous healings, by his own power. He claimed with incontrovertible authority that the reign of God had arrived and saw himself as uniquely sent to bring that reign about, even through his death. Though Jesus never seems explicitly to have claimed that he was God, and at best may have used the titles "Son of God" and "Son of Man" (understood in their Semitic context), he showed by his way of life and by the consistent tenor of his ministry that he perceived himself not only as specially, but as uniquely, related to God who was his *Abba*. In the depth of his own mind, he understood himself as God's unique emissary in bringing about universal salvation and therefore acted consistently and with power in accord with this self-awareness.[38]

Systematic Reflections Regarding Jesus' Human Knowledge
Our efforts to understand Jesus' human knowing, and particularly his consciousness of himself, have led us to fashion a fundamental distinction, the distinction between Jesus' non-verbalized awareness of himself and his expression of that awareness, whether in explicit words or in action. This distinction between inner implicit awareness and externalized expression in explicit word or intentional action is characteristic of all human knowing. A moment's reflection will make this clear.

Anyone who has ever fallen in love and has felt the deep desire to spend oneself in promoting the well-being of another, knows what it is to experience profound energy and life within oneself without immediately being able to fathom, much less explicitly articulate, the full meaning of that energy for one's own identity and future life. Even as we express this newly discovered energy in selfless acts toward another, we will not be able to grasp, clearly and explicitly, the paths that love will open up for us as we strive to live faithfully to this love over time. This scenario is true whether we are speaking of the love of friendship, love that leads to marriage, love that beckons us to some form of service of neighbor (doctor, counselor, teacher, religious minister) or love of nature, of science or, above all, the love of God. Though we may sense the genuine significance of such love even in its beginnings, only over a period of time will we discover its full meaning, its power to lead us out of ourselves toward another or several others, and its capacity to disclose our own identity, our personal meaning before God and before others. Human beings know themselves and the deep movements of their hearts implicitly long before they can articulate their own personal identity and express the import of these movements explicitly.

Thus, we should expect that Jesus would have been aware, *in an implicit manner*, of who he was long before he would have been able to *express that identity explicitly and verbally*. He would have been consciously present to himself and the deepest movements of his being long before he would have seen their implications for his active relationship to *Abba* and to God's people. Like our own, his identity also would unfold explicitly as he sought to be faithful to himself in relating to God, to people, and to the society and world of his own day. Said in another way, Jesus did not know, clearly and explicitly, who he was from the outset of his life. Only through time, through prayer, through his alertness to people's needs and the needs of his society, through a responsible assessment of the opportunities before him, and through constant attentiveness to the energy of his deepest self (the movements of his own heart), could he discover who he was in relationship to *Abba* and to God's people, and how he should express that identity in action. And only through repeated similar and ever deepening decisions and actions, well into his public ministry, could Jesus have known *explicitly* and *completely* who he was: the one uniquely sent by the Father, commissioned to establish forever the reign of God; God's uniquely beloved Son, sent to bring the life he received from *Abba* to all persons; the uniquely faithful servant, called to bring about God's kingdom by way of the cross.

At this point then, we can return to one of the questions we asked at the outset of this section: "What happens when the Word becomes flesh?" In general, we must respond that when the Word becomes flesh, humanity is divinized. But such a divinization of Jesus' humanity has immediate implications for Jesus' self-consciousness. For, to borrow from the theology of Karl Rahner, human being is "spirit in the world," embodied spirit. But spiritual being is being that is "present to itself," that is, being that is aware of itself in each act of knowing and in each act of freedom in the world. Whatever one knows and whatever one chooses, one is also aware of oneself as knowing and as choosing.

Hence, when the Word becomes flesh, humanity, in Jesus, becomes alive with a new and unprecedented awareness. In being present to himself, Jesus is immediately aware of the self-emptying energy of divine love. When the Word becomes flesh, a human being, Jesus, becomes gifted with the resource (within himself) to perceive what love, genuine love, truly means for human beings. When the Word becomes flesh, God provides a human being with an inner presence against which he can see and judge the actions of all persons. Therefore, Jesus, in knowing himself and his own inner dynamism, has immediate access to God's own standard of action. And so, the divinization of the man Jesus, in its primary effect, means that Jesus will look at life and see the world against the horizon of his unique personal self-awareness, an awareness that reveals to his human consciousness the nature, the power, and the wisdom of living by divine love for all people. God's love becomes fully alive in the world, and the world becomes transformed by the presence and power of God's love.

What is so important for this section of our study, however, is precisely this: Jesus' awareness of his personal center and personal identity is truly a human awareness. Jesus' efforts to understand himself and act faithfully to himself are genuinely human efforts. Jesus' struggle to discover and follow *Abba's* will involves a truly human struggle. All of Jesus' efforts to process the meaning of his own identity and the desires of the Father follow the laws of human processing. The unity of the Person of the *Logos* with the humanity of Jesus requires that Jesus process all of the energy of his deepest self, his divine sonship, through human effort, through human darkness, in an ongoing program of discernment, until he hands all back to *Abba* in faithful love. Thus, on the one hand, it is precisely his human life of discovery and fidelity which reveals and manifests the presence of the *Logos* as the deepest center of Jesus of Nazareth. And, on the other hand, it is the human struggle and journey which enable us to say that, in Jesus, God has truly entered the human world. When the Word becomes flesh, God's Love becomes present to a human being in his personal human consciousness, and, in that human being, humanity itself is transformed.

Jesus' Freedom and Sinlessness

Human beings who are, by nature, "spirit in the world," not only enjoy a presence to themselves in self-consciousness; they also enjoy the capacity to communicate with others in the world in self-initiated openness to them and self-giving action before them. In a word, they EX-ist (go out of themselves) in relationship to others; they express themselves in freedom.

Most often we think of freedom as an ability to choose; that is, to select from among things we might acquire, persons we desire to be with, or tasks we wish to or need to engage in. We experience our freedom as a capacity to do as we will, without inner compulsion or external coercion. Philosophers and theologians name this type or level of freedom, "freedom of choice."

Human experience, however, discloses to us another, deeper level of freedom: "transcendental freedom." Karl Rahner has defined this level of freedom, present in every human being, as the capacity "to effect oneself once and for all into finality,"[39] to give oneself away, once and for all, for an Absolute (value). Transcendental freedom refers to the human capacity to effect ourselves, that is, to make something of ourselves. We can exercise this capacity to make something of ourselves at various levels. We can make ourselves something on a professional level (for example, a doctor, a lawyer, a social worker, a judge). We can make ourselves something on a religious level (for example, a Buddhist, a Jew, a Christian). And, we can make ourselves something on an all-embracing personal level (for example, a dedicated servant of

-314-

others, a person who consistently places his or her trust in God, a person who seeks to act toward others with forbearance and reverence).

Further, transcendental freedom refers to the human capacity to effect oneself once and for all. Making ourselves something on each of these levels obviously involves making many choices and making them with consistency. If we are going to make something of considerable value of our lives and of ourselves, we must choose that value, that "something," with firmness. We cannot waver. We cannot give in to competing opportunities or make contradictory decisions. For example, we cannot vacillate between pursuing the professions of a lawyer and a social worker; we will become neither. We cannot vacillate between being a knowledgeable and committed Buddhist and a knowledgeable and committed Christian; neither will have our loyalty. We cannot waver between being dedicated servants of others and dedicated servants of our own comfort and convenience; our freedom and our hearts will be divided. To make something of value of ourselves demands that we choose that value again and again until we become firm and consistent in that choice. We cannot waver; we must reach the point of making these decisions once and for all.

Further still, transcendental freedom involves the human capacity to effect ourselves once and for all into finality. As we seek to make something of value of ourselves with firmness, we become one with the value which we seek. We become the lawyer and no other professional. We become a Christian and espouse no other religious persuasion. We become characteristically servants of others and/or persons whose lives consistently reflect trust in God; and we avoid even the appearance of selfishness. There is no "going back" on what we have made of ourselves. We have effected ourselves, made something of ourselves, once and for all into finality.

Finally, transcendental freedom involves the human capacity to give ourselves away, once and for all, for an Absolute (value). In the examples which we have presented, we have observed that transcendental freedom refers to the capacity to make something of ourselves at various levels. What we should also notice is that these levels are interrelated: the latter embrace the former. For example, one can be a dedicated Christian and be either a lawyer or a social worker or any other worthy professional person. And, one can be a dedicated servant of others and a person trusting the Transcendent either as a Christian, or a Jew, or a Buddhist, or as a person of some other worthy religious persuasion.[40] Hence it is clear that what we have called the all-embracing personal level of self achievement is the level of overriding decisions and values. This level represents the ultimate level of decision; it expresses the level of absolute, unconditional, value for us. It is the level of choice that is the deciding factor in all other levels of choice. All other choices, even professional and religious choices, foster and express these overriding values and the decisions we make in favor of these all-embracing values.[41] Transcendental freedom refers to the capacity to give ourselves away to an unconditional, all-embracing, overriding value once and for all as our life's fullest and final achievement.

Thus, we can see that transcendental freedom refers to the deepest level of the human dynamism which, in every act, reaches out for that which is ultimately and totally satisfying, that which we name our "ultimate good." We can recognize this level of freedom in noticing the fact that no matter how wonderful another person, a singular event, or a most meaningful task may be, he, she, or it never satisfies us totally or permanently. We always long for more, for what will enable us to feel complete, in full communion with ourselves and our world forever. At heart, we wish to surrender ourselves, once and for all, to that value, that task, that person which will satiate our longing without end. Within ourselves we can recognize the deep and dynamic movement of what philosophers call "transcendental freedom."

Transcendental freedom is so named because it is present in every conscious free human act; it transcends each particular decision and action. As such, it actually constitutes the ground of freedom of choice. Because we desire that which is ultimately and totally satisfying, we experience, more or less, a freedom of choice when we face anything created. For, on the one hand, created reality is limited; it is not fully satisfying.[42] We are free to pass any particular person, any created opportunity, by. On the other hand, all created reality, every opportunity for action, each person, to some degree has something to offer us. Each possesses some element of goodness, some quality which can attract us and bring us some degree of satisfaction. Hence, we feel ourselves drawn by them though not compelled to engage them. Our deep desire for ultimate and total completion draws us forward in ever deeper relationships with our world and particularly with concrete persons within it, while leaving us quite free to choose to whom we will relate and how we will craft those relationships. Transcendental freedom is the ground of freedom of choice as we live human lives in the midst of a world of genuine but relative values.

Jesus' Human Freedom

Jesus, the Word made flesh, enjoyed both levels of freedom. When the Word became flesh, he experienced the same human incompleteness and longing that we experience. He is portrayed in each of the Gospels as expressing that insatiable human longing. In the midst of temptation, he is presented quoting Deuteronomy to this effect, stating: "Not by bread alone does one live, but by every word which flows from the mouth of God" (Mt. 4:4; see Deut. 8:3). Later, as his life unfolded, he declared "I have a baptism to be baptized with; how anxious I am for it to be accomplished" (Lk. 12:50; see also Lk. 9:58), a statement which reflects longing both for release from imminent danger and also for the fullness of life Jesus expected at the end of his journey. As the end neared, Jesus again expressed this longing, telling his disciples: "I will not drink of the fruit of the vine again until the coming of the reign of God" (Lk. 22:18). And the fourth evangelist captures this dimension of Jesus' self-experience as he portrays the Lord at prayer, calling upon *Abba*: "Father, the hour has come! Give glory to your Son.... I have given you glory on earth by finishing the work you gave me to do. Do you now, Father, give me glory at your side, a glory I had with you before the world began" (Jn. 17:1, 4-5). Jesus earnestly longed for a better world, for the healing of his people, for communion with others in love, for a life in union with the Father, and for the ultimate transformation which could take place only through his death, a transformation which he confidently hoped would bring him the fullness of divine life, in his humanity. Jesus, human as we are, longed for *Abba's* total Self-Gift, God's loving response to Jesus' total surrender of himself in trust to the One who is absolute love.

Likewise, Jesus experienced freedom of choice. No created value, no deed, no person, compelled his freedom; yet everything created could, to some degree, attract him and draw from him his free response. Hence the synoptic Gospels record Jesus' temptations in the desert at the outset of his ministry. In them, the evangelists recognize that Jesus truly faced the challenge of deciding between a variety of attractive paths of ministry, including the possibility of aligning himself with one of the established religious groups prominent in the Israel of his day. Each of them held some appeal, though ultimately Jesus recognized that choosing any of them would have ultimately led to compromising his deepest self. Further, Jesus' relationship to the Twelve clearly engaged him in freedom of choice. He took time for prayer and discernment before he selected them from among the wider group of those following him and he continued to nurture them in spite of the fact that they were at times obtuse, hard-headed, and disloyal. Each step of his developing relationship with the Twelve called forth from him new decisions, expressing a renewal of his original choice at deeper levels. Finally, the anguish which he experienced in the Garden before he died, and the prayer he uttered to his *Abba*, reveal a person struggling, torn, but ultimately making a free decision in favor of God's will whatever that will might show itself to be. Jesus experienced genuine freedom of choice as he moved through his earthly life. And he knew the struggles inherent in that freedom as he sought to be faithful to himself and to the deepest movements of his heart, the thrust of transcendental freedom, in negotiating the joys and pains of human life in a good but imperfect world.

Jesus' Sinlessness
The contemporary question of Jesus' sinlessness arises out of a desire to acknowledge the truth of his humanity and the authenticity of his human freedom. Stated succinctly: if Jesus were humanly free, how is it that he did not sin? Human freedom would seem to include, of its very nature, the possibility of sin. In a certain sense,

his sinlessness would seem to render the genuiness of his freedom, and even of his humanity, unbelievable.

The question becomes all the more complex when we take as our starting point an affirmation of precisely who Jesus is: he is the divine Son of God. When we begin from the perspective of Jesus' divine personhood, we move quickly not only to affirm Jesus' sinlessness *as a fact*, but also to maintain as a principle that Jesus *could not sin*. In traditional language, not only was Jesus sinless; he was *impeccable*. This affirmation, however, once again raises the question: "Was Jesus truly human, like us in all things but sin?" If he could not sin, can he be said to be truly human?[43]

In placing the question as we have done in the first of the two paragraphs above, offering an approach which favors Jesus' humanity, one tends to regard sin as a genuine possibility for Jesus.[44] The question then becomes one of explaining Jesus' factual constancy in avoiding sin. One must seek to illuminate his factual consistency in being faithful to *Abba* and to *Abba's* will. One asks how Jesus, in his humanness, found the light and strength to maintain his stance of consistency in loving.

But if we take our lead from a recognition of the personal center of Jesus and from an acknowledgment that he always was the divine Son of God (as discussed in the second paragraph above), we find ourselves led to regard sin as impossible for Jesus. If this is the case, then we must reexamine the question of Jesus' freedom of choice and the overall influence of the incarnation of the *Logos* upon Jesus' human becoming.[45] Recognizing the legitimacy and the importance of both perspectives, we would argue that the question of Jesus' sinlessness can best be addressed by situating sin in the context of human freedom and then by returning to the question of "What happens when the Word becomes flesh?" We will pursue both of these areas of concern consecutively.

To situate the relationship of sin to freedom of choice, we should recall that such freedom flows from the fact that concrete created realities always have the dual quality of being partially satisfying but not fully satisfying. When we make any concrete decision, the best one can hope for will be to make a choice which will yield the *greatest and deepest personal satisfaction POSSIBLE at the given time*. Much of that decision, in so far as it is truly free, will rest upon how we see and evaluate each concrete possibility that we face. In the last analysis, each person will choose, from among varied possibilities, the one which he or she thinks or estimates will bring the deepest and fullest possible satisfaction.[46] Two things, however, may go awry as one comes to this decision: On the one hand, we may make a mistake in our weighing of the possibilities, and unwittingly choose a less satisfying course of action. Or, on the other hand, in spite of our accuracy in weighing the merits of the opportunities we have, we may decide in favor of an immediate lesser gain, knowing that, in the long run, a different choice would be the most satisfying.

But how do such choices relate to growth in holiness or, on the contrary, to engagement in sin? Concrete choices which harmonize most fully with the movement of transcendental freedom and with the absolute value which one seeks in that movement of freedom, concrete choices in which one elects the way of acting (among limited possibilities) which most participates in or reflects the ultimate value which will fulfill human being, constitute what we term morally good acts, acts of holiness, genuine acts of human love. In actual fact, such acts best mediate authentic selfhood, one's deepest self; they express best the striving of transcendental freedom and they offer us the fullest measure of ultimate value and satisfaction at the given moment. On the other hand, concrete choices which fail to harmonize with or tend to stifle the full movement of our deepest freedom and our authentic self constitute actions which we name as morally evil or "sin." Such choices are, at root, largely self-defeating. At best, they participate in and mediate in a very meager way the measure of satisfaction we truly yearn for. They manifest a disregard for the richer and more deeply satisfying quality of the other possible choices at hand. In this sense, such choices can be said to disregard or to offend the deeper values before us and, when we define the ultimate value by the name "God," one can be said in such choices to offend God.

Jesus, being human as we are, perceived the relative values of all concrete things, persons, and ways of acting which confronted him at every moment of his historical life. He could be (and was) repulsed by some, but enticed by others and strongly attracted to a few. He knew that estimating the relative worth of some ways of acting in comparison to others was not always an easy task. Such a process of evaluating required sensitive perception, patient reflection, and genuine insight. Like us, Jesus experienced freedom of choice and, within that freedom, an inner calling to choose that which would provide the *greatest satisfaction possible for him from among the concrete possibilities which lay before him*. Like us, Jesus knew the call to choose what appeared to harmonize best with his deepest Self and the movements of his deepest, transcendental freedom searching for absolute value in the human journey. And like us, he, at least at times, found sorting through the concrete possibilities which lay before him time-consuming and difficult. One might say he made a "desert retreat" early in his adult life in order to accomplish this task.[47]

Jesus, however, in not just like us; he is also different from us. He exists by way of the incarnation of the *Logos*. In him, the Word became flesh. He knew within himself the movement of divine love in its fullness. Hence, when deciding among concrete possibilities, Jesus, seeking to be faithful to himself and his inner fundamental striving, found himself able, better than other humans, to appreciate how truly and fully a given way of acting participated in, and mediated, the ultimate value of life which he deeply sought. Though *from a human point of view* he was not compelled to choose what best mediated divine love, yet *because of who he was*, from his being personally and deeply the Word made flesh, he would always find within himself a deep call to be authentic to himself. He would always have available to himself, a deep source of clarifying light enabling him to judge the true worth of any concrete opportunity for action. He would always have within himself an initial dynamic movement toward God-like loving seeking to express itself in all his actions. He would always experience an initial inner invitation which called him to search for and to find the paths of action which would best express the Selfless love of God.

Jesus was, in fact, sinless. From the viewpoint of his humanity, however, that sinlessness could not be presumed. It could be known only after the fact. Nonetheless, from the viewpoint of his divine personhood, he had the inner profound resource, his deepest Self, to prompt him and to guide him to make the most life-giving and loving decisions that were possible along the way. Thus, he lived a truly human life. And he lived always in utter fidelity to his deepest Self, and to *Abba*, who communicated the fullness of his life to Jesus. In every action, Jesus, born of Mary, was the Word become flesh.[48]

JESUS: MEDIATOR OF SALVATION FOR ALL PEOPLE

The unity of the eternal Word with humanity in the womb of Mary expressed itself in a dynamic and inseparable unity apparent in the unfolding of the historical life of Jesus. When the Word became flesh in Jesus, the world came to witness a human being who manifested a divinely human vision of life and a divinely human energy for love of all people. All of Jesus' concrete and manifold conscious and free human activities, his opening of himself to *Abba*, his consistent efforts to discern his personal calling, his undying energy in pouring himself out in visible, historical acts of healing, forgiving, selfless generosity for all sorts of persons, especially the marginalized: all show forth an inseparable unity of Godly life in human becoming. All manifest the gift of the reconciliation of God and humankind. Hence, Jesus of Nazareth constitutes the reconciliation of God and humankind by the very fact that he is the Word made flesh, by the very fact of the incarnation (always understanding that "incarnation," becoming human, means being which is complete only through expressing itself in ever deeper measure through the journey of time). For in the moment of the incarnation, God's eternal love united itself with time. God established an inseparable partnership with a human being; God broke into human history to live the earthly journey; and a human being came to know the transforming power of living human life strengthened by the inexhaustible energy of God. The gift of the reconciliation of eternity and time became historically real when the Word became flesh.

But Jesus of Nazareth, by the fact of the incarnation, is not only *the manifestation and the realization* of the reconciliation of God and humankind in himself; he is also *the instrument and the agent* of that reconciliation for all who follow him. Jesus is the universal and absolute Reconciler, the universal Mediator of salvation. As Irenaeus had expressed it: "The Son of God became human so that human beings might become sons (and daughters) of God."[49] God became human so that human beings might become divine.

But how is it that the very incarnation, the very presence of Jesus in our history, effectively brings about the salvation of all? Or, to put the question another way, if salvation consists in our being alive in God as Jesus is alive in God,[50] how do Jesus' life, death, and resurrection effectively communicate to us the life of God? In order to respond to these questions, we will reflect upon the dynamics of interpersonal communication.

When any of us speaks sincerely with another person who is openly receptive to us, we communicate something of ourselves to the hearer. We lead others to see, to understand, to appreciate things, persons, life itself as we do; we give the other person something of ourselves. Likewise, when any of us spends time, talent, and energy in dedicated love and service of another, we also give something of ourselves to the other person. The expression of service and love may be in the form of teaching, counseling, parenting; it may be by way of honesty in business or professional services; it may take place in the contexts of friendship or marriage; it may be concretized in acts of listening, challenging, encouraging, forgiving or advising. In each of these instances we give something of ourselves to the other person; the other person's life is, to some degree, imbued with new energy; he or she is transformed. In truth, they take on a fuller life, sharing something from us; and, we, also in truth, live in them. Through our honest and genuine loving interpersonal relationships, we communicate something of our true selves, even the deepest dimensions of our lives, to others. We and they become one.

By the very fact that Jesus of Nazareth is the presence of the *Logos* in the flesh, he, in expressing himself in words and actions of genuine love, personally communicates himself to us. But, given the core depth of his own personal being, his self-giving to us communicates none other than the God of everlasting life and love. We name that Gift of his deepest life, communicated to and dwelling within us, the Spirit of God (the personal dynamic energy of God's Love moving us to love and to respond to *Abba* and his Son in gratitude and joy). Jesus is the one Mediator of God's life to humankind, the one through whom God becomes alive for us; Jesus is the one through whom God mediates God's own Self to us, so powerfully that we, open to his gift, become transformed. We become empowered to live by the Spirit of God, to see as Jesus saw, to love as Jesus loved. We become one with and alive in God.

But there is still one other significant dimension of Jesus' role as Mediator. Jesus not only communicates the Spirit, God's personal energy for light and love, deep within us; Jesus also shows us how to live by that Spirit. We find God alive, not only through him, but also in him and with him. By his prayer, by his way of searching for *Abba's* will, he shows us that it is possible for us, human beings, to discern God's presence within ourselves, and with that, to discover more fully our own true and authentic selves. He leads us to see that we truly are persons created, and constantly being re-created in and through the Word. Further, by his surrender to *Abba*, by his faithfulness to the call to love, by the breadth of his forgiveness, by the risen life he finally manifests, he shows us the ever deepening potential for life and love which is ours as we allow the energy of his Spirit to move us forward in love just as he did. And by the overall outline of the way of discipleship which he counseled, he offers continual and concrete guidance, giving us his constant word of light and support, so that we might discern well the paths of Godly life in this world until we meet the risen Lord in everlasting glory. Jesus is the Mediator in whom we find God alive for us, the Mediator manifesting who we are and who we are destined to become.

By the very fact of the incarnation, completed in Jesus' death and resurrection, then, Jesus of Nazareth manifests the divinization of human being. He is the reconciliation of God and humankind in person. He is the true Mediator between God and humankind. He is the one in whom and through whom we find God alive for us and communicated to us, the one in whom and through whom we too become alive in the Spirit of God. In him and through him, we too become empowered to live the human journey in a Godlike way, seeing the world as God sees the world and loving other persons as God loves them. Jesus of Nazareth, Word made flesh, crucified and risen, is the one in whom and through whom God's Spirit is poured forth upon the earth. He is the one in and through whom we are made one with God so that, as members of Christ's living Body on earth, we may walk with him in lives of conscious freedom in the ongoing task of bringing about God's kingdom. Jesus is the one Mediator between God and humankind.

Reflections for Doing Christology

Our consideration of the personal unity of Jesus, the Word made flesh, a unity in Christ's concrete being, consciousness and freedom, brings us to our final set of observations concerning the process of doing Christology, the task of every Christian. We will unfold these observations in two stages.

THE PROCESS OF DOING OF CHRISTOLOGY
From the repeated efforts Christians have made to come to an adequate understanding of Jesus' personal unity, and from the multiple ways they have striven to express that unity, it becomes clear that one needs a refined language, a carefully crafted philosophical idiom to speak accurately of transcendent mystery in general and the mystery of Jesus, the appearance of the transcendent One among us, in particular.

Further, it also becomes clear that the words and the language we use to express divine mystery in general, and in this case, the unity of God with the human in the man Jesus, grow out of a particular culture and history. As culture and history change, so do the meaning of the words and the statements we had used to convey faith-understanding. Beliefs, statements expressive of a profound experience in faith, carefully crafted in a given age, become unintelligible to a later age. Hence, the Church is charged with the task of doing Christology again for every succeeding age. It is charged with reinterpreting the mystery of Christ's and God's transcendent love for another culture and another era. By its nature, Christology is always an unfinished business. In its very essence, it is a process by which Christians strive to describe for themselves and for their own age the mystery which has unfolded in the historical Jesus and which, through him, unfolds again and again in every new context.

Nevertheless, in doing Christology in any age, one cannot ignore the questions and responses of past generations. For, in spite of changes, human nature, the concerns of human beings, and the mystery which perplexes and challenges their understanding and stirs human beings to inquire further, remain very much the same, even if we ask the questions in different terms. Hence, before giving answer to the question "Who do you say that I am?" Christians wisely seek to respond to the question "Who do people say that I am?"

At the same time, it also becomes clear that no language, no matter how refined, can be adequate to express the mystery which always lies beyond the limits of human words. Hence, we must keep in touch with the mystery itself, we must maintain a contemplative stance, we must be open to the Transcendent and must actually experience the transforming power of transcendent Mystery and the crucified and risen Lord ourselves, if we are truly to understand *Abba* and the One whom *Abba* has sent. Language and the beliefs of the Church are meant to guide and to lead into the experience of God; they can never be a substitute for that experience, or worse, for God in God's Self.

DOING CHRISTOLOGY AND
THE AFFIRMATION OF THE UNITY OF JESUS
The tasks of meeting God in Christ, of maintaining a contemplative stance before transcendent Mystery whom Jesus and we name *Abba* and of continuing the process of interpreting this mystery may seem overwhelming. The message of this book, and particularly this chapter, however, points to the clear possibility of engaging in these tasks fruitfully and successfully. For, just as Jesus experienced *Abba* and spoke clearly of him, so the Christian, alive in Christ, comes to know God and is empowered to show forth what God in

Christ wills to do in this world with and through us. The uniqueness of Jesus should not be taken as a truth which reduces the Christian to powerlessness in this task. For the Church's efforts to uphold the personal unity of Jesus - God and human - while certainly attesting to Jesus' uniqueness among us, must not be seen as a way of separating Jesus from us. For, not only do Christians walk the same human life as Jesus did, they also are begotten of God, *Abba*, in and through Christ.[51] Gifted with the Spirit of Christ, Christians too enjoy a profound union with God at the level of their deepest selves, a unity at the personal level, begetting a dynamism for life in Christ's likeness. In each Christian, reborn in Christ, there exists a wellspring of life and love reaching to life eternal. Hence the true self of every Christian already springs forth from the creative and re-creative hand of God who is *Abba*. We too are rooted in God's eternity from the very beginning; we too have been created and re-created in the eternal Word. Believers have a source of life and love within that enables them to live and to love as Jesus did. They form the Body of Christ on earth.

Therefore, Jesus' ways of discernment and of love model paths which we too can and must take, paths which will lead us to become more fully conscious of God's being alive in and one with us, paths which will enable us to express that unity of God and us in life-giving action in our world. Like Jesus, then, we can seek and find God's will by prayerfully considering the needs of our own time, the light of God's word, and the power of God's presence and love stirring us to fruitful action. Like Jesus, we can and will find ourselves nourished in our surrender to the movements of God's Spirit within and in our efforts to extend ourselves in selfless and generous love of neighbor. We can find in our lives a growing and deepening unity with the divine. The "Good News" of the life, death, and resurrection of Jesus is that through him, we and God have become one, one in being, one in mind, and one in heart. The unity of God and humankind in Jesus models the unity which all Christians can experience. As has been true since the Apostles first gave witness to the risen Lord, the Church has concerned itself and continues to concern itself with the question of who Jesus is in order to preserve and to foster the experience of salvation which all are to enjoy. The mystery of Christ and the mystery of Christian salvation are one.

In light of these observations, we can bring this book to a close. For all that we have tried to do was to introduce the reader to the personal task of doing Christology, the task that begins in the experience of God alive in and through Jesus, the task that is enlightened and shaped by the reflections and beliefs of many generations of believers who themselves have processed and handed on this experience of Jesus, the task that always remains "open-ended" and necessarily ongoing if the Word is to continue to become flesh in believers of each age until the end of the world. What we have attempted to do in writing this book is merely to give the reader a fuller understanding of who people say that Jesus is together with an appreciation of what lay behind their beliefs; to offer the reader some light concerning the process itself of doing Christology; and thereby to enable the reader to give an intelligent and personally fulfilling account of who he or she says and believes Jesus to be. In doing so, we, hopefully, have convinced the reader that, like the Church as a whole, no one of us can consider him or herself to have finished the task. For, as our lives change and grow, we must once again ask who Jesus is for us. We must seek to understand the mystery ever more deeply as Christ himself invites us to meet each new stage of life and each new moment of history supported by the power, the light and the energy of his presence. Thus the Church as a whole, and each believer within it, must continue to do Christology if we are to find life in Jesus' Name...life which lifts up the heart, prompts Christian action and brings about God's kingdom in the crucified and risen Lord for the transformation of the entire world.

Questions for Reflection

1. Having read this chapter, how have you come better to understand the classical distinction between "person" and "nature?" Can you identify the dimensions of human experience which these terms point to in your own life? Explain.

2. The struggles which the Church endured in the fifth century and beyond in its effort to uphold the unity of Jesus while also giving adequate account of both his divinity and his humanity represent a struggle inherent in any human effort to express the experience of the union of the transcendent God with human beings. In what way(s) do you notice the Church and Christian believers within it engaged in that same struggle today? Explain.

3. From your reading of the Gospels, in what ways do you see the unique and personal character of the Logos *manifested in the life of the historical Jesus? How do these aspects (words, deeds, attitudes) of the life of the historical Jesus enable one to maintain the absolute unity of Jesus while also enabling one rightly to speak of the "human personality" of the divine Person? Explain.*

4. Having read and reflected upon the material of this chapter, what would you name as the principal elements within Jesus' historical life and experience which enabled him to discern clearly the will of Abba*? In what way do these elements offer Christian believers a workable pattern by means of which they can discover, in their own lives, the will of* Abba *and their most authentic selves re-created in Christ?*

5. In what way(s) does the historical Jesus' pattern of exercising human freedom reveal the true nature of human freedom? What do you find especially "freeing" for yourself in Jesus' way of life and example of freedom?

6. As you and the Church move into the future, what concrete experiences and/or issues stand before you "begging" for God's saving light and love? What guidelines have you gleaned from this study which will help you discover some answers to the questions which those experiences and/or issues present? How do you see the words, the deeds, the life and the person of Jesus bringing light and salvation to those experiences and issues?

ENDNOTES

CHAPTER 1

1.Any number of theologians, including those of considerable stature, initiate their discussion of Christology adopting this starting point. Raymond Brown, for example, writes: "In its most literal sense,... 'Christology' would discuss how Jesus comes to be called the Messiah or Christ and what was meant by that designation.... In a broader sense... 'Christology' discusses any evaluation of Jesus in respect to who he was and the role he played in the divine plan - and this is the way the term shall be used henceforth." *An Introduction to New Testament Christology* (Mahwah, NJ: Paulist Press, 1994), p.3.

Likewise, Gerald O'Collins offers the following definition: "*Christology*: The theological interpretation of Jesus Christ, clarifying systematically who and what he is in himself." *Interpreting Jesus* (London: Geoffrey Chapman, 1983), p. xv. And further: "An intelligent Christology can help them (Christians) clarify and express just what it is they believe about him (Jesus)" *Ibid.*, p.2.

Finally, most recently, Brian McDermott wrote: "Christology is the word about Jesus, the Word of God: orderly speech (*logos*) about the Christ or 'anointed one' of God." And further: "Christology is the reasoned account of Christians' faith in Jesus of Nazareth as the Christ of God." *Word Become Flesh* (Collegeville, MN: Liturgical Press, 1993), pp.15, 17.

2.Daniel A. Helminiak, *The Same Jesus* (Chicago: Loyola Univ. Press, 1986), pp. 19-20.

3.O'Collins also moves in this direction, not in defining Christology, but in discussing the motives for this study: "Understanding, accepting and interpreting Jesus of Nazareth as Son of God and this world's Saviour immediately touches upon our personal identity, deepest needs and final destiny." *Interpreting Jesus*, p.2

4.Avery Dulles underscores this point in his book *The Craft of Theology* (New York: Crossroad, 1995), p.53: "The foundation (of theology) is not a set of objective statements, but rather the subjective reality of the persons who reflect upon their religious experience and especially upon the basic process we call conversion."

5.Richard P. McBrien follows this path, writing: "Theology comes into play at that very moment when the person of faith becomes intellectually conscious of his or her faith.... For the interpretation of one's faith is theology, itself.... More specifically, theology is that process by which we bring our knowledge and understanding of God to the level of expression. Theology is the articulation, in a more or less systematic manner, of the experience of God within human experience." *Catholicism, I* (Minneapolis, MN: Winston Press, Inc., 1980) p.26.

6.Reflecting upon the nature of theology, Roger Haight highlights three inter-related characteristics of interpretation. "Interpretation must be faithful, intelligible and empowering.... All three are necessary. Interpretation that is faithful and intelligible but does not empower human freedom is irrelevant. Interpretation that is faithful and empowering but unintelligible is demagogic and a contradiction to human freedom. Interpretation that is intelligible and empowering but unfaithful to Christian origins is, by definition, in that measure non-Christian." *Dynamics of Theology* (Mahwah, NJ: Paulist Press, 1990), p.188.

7.Richard McBrien (*Catholicism, I*, p.25) "tentatively" defines faith as "personal knowledge of God." Further on, he expands his description of faith (pp. 31-46, but see especially his synthesis on pages 45f). We prefer to use the terms "awareness" and "disposition" at the outset, because the word "knowledge" can be too quickly understood to mean "explicit thought, concept and/or judgment."

8.Soren Kierkegaard describes this dimension of faith in very dynamic terms, calling it an "infinite passion," thereby emphasizing its powerful and profoundly energizing quality. See *Concluding Unscientific Postscript*, trans. by David F. Swenson and Walter Lowrie (Princeton: Princeton Univ. Press, 1941), p.182.

9.Paul Tillich has summed up the experience of God in faith as the experience of and commitment to an "Ultimate Concern." See his *Dynamics of Faith* (New York: Harper Torchbooks, 1958), pp.1-4.

10.Further reading on the experience of God as source of theology can be found in Dermot A. Lane, *The Experience of God: An Introduction to Doing Theology* (New York/Ramsey, NJ: Paulist Press, 1981), especially pages 4-31.

11.McBrien defines "Beliefs" in this fashion: "In the theological sense of the word, a belief is a formulation of the knowledge we have of God through Faith." *Catholicism, I*, p.27.

12.*Ibid.*

13.False beliefs are often referred to by the term "heresy". Within the Roman Catholic Church, however, in its official law (Canon 751), the term heresy is applied only to a very specific group of persons (baptized Christians) and is reserved to the obstinate denial or doubt of a very specific group of beliefs (those which the official Church formally teaches and proposes as divinely revealed). See *The Code of Canon Law: A Text and Commentary*, James A Coriden, Thomas J. Green and Donald E. Heintschel, eds. (Mahwah, NJ: Paulist Press, 1985), pp. 547-548.

14.For a further analysis of the interrelationship of faith and beliefs, see Haight, *Dynamics of Theology*, pp.26-29

15.Ultimate Reality, if it is truly ultimate, cannot be two (or more). If the latter were the case, neither would be truly ultimate.

16.These two points will be developed more fully below on page 22f in the discussion of "Personal Faith and the Transcendent Object of Faith."

17.Roger Haight grounds the relationship between personal faith and the community of beliefs in the nature of truth itself. "On the one hand there is a dimension of everyone's faith that is individual and uniquely his or her own. But on the other hand it cannot remain merely or purely private; it inevitably and inescapably shares in the public sphere.

"It is not difficult to understand why this is necessarily the case. The object of faith concerns ultimate truth, and both the nature of truth and its ultimacy demand that faith become a public act. For truth cannot remain 'truth for me'. The inner logic of a search for truth cannot accept and necessarily rejects an absolute relativism that negates the idea of truth itself. This is especially apparent in matters of ultimate importance. They cannot remain purely private matters. Thus...this object of faith is rendered public by the use of common language." *Dynamics of Theology*, pp.32f.

18.For a fuller discussion of this process, see Haight, *Dynamics of Theology*, pp.32-39.

19.This material will be considered more fully in Chapter 2 below.

20.In this respect, Jesus was and is the "premier theologian."

21.Fuller development of the material in this section can be found in John F. Haught, *What is God? How to Think of the Divine* (Mahwah, NJ: Paulist Press, 1986).

22.It is true that some persons can hide from or ignore these evils and from the desire to be freed from their threat. They can do so by keeping busy and/or by engaging in passing satisfactions. But given a short period of reflection, a temporary respite from such busyness and passing satisfaction, the pain of the presence of evil and the desire for an existence which is more abiding and satisfying will readily emerge in consciousness. Everyone, at least from time to time, must ask: "How shall I die?" and "How will I face death?"

23.The experience of self-transcending openness in knowledge and freedom, the desire for the Transcendent, and the experience of the Transcendent itself form a unity in human experience, so much so that it is difficult to distinguish the longing for transcendent reality from an awareness of the Transcendent One. This becomes even further complicated when the longing is suffused with a sense of the Presence, yet surpassing Otherness, of the Transcendent. For these reasons, Karl Rahner names the Transcendent "Holy Mystery." On this entire issue, see his *Foundations of Christian Faith*, trans. by William V. Dych (New York: Seabury, 1978), pp.44-89, 116-126, and, regarding the name "Holy Mystery," especially pp.57-66.

24.For this reason Dulles, reflecting upon the insights of Bernard Lonergan, speaks of the foundation of theology as being not just "religious experience," but more especially "the basic process we call conversion." He then defines "conversion" as "a radical shift in a person's apprehensions and values, accompanied by a similar radical change in oneself, in one's relations with other persons, and in one's relations to God" (*The Craft of Theology*, p.53). He further notes that the process of conversion "is a continuous process, demanded at every stage of the Christian life," making the doing of theology of existential importance for all believers (p.54f).

25.The nature and theological understanding of salvation, as well as the nature of the human longing for salvation, will receive fuller attention below in Chapters 5 and 7.

26.If the original experience of Moses would have been less specific and detailed than the text immediately suggests, one may ask, "What manner of knowing, what kind of knowledge, does an experience of the Transcendent entail?" One does not detect the presence of the self-giving God through sense knowledge or empirical observation. Rather one becomes aware of God, present in the freedom of God's love, through the self-transcending openness of one's deepest longings as a spiritual person. This type of knowing might well be described as "contemplative" knowing. It is distinguished from empirical knowing and even from rational, deductive knowledge. Contemplative knowing requires the willingness to be quiet within oneself and to allow one's desire for and openness to the fullness of reality to be consciously awakened. This is why periods of meditation and prayer are more likely to afford opportunities for such awareness than are the busy periods of the day. Knowledge of the Transcendent is contemplative knowledge, not empirical knowledge; it is an awareness born in the openness and readiness of faith.

CHAPTER 2

1.We say *dimension* because, as we have seen above in Chapter 1, in every generation the experience of God in personal faith is another necessary dimension of the starting point of doing Christology.

2.The earliest version of the Gospel of Mark ends with the promise of his future appearance.

3.More synthetic pictures of Jesus' life, ministry, death, and resurrection, gleaned from reflections on the Gospel traditions taken as a whole, can be found in Brennan Hill, *Jesus the Christ: Contemporary Perspectives* (Mystic, CT: Twenty-Third Publications, 1991) and in Donald Senior, *Jesus: A Gospel Portrait* (New York: Paulist Press, 1992).

4.On the following, see Daniel J. Harrington, "The Gospel According to Mark", *The New Jerome Biblical Commentary*, ed. Raymond E. Brown, Joseph A. Fitzmyer, and Roland E. Murphy (Englewood Cliffs, NJ: Prentice Hall, 1990), pp. 597-614.

5.For a full development of the biblical figures of "Suffering Servant" and "Son of God", see Oscar Cullmann, *The Christology of the New Testament* (Philadelphia: Westminster Press, 1963), pp. 51-82, 270-305.

6.On the title "Son of God", see Walter Kasper, *Jesus, the Christ* (New York: Paulist Press, 1976), pp. 163-172, and Raymond E. Brown, *Jesus God and Man* (Milwaukee: Bruce Publ. Co., 1967), pp. 86-88.

7.Is. 42:1-4; 49:1-7; 50:4-11; 52:13-53:12

8.Mk. 8:31; 9:31; 10:32f

9.Raymond E. Brown, *A Crucified Christ in Holy Week* (Collegeville, MN: Liturgical Press, 1986), pp. 21-33.

10.*Ibid.*, p. 23.

11.Mk. 14:60-61; 15:1-5; compare Mk. 14:45f with Mt. 26:49f.

12.The infancy narratives (chapters 1 and 2) of both Matthew's and Luke's Gospels serve as prologue for their respective Gospels as a whole. Each infancy narrative shows the distinctive theological cast which characterizes the remainder of the books of these authors.

13.Raymond E. Brown, *A Coming Christ in Advent* (Collegeville, MN: Liturgical Press, 1988), pp. 7-39, especially 27-29.

14.Raymond E. Brown, *An Adult Christ at Christmas* (Collegeville, MN: Liturgical Press, 1978), pp.10-14.

15.On this entire section, see John P. Meier *The Vision of Matthew* (New York/Ramsey, NJ: Paulist Press, 1979), pp. 62-66, 222-239.

16.This particular emphasis of Matthew is further highlighted by contrasting this episode with its Lucan parallel, Christ's teaching *on the plain* (Lk. 6:17).

17.Mt. 5:21f, 27f, 31f, 33f, 38f, 43f.

18.Mt. 5:3,6; compare with Luke 6:20f, 24f.

19.Raymond E. Brown, *The Churches the Apostles Left Behind* (New York/Ramsey: Paulist Press, 1984), pp. 131-135.

20.John P. Meier, *The Vision....*, pp. 106-121.

21.*Ibid.*, pp. 127-135.

22.*Ibid.*, pp. 210-219.

23.For a comprehensive treatment of Luke's Christology, see Joseph A. Fitzmyer, *The Gospel According to Luke I-IX*, Anchor Bible 28 (Garden City, NY: Doubleday, 1981), pp. 192-227.

24.*Ibid.*, pp. 247-251.

25.As Joseph Fitzmyer points out (*The Gospel...*, pp. 379, 387), "Daybreak (Dawn) from on high" is a Messianic title. The Greek word *anatole,* here translated by the term "daybreak" or "dawn" occurs three times in the Septuagint: in Jer. 23:5; Zec. 3:8, 6:12. There it is used to translate the Hebrew, *semah,* meaning "sprout," "shoot" or "scion" in obvious Messianic contexts. (For example, Jeremiah 23:5 reads: "Behold the days are coming, says the Lord, when I will raise up a righteous shoot to David.") Thus the Messianic heir to the Davidic throne is here referred to at the "Daybreak (Dawn) from on high" mediating the compassion and mercy of Yahweh for those who sit in darkness and the shadow of death, leading all to God's peace.

26.Joseph A. Fitzmyer, *The Gospel....,* pp. 529f.

27.Compare Luke 6:20-26 with Matthew 5:3-11.

28.Joseph A. Fitzmyer, *The Gospel....,* pp. 1043-1048.

29.*Ibid.,* pp. 1124-1136.

30.*Ibid.,* pp. 1201-1206, 1218-1227, 1319-1322.

31.Robert J. Karris, "The Gospel According to Luke", *The New Jerome Biblical Commentary,* ed. Raymond E. Brown, Joseph A. Fitzmyer, and Roland E. Murphy (Englewood Cliffs, NJ: Prentice Hall, 1990), p. 697.

32.Joseph A. Fitzmyer, *The Gospel....,* pp. 882-890.

33.*Ibid.,* pp. 1071-1094.

34.*Ibid.,* pp. 1507-1511.

35.His "going forth to his Father." On the meaning of the term and its significance, see Chapter 3, page 84.

36.On the role of the Spirit in Luke see Joseph A. Fitzmyer, *The Gospel....,* pp. 227-231.

37.In this respect, he is one with Matthew 1:18-20.

38.That same Spirit enables Elizabeth to recognize Jesus in his mother's womb (Lk. 1:41), a foreshadowing that all who recognize him will do so because of that Spirit's presence.

39.Joseph A. Fitzmyer, *The Gospel....,* pp. 864-876.

40.Note the distinctive character of Luke's version of this pericope as compared to Matthew's version. See Mt. 7:11.

41.Joseph A. Fitzmyer, *The Gospel....,* pp. 962-967.

42.*Ibid.,* pp. 1578-1585.

43.Compare, for example, Proverbs 8:22-31 with John 1:1-13. Biblical scholars point out the identity of this Word with Wisdom. See Elizabeth A. Johnson, *She Who Is* (New York: Crossroad, 1994), pp. 94-100, 156-161.

44.Glory in John refers to the visible manifestation of God's presence and power, dwelling first in the tabernacle (Ex. 40:34) and later in the temple (I Kings 8:10-13).

45.Compare with Ex. 34:6.

46.On the theme of Wisdom in the fourth Gospel in general, and on the following passages in particular, see Raymond E. Brown, *The Gospel according to John, I-XII,* Anchor Bible, 29 (Garden City, NY: Doubleday, 1966), pp. cxxii-cxxv, 128-149, 156-163, 178-180, 262-280, 339-345.

47.Verses are numbered according to NRSV version of the Bible.

48. See also Jn. 7:37-39

49. In this passage Wisdom is identified with the starry flame guiding Israel by night. See also Wisdom 18:3-4, where Wisdom is identified with the "imperishable light of the Law," continuing the saving work of that Law.

50. As in Mark 1:27; 2:12; 5:20, 42; 7:37; and parallels.

51. As in Matthew 11:2-5; 12:28.

52. This sign foreshadows the bread which he will give for the life of the world (6:22-59).

53. Jn. 9:13-17, 24-41.

54. Jn. 8:12

55. Raymond E. Brown, *The Gospel according to John I-XII*, pp.533-538.

56. This section describes Jesus' final words to his disciples, often called his "Farewell Address" (chapters 13-16) and his final prayer (17), in addition to embracing the Johannine passion (18-19) and resurrection (20-21) narratives.

57. See Raymond E. Brown, *The Gospel of John, XIII-XXI*, Anchor Bible 29A (Garden City: Doubleday, 1970), pp. 607, 612-614.

58. *Ibid.,* pp. 1102-1120.

59. For an analysis of the identity and functions of the Spirit in the fourth Gospel, see Raymond E. Brown, *The Gospel of John, XIII-XXI*, pp. 1135-1143.

60. Often such a change is called "conversion." From what is being said here, it should be clear that such conversion is more God's doing than the individual's doing.

61. Again, it should be noted that it is the experience of God in faith that will be the driving force behind the fashioning of the new image. Without the experience of God, any representation of the transcendent would be merely an empty shell, containing no life or inner vitality.

62. This point has relevance also for the development of the tradition after the New Testament period, a development which we will trace in Chapters 9 and 10. For it is not only the individual disciple but the Church as a whole which necessarily faces new circumstances, new questions, and new challenges in its beliefs and in its communal life of faith. This "newness" in the ongoing life of the community itself prompts and requires further understandings and representations of the Transcendent and of God's Christ, so that the genuineness of one's interpretation of the faith experience of God in Christ be preserved and an ongoing life with God in Christ be fostered.

CHAPTER 3

1. The phrase "community of beliefs" can actually be used in two related senses: 1) a "communion of persons united and driven by common faith and common beliefs"; 2) the "collection of beliefs which the community shares and hands on." Here we intend the first sense of the phrase and will use the term "tradition" or "traditions" for the second sense.

2. This method, in so far as it is employed in analyzing and interpreting the Gospels and their formation, seeks 1) to identify and to distinguish the various stages of the historical development of the Gospel texts as we now have them and 2) to place the portions of the overall texts which it has distinguished in the churches and historical moments which produced them. Thus, the "historical-critical" method would distinguish (a) elements of

the Gospel which the final writer (technically referred to as the "redactor") is responsible for (e.g., the differences in the theologies which can be discerned by comparing and contrasting similar passages in different Gospels, one with the other); (b) elements of the Gospels which reflect the post-resurrection insights of the living churches as they handed on and interpreted their living memory of Jesus orally and/or in brief written forms (e.g., allegorical interpretations of some of Jesus' parables; clarifying details within Jesus' own predictions of his forth-coming passion, death and resurrection); (c) elements which reflect the actual setting of Jesus' earthly life (e.g., the actual unfolding events of Jesus' historical life as well as the (substance of the) sayings, the miracles, the pronouncements and the parables of Jesus himself). By using this method, scholars are able, among other things, to discern more clearly the intent of each individual evangelist, the development of faith and belief within the early church, and the concerns which Jesus himself faced as he executed his mission.

We are presupposing the legitimacy and the value of this method in this book in general, and particularly in the work of this chapter. The usefulness and the value of the method will become clearer throughout the chapter.

3.*Sitz im Leben Jesu*, in German, the language of the biblical scholars who first distinguished the stages of the formation of the Gospels as we know them.

4.*Sitz im Leben der Kirche*, in the German.

5.Such preaching and catechizing may have initially consisted simply in the proclamation of Jesus' death and resurrection in rather short dogmatic formulas (see, for example, Acts 2:36 and Romans 4:25). But soon, the "telling of the story" of Jesus was amplified and filled out so as to preserve the memory of Jesus in greater detail. Thus, the disciples would have developed what are now called "passion narratives," giving fuller account of Jesus' last hours. To that would have been added narratives of his post-resurrection appearances, accounts of the sayings, the parables, the pronouncements and the miracles of Jesus, each addition serving well to "preserve the memory of Jesus" for subsequent generations. Finally, still during this period, leading figures in the churches would have begun to write these memories down, largely to preserve them more carefully as the original witnesses of Jesus began to die. Nonetheless, during this period, the mode of handing on the good news of God's love accomplished in and through Jesus, consisted largely in communicating an oral tradition.

6.*Sitz-im-Evangelium,* in the German.

7.Very readable and informative summaries of the historical background within the field of contemporary biblical criticism and also of insightful presentations of current methodology can be found in Norman Perrin, *What is Redaction Criticism?* (Philadelphia: Fortress Press, 1969) and also in Edgar V. McKnight, *What is Form Criticism?* (Philadelphia: Fortress Press, 1969).

8.We will leave further consideration of the first period of Gospel formation, namely the establishment of the original revelation in the time and life of Jesus, to chapters five through eight.

9.Because of its complex and different development, we will treat the Johannine community and the fourth Gospel in the next chapter.

10.In the next chapter, where we will reflect upon the Johannine community, we will attend at some greater length to the "life-situation" of that community prior to, as well as at the time of, the final composition of the fourth Gospel.

11.See Raymond E. Brown and John P. Meier, *Antioch and Rome* (New York: Paulist Press, 1983), pp. 196-197 for a summary of the evidence which establishes the location of the community for which this Gospel was written.

12. Vincent Taylor, *The Gospel According to Mark*, 2nd ed., (London; Macmillan, 1966), pp. 31-32; Daniel J. Harrington, "The Gospel According to Mark", *The New Jerome Biblical Commentary*, p. 596; Brown and Meier, *Antioch...*, pp. 191-194.

13. Tacitus thought Christians to be a "notoriously depraved group," a people who sponsored "pernicious superstition," exhibiting practices and behaviors which he likened to "all the degraded and shameful practices (which) gather and become the vogue" at Rome. See *Annals*, 15:44, cited in Raymond E. Brown and John P. Meier, *Antioch and Rome*, pp. 98-99.

14. Brown and Meier, *Antioch...*, pp. 97-99. The context of Nero's action involved a fire which lasted nine days and which destroyed, in whole or in part, ten of the fourteen districts of Rome. The emperor himself was suspected of having instigated the fire. To suppress the rumor, Nero arrested and persecuted the Christians, making scapegoats of them.

15. C. S. Mann, *Mark, Anchor Bible 27.* (Garden City: Doubleday, 1986), pp. 73, 79.

16. By the first century, Jews of Rome, numbering between 40,000 and 50,000, were free to associate with one another for their own religious purposes (See Brown and Meier, *Antioch...*, p. 94). It was among such groups that Jewish Christian missionaries from Jerusalem made converts and it was within these Jewish Christian communities that Gentiles were subsequently admitted.

17. Each community of Jewish Christians held varying opinions with regard to which aspects of their Jewish heritage remained in force in their lives as Christians. The most conservative group insisted upon full observance of the Mosaic Law, including the circumcision of Gentile converts. (See Acts of the Apostles 11:2, 15:5. Paul writes of this group, manifesting disdain, in Galatians 2:4 calling them "false brothers" who were "secretly brought in [to the Council of Jerusalem] to spy on our freedom which we have in Christ Jesus, that they might enslave us.")

A moderately conservative group relaxed the demand for the circumcision of converts, but required that both Jewish and Gentile Christians continue to observe the Jewish Laws governing both foods and Jewish Feasts. (See Acts... 15:14-29, Galatians 2:11-14, and I Corinthians 8.)

A third, more liberal, group regarded laws governing foods as no longer binding, but continued to demand the observance of Jewish Feasts. (Paul himself would seem to have represented this group as is evident from the tone of his writing in Galatians and I Corinthians as cited above. See also Galatians 3:10-25.)

Finally, a fourth, ultra-liberal group sponsored the replacement of Jewish feasts with Christian celebrations. (See John 2:19-21, 4:21, 5:1, 5:9b, 6:4, 7:2.)

Although the larger number of Jewish/Gentile Christians most likely maintained the characteristics of the moderately conservative group, other groups of Jewish/Gentile Christians would also have existed within the confines of Rome. (This would be true particularly because these communities were founded by the Church at Jerusalem, itself moderately conservative. See Brown and Meier, *Antioch...*, pp. 97-104.)

18. Brown and Meier (*Antioch...*, pp. 124-127) offer evidence indicating that, out of jealousy and envy, fellow Christians betrayed both Peter and Paul into Roman hands, thereby leading them to their martyrdom.

19. Some scholars also speak of the figure and concept, developed in Hellenistic culture, of a "Divine Man", one who shared the Divine Nature and had the ability to work miracles. (See Norman Perrin, *What is Redaction Criticism?* [Philadelphia: Fortress Press, 1969] pp.55-56, and also Reginald H. Fuller, *The Foundations of New Testament Christology*

[New York: Charles Scribner's Sons, 1965], pp. 98, 227-228.) If such a concept were circulating in the time of Mark's community, it would prompt the question of how to understand Jesus, worker of wonders, filled with divine power. It would challenge Christians to articulate their faith in Jesus in terms which stood in clear contrast with pagan and Hellenistic beliefs. The existence, however, of a clear and widespread concept of a "Divine Man" and, therefore, its possible influence upon Mark's Gospel is largely discredited among most recent scholars. (See John P. Meier, *A Marginal Jew: Rethinking the Historical Jesus, Vol.II* [New York: Doubleday, 1994], pp. 595-601, and also C. S. Mann, *Mark, Anchor Bible, 27* [New York: Doubleday, 1986]).

20.For a fuller development of the interrelationship of the Marcan Jesus and the way of discipleship in the Marcan community, see Ernest Best, *Following Jesus: Discipleship in the Gospel of Mark* (Sheffield, England: University of Sheffield, JSOT Press, 1981).

21.This concern of the Marcan Jesus to hide his identity is referred to by scholars as the "Messianic Secret" in Mark's Gospel. This secrecy of Jesus concerning his Messiahship is clearly Mark's way of underscoring Jesus' efforts to draw attention to (what Mark regards as) the deepest dimension of Jesus' identity, his suffering.

22.Further, while the author unfolds this curious tension between Jesus' manifestation of divine power and his concerted effort toward maintaining secrecy, he simultaneously introduces another conflict: the disciples' inability to understand Jesus and Jesus' repeated rebuke of them for their lack of understanding. They do not understand the parable of the sower (4:10, 13), Jesus' power over the wind and the sea (4:40-41), the meaning of Jesus' miraculous feeding of the multitude and his walking on the water (6:50-52), Jesus' teaching about what constitutes cleanliness and uncleanness (7:17-18) or Jesus instruction concerning the "leaven of the Pharisees" (8:16-21). Jesus first rebukes tend to be mild: "Do you not understand this parable? Then how will you understand any of the parables?" (4:13); but gradually, his response seems to be marked with clear frustration: "Do you not yet understand or comprehend? Are your hearts hardened? Do you have eyes and not see, ears and not hear?" (8:17-18). (The theme of the disciples' lack of understanding continues through the entirety of the Gospel. See 8:32, 9:5-6, 9:30-32, 10:24-26, 32, 35-40 culminating in 14:37-41. This is most striking in that, as we shall see, the Marcan Jesus begins to reveal his identity in 8:31.)

23.For this reason, we also hear Jesus rebuking the disciples for lack of understanding. They need to know that they have not truly understood. Jesus makes sure that they, and the community at Rome, recognize that he is not readily or easily understood. It would be dangerous if they did not come to see that everything about him and his life falls within the ambit of God's unfolding for them the true way toward life.

24.This phase extends from 8:27 to 10:45 and is considered to be the heart of Mark's teaching regarding the meaning of Jesus in himself and the meaning of Jesus for discipleship within the community of Mark. The two meanings are intrinsically related: One can not understand Jesus without seeing his import for the community and one can not understand the way of the disciple without understanding the way of Jesus, for essentially the disciple is a follower of the Lord. See Ernest Best, pp. 15f.

25.This threefold structure of prediction of the passion, misunderstanding and/or resistance of the apostles, and instruction of the disciples by the Lord, a pattern itself repeated three times, clearly shows the evangelist's touch. He has selected and gathered sayings and memories of events from the community's tradition and carefully arranged them, linking them in this fashion, to highlight the interrelationship of Jesus' destiny and the way of discipleship.

26.On this passage and the interpretation which follows, see Ernest Best, pp. 37-44.

27. Jesus' understanding of this all-embracing perspective will become clearer through his subsequent instructions, but because the terms of his instruction are so generic and so open to contemporary misunderstanding, a few comments may be in order here. What does the Marcan Jesus mean by "taking up one's cross?" What is the import of the injunction to "deny oneself?"

Mark knows that, although persecution clearly stands as a threat to every Christian, it does not threaten every day. He knows that, should persecution strike, not every Christian will suffer martyrdom, and that, among those who do die, not each will die by way of crucifixion. Yet each disciple must take up his (her) cross. What is this cross? The cross, inevitable and necessary, which each disciple must take up refers to the hardships of being a disciple. The intent of the Marcan Jesus is to call each Christian to suffer whatever losses, whatever hardships, following Christ and his way will entail. Choices always involve letting go of one value, one relationship, one opportunity or goal in order to pursue another. Following Christ will involve concrete choices and hardships; it may even demand letting go of one's life. The Christian, and especially the Roman Christian of Mark's day, must be willing to live under the shadow of the cross. The disciple must be ready and willing to suffer whatever hardships fidelity to Christ may require.

This command stands in contrast with, but is nonetheless supported by the accompanying phrase, the command to deny oneself. Once again, the meaning of self-denial may not be immediately evident. Self-denial does not refer to denying oneself some thing (food), some pleasure (recreation) or some pursuit (leisure, reading, study of some topic which is of personal interest) which one may deeply desire but must let go of; rather it refers to the denial of one's very self. It invites the disciple to avoid focusing primarily on one's self, on one's own concerns, but rather to focus one's interest and concerns on Jesus. It invites one to abandon one's own limited vision of life and of the self and, rather, to adopt Christ's more profound vision of life and of the self (which actually reaches to eternity). In effect, it calls one to find one's "true and authentic self" in Jesus by rejecting the "false self" (a "lesser self") which status and comfort in this world and society tend to promote.

These two injunctions, the basic expressions of how the disciples must understand their journey in light of Jesus, the suffering Son of Man, then, correspond to one another as two dimensions of the same call: They refer to individual concrete actions and choices (taking up the cross: bearing concrete hardships which following Christ entails) and an abiding inner attitude (denial of self: humbly directing one's concern and attention away from the self and toward Christ), an attitude which will enable one to choose life through the cross of Christ with consistency. One must lose, let go of, one's lesser self through this self-denial in order to find one's true and authentic self, that is, to find and to accomplish all that one can be in Christ.

28. On this passage and the interpretation which follows, see Ernest Best, pp. 75-85.

29. See Ernest Best, pp. 99-101, 110-115.

30. In face of such radical self-surrender, the disciple might ask (as Peter intimates in the text): "What shall we receive?" (see 10:28). To such a question, the Marcan Jesus gives unqualified assurance: The disciple who lets go of all that stands in the way of servant-love can anticipate innumerable blessings even in this life, provided that that disciple be ready and willing also to accept the inevitability of persecution (10:29-30). The Marcan community needs to be a servant-community; in such service it will find its true greatness. In this way, they will find blessing now, and eternal life in the future (10:30).

31. For fuller analysis of this passage, see Ernest Best, pp. 123-130.

32. Unlike Matthew and Luke, Mark does not clearly separate these two events. Compare Mk. 13:4 with Mt. 24:3; compare Mk. 13:14-27 with Lk. 21:20-28, especially at verse 24.

33. The notion of "false Messiahs" may refer to revolutionaries or zealots, or other Jewish sectarians. On the difficulty of identifying precisely which group and/or individual this designation is referring to, see C. S. Mann, *Mark*, pp. 513-514.

34. On the theme of watchfulness in Mark's Gospel, see Ernest Best, pp. 147-161.

35. The reader would note that the instructions to watch and to pray are the same counsels which Jesus, in his moment of trial, gave to Peter, James and John as he brought them with him into the Garden of Gethsemane ("Remain here and watch" [14:34]). And that reader would also be aware of the fact that Peter, a hero of the Roman church, failed Jesus in this hour, even to the extent of cursing Jesus (Raymond E. Brown, *A Crucified Christ in Holy Week* [Collegeville, MN: Liturgical Press, 1986], p. 27). This memory would have special import for them. They too would be questioned regarding their allegiance to Jesus and would be challenged to curse him in order to save their lives (I Cor. 12:2-3, Rom. 10:9-13.). Remembering Peter's lack of courage and the extent of his capitulation to the forces of evil, together with recalling that same disciple's subsequent repentance and courage in proclaiming Jesus, would serve as warning and also would provide hope for any Roman Christian who may have so seriously succumbed to Roman inquisition.

36. On these two verses, see Ernest Best, pp. 199-101. For further reading with regard to Jesus' earlier commissioning of the apostles, see Best, pp. 166-196.

37. For discussion of the place and date of composition of the Gospel according to Matthew, see Raymond E. Brown and John P. Meier, *Antioch and Rome* (New York: Paulist Press, 1983), pp.15-27.

38. For fuller treatment of the church in Antioch during this period, see Brown and Meier, *Antioch...*, pp. 45-51.

39. Mt. 13:52 ("Every Scribe who has become a disciple of the kingdom of heaven is like a householder who brings out of his treasure what is new and what is old") is most probably self-descriptive. See Brown, *The Churches...*, pp. 126-127.

40. The party of the Sadducees, the more conservative of the Jewish leaders and the party so significant during Jesus' time had declined in importance in Judaism after the destruction of the Temple in the year 70. The party of the Pharisees, the teachers who had interpreted the law more liberally in Jesus' day, were the Jewish leaders commanding the greater respect at the time of Matthew's composition.

41. The latter is referred to as the "Sayings Source" or "Q", "Q" standing for the German *Quelle*, which, translated, means "source".

42. The narrative sections of the five books each move toward the five discourses so as to present the reader with the teachings of Jesus gathered into five coherent groups, broadly dealing with five basic themes: The Sermon on the Mount, dealing with the life of the disciples and giving the basic "plan" of the Kingdom of God which Jesus preached (5-7); the Missionary Discourse (10); the Discourse in Parables (13); the Discourse on Church Order (18); and the Eschatological Discourse (24-25). The ending of each discourse is marked by the phrase: "When Jesus finished these words, giving these commands, these parables,..." (7:28, 11:1, 13:53, 19:1, 26:1), facilitating a clear transition into the next book (or, for the last, into the passion narrative).

The basic themes contained in each book (narrative and discourse) can serve to highlight Jesus' responses to the questions presented above, although the author deals with the needs of the community and with Jesus' teachings in their regard in a progressive manner throughout the five books and through the Gospel as a whole.

43. For fuller treatment of the following, see Meier, John P. *The Vision of Matthew* (New York: Paulist Press, 1979). For briefer treatments, see Brown *The Churches...*, pp. 129-145 and Brown and Meier *Antioch...*, pp. 15-18, 57-72.

44. The Pharisees had striven to update the Law for a contemporary setting within Judaism, but their interpretations had become fixed tradition, rigid. As Raymond Brown (*The Churches...*, p. 127.) points out, the Jesus, who says again and again: "You have heard that it was said in the past..., but I say to you..." is making sure that a previous effort (that of the Pharisees themselves) to update God's law and will is not going to be regarded as if it were exhaustive of that law and will. It is not only the New Law which is at stake; it is freedom to move beyond the Old Law, the law which, as Jesus teaches, is not being cast aside but is reaching its higher fulfillment. Matthew invokes Jesus, the Teacher of the New Law, to move the community along the path to growth in its own identity precisely as Christian.

45. John P. Meier, *The Vision of Matthew*, pp. 84f.

46. John P. Meier, *The Vision of Matthew*, pp. 70-72.

47. John P. Meier, *The Vision of Matthew*, p. 106.

48. The author recognizes that Jesus' missioning his disciples to all nations reflected a marked change from the mind of the historical Jesus. It is a change in what seemed to have been God's plan of salvation. Hence, he underscores the fact that a radical change has happened within history in and with Christ's death and resurrection. He does this by surrounding both events with apocalyptic imagery: At Jesus' death, the veil of the sanctuary is torn in two, the earth quakes, tombs are opened, the dead are raised (27:51-54). At his resurrection the earth quakes again, an angel with an appearance like lightning descends upon the tomb, and the guards, shaken with fear, become like dead men (28:2-4). Clearly, the very foundations of the world are shaken and divine intervention is at its height. Jesus' death and resurrection establish a new age, and the disciples are rightly called to move that age forward (28:16-20). (See John P. Meier, *The Vision of Matthew*, pp. 33-38.)

49. See Mark 12:1-11. Matthew 21:33-42 follows Mark; Matthew 21:43 is peculiar to Matthew.

50. For further examples, see Brown *The Churches...*, pp. 133-134.

51. On the significance and meaning of this proclamation of faith and its difference from Peter's confession in Mark 8:29, and for further development and exegesis of the Matthean Jesus' words of commission to Peter, see John P. Meier, *The Vision of Matthew*, pp. 106-114.

52. The death of Peter and Paul in 64 would have left the community even more deeply vulnerable to factions and subject to greater disruptions than it would have been during an earlier period. Matthew's teaching about Peter may have been either confirming a leadership by way of succession already in place in Antioch or it may have been an effort to lay the ground for such leadership as the way to preserve unity. By 110, in the ministry of the monarchical bishop, Ignatius, this leadership was clearly in place. (See Brown and Meier, *Antioch...*, pp. 66-68.)

53. Mark's Gospel was written before the destruction of the Temple and the subsequent fall of Jerusalem to the Romans. Unlike Matthew and Luke, Mark does not clearly separate these two events. Compare Mk. 13:4 with Mt. 24:3; compare Mk. 13:14-27 with Lk. 21:20-28, especially at verse 24.

54. since the Gospel as well as Acts was composed in the mid-80's, after the events described in Acts.

An Introduction to Christology: Notes

55.Brown, *The Churches...*, pp.61-61; Joseph A. Fitzmyer *The Gospel According to Luke I-IX Anchor Bible 28* (Garden City, NY: Doubleday, 1981), pp. 53-59.

56.See Brown *The Churches...*, pp. 63-70; Fitzmyer *The Gospel According to Luke I-IX*, pp. 57-59.

57.The Lucan Jesus counsels the communities whom Luke envisions as his audience to deal with the interim period between his ascension and his second coming in a manner similar to the Matthean Christ. Luke downplays the persecutions and the second coming by stressing the importance of "taking up one's cross *daily"* (9:23, compare with Mk. 8:34) and by emphasizing that the time of the Gentiles must be fulfilled before he returns (21:24).

58.This lack of a sense of having a long-standing tradition, a lack of a sense of their roots, would have become even more troublesome given the fact that these communities would suffer from the general disregard that Romans had of Eastern religions, thinking of them as "superstitions." What would give them a sense of self-worth as religious people?

59.See Romans 1:18-32 for Paul's view of the Gentiles and sin.

60.In order to do this, Luke shows that God's plan of salvation is divided into three periods centered in Christ and his death and resurrection: The age of Israel prior to Christ (1:5-3:1), the age of Jesus (3:2-24:51) and the age of the Gentiles (Luke 24:52 - Acts 1:3-28:31). For fuller development of this perspective, see Fitzmyer, *The Gospel...*, pp. 179-192, especially pp. 181-185.

61.1:5-25, 57-80; 2:25-40.

62.Acts 2:14-36, 3:12-26, 13:16-41, 24:10-21, 26:2-23.

63.3:23-38, compared with Mt. 1:1-17.

64.Luke continues this theme in Acts beginning with Jesus' promise and commission to his disciples: "You will receive power when the Holy Spirit comes upon you and you will be my witnesses in Jerusalem throughout Judea and Samaria and to the ends of the earth" (1:8) and ending Paul's proclamation in Rome, affirming "that this salvation of God has been sent to the Gentiles; they will listen" (28:28).

Other adaptations which Luke has made in order to accommodate his Gospel to a predominantly Gentile audience include his omission of the controversy over what is clean or unclean (see Mark 7:1-23) and his failing to record the antitheses (Jesus' "updating" the Mosaic Law) of Matthew 5:21-48. For further Lucan adjustments, see Fitzmyer, *The Gospel...*, pp. 57-59.

65.So Peter and the apostles (1:5,8; 2:33; 4:8,31), then Stephen (6:8,10; 7:55), next Paul (9:17-20), and finally the presbyters at Ephesus (20:28).

66.The Spirit moves Philip to speak with an Ethiopian eunuch, whom he baptizes (8:29,38) and then guides him from Azotus to Caesarea (8:39-40); the same Spirit had directed Peter to accept the conversion of the Roman Gentile, Cornelius (11:12-15); while at worship, the Spirit indicated to Christian leaders in Antioch that they should send Barnabas and Saul to Seleucia and Cyprus (13:2,4); in council, the Spirit leads the apostles and presbyters of the Jerusalem church to come to a decision regarding admission of the Gentiles and circumcision (15:28); and ultimately it was the Spirit who guided Paul to Rome (20:22-23; see 19:21).

67.Everyone heeding Peter's counsel to "repent and be baptized...in the name of Jesus Christ for the forgiveness of sins...will receive the gift of the Holy Spirit. For the promise is made to you and to your children and to all those far off, whomever the Lord our God will call" (2:38-39). Through Peter and John, converts in Samaria received the Spirit (8:14-17); as Peter preached, the Spirit descended upon the Roman centurion Cornelius, a Gentile (10:17,44-48); and, as Paul baptized some inquiring new disciples at Ephesus, they received the Holy Spirit, spoke in tongues and prophesied (19:1-7).

68.As Luke unfolds the way of the disciples into the future, he gives ample evidence that the communities relied frequently upon the word mediated through the apostles and through their successors. Thus, the Jewish Christian converts, after having initially heard the word through Peter on the first Pentecost "devoted themselves to the teaching of the Apostles" (2:42). Paul received his commission, like the twelve, from the risen Lord (9:3-6) and later conferred with the apostles (9:27; 15:2) guaranteeing the authenticity of his preaching and teaching. Indeed Paul himself spent three years with the presbyters of Ephesus, proclaiming to them "the entire plan of God" and departed from them commending them to that word of God (20:31-32; see also 14:21-23). And he continues that ministry in Rome, remaining with these disciples two full years...and with complete assurance and without hindrance, he proclaimed the kingdom of God and taught about the Lord Jesus Christ" (28:28-31).

69.Peter (3:6-10; 9:32-41), all the apostles (5:12-16), Philip (8:4-8), Paul (8:8-10; 19:11-12; 20:9-12; 28:7-10) healed the crippled, raised the dead and cast out evil spirits, continuing the wonderful works of Jesus.

70.This understanding is clear from the fact that Luke, in anticipation of the beginning of Jesus' journey to Jerusalem, refers to that journey as Jesus' "movement beyond this life." In his account of Jesus' transfiguration, Luke describes Jesus as "conversing with Moses and Elijah, who...spoke of his exodus that he was going to accomplish in Jerusalem" (9:30f; contrast with Mk.9:4 and Mt.17:3). The author then makes this understanding explicit as he introduces the journey with the statement: "When the days for his being taken up were accomplished, he resolutely determined to journey to Jerusalem" (9:51). It is not Jesus' suffering and death which is the focus, but the outcome of his suffering which captures attention.

71.The figure of Jesus' journey to Jerusalem and the theme of Jesus' being the center of history are deeply inter-related. If Jesus is the center of history, the core event by which he assumes all of history to himself and becomes its center consists in his passage from death to life in his death and resurrection. He actually becomes the center of history by gathering everything of his life together and by bringing it to new life as he dies and rises, as he "enters into his glory" (Lk. 24:26). In this process, the figure of Jerusalem, the Holy City representing all of Israel, plays a central role.

In this light, Jesus must journey to Jerusalem (9:51; 13:22, 33; 17:11), enter that city (19:28-38), take its life "under his tutelage" (13:34b; 19:45-48) and, in its midst, with its people, die (13:33; 23:27-31), rise (24:1-6a), appear (24:33-40) and pour forth new life for all (24:46-49). By doing so, Jesus truly becomes the center of history. His accomplishing of his role of transforming human life, human freedom, and human history before, with, and in God must take place in the center of God's world, the center of Israel's world: the Holy City.

Hence Luke presents Jesus' life, and the way of discipleship, both as a journey through the world to a fuller life and world beyond. And he also presents Jesus' life and the disciples' way as a journey to Jerusalem. The latter enfleshes, expresses in history, what is taking place more deeply at the level of the spirit. In actuality, it is one journey which unfolds in two dimensions: the historical, this worldly dimension and the transcendent, other worldly, Godly dimension. By accomplishing the historical dimension of the journey, Jesus embraces the transcendent dimension of that journey. He becomes, in all reality, the center of history, the center and the mediator of all people's lives with God and of God's life with them.

The way of discipleship, too, must be understood as embracing a twofold dimension. It is (figuratively) a journey with Jesus to Jerusalem; in walking this journey, they too will move through this world, through their history, to everlasting life and glory with Christ.

72.Other instructions which the Lord gives his disciples along the journey include the parable of the rich fool (12:16-21); the parable of the wedding banquet and the advice to invite the poor (14:7-14); and the call to the rich official (18:18-23) together with Jesus' comment underscoring the difficulty which wealth presents as a person is called to become a full-fledged disciple (18:24-25).

73.In the book of Acts, Luke shows the community as having "taken to heart" these instructions regarding the way of discipleship. He calls attention to the fact that the model community held all things in common; members would sell their property and possessions and divide them among all according to each person's needs (2:44-45; see also 4:32-37). And the author indicates that Gentile converts continue such generosity, citing as examples Tabitha (9:36) and Cornelius (10:2, 4, 31). Further, he shows that Paul likewise urged the presbyters of Ephesus to "keep in mind the words of the Lord Jesus who himself said 'It is more blessed to give than to receive'" (20:35).

74.Luke records the apostles' faithfulness to this command frequently in Acts; see 2:38, 3:19, 5:31, 8:22, 11:18, 13:24, 17:30, 19:4, 20:21, 26:20.

75.Following through on this teaching, Luke, in the book of Acts, depicts the disciples as faithful to Jesus' call to prayer and their sustenance in the Spirit. Awaiting the Spirit on the first Pentecost, Mary and the apostles, some other women and Jesus "brothers" returned to the upper room where they were staying and "devoted themselves with one accord to prayer" (1:14). Before significant events and decisions, such as choosing Matthias as a successor to Judas (1:24), before appointing seven "deacons" to assist the apostles (6:2, 4), before missioning Barnabas (13:2), and before appointing elders in a number of cities (14:23), the disciples give themselves to prayer. The author further points out that Peter (3:1; 10:9, 30; 11:5), Paul (9:11; 20:36; 21:5) and the community as a whole (2:42; 4:31; 12:12) remain consistently faithful in prayer, clearly keeping open to Christ's guidance and the movement of the Spirit which Christ had promised them.

76.On this material, see Fitzmyer, *The Gospel...,* pp. 231-235.

77.Note how he clearly refers to Jerusalem's being surrounded by armies and to her desolation's being near (21:20; contrast with Mark 13:14), altering Mark's allusion to Daniel 9:27, 12:11, an allusion that his Gentile audience would not have understood.

78.Note 21:10c-11: "'but it will not be immediately the end.' Then he said to them...."

79.But note that this thought, too, can be detected, albeit in a weaker fashion, in Mark 13:10.

80.the text reads: "give us each day our daily bread."

81.The Lucan Jesus emphasizes this perspective even though he preserves some of the Marcan Jesus' sense of the imminence of the last days (22:32, 36; see also 18:7-8).

82.Note that this parable and its intent is similar to Matthew 25:14-20.

83.In the context of its fuller awareness of the role of Christ's Spirit in shaping the early church, the later church came to recognize the writings of the evangelists as "inspired," prompted by the Spirit. In part this awareness grew out of the disciples' experience of the presence of the Spirit offering light, strength, guidance and peace through the reading and proclamation of these writings (see II Tim. 3:16-17).

CHAPTER 4

1.Raymond E. Brown, in *The Community of the Beloved Disciple* (New York: Paulist Press, 1979) has given us a most comprehensive treatment of the origins, character and development of the Johannine Community together with an assessment of the contributions of several other scholars. The following is largely dependent on Father Brown's work.

2.Some would suggest Syria or even Alexandria. For discussion of the place of composition and reasons supporting the preference of Ephesus, see Raymond E. Brown, *The Gospel according to John, I-XII, Anchor Bible, 29* (Garden City, NY: Doubleday, 1966), pp. ciii-civ.

3.See *ibid.,* pp. lxxx-lxxxvi for discussion of the date of composition and pp. xxxiv-xxxix for the presentation of the stages of the development of the Gospel material prior and up to its final composition.

4.We are aware that Raymond Brown rightly distinguishes between the evangelist and the final redactor. He attributes to the evangelist the major work of developing, gathering, selecting, and organizing the preached and written materials which formed the earliest editions of the Gospel text and designates the final redactor as the person who has composed or compiled the text as we now have it. This person would have added Chapter 21 and also, most probably, the Prologue (1:1-18). See Brown, *ibid.,* pp. xxxiv-xxxix. Since we will be referring principally to the community addressed by the Gospel prior to its final redaction, and since the major work of composition of the Gospel was done by this first author, we will continue to refer to the author of the fourth Gospel as "the evangelist," unless it be certain that the portion of the text under consideration should be attributed to the final redactor.

5.The purpose of the Gospel clearly reflects a context of such struggles, whether Ephesus be the setting of the composition of the Gospel or not. The fact that Ephesus was the seat of such bitter strife in the early church, however, has led many scholars to prefer this city, among other proposed places, for the composition of the fourth Gospel. See Brown, *The Gospel*, pp. lxvii-lxxix, ciii-civ.

6.New York: Paulist Press, 1979. For the following we are largely dependent upon and very much indebted to this work.

7.See Jn. 1:35-51.

8.First called in the synoptics are Peter, Andrew, James, John (see Mk. 1:16-20; 3:13-19).

9.See 1:35-49.

10.Although, as we shall see, the fourth Gospel presents "the Jews" most often as bitter opponents of Jesus, it also retains remnants of more favorable relationships of Jesus (and of the community) with their Jewish ancestry. The evangelist records Jesus as saying to the Samaritan woman: "You people worship what you do not understand; we worship what we do understand, because salvation is from the Jews" (4:22). Likewise, the author preserves the memory that many Jews came to believe in Jesus after the raising of Lazarus (11:31-37,45; 12:9).

11.A reaffirmation of the Baptist and of his testimony is given in a summary statement (10:40-42), evidently meant to bring the public ministry of Jesus to a close in an earlier edition of the Gospel.

12.*The Community*, p.30. See also *The Gospel*, pp. lxii-lxiv.

13.On the figure of the "Beloved Disciple" and his influence on the development of the Johannine Community and its distinctive understanding of Jesus, see Brown, *The Community*, pp.31-34 in which he synthesizes, with some significant modification, material he previously presented in *The Gospel*, I-XII, pp. xcii-cii.

14.The early description of an unnamed disciple, companion of Andrew (1:35, 37, 40), indicates the contrary. But he is the disciple who was able to grow while others lagged behind, exhibiting a growth which the community saw as sign of Jesus' own love for him.

15.The Acts of the Apostles records early Christian missionary efforts in the region of Samaria (8:1b-8, 9:31, 15:3), explaining that the initial movement into that territory grew out of a persecution of the church in Jerusalem. The fourth Gospel, in its fourth chapter, also records a mission into Samaritan territory, although it pictures Jesus himself (in dialogue with a Samaritan woman) as the missionary! Thus, while each author seeks to "justify" Jewish-Christian efforts to convert Samaritans, the fact of the early inclusion of Samaritan converts within the church is genuine history. The author of the fourth Gospel, however, places greater significance upon this missionary movement than does Luke in his composition of Acts, for he includes the Samaritans among the first believers in Jesus (4:39-42). (See, Raymond Brown, *The Community*, pp. 36-40.)

16.Raymond Brown (*The Community*, pp. 43, 45) speaks of the views of the Samaritans (and of a group of anti-temple Jews, whom we will consider next) as constituting a catalyst for the development of Johannine beliefs. The term "catalyst" is especially helpful in that it brings out the influence which these groups had upon the development of the Johannine tradition, while it also recognizes that these earlier beliefs are not the source of that tradition. The tradition ultimately affirms Jesus as the preexistent One, the One who is before even Abraham existed, the One therefore who came down, not from the mountain (as did Moses) but from heaven. All these beliefs express a faith far beyond that of the Samaritans (and/or anti-temple Jews). Rather they stem from an experience of Jesus whose preexistence is explicitly recognized and affirmed when such reflection is prompted by the Samaritan heritage.

17.We have noted the existence of this, the most liberal group of Jewish Christians, earlier in this chapter. Acts presents Stephen as including anti-temple attitudes (7:47-48) within his proclamation of Jesus. Bitter hostility between him and Greek-speaking Jews (Hellenists), on the one hand, and more conservative Jerusalem Jews, on the other hand, led to his martyrdom (7:54-60).

18.See Brown, *The Community*, pp. 37-39.

19.It was most likely the Greek-speaking Jews who were responsible for the conversion of Samaritans. The Acts of the Apostles (7:48-50) recounts the fact that the Jerusalem Hellenists (i.e., Jews who spoke only Greek) spoke strongly against the temple. Brown and others (see *The Community*, pp. 38f) suggest that these Jerusalem Hellenists were the source for the conversion of the Samaritans, given the fact that Acts 8:1 affirms that many Christians fled to Samaria when persecution broke out in the church after the martyrdom of Stephen.

20.See also John 5:45-47, 7:14-24, 8:34-58, 10:24-39.

21.On the following and on the antipathy to "the Jews" in the fourth Gospel in general, see Raymond Brown, *The Community*, pp.40-43, 46-47, 66-69, and also *The Gospel*, lxx-lxxv.

22.See Deuteronomy 6:4: "Hear O Israel, the Lord our God, the Lord is one".

23.Because of the desire to defend the high Christology which the community of the fourth Gospel espoused, the evangelist adds a number of passing observations to explain away any aspects of Jesus' life and/or behavior which might seem to weaken the defensibility of his divinity. In this light see John 6:5-6, 70-71; 10:18; 11:41-42; 12:27; and 18:6 and, Brown, *The Churches*, pp.105-106.

24. See Brown, *The Community,* pp. 55-57.

25. Raymond Brown (*The Churches,* p. 106) brings out the fact that the failure of the Johannine Jesus to articulate a more detailed ethic flows from and illustrates the fact that the community was wholly taken up in defense of its understanding of Jesus before all adversaries. Hence, though it possessed and adhered to known ethical standards, these standards needed little reaffirmation; they were agreed upon by all. The one standard, however, which was not agreed upon was that of following Jesus, precisely as the Johannine community understood him.

26. On the centrality and the significance of the personal relationship between Jesus and the disciples in the fourth Gospel, see Raymond Brown, *The Churches,* pp. 86-94.

27. On the sacramentalism in the fourth Gospel, see Raymond Brown, *The Gospel,* pp. cxi-cxiv, and *The Churches,* pp. 88-90.

28. NRSV translation.

29. For a discussion of the Spirit in the fourth Gospel, and of his role as "Advocate," see Raymond Brown, *The Churches,* pp. 106-108 and *The Gospel,* pp. 1141f.

30. Note the description of the Spirit's work described in 16:8-11.

31. Raymond Brown underscores the fact that the Spirit in the fourth Gospel serves to continue and to deepen Jesus personal relationship with the disciples, showing how much of what is said of Jesus' origins from the Father, of Jesus' witness to the Truth, of Jesus' presence to the disciples, finds its parallel in affirmations about the Spirit. See *The Gospel,* pp. 1140-1141 and *The Churches,* p. 106.

32. For a fuller development of the eschatology of the fourth Gospel, see Raymond Brown, *The Gospel,* pp. cv-cxxi.

33. On the many signs of Jesus and the revelation of his glory, see Chapter 2 above.

34. The simplicity, together with the exalted spirituality, of the way of life of the Johannine community was not without its weaknesses. Chief among these was its lack of structured leadership. While the prominence of the call to a personal relationship with Jesus and the possibilities of developing a life of inter-personal love with the Lord reflect the profound richness and depth of the Christology of the Johannine community, the lack of any significant reliance on a leadership appointed and entrusted with authority by Jesus left these disciples quite vulnerable to inner conflicts and to divisions within the community, as the subsequent Epistles of John testify (see I John 2:18-19, 4:1-6; II John 7-11; III John 9-10). Without a decisive voice to guide the disciples, among whom all could claim the "anointing of Jesus' Spirit," the community itself became sharply divided in its understanding of Jesus. As a result, the larger number of disciples fell into Gnosticism while the remainder found refuge in joining the apostolic churches. The profound Christology of the Johannine Community was not without its weaknesses. (See Raymond Brown, *The Community,* pp.93-162 and *The Epistles of John, Anchor Bible volume 30* [Garden City, NY: Doubleday, 1982], pp. 69-86, 103-115.)

35. By "existential/moral" we intend to underscore the dimension of the personal responsiveness (or personal responsibility) to the claim which Jesus and following Jesus placed on the disciples and their personal freedom.

36. On the contrary, if one were to seek to do Christology without a readiness to be transformed through one's study, one would seriously hamper one's capacity to come to know and appreciate Jesus. In effect, one would negate the heart of the very experience of who and what Jesus is for the disciple and for the world: the bearer of God's personal saving love. One would empty the process of doing Christology of the foundational power which it presumes; namely, the one who engages in the process has experienced the saving love of God, which, of necessity transforms the individual. One's naming of God and

one's understanding of Christ would, then, at best be a purely conceptual endeavor, divorced from one's real life. One would come to know about Jesus, gleaning largely a knowledge from what others think, but one would not truly know him who is life-giving Lord.

37.Mk. 14:17, 22-25; Mt. 26:20-21, 26-29; Lk. 22:14-21; Jn. 13:1-20.

38.The Johannine community also, at least in some manner, came to recognize the importance of such leadership in Peter, even though, as we indicated above in discussing the twenty-first chapter of the Gospel, its recognition of that need was apparently too weak and/or too late.

39.In the Roman Catholic tradition, this leadership has become structured in the form of papal and episcopal Magisterium. The interested reader might want to consult the following texts dealing with various aspects of this question: Francis A. Sullivan, *Magisterium* (New York: Paulist Press, 1983); J. M. R. Tillard, *The Bishop of Rome* (Wilmington, DE: Michael Glazier, 1983); Raymond E. Brown, Karl P. Donfried, and John Reumann, *Peter in the New Testament* (Minneapolis: Augsburg Publ. House, 1973).

40.The distinction between these two terms, to be refined in the next chapters, in its most fundamental sense is based on the fact that, once Jesus died, he lives beyond history. Hence, the phrase "Jesus of history" refers to the Lord, including his life, his words, and his deeds, from the first moment of his conception until his death on the cross. The phrase "the Christ of faith" refers to the Lord, immediately after his death, including the Lord in his resurrection and post-resurrection appearances.

CHAPTER 5

1.See Avery Dulles, *The Craft of Theology* (New York: Crossroad, 1995), pp. 211-224 for a summary of a variety of approaches to this question. See also Luke Timothy Johnson, "Who is the Real Jesus? The Academy vs. the Gospels," *Commonweal* vol. 82, No. 22 (December 15, 1995) pp. 12-14 for a brief reflection by a scholar who wishes to challenge the contemporary effort of the "historical-critical" method in general and of its use in "seeking the historical Jesus" in particular.

2.John P. Meier, in his article entitled "The Historical Jesus: Rethinking Some Concepts" (*Theological Studies*, 51[1990], pp. 3-24), has clarified the meaning of the designation "historical Jesus" by distinguishing this phrase from the designation "the real Jesus" as follows: "The Jesus of history is a modern abstraction and construct, not to be equated with the 'real Jesus,' whether that reality be understood as 'total' or just 'reasonably complete.' By the Jesus of history I mean the Jesus whom we can 'recover' and examine by using the scientific tools of modern historical research." (p.18) By contrast, the real Jesus refers to the totality of Jesus' full earthly life, including Jesus' human and psychological development, his vision of life, his religious intentions, and his personal decisions along his historical journey of some thirty-three years. "The real Jesus is not available, and never will be, by historical-critical methods. This is true not because Jesus did not exist - he certainly did - but rather because the sources that have survived do not and never intended to record all or even most of the words and deeds of his public ministry - to say nothing of the rest of his life." (p.16)

3.John P. Meier, in his work *The Marginal Jew: Rethinking the Historical Jesus* (Garden City: Doubleday, 1991) Vol. I, pp. 167-195, offers five such criteria: (1) The criterion of Embarrassment (e.g., the faithful recording of Jesus' baptism by an inferior, namely by John the Baptist); (2) The criterion of Discontinuity (Dissimilarity) which "focuses upon words or deeds of Jesus that cannot be derived either from Judaism or from the early Church after him" (e.g., Jesus' sweeping prohibition of all oaths; and possibly Jesus' use of the term *Abba*); (3) The criterion of Multiple Attestation which "focuses on those sayings and deeds of Jesus that are attested to in more than one independent literary source and/or in more than one literary form or genre" (e.g., Jesus' speaking of the "kingdom of God"; the substance of Jesus' sayings over bread and wine at the Last Supper); (4) The criterion of coherence which "holds that other sayings and deeds of Jesus that fit in well with the... 'data base' established by using the first three criteria have a good chance of being historical" (e.g., sayings concerning the coming of the kingdom of God); and (5) The criterion of rejection and execution, which "directs our attention to the fact that Jesus met a violent end...and then asks us what historical word and deeds of Jesus can explain his trial and crucifixion as 'King of the Jews.'"

4. For fuller discussion of the usefulness and values of describing the "historical Jesus" with precision see John P. Meier, "The Historical Jesus...", pp. 22-24, and/or *The Marginal Jew...*, Vol. I, pp. 199-200.

5. For fuller development of this theme and the material which follows, see Marcus J. Borg, *Jesus: A New Vision*, (San Francisco: Harper, 1987), pp. 39-56 and, by the same author, *Meeting Jesus Again for the First Time* (San Francisco: Harper, 1994), pp. 31-36.

6. See Chapter 2, pages 42-43..

7. See also 5:16 and 10:21f as well as Luke's universalizing comment in 22:39 where he states that Jesus' retreat into the Garden on the Mount of Olives, the place of his final prayer, reflected his *custom*.

8. See also 5:19; 8:26; and 12:49.

9. Sometimes a freer translation reads "a mighty wind" but a strictly literal rendering of the text reads "a wind of God" or "a Spirit of God". The Hebrew *ruah* can be translated "wind," "breath," or "spirit".

10. Note especially that the voice from heaven, as recorded in Mark and Luke, is addressed directly to Jesus: "You are my beloved Son; with you I am well-pleased" (Mk. 1:10f; Lk. 4:22), whereas in Matthew's account, the voice is directed to witnesses of the Baptism: "This is my beloved Son...." (Mt. 3:17), while in the fourth Gospel, the revelation, with clear Johannine emphases, is given to John the Baptist (Jn. 1:29-34).

11. See also the three other "Servant Songs" of Isaiah (49:1-7; 50:4-11; 52:13-53:12) which the evangelists may also have had in mind.

12. at Nicea (325), Ephesus (431) and Chalcedon (451), as we shall see below in Chapters 9 and 10.

13. Hence, none of this is to say that Jesus had explicit human awareness of all of the details of these texts nor of their fulfillment in his ministry. It is simply to state that Jesus was deeply conscious of God's love for him, a consciousness which strengthened Jesus' desire to share that love. The full implications of this closeness of God to Jesus would become explicitly clear only through time, as Jesus' own concrete history would unfold.

14. We say theology of the infancy narratives, recognizing that the details of these narratives are not historical record, but that, within these accounts of Jesus' infancy, the authors wish principally to give a faith-inspired interpretation of Jesus' origins. Hence we would affirm that the substance of these accounts and the meaning which the authors intend to convey in these early chapters of their Gospels accurately reflect the movements and the meaning of Jesus' origins and generalized development within historical reality.

15. See in particular Mt. (1:18-25 and 2:13f, 19-21, 22b-23) who carefully emphasizes that God guided Joseph (through dreams and angels) to understand and to follow God's special initiative both in the conception and birth of Jesus and further in protecting the child Jesus from those who would kill him. See Luke (Lk. 2:21, 22-24, 39-43) who underscores

Mary's and Joseph's fidelity to the Law in bringing up Jesus, a fidelity which would have given Jesus both a recognition of the importance of faithfulness to God and also a sense of God's love for him and his family.

16.It is important to note two things regarding what might at first reading appear to be a rather strong, judgmental, and perhaps generalized statement concerning Israel. First, this and the foregoing sets of contrasts between Israel and Jesus are not simply contrasts created by contemporary theologians. Rather, they are contrasts which the sacred authors themselves sought to enunciate. Secondly, in underscoring thee contrasts, the sacred authors did not intend to repudiate or judge the integrity of particular individuals. Rather they intended to show the limits inherent in the (God-given) religious program and religious potential of God's people prior to the coming of Jesus in comparison with the potential and achievement of Jesus. In this way, the sacred authors wish to highlight the fact that Jesus, himself an Israelite, fulfills the religious call and the religious strivings of Israel in an unsurpassed and unsurpassable manner.

17.Note, therefore, the plight of the widow who had lost her only Son, someone who would continue the family line of her deceased husband, the only way she and the husband's family would retain status (Lk. 7:11-17); on the Levirate law, see Deut. 25:5-10 which provides background for Mt. 22: 24 and Lk. 20:28.

18.Hence the marvel of Jesus' welcoming Zacchaeus (Lk. 19:1-10).

19.Note how, in opposition to this disregard for the leper, Jesus does not keep this supposedly "unclean" person at a distance, but rather comes closes to the man and touches him. Jesus heals with a gesture of acceptance of, and personal closeness to, a person rejected by the masses (Mk. 1:40-42).

20.For a fuller description of the marginalized persons within Israel and a careful presentation of the reasons underlying their helplessness, see Albert Nolan , *Jesus Before Christianity* (Maryknoll, N.Y.: Orbis Books, 1976), pp.21-29.

21.This "fourfold peace" constitutes the heart of the "eschatological hope" of Israel, Israel's expectation of what God, the Just and Benevolent Ruler, would bring about in the "Last Days". For a brief description of this hope, see Walter Kasper, *Jesus the Christ* (New York: Paulist, 1976), p.73.

22.For fuller treatment of what follows, see Raymond E. Brown, *An Introduction to New Testament Christology* (New York: Paulist, 1994), pp. 155-161.

23.Psalms 2 and 110 which also represent Israel's prayer for the king on the day of his inauguration. As God's representative, the king is described as "God's Son," "begotten of God."

24.See also Isaiah 7:14-17.

25.In this way, Jesus used Israel's expectation and the image of the kingdom as an "interpretative metaphor." He took the image and transformed it, giving it fuller meaning in light of his own experience of God. This "fuller meaning" which Jesus gave to the image of the kingdom will be the theme of the next section of this chapter.

26.*Jesus the Christ*, pp. 73f.

27.See Chapters 3 and 4 above.

28.The original parable ends at this point with this emphasis. The post-resurrection church, recognizing that many refused to hear, developed the allegorical interpretation which follows, leading the reader to focus on the types of persons who receive the gift rather on the graces of God the divine initiative and the power of the gift itself.

29. Additional material on the following can be found in Walter Kasper, *Jesus the Christ*, pp. 74-88.

30. (Mt. 5:7; 6:12-14; 26:27-29; Lk. 6:36; 11:4)

31. *Jesus the Christ*, p. 81.

32. In underscoring Jesus' use of the name *Abba* (Father) to describe God, we do not intend to provide a defense for those who wish to assert an exclusive use of masculine over-against feminine images in order to describe God. On the contrary, we would recognize that Scripture clearly uses feminine as well as masculine images to describe God. (See Prov. 8:1-3; Is. 49:14f; 66:33.) Indeed, Jesus himself describes God as a woman searching for what has been lost, restless until it be found (Lk. 15:8-10). What we are concerned with here, rather is to penetrate the meaning of the more frequent name by which Jesus calls upon, as well as describes, God. His choice of the masculine, in fact, may have, in part, been influenced by his situation in a patriarchal culture; for it was that culture, not some other culture distant from Jesus' own historical life and setting, which needed transformation.

33. *Jesus the Christ*, pp. 81f.

34. See Ecclesiastes 3:1-8. The notion of "time for" illustrates well the Hebrew understanding of time. Time is not to be equated with the regular ticking of a clock but is related to the quality, possibilities, opportunities, and purposes inherent within a given moment, season, or event of history. Hence, though from the point of view of an abstract calendar, the day of Jesus simply followed the day before Jesus, from the point of view of the quality, opportunities, and purposes made available because of Jesus' presence and life, the "day of Jesus" was qualitatively a singularly new time and age.

CHAPTER 6

1. Readers who might wish to inquire into the fore-mentioned aspects of Jesus' miracles (and even of miracles in general) could consult Louis Monden, *Signs and Wonders* (New York: Desclee Company, 1966); Rene Latourelle, *The Miracles of Jesus and the Theology of Miracles*, translated by Matthew J. O'Connell (New York: Paulist, 1988), and John P. Meier, *The Marginal Jew: Rethinking the Historical Jesus, Vol. 2* (Garden City: Doubleday, 1994), pp. 509-1038.

2. For a brief treatment of philosophers and philosophical positions which prompted a denial of the very possibility of God's working miracles, see Louis Monden, *Signs and Wonders*, pp. 48-51, 184-193 and Rene Latourelle, *The Miracles...*, pp. 24-30.

3. For a summary of the questions raised by this research together with a brief list of scholars who have brought forth these questions, see Walter Kasper, *Jesus the Christ* (New York: Paulist, 1976), pp. 89f and endnote 1, pp. 98f.

4. Chapter 4.

5. For fuller analyses of this miracle story by exegetes faithful to the principles of the historical-critical method of interpretation, see John P. Meier, *A Marginal Jew: Rethinking the Historical Jesus, Vol. 2* (Garden City: Doubleday, 1994), pp. 798-832 and Raymond E. Brown, *The* Gospel According to John, I-X2, Anchor Bible Vol. 29 (Garden City: Doubleday, 1966), pp. 420-438. Both authors manifest careful scholarship in distinguishing pre-resurrection from post-resurrection elements within the narrative.

6. For fuller reflection upon this miracle story, including the evidence for affirming the fact that the narrative originated in an historical deed worked by the historical Jesus, see John P. Meier, *A Marginal Jew...., Vol. 2*, pp. 950-967.

7.See, for example, Rene Latourelle, *The Miracles of Jesus...*, pp. 39-69; John P. Meier, *The Marginal Jew...., Vol. 2*, pp. 617-645; and, Walter Kasper, *Jesus, the Christ*, pp. 89-91 to name but a few.

8.*The Marginal Jew...., Vol. 2*, pp. 617-622.

9.*Ibid.*, p.622.

10.*Ibid.*, pp. 622f. Note especially Mk. 3:27 and parallels; Lk. 11:20 and parallel; and Jn. 6:34-51, the latter reflecting back to the multiplication of the loaves in Jn. 6:1-15.

11.*Ibid.*, p.630.

12.For a treatment of the manner in which each particular evangelist, intent on developing his specific portrait of Jesus, wove his own interpretation of Jesus' miracles into these narratives, see Rene Latourelle, *The Miracles of Jesus...*, pp. 248-256.

13.The early Church gives explicit affirmation, in each Gospel, of its belief that its developing understanding of the meaning of Jesus life, death, and resurrection for its own life actually came from Jesus, present and alive in its midst. See Mk.13:11; Mt.10:19f; Lk.12:11f; Jn.14:26 and 16:12-14.

14.Thus the efforts of persons like John P. Meier and Raymond E. Brown, as indicated in endnotes 5 and 6 above. It should be noted that the historical-critical researcher does not claim to be able to discover precisely what happened in all its drama and concreteness in the historical moment pointed to by the narrative. All that he or she can establish is that something truly did happen, something did flow from Jesus' words and actions, in the historical moment alluded to, something which was truly extraordinary and surprising enough to evoke wonder from the spectators, something which was extraordinary enough to lead many to perceive that God was acting in and through Jesus among God's people, something worthy of being described as "healing," "casting out of evil spirits," "feeding," "restoring life," etc.

The report of Jesus miraculous deeds is therefore intended to recall the fact of the wonder and to foster a faith-inspired interpretation of the event. Modern minds often would like to know in detail precisely what the event looked like or how Jesus accomplished it. Neither the original witnesses nor the post-resurrection Church, however, were concerned to describe the event in its precise, concrete, dramatic appearance. Rather, the original witnesses were struck by the extraordinary power of Jesus' deeds and were given to seek the God-intended meaning which they mediated. It made little difference to them how precisely these transformations came about; what made a difference to them was that they were in the presence of a loving, dependable, surprisingly healing, saving God (Lk. 7:16).

15.Still other scholars have questioned the historicity of miracles on the grounds that these stories parallel wonders worked by other prophetic or religious figures within history. Such persons were "expected" to work such wonders to verify their own status as reputable religious teachers, divinely approved. Raymond Brown (*Introduction to New Testament Christology*, pp. 63-66) brings out the dubiousness of this presumption. The work and existence of such figures is not clearly attested to in recorded history; whereas Jesus is truly an historical figure and his events are reported as historical, the wonders supposedly worked by other figures are reported simply as legend.

In this regard, Walter Kasper (*Jesus, the Christ*, p. 90) notes further: Other "wonder workers" used miracles to call attention to themselves; Jesus, however, works miracles, not to call attention to himself, but rather to call attention to the coming of the reign of God (Mt. 12:28). For fuller treatment of this question, see John P. Meier, *The Marginal Jew....*, *Vol. 2*, pp. 535-616 and his summary of his findings, presented under the criterion of discontinuity and the historicity of Jesus' miracles considered globally, pp. 623-625.

16. See *The Marginal Jew...*, *Vol. 2*, pp. 967-970, where he gives a summary of his findings after his detailed analysis of each story of a nature miracle considered individually (pp. 646-967).

17. See *The Miracles of Jesus...*, pp. 70-238.

18. See *Jesus, the Christ*, pp. 89-91. Kasper classifies resurrection miracles among nature, not healing, miracles and regards them as secondary accretions to the original tradition (p. 90).

19. Since a good portion of the stories of Jesus' exorcisms and of Jesus' acts of physical healing meet the criteria of multiple attestation (both of sources and of literary forms) and of coherence (and in some manner, other criteria supporting historicity), and since so many contemporary exegetes employing the historical-critical method of analysis of texts regard these types os stories as grounded in actual events of Jesus' public ministry, we need not consider the historicity of the narratives reporting exorcisms or physical healings in any detail. For such an effort, we refer the reader to John P. Meier, *The Marginal Jew...*, *Vol. 2*, pp. 404-407, 648, and 678-679.

20. For a fuller presentation of the foregoing, see John P. Meier, *The Marginal Jew...*, *Vol. 2*, pp. 773-775.

21. See John P. Meier, *The Marginal Jew...*, *Vol. 2*, pp. 622 and 638, endnote 23. His classification is decidedly different in this regard from that of Walter Kasper, *Jesus, the Christ*, p. 90.

22. For fuller development, see Meier, *The Marginal Jew...*, *Vol 2*, pp. 784-788.

23. For an analysis of the historicity of the narratives concerning Jesus' raising the son of the widow of Nain (Lk. 7:11-17) and the raising of Lazarus (Jn. 11:1-45), see Meier, *ibid.* pp. 788-832,

24. Raymond E. Brown argues similarly in his *Introduction to New Testament Christology*, p. 62, endnote 79.

25. On the meaning of "nature," of its ambiguities as a philosophical concept, and of its usefulness in defining and classifying miracles, see below, **The Nature of Jesus' Miracles** and also John P. Meier, *The Marginal Jew...*, *Vol. 2*, pp. 512f and 874f.

26. The two stories recounting the miraculous catch of fish (Jn. 21:1-14; Lk. 5:1-11) would appear to originate from an event recounted in the Johannine version which reports an action of the risen Lord, not of the historical Jesus (See Meier, *The Marginal Jew...*, *Vol. 2*, pp. 899-904) and so would not be relevant to our precise question.

27. Such also is Paul's understanding in I Cor. 15:20-28. See also Eph. 1:7-10 and Col. 1:15-20.

28. We are aware that these conclusions may be surprising, even dissatisfying, to a number of readers. On the one hand, for some, they may not affirm enough about what Jesus may have done; they may seem to underplay the image of Jesus which one has "grown up with." On the other hand, for others, these conclusions may seem to be extravagant. They may purport to establish as factual history, events which some readers may feel we do not have literary access to.

In light of these two types of misgivings, it is helpful to recall what, by definition, one hopes to find when one seeks "the historical Jesus": One hopes to uncover events, sayings, and deeds which, by means of contemporary historical-critical methodology, one can affirm of Jesus of Nazareth with significant historical certitude (that kind of certitude which one can have in any historical investigation). One does not claim to have discovered all that Jesus said or did. Such would be impossible. He said and did much more, as the author of the fourth Gospel himself affirms (21:25). Nevertheless, the effort, limited though its results be, has a significant degree of fruitfulness: In the end, one can feel secure in knowing that one has established, through rigorous methodology and objective criteria that certain remembrances of what the earthly Jesus did, what he said and what he was like, are true to him in his historical being. Such rigor has significant value in that it preserves us from building Christology upon conjecture or whim rather than on fact and originating faith-experiences.

29. We can perceive immediately that this definition underscores two inter-related but distinguishable dimensions of the miraculous event: the fact that the event can not be explained by the laws of nature and the fact that it is caused by God. The first element could be perceived by persons without faith. Hence some claimed that Jesus cast out devils by the power of Satan (Mt. 12:27f). The second element could be perceived only by persons of faith. Hence, it can not be discerned by reason alone, nor by means of scientific or historical methodology; the most a scientist or an historian could affirm, speaking from his or her professional competence, would be that he or she can attest to no known cause which could adequately explain the event.

This distinction within the definition is worth making, particularly if one wishes to designate the kind of event which can be a candidate for a miracle, as one wishes to join with non-believing professionals in making an historical or scientific inquiry into a questionable event. John P. Meier (*The Marginal Jew..., Vol. 2*, pp. 512-515) does just that in offering an "non-theological" definition of a miracle for the purposes of engaging in historical critical research. At this point in our essay, however, we wish to give a fuller, explicitly theological, definition to a miracle, the miracles of Jesus, to be precise. We wish to do this because our task is to do theology: We seek to interpret faith-experience.

30. *Jesus the Christ*, pp. 91-94.

31. *Jesus, the Christ*, p.92.

32. The Sacred Author recounts this affirmation no less than seven times in the first chapter of the Book of Genesis (in verses 4, 10, 12, 18, 21, 25 and 31).

33. *Jesus, the Christ*, p. 95.

34. For additional reading developing the notion of miracle in general as sign of the transcendent Presence and in particular as sign of the kingdom, see Louis Monden, *Signs and Wonders*, pp. 24-40, 106-115 and Rene Latourelle, *The Miracles of Jesus....*, pp. 280-293. For a more detailed effort at developing a theological definition of a miraculous event, see Latourelle, pp. 276-280.

35. Of course, further reflection on what Jesus did and what he said, reflection done in light of the resurrection, did, in fact, allow the Church to focus on who Jesus was in himself. We will develop that trajectory in the Church's belief and that deepening of the Church's faith-experience in Part IV below. What is significant here, and what must always be held firmly in the forefront of one's understanding of Jesus, is that God's gift of God's Self in "saving love," the experience of salvation, expresses the overriding intention of God as well as the overriding experience of faith which contextualizes all further reflections upon an understanding of Jesus and of his mission. The reign of God remains central to the understanding of Jesus, of his work, and of his person.

36. For further reading on the characteristics of the miracles of Jesus, precisely as revelations of his mission and his power, see Monden, pp. 115-130; Latourelle, pp. 257-262 and Kasper, pp. 96f.

37. Louis Monden (*Signs and Wonders*) calls attention to this dimension of faith as pre-requisite for the recognition of miracles in stating: "The discernment of signs requires, above and beyond any other form of cognition, an *inner attitude* (emphasis his) compounded of honesty, spiritual health and unprejudiced openness" (p.88). He discusses the relationship of miracles to faith at length (see pages 80-99).

38. Louis Monden, pp. 122-129; Walter Kasper, pp. 97f.

39. Mk. 2:18-3:6.

40. Mk. 2:15-17; Lk. 7:36-39; Jn. 8:1-11.

41. Mk. 2:5-7; Lk. 7:48-49.

CHAPTER 7

1. Peace within the self, peace with one's neighbor, peace among nations, and peace within the world.

2. Mark 8:31, 9:31, 10:33 and parallels.

3. See Mark 14:22-26; Matthew 26:26-30; Luke 22:14-20. See also I Cor. 11:23-25.

4. Chapter 3, pages 64-68, and note 2 above.

5. See, for example, Raymond E. Brown, *Jesus: God and Man* (Milwaukee: Bruce Publ. Co., 1967), pp. 61-68 and, by the same author, *An Introduction to New Testament Christology* (New York: Paulist, 1994), pp. 44-49.

6. See, for example, Acts 23:6-8 and Matthew 22:23. Pharisees believed in a future resurrection; Sadducees did not.

7. In this light, it should also be noted that the Johannine community, too, while reflecting a different tradition, recalls Jesus' making a threefold prediction of his passion, death, and resurrection as Jesus, in the more triumphant tones characteristic of the fourth Gospel, proclaims "If I be lifted up, I will draw all to myself" (Jn. 12:32; see also 3:14f and 8:28). The validity of the conclusions which we have arrived at here, therefore, are further supported by the fact that they meet the criterion of multiple attestation of sources.

8. For a complementary treatment of this theme and the interpretation of the Gospel texts which follow, see Walter Kasper, *Jesus the Christ*, pp. 119-121.

9. See II Macc. 7:18, 37ff; IV Macc. 1:11, 6:29, 9:23f, 17:22.

10. Walter Kasper, *Jesus, the Christ*, p. 115.

11. It should be noted that scholars regard this verse, situated within the so-called "institution narrative" as a true representation of the words of the historical Jesus. Although the verses surrounding these words manifest the influence of the early Church and its celebration of the Eucharistic liturgy, this particular saying was never reflected in those liturgies. Nor does this verse reflect any theme of the Hebrew Passover Meal, the context within which the synoptic evangelists interpret Jesus' actions. The origin of these words, therefore, must rest in the thought and action of the historical Jesus. Otherwise there would be no reason for their inclusion in the "Last Supper" narrative.

Elements of the fourth Gospel confirm this view: The fourth evangelist presents Jesus, prior to his death, as speaking about that event as the moment of his glorification. Though the terminology is distinctly Johannine, the substance of Jesus' statement is essentially the same as that of Jesus' pronouncement recorded in the synoptics. Jesus sees his death as the moment in which all will be accomplished; he is stating his view that the reign of God is about to be established with Jesus himself at its center.

12. It should be noted that, although the Johannine tradition does not record "words of institution of the Eucharist" in the context of Jesus' final meal with the twelve (Jn. 13), that tradition does present Jesus, in the Eucharistic discourse of the sixth chapter of the

fourth Gospel, as speaking of his "body given over for the life of the world" (6:51; see also 6:53-57). Further, the author of the fourth Gospel recalls Jesus as viewing his death as the greatest act of love and service one can express for a friend (Jn. 15:13). The substantial similarity of the synoptic (basically Marcan) tradition and the Johannine tradition strongly support the historical authenticity of this presentation of Jesus' understanding of the meaning of his death.

13. These passages are particular to the Marcan and Lucan traditions respectively. Yet, the substance of these verses coheres with the substance of the traditions unfolded in the previous paragraph. Hence, they lend further support to the position that the historical Jesus understood his death as the way in which God would establish salvation for all people.

14. To assert that Jesus understood his death as the vehicle of salvation for all touches upon, not only Jesus' mind and heart, but also upon the nature and integrity of the very God whom Jesus claimed to know and to reveal. For, in every other incident in which God had extended God's saving love through Jesus, God respected and enlisted Jesus' conscious and free cooperation. For God to have acted otherwise at this moment would have been contrary to God's wisdom and love. God would have, in effect, used Jesus somewhat as a puppet. Such an action would be an abuse of Jesus' human dignity; it would be to leave Jesus, who is light for the world, in darkness regarding the ultimate value of the surrender of his life on earth. It would be to harness Jesus' freedom for a purpose of which Jesus would not have been able to intend.

Further, such an act on God's part would contradict the very reality which God intended to achieve through Jesus' death. God's action in regard to Jesus would not be a saving action, for it would not have been an action by which God truly sets freedom free. But, in actual fact, God did work salvation fully in, through, and for Jesus. God respected Jesus' human freedom. God revealed God's Self as the God who wishes to liberate freedom from darkness, deceit, and the slavery of sin; God manifests the truth that God wishes to engage human beings in the conscious and free sharing, with God, of a life of Godly love. And Jesus is the first and foremost person in and with whom God accomplishes that desire. In Jesus, saving love and freedom are accomplished as Jesus walks the journey of human life freely and consciously engaged in the saving plan of God.

15. We are following the careful, literal, translation of C. S. Mann (*Mark* [Garden City, NY: Doubleday, 1986], *Anchor Bible vol. 27*, p. 587) at this point. The New American Bible, revised edition, softens the original Greek by translating these two verbs as "troubled and distressed."

16. Mann renders the addition "unto death" (literally: "almost as to death") as "it almost overwhelms me." He comments further: "The sorrow of Jesus is such that it takes hold of life itself; death is not here a desired cessation from unbearable pain." (See: *Mark,* pp. 587, 589).

17. Of this entire passage, Mann (*Mark,* p. 589) writes: "(The phrase) he began to be must be given its full force; ...the two following verbs give us a picture of ever-increasing horror and agitation.... Distressed...covers a whole realm of emotions, from amazement to overwhelming distress. The verb full of dread...describes a state of mind in which mental anguish produces a confused and restless state of shock and even terror."

Further, addressing the issue of the historicity of this description, he writes: "It is in the highest degree probable that the very force of the words guarantees that we are dealing with a primitive tradition. Luke does not have this dramatic depiction of Jesus' distress (nor does) Matt. 26:37...."

18. Commenting upon this verse, Mann (*Mark,* pp. 591-592) writes: "The word test is used generally in two senses - proving and testing by suffering (cf. Luke 22:28, Acts 20:19, Gal. 4:14, Jas. 1:2, I Pet. 1:6); and also tempting to sin, resulting from desire or from suggestion by Satan (cf. Mark 1:13, Jas. 1:13-15), but neither sense fits this context. There is a note here of a peril far beyond that of a lapse in awareness or fear of arrest. The air of grim foreboding much more akin to the language of Chapter 13 and its atmosphere of eschatological turmoil is reminiscent of Rev. 3:10....

Underscoring the fact that, at this moment, Jesus is actually engaged in "summing up" his entire life, his personal meaning and ministry, Mann continues: "(A)t this point...all the concerns expressed in the comment to this section come together: the hour, the dread of v. 33, the sayings in v. 34, the cup of v. 36, even the cry of desolation in 15:34 all combine to indicate that one of the factors at work here is the realization by Jesus that all the conflicts of the ministry, and especially the conflicts with evil in the healings and exorcisms were now coming to a single, inexorable point. He was face to face at this hour with the power of evil manifested in the sharpest way, and he saw the disciples as faced with the same menace."

19. Jesus' prayer echoes the prayer he taught the disciples as a model (Mt. 6:9-13; Lk. 11:2-4). There Jesus urged his disciples also to pray "Do not subject us to the final test (Mt.6:13a, Lk.11:4); but deliver us from the evil one" (Mt. 6:13b) as they begged God "Your Kingdom come." For the reign of God is diametrically opposed to the ways of Satan, as Jesus' life and ministry have shown. Any effort to establish the reign of God would place one in conflict with Satan. Hence, in the final stage of the coming of the kingdom, the conflict would necessarily reach its greatest pitch. God's emissary and the disciples must be prepared to meet the full forces of evil in the final moment before the kingdom's realization. Therefore, Jesus, realizing at great depth the struggle of this moment urges the disciples to pray: Only in God can one be victorious.

20. Karl Rahner has developed this point in "The Theological Concept of Concupiscentia," *Theological Investigations*, Vol I, (Baltimore: Helicon Press, 1963), p. 368 at note 1.

21. While being truly human, that courage also has a divine dimension within it. For, since Jesus' courage itself was born of his unshakable confidence in *Abba* and his conviction that *Abba* would vindicate him, his courage is an expression of the presence and victory of God's life and love, strengthening the mind and heart of Jesus as he entered and endured this trial.

22. See Mk. 11:1-11; Mt. 21:1-11; Lk. 19:28-40.

23. This, in itself, provides strong support for its historical authenticity. Embarrassing references would not be created by a community or author striving to promote faith in Jesus, God's divinely appointed emissary.

24. See, for example, Walter Kasper, *Jesus the Christ*, pp. 118-119.

25. Theologians have wrestled with this issue in various ways. It has been a particularly troublesome issue for those theologians who, from the time of St. Thomas Aquinas, have felt it necessary to maintain that Jesus, throughout his earthly life, enjoyed the beatific vision. For a contemporary treatment of this issue, see Karl Rahner, "Dogmatic Reflections on the Knowledge and Self-Consciousness of Christ," *Theological Investigations*, vol. 5 (Baltimore: Helicon, 1966), pp. 193-215, especially page 203 and note 10.

26. or at least experiences what the evangelists intend to convey with these words.

27. Again, it is important to allow these words (and the experience of Jesus) to have their full force. To one who had known and lived by the profound closeness of God, as Jesus had, the felt absence of God would be, not less painful, but the deepest pain of all. For this

reason, the sense of God's abandonment would have enveloped Jesus' consciousness and wounded his heart far more deeply than it would have enveloped and wounded someone who had not known God very well or even at all.

28.It is noteworthy that this confession of faith emerges from the mouth of a Roman Centurion, a Gentile, rather than from the voice of a disciple of Jesus. Clearly it reflects, once again, the belief of the post-resurrection Church and Mark's own conviction that, whereas God's chosen people failed to understand Jesus, the Gentiles, pagans, came to understand him well.

29.The reader will find a similar and somewhat complementary treatment of what follows in Daniel A. Helminiak, *The Same Jesus* (Chicago: Loyola University Press, 1986), pp. 225-272.

30.See Chapter 5, pages 143-145.

31.Thus, the transcendent dimension of salvation, Transcendent Love, has a threefold dimension: It is inexhaustibly giving, fully revealed, and wholly living in us. In the language of the Christian Tradition, Transcendent Love is Triune: Transcendent Love is Father (*Abba*), Word, and Spirit; the Divine Being is Transcendent Love inexhaustibly Self-communicating (or Self-giving), perfectly shown forth, and personally indwelling in each believer.

32.For fuller analysis of this image, see Stanislaus Lyonnet, "Redemption," in *The Theology of the Atonement*, John R. Sheets, ed. (Englewood Cliffs, NJ: Prentice Hall, 1967), pp. 112-119.

33.See also Is. 62:11f; Jer. 31:32.

34.Consistent with this understanding,, Jesus, through his death, is thought of as "having paid a great price" (I Peter 2:9; I Cor. 6:20; 7:23), though the authors do not mean that Jesus literally paid a fee in any form to anyone but simply that his dedicated love and fidelity was costly. With that understanding, Jesus himself tells his disciples that he has come to give his life as a ransom for many (Mk. 10:45), without intending to imply that he needed to pay anyone for the release of humankind from its slavery to sin. In like manner, Paul speaks of Jesus as ransoming sinners (Gal. 3:13, 4:5) as do the authors of I Timothy (2:5-6) and Titus (2:13f).

35.See Leviticus 4:19f, 31.

36.For fuller development of this image, see Stanislaus Lyonnet, "Expiation," in *The Theology of the Atonement*, pp. 99-101.

37.By symbolic we mean "outwardly, or visibly, expressive of one's inner self." So deep is that self that words alone can not express the fullness of its desires and feelings. Hence we give gifts; we use handshakes, hugs and kisses; we weep and smile; we may sing the national anthem as a sign of patriotic dedication and unity. Each gesture attempts to give fuller expression to the depth of our true selves. Just as we use metaphors and images to express reality which is too deep to be captured by the literal meaning of the words we may use, so also we use symbolic gestures to express the deepest feelings, convictions, and longings of our hearts. Far from being unreal, symbols are most deeply real. (For a fuller treatment of the notion, nature, and reality of religious symbols, see Roger Haight, *The Dynamics of Theology*, pp. 129-166, especially pages 132-142, 147-163.)

38.For a complementary analysis and development of the import of this image, see Gerald O'Collins, *Interpreting Jesus* (Ramsey, NJ: Paulist Press, 1983), pp. 162-165.

39.See also Mk. 14:24; Mt. 26:28; Lk. 22:20; Jn. 19:34; I Cor. 11:25; Heb. 9:12-14; Rev. 5:6ff.

40.the sacred pledge of mutual fidelity and union between God and God's people.

41.perhaps also prompted by Christ's words over the cup at his Last Meal (See Mk. 14:24; Mt. 26:28; Lk. 22:20; I Cor. 11:25).

42.For a manageable summary of earlier tradition in the post-apostolic Church, see H. F. Davis, "A Survey of the Theology of the Redemption" in *The Theology of the Atonement*, pp. 10-19. For an explicit treatment of the perspectives of specific medieval theologians, particularly St. Thomas Aquinas, see the survey of John R. Sheets (editor) in the same volume, pp. 57-84.

43.There is necessarily a certain subjectivity involved in anyone's attempt to create a synthesis or to propose models. The reader can find another approach to summarizing this material in Gerald O'Collins' *Interpreting Jesus* (Mahwah, NJ: Paulist Press, 1983), pp. 142-160, where the author proposes a threefold synthesis: a "liberation" model, an "expiation" model, and a "transforming love" model.

44.O'Collins recasts this theory in a model described as "transforming love" (pp. 157-160). Reference to the particular theologians advocating this theory can be found there.

45.O'Collins sees the "Satisfaction Theory" as the classical example of his "second" model of redemption: his "expiation" model. Therefore, for fuller development of the satisfaction theory and for reference to its proponents, see O'Collins, pp. 145-150.

46.in Anselm's mind, Jesus, because he was sinless, did not have to die.

47.Sinful human beings were powerless, in Anselm's mind, to restore God's honor, for the degree of honor given depends upon the status and worthiness of the one giving the honor.

48.See Walter Kasper, *Jesus the Christ*, pp. 219-221.

49.For fuller elaboration, see O'Collins, pp. 150-156.

50.See O'Collins, pp. 156-157.

51.See his *Theology of Death* (New York: Herder & Herder, 1961).

52.*Ibid.,* pp. 21-34.

53.*Ibid.,* pp. 71-75.

54.*Ibid.,* pp. 35-39.

55.*Ibid.,* pp. 69-71.

56.*Ibid.,* pp. 40-57, 61-63.

57.*Ibid.,* pp. 65-74.

58.Other human beings, experiencing sin in their lives may not approach death with the same depth of confidence or the same swiftness in coming to inner peace as Jesus' death witnesses to. But given the grace of Christ, and given the possibility of living lives of deepened trust in God and love of neighbor, many persons can and do ultimately face death in confident surrender to God. They, too, seem to approach death as a transition to life, gradually negotiating the darkness in a movement to inner peace, convinced in faith that they have been freed from the *penalty of sin* and even healed of much of the *consequences of sin*. With Christ, the redeemed person lives and dies, saying "*Abba*, into your hands I give my spirit."

59.*The Same Jesus*, initially on pages 228-229 and more fully on pages 234-237, 241-245.

CHAPTER 8

1.For more detailed treatment of the material presented in this section, see Raymond E. Brown, *The Virginal Conception and Bodily Resurrection of Jesus* (New York: Paulist Press, 1973), pp. 69-129. See his note 120 (pp. 69f) for fuller bibliography.

2.See also Gal. 1:1 and I Cor. 6:14.

3.See also 8:11 and 10:9.

4.Daniel Helmeniak (*The Same Jesus*, pp. 165, 173-178) speaks of this "filling Jesus, in his humanity, with the transcendent life and love of 'Abba'" as the "divinization" of Jesus' humanity, a term which has its origins in the language of the Greek Fathers of the Church. To speak in this manner does not imply that Jesus "became divine" only at the moment of his resurrection, but rather that his divinity, always as the One begotten of *Abba*, was able fully to permeate his humanity only after he reached the point of death and was glorified in his resurrection. This understanding of the way Christ's divinity affected his humanity respects the genuine integrity of his humanity. It recognizes that, as a human being, Jesus came to fullness of life, even in his capacity to reflect his Godliness, only gradually, only by passing through time. This understanding is fully consonant with Luke's teaching about Jesus, given early in his Gospel: "Jesus grew in wisdom, age and favor (grace) before God and man" (2:52). We will develop this point more fully in Part IV of this work.

5.Walter Kasper develops this point emphatically in *Jesus, the Christ*, pp. 144f.

6.A brief reflection many help us more fully appreciate the way in which the Apostles' experience of the risen Lord led them immediately to recognize in Jesus God's fully realized intention to gift them with salvation. In the risen Christ, the Apostles saw Jesus, in his humanness, filled forever with divine life. In that experience, they perceived that God reigned in the very person of Jesus; the reign of God had been definitively given to Jesus. But, by that very action, God's reign has forever been given to history and to humanity; for what Jesus has so fully received, Jesus can share with others. Thus, he stands inviting others to participate in his divinized human life. He calls others to walk with him; he empowers them to be faithful as he is faithful; he gifts his fellow human beings with new God-like life which is the life and love by which all enter and co-create with God the final kingdom. Jesus embodies and ushers in the reign of God. He is the Messiah. The Apostles recognize this dimension of the life and person of the risen Lord immediately as they experience his glorified presence.

7.For a clear and detailed presentation of the Pauline witness, see Raymond Brown, *The Virginal Conception...*, pp. 70-96.

8.See, for example, W. Marxsen, *The Resurrection of Jesus of Nazareth*, (Philadelphia: Fortress Press, 1970).

9.See also Eph. 4:10 and I Tim. 3:16

10.In this vein, see also Hebrews 4:14, 6:19f, 9:11f.

11.It is noteworthy that in making this affirmation, Paul claimed that this belief had already become tradition when he had first preached to them sometime prior to his writing this letter.

12.*The Virginal Conception and Bodily Resurrection of Jesus,* pg. 76.

13.For example, assumption into heaven in the likeness of Elijah or immorality of a soul-like principle (Wis. 3:1-8).

14.(1 Cor. 15:42-44; see 2nd Cor. 4:6).

15. See Mk. 16:12 which speaks of Jesus appearing "in another form".

16. 1ˢᵗ Cor. 15:35-41.

17. Mk. 16:14-16; Mt. 28:16-20; Lk. 24:36-49; Jn. 20:21-23.

18. Mk. 16:14-16; Mt. 28:16-20; Lk. 24:36-49; Jn. 20:21-23.

19. It is not only the appearance narratives which record the significance of the risen Jesus' utterance of a personal word to his witnesses. Luke, in the Acts of the Apostles, describes Jesus and Paul in dialogue as he (Luke) reports and retells the episode of Paul's encounter with the risen Christ (Acts 9:3-7; 22:6-8; 26:12-15). Each of these accounts, like the Gospel narratives, includes Jesus' personal address to the witness and the Lord's giving his hearer a mandate or commission to proclaim the "Good News". Paul himself reports a verbal component within his recollection of his experience of the risen Lord in his letter to the Christians of Galatia (1:11-24).

20. It should be noticed that only Luke is so graphic that he states that Jesus actually ate food before them (24:41-43), but then Luke tends toward graphic physical descriptiveness in his narratives (see also Lk. 3:22 where he describes the baptism of Jesus, stressing that the Spirit descended upon Jesus bodily "in visible form" like a dove).

21. Peter (Lk. 24:12) or Peter and the Beloved Disciple (Jn. 20:3-9) come later to the tomb. They, too, "did not yet understand that he (Jesus) had to rise from the dead" (Jn. 20:9).

22. Mk.16:5f, Mt. 28:2-5, Lk. 24:4-7, Jn. 20:12. There are some clear differences in each of the empty tomb narratives. John (20:12) recalls the presence of angels at the tomb but does not have them attest to Jesus' resurrection; rather, the Johannine narrative moves immediately to an appearance of the risen Christ to Mary, making an angelic proclamation unnecessary (20:14-18). Mark and Luke do portray the angels as proclaiming Jesus' resurrection. They, however, depict the angels in "human form," Mark recording the presence of "a young man," Luke telling us that there were "two men". The fact that some narratives speak of "men" while others recall "angels" at the tomb should not be regarded as contradictory; the Scriptures readily describe angels as human in appearance. Compare, for example, Gn. 18:2, 16, 22 and 19:2 with Gn. 19:1, 10-12. On this last point, see Raymond E. Brown, *The Virginal Conception and Bodily Resurrection of Jesus*, p.119 and his note 199.

23. The early church, itself, had to deal with such an hypothesis (Mt. 28:11-15), showing clearly that any hypothesis about the reasons for the tomb's emptiness would be inconclusive.

24. described as "men" in Mark's and Luke's accounts.

25. Such a reading of these texts would be grounded in the fact that Scripture often uses the figure of "angels" to portray God, in the act of revealing. In these instances, angels and God are spoken of interchangeably. Compare, for example, Ex. 3:2 with Ex. 3:4; Gn. 18:1, 13f with 18:2, 9-12; Gn. 18:16, 22 and 19:1, 12 with 18:17-33 and 19:10-12, 14, 27-29.

26. On this interpretation, see Raymond E. Brown, *The Virginal Conception...*, pp. 120-122. Further bibliographical references are given there.

27. The New Testament invariably sees this new life and this deepened faith, called forth by the resurrection, as a manifestation of the Spirit. Thus Paul writes to the Christian of Corinth: "No one can say 'Jesus is Lord' except by the Holy Spirit" (I Cor. 12:3). He rejoices in a letter to Roman disciples: "If the Spirit of the one who raised Jesus from the dead dwells in you, the one who raised Christ from the dead will give life to your mortal bodies also, through his Spirit that dwells in you" (Rom. 8:11). In the same line of thought, Paul recognizes the Spirit enabling Christians to name God *Abba*, as Jesus did: "God sent the Spirit of his Son into our hearts, crying out *Abba*, Father!" (Gal. 4:6; see

Rom. 8:14-17). The Spirit is God's and Jesus' Easter gift to the Church, empowering God's people to live a fuller, divinized life, faithful and loving as Jesus is faithful and loving.

28. The evidence of the writings of the early post-apostolic Church leaders like Clement of Rome, Origen, Tertullian, and Cyril of Jerusalem, as well as the systematic reflections of Medieval Theologians, such as Thomas Aquinas, illustrate that Christians of every age needed to process their understanding of Jesus' resurrection from a variety of perspectives in response to a variety of challenges. For a clear and concise exposition of the development of the theology of the resurrection of Jesus in Christian Tradition from the Patristic Era through the Scholastic Period, see Gerald O'Collins, *Jesus Risen*, (New York: Paulist, 1987), pp. 7-33.

29. For an exposition of the theological insights of eight specific contemporary scholars concerning Christ's resurrection, see Gerald O'Collins, *Jesus Risen*, pp. 34-98.

30. It is the fourth evangelist who most clearly underscores the unity of Jesus' death and his glorification. In the fourth Gospel, the "hour" of Jesus' death is the "hour" of his glorification (Jn. 12:23-28; 17:1-5). Jesus' death and glorification take place in one moment at the juncture of time and eternity; they are two dimensions of what is essentially a profoundly transforming interpersonal experience, an experience of mutual self-giving love between Jesus and *Abba*.

31. Karl Rahner develops this understanding of Christ's death and Christ's resurrection precisely as two sides of one event. See his *Foundations of Christian Faith* (New York: Seabury Press, 1978), pp. 266-268.

32. Walter Kasper, *Jesus the Christ*, pp. 139f.

33. Raymond E. Brown, *The Virginal Conception...*, p. 112.

34. Ex. 14:10-31; 15:1-10; Num. 34:1-29.

35. Lk. 4:36f; Jn. 2:11, 6:67.

36. Lk. 7:16; see also Lk. 1:68 and 19:44.

37. These reflections can help us better to appreciate the reasons why Paul and the evangelists struggled both in their attempts to describe the risen Lord and also in their efforts to record the total experience of the witnesses of the glorified Jesus. In the last analysis, what these authors seek to describe is, from God's side, the fuller in-breaking of the transcendent Power who can never be adequately defined, and, from the human side, an experience of the Transcendent, which is always primarily and deeply an experience of faith, no matter what tangible event contextualizes that experience. This is true, first and foremost, for the historical Jesus himself. In his passion and death, he came to encounter and to experience *Abba* and the transforming effects of God's presence, as never before. And it is true, consequently and secondarily for those who witnessed the risen Lord. In perceiving the risen Christ appearing before them, they experienced the transcendent God, the One whom Jesus named *Abba*, to a degree never before given to them. Thus, in describing Jesus, risen and bodily glorified, and also in relating the Apostles' experience of his glorified presence, Paul and the evangelists were attempting to "hand on" what was essentially a transforming faith-experience of the transcendent God, an experience of the One who, known only by faith, escapes empirical description and verification. In proclaiming the resurrection of Jesus, the writers of the New Testament sought to proclaim the definitive transformation, first and foremost, of Jesus. Secondly, in him and with him, they wished to proclaim the transformation of those who became witnesses of his glorified life, and, indeed, of all who come to know the risen Lord in ongoing faith. All, Jesus included, are changed because of an encounter in faith with the transcendent, saving God.

38.Conversion does not actually denote an experience totally different from that enjoyed in hearing the Word and celebrating the Eucharist. Rather it underscores a central dimension of every experience of the risen Lord, whether one encounters Christ in the very formal moments of listening to a preacher or celebrating the Lord's Supper, or whether one meets the risen Lord in private prayer, in informal conversation with a fellow believer, or in meeting the everyday challenges of living the Christian life as a whole.

39.This call to conversion, as a primary way of experiencing God's reign in the living Christ reflects the central imperative within the historical Jesus' proclamation of the Good News itself. We need simply recall the fact that the Synoptic Gospels summarize Jesus' preaching with the injunction: "The reign of God is at hand; repent, and believe the Good News," an injunction which is continually specified and unfolded throughout the Gospels. It is in the experience of conversion to living according to the way of Jesus, and in the deepening and strengthening of that experience, that one meets the risen Lord, alive in the Church. In this experience of ongoing and deepening conversion, fostered by hearing the word and celebrating the memory of Jesus, that the contemporary Christian both experiences and also recognizes the presence and power of the same risen Lord proclaimed by the apostles and the early Church. Now as then, disciples are made through the experience of the risen Lord and in no other way.

40.See also Acts 2:37f; I Thess. 1:5-7; II Tim. 3:16.

41.See also Acts 2:42-47; Mk. 14:22-26 and parallels, I Cor. 11:23-29; Jn. 6:48-58.

42.See his *Foundations of Christian Faith*, pp. 268-278.

43.Both in Chapter One and in this chapter.

44.*Jesus the Christ*, p. 150. See pp. 149-154, where the author develops his understanding of the corporeality of Jesus resurrection and its significance for the fulfillment of humankind and history in heaven.

45.Gerald O'Collins develops this point carefully in his *Risen Jesus* (New York: Paulist, 1987), pp. 179-187.

CHAPTER 9

1.The question "What is required of Jesus that he be the Mediator of salvation?" (and also the definitive revelation of the Father) rests upon the Christians' experience of that salvation and their understanding of its profound nature, an experience which itself was clarified together with the Church's fuller understanding of Jesus. Hence, this question concerning Jesus was intimately connected with the Church's insight into and desire to safeguard the experience and understanding of salvation itself. This point will be developed further in the pages which follow.

2.The recognition of a divine power in Jesus also prompted the questions: "Is Jesus fully human?" and "How are the divinity and humanity of Jesus related?" These questions became all the more pressing after the solemn proclamation of Jesus' divinity, as we shall see below.

3.On the question of whether and where the New Testament applies the name "God" directly to Jesus, see Raymond E. Brown's essay entitled "Did New Testament Christians call Jesus God?" in his *Introduction to New Testament Christology*, pp. 171-195. After considering a number of passages which seem to distinguish Jesus from God (Mk. 10:18; Mk. 15:34 and Mt. 27:46; Eph. 1:17, II Cor. 1:3 and I Pet. 1:3; Jn. 17:3; I Cor 8:6; Eph 4:4-6; I Cor. 12:4-6 and II Cor. 13:14; and I Tim. 2:5), he lists five pericopes which most probably call Jesus God (Jn. 1:18, not completely conclusive because of variant readings;

and Tit. 2:13, Rom 9:5; and I Tim. 5:20, not absolutely certain because of ambiguity of syntax) and three texts which certainly call Jesus God (Heb. 1:8-9, Jn. 1:1, and Jn. 20:28).

4. The Marcan Tradition, too, recalls Jesus acknowledging himself to be less than the Father in terms of Jesus' lack of knowledge of the "day and the hour" when the end will come (13:32).

5. Hence, the Greek mind would have found it most difficult to conceive of God's becoming human precisely because "becoming" implied change (which itself is imperfection) and to be human implied acceptance of change, movement from imperfection to perfection, again and again.

6. Because of this difference, an Israelite would judge that one could truly and adequately know a reality only after its historical unfolding reached completion (see 1 Jn. 3:2) whereas a Greek would judge that every reality could be known in its full truth right in the beginning. This difference of perspective would, at least in part, explain why the Jewish Christians would maintain emphasis on the historical with regard to Jesus (who can be known fully only in his crucifixion and resurrection), while the Greek Christians would begin to emphasize the incarnation of the *Logos* and Jesus' conception in the womb of Mary (everything having been accomplished in the beginning in the very truth of the incarnation itself.)

7. As one might expect, these differences reflect the diversity within the ways of thinking within each of these cultures. Thus, they become the expression, not only of religious differences and beliefs, but also of the unreflected cultural and intellectual processes of a given people. The deep-seated nature of both dimensions of these differences make them powerful sources of disagreement and conflict.

8. Since the very name of God and Israel's understanding of God are expressed in terms of God's relationship with and God's ways of acting toward Israel, the type of theology evidenced among the Semites is called functional theology; that is, the way of interpreting their faith-experiences of God and of naming the God behind that experience emphasizes the way God functions. This is clearly distinguished from the Greek way of understanding God. Since God is non-relational (in the Greek way of thinking), Greek philosophy described God in God's Self, in God's being. This type of theology is called ontological theology. Obviously, both types of theology flow from the ways these two cultures initially experienced and then came to understand God.

9. See Richard A. Norris, Jr., *The Christological Controversy* (Philadelphia: Fortress Press, 1980), p.5.

10. It is noteworthy that Ignatius speaks of Christ as "physician"; in doing so, he indicates that his ultimate concern is to ground firmly the experience of salvation, that is, to establish securely the Divine healing mediated through Jesus.

11. *De Principiis* 1:2:9.

12. Acceptance of distinction within God would appear to violate the necessary simplicity and perfection of God in the traditional way of Greek thinking. As we have mentioned above, Greek thought proceeded from firmly held principles to a knowledge of reality. In this case, Greek philosophy held that God is absolutely one and indivisible. No matter how God had revealed God's Self to persons of faith, the Greek mind felt compelled to measure that revelation by this principle of its own philosophical reason.

13. Hence Arius' position would be classified as a "deutero-theological" (a "secondary God-affirming") position as opposed to a "monarchical" ("one principle") position which maintained that everything of the divine consisted in only one level, one source (or principle).

14.Arius could find grounding for this interpretation in both Old and New Testaments. Prime passages would have been found in the Book of Proverbs (8:22-31) and the Letter to the Colossians (1:15-17). The text of Proverbs, however, in speaking of Wisdom as "the firstborn of God's Ways" does not clearly affirm whether that Wisdom, "begotten of the Lord," is begotten in the beginning of time or in eternity. Likewise, the text of Colossians can be taken to mean that the Son ranks first in creation or that he exists before creation.

15.The word *ousia*, had material connotations, occasioning some misgivings among the Council fathers, but it was sufficiently abstract to avoid misunderstanding.

16.Hence its formula reads as follows: "We believe...in one Lord, Jesus Christ, the Son of God, born as only-begotten of the Father,...God from God, Light from Light, true God from true God, begotten not made, one in being (*homoousios*) with the Father, through whom all things came to be, those in heaven and those on earth, who for us men and for our salvation came down, became flesh and became man..." (DS 125).

17.Walter Kasper expresses this perspective particularly well. In his book, *Jesus, the Christ*, p. 175, he writes: "To think of God and history together is not as difficult for the Bible as it is for Western philosophy under Greek influence. In Greek metaphysics from the pre-Socratics to Plato and Aristotle and on to neo-Platonism, immutability, freedom from suffering and passion (*apatheia*) were always regarded as the supreme attributes of the divine. The God of the Old Testament on the other hand is known as God of the way and of guidance, as God of history.... The fact that Yahweh is a God of history of course does not mean, even for the Old Testament, that he is a God who comes to be. On the contrary,...God in the Old Testament has no beginning and as a living God he is not subject to death. God's eternity is something taken for granted in the Old Testament: it does not mean however immobility, unchangeability and timelessness; it means mastery over time, proving its identity, not in unrelated, abstract self-identity, but in actual, historical fidelity. God's becoming man and thus becoming history in Jesus Christ, is the surpassing fulfillment of this historical fidelity to his promise that he is the one who is present and the one existing with us."

18.Already in the late New Testament, the author of the first letter of John had to insist that Christian faith centered on "what we have heard, what we have seen with our eyes, what we looked upon and touched with our hands...the Word of life - for the life was made visible" (1 Jn. 1:1f.).

19.*Letter to the Trallians* 9:12; see also *Letter to the Ephesians* 7:2, cited above.

20.The name is taken from the Greek *dokein*, "to seem" or "to appear".

21."We could not learn the things of God unless our teacher, already existing as God's *Logos*, became a human being.... We could not learn the things of God, unless by seeing our teacher and hearing his voice for ourselves, we became imitators of his deeds and doers of his words. In that way we have communion with him.

"The Lord redeems us by his own blood,...gives his life for our life and his flesh for our flesh,...pours out the Spirit of the Father to unite God and humanity and bring them into communion, bringing God down to human beings through the Spirit and, conversely, bringing humanity up to God through his own incarnation" (*Adversus Haereses.* 5:1:1).

22.*On the Flesh of Christ*, 4:1-3.

23.See his *Letter to the Romans*, Chapter 8.

24.This indwelling, Theodore states, takes place by way of "God's good pleasure," that is "by the best and noblest will of God, which he exercises when he is pleased with those who are zealous to be dedicated to him...." (*On the Incarnation, Book 7, Fragment 2*; English translation by Richard Norris, *The Christological Controversy*, pp. 115f.)

25.*On the Incarnation, Book 7, Fragment 2* (Translation by Richard Norris, *The Christological Controversy*, pp. 116f.)

Theodore, like Apollinaris, also felt the need to explain how this indwelling of the *Logos* secured the sinlessness of Jesus. Norris sums up his teaching in this regard as follows:

> The *Logos* unites himself to Jesus from the moment of Jesus' conception, and as Jesus' human life goes on, maturing and fulfilling itself more and more through his struggle against evil, the reality of this union comes to fuller and fuller expression until, in the resurrection, the human being and the *Logos* show that they have always been, so to speak, one functional identity - one *prosopon* or, to use the inadequate English equivalent, one "person" *(The Christological Controversy*, p.25; See *On the Incarnation, Book 7, Fragments 3-4; Book 8, Fragments 7 & 8*).

26.*Letter 137:3,11; Letter 140:4,12* (PL 11, pp. 520, 543); *De Fide et Symbolo, 4:10* (CSEL 41, pp. 13f).

27.*Conversation with Heracleides, VII,5 (Source Chretienne, vol.67, p.70.)*

28.*DS* 150.

29.On this development, see Walter Kasper, *Jesus the Christ*, pg. 177.

30.In this vein, Kasper writes: "As the significance of Jesus' humanity in mediating salvation was forgotten, the intercessory salvation-mediatorship of the saints - especially Mary - became more prominent. The consequences appeared also in ecclesiology where the one-sided emphasis on the divinity of Christ meant that excessive importance was attached to the authority of the Church's ministry. The more it was forgotten that Christ is our brother, the more the fraternal dimension in the Church was ignored and the authoritative factor was stressed exclusively. These consequences were naturally most obvious in the Christology generally prevailing in the minds of ordinary Christians. (*Jesus, the Christ*, pg. 211.)

31.Walter Kasper makes a similar observation in his work *Jesus, the Christ*, pg. 212, as he writes: "A more philosophico-metaphysical argument was adopted (by the fathers) in addition to the soteriological arguments. It was used against Apollinaris' first objection that two complete substances cannot in turn form a higher unity. Against this, the Fathers...tried to show that Apollinaris' basic mistake lay in his conception of man's nature as a self-contained reality. Under this assumption, the union of God with a whole and complete man is obviously inconceivable. But if we start out from the fact that the human spirit as such has an openness transcending everything finite, then it is not only capable of union with God, but is even the sole possible presupposition for the Incarnation of God. Since the spirit alone is really open for God, a union of God with an unanimated body is in the last resort impossible. If God wills to be corporeally present in the world he cannot achieve this except by becoming a complete man, endowed with human freedom. Human freedom is the condition set by God himself for the Incarnation. This led to the famous formula: 'The Word assumed the body by the intermediary of the soul.'"

32.Thus, hurt and anger need not lead to hostility, life-long animosity, or worse, violence (verbal, emotional, or even physical). Rather it can yield to light, compassion, perhaps constructive dialogue and critique, and ultimately forgiveness and reconciliation. Loss and grief need not lead to hopelessness and despair; they can initiate a process of coming to new vision, genuine hope, and a new phase of energetic and fruitful life. Love of another human being need not lead one to place persons on pedestals and to make excessive demands on them, demands that can yield disappointment and fuel hurt and anger; it can mature to a realistic acceptance of the other, in that person's gifts and liabilities, as a fellow traveler in the process of ongoing conversion as we all seek, in Christ, entrance into

God's kingdom. God's own faithful and loving wisdom can lift up any human situation, every dimension of the human.

CHAPTER 10

1.Indeed, this latter question already had become an issue at Nicea and even prior to that Council. As we have seen, the question of the relationship of God to creation was so difficult that it readily prompted Hellenistic Christians, first, to contest the divinity of the *Logos* and, later, to deny the full humanity of Jesus. Hence, only after the authoritative statements of Nicea and Constantinople I concerning these two natures, could the Church give focused attention to, and an accurate account of, their interrelationship.

2.For example, we think of "persons" as denoting relatively autonomous individuals, men and women, who actively see, hear, think, choose, and act in the world. We rarely make the distinction between "the person" and "the capacity to see, hear, think, choose, and act." But, with a bit of reflection, we easily recognize that by the term "person" we seek to call attention to the one who acts and by the word "nature" we refer to the capacity for specific kinds of acts.

The meaning of the latter word becomes clearer when we recognize that we use the term "nature" to mean "that which grounds the ordinary way things act," so that we might say: "Dogs bark because it is their nature to bark"; or "Fish swim and breathe in the water because their nature enables them to swim and breathe in the water"; or "People see, hear, think, choose, and act, because they have a human nature." Hence we do make a distinction between the "person" (the one who acts; who one is) and the "nature" (the capacity for specific acts; what one is).

Nevertheless, the terms "person" and "human nature" imply one another. Therefore, we often use the word "person" to include the reality "human nature." This creates a difficulty in speaking of Jesus, for to say "Jesus is one Person in two natures" roughly seems to us to state that Jesus is an autonomous, conscious, and free individual, who consciously and freely chooses whether he will use his divine or human nature. Such an understanding of Jesus, however, is not what the formula "one person in two natures" is meant to convey. Our effort here will be to overcome this misconception borne of linguistic confusion and to foster an intelligible appreciation of the unity of God and the human which the formula is intended to promote.

3.The challenge to develop and to redefine a word is not unique to the theological endeavor. Empirical sciences, agriculture, and medicine (to name only some areas of life and study) develop their own words and concepts in order that persons involved in these areas of life and learning can speak accurately of their experiences and discoveries with one another.

4.For further reading concerning the linguistic analysis which follows, see Walter Kasper, *Jesus, the Christ,* p. 241 and John C. Dwyer, *Son of Man and Son of God,* pp. 59-63.

5.Walter Kasper notes that in this latter sense the Greek Old Testament used the word *prosopon* to express the "face of God," God's Self-manifestation (*Jesus the Christ,* p. 241).

6.For this reason, the Latin comfortably translated *ousia* with the word *substantia,* even though *substantia* literally corresponds to the Greek *hypostasis.* Hence the Greek *homoousios* of the Council of Nicea was translated by the Latin *consubstantialis* (English "same substance).

7.For a development of the Trinitarian theology of the Cappadocian Fathers, see J. N. D. Kelly, *Early Christian Doctrines*, 2nd edition (New York: Harper and Row, 1960), pp. 263-269. For the development of this theology in Augustine, see *ibid.*, pp. 271-279.

8.Nestorius developed his position out of that already articulated by Theodore of Mopsuetia. Theodore himself had previously argued from the Antiochene stance which emphasized the concreteness and wholeness of Jesus' humanity.

9.Cyril found this phrase in a work attributed to Athanasius, but which, in fact, had been written by Apollinaris. In this regard, Richard Norris (*The Christological Controversy*, p. 27) writes; "Cyril...was no Apollinarian. His writings from the period of the Nestorian controversy and after show that he affirmed the fullness of Jesus' human nature, its possession of soul as well as of body. What Cyril saw in this Apollinarian phrase was an affirmation of the view which, he insisted, was stated in the creed of the Council of Nicea. The language of that creed makes it clear that the *Logos*, the divine Son, is the one who was born, suffered and died, and (was) raised from the dead. As Cyril sees it, one must therefore affirm that Jesus is the *Logos*, but the *Logos* existing under the conditions of the human way of being–'incarnate'."

10.Neuner and Dupuis, *Christian Faith in the Doctrinal Documents*, p. 155, n. 615.

11.The advance beyond Nicea might be expressed this way: from the teaching of Nicea, one might conclude that the *Logos* acted through Jesus, influencing him deeply, though Jesus himself remained simply a human being, a fully independent person. As a human being, Jesus would be acknowledged as wondrously responsive to the influence of the *Logos* and unsurpassably faithful to *Abba*. With the teaching of Ephesus and Chalcedon, however, one must conclude that the *Logos* not only influences Jesus but is the one who acts in each conscious, free moment of Jesus' life. Jesus is not simply a human being, but one in being with the *Logos*. Therefore, we meet the Father *through* Jesus but we meet the Son of God *in* Jesus.

12.St. Thomas, seeking to foster fuller understanding of this teaching and the distinctions which undergird it, offered further insight using his philosophy of being. In his systematic philosophy and theology, Thomas noted that all created reality was composed of "essence" and "existence." The "essence" of any reality is the factor that makes it what it is. (In this respect, essence is the same as "nature" and "substance.") "Existence" is the factor that makes the reality truly real, not just an idea. Therefore the fact that a dog, or a cat, or a person is, flows from the act of "existence"; what (or the way) it is, namely dog, cat, person, flows from its "essence." Every created reality is truly real because its nature has existence.

And everyone recognizes existence, even though we find it difficult to define. We affirm existence in every judgement we make about anything. When we say: "That man is tall," we affirm the existence of the man (his essence or nature) and also the existence of the quality of tallness. When we say: "That woman sings beautifully," we affirm existence of the woman, of her action of singing, of the sound and of the quality of the sound (beautiful). Without existence, nothing is. Existence is the dynamism of all that is.

In Thomistic philosophy, God gives every creature a created act of existence, making that creature real and able to act. In the incarnation, however, God, whose very nature is to exist, communicates the divine existence of the *Logos* to the human nature of Jesus. For Thomas, then, Jesus of Nazareth, in his humanity exists, not by way of a created act of existence, but by way of the uncreated existence of the Word. If existence is the dynamism of all that is, the uncreated existence of the *Logos* becomes the dynamism of Jesus of Nazareth.

13.In contemporary language, following the theological insight of Karl Rahner (*The Trinity*, trans. Joseph Donceel [New York: Herder and Herder, 1970], pp. 87-101), one might speak of the one divine Love consciously manifesting itself to itself and freely loving itself eternally. Thus, the divine Love relates to itself in a threefold manner: 1) the divine Love actively expressing itself consciously and loving itself (*Abba*, the origin of the Three), 2) the eternal manifestation of God's Love to God's Self (God's Word, God's perfect Self-Image, God's "Son"), and 3) the eternal grateful and joyful Response of being loved so fully (the Spirit, the Gift of God's loving, God's Joy in God's Self). The Three are three ways in which God eternally relates to God's Self, in full consciousness and grateful joy.

For Rahner, the three inner ways in which God is Self-expressed make it possible for God to be similarly Self-expressed "outside" of God's Self. Thus, God continually manifests and communicates God's Self in history through God's Word and abides in God's people who receive God's love in the dynamism and joy of God's Spirit.

14. What becomes evident in this analysis is the fact that the term *hypostasis* (and, therefore, the concept of person which has grown out of it) is analogous.

15. *Liber de persona et duabus naturis*, III (PL 64:1343). His definition fell short of being useful in regard to offering an understanding of the Three in God since God is one substance (if one were to use that word) not three individual substances. Boethius' contemporary, a Roman deacon by the name of Rusticus (*Contra Acephalos disputatio* [PL 67:1239 B]), criticized Boethius' definition precisely on that account.

16. *Contra Nestorianos et Eutychianos*, I (PG 86:1280 A).

17. *De Trinitate*, 4 (PL 196:944-47).

18. In emphasizing the relational aspect of being a person, Richard retrieves an element implied in the Greek word *prosopon*, for the notions of "face" and "mask" both implied the movement of manifesting and expressing oneself in relationship to others.

19. Richard's views are of particular importance since all later theologians from the thirteenth to the early seventeenth centuries tended to emphasize and further to refine one or other of the two dimensions of personhood which he captured in his own reflections. For a synthesis of the views of these theologians, see Walter Kasper, *Jesus the Christ*, pp. 242f. and after him, Brian McDermott, *Word Become Flesh*, pp. 267f.

20. In accord with this position, two late sixteenth century theologians understood the distinctive character of personhood as consisting of a "distinct mode of existence" (the Jesuit Suarez, died in 1617) or "a distinct mode of subsistence" (the Dominican Banez, died in 1604). For commentary on their positions, see Kasper, pp. 242f and McDermott, p. 268.

21. see Chapter 8, especially pages 242-251.

22. This notion is more fully developed by Hans Urs von Balthasar in his short essay entitled *A Theology of History* (New York: Sheed and Ward, 1963), pp. 23-45.

23. See Richard Norris, *The Christological Controversy*, pp. 28-31 for a fuller account of the intricacy of the events detailed here.

24. from the Greek *mono*, "one" and *physis*, "nature."

25. Neuner and Dupuis, *Christian Faith in the Doctrinal Documents*, p. 155, n. 615.

26. One should note carefully that neither Thomas, nor we, are speaking here of the divine knowledge of the *Logos*, the knowledge which the *Logos* shares with the Father and the Spirit in the mind of God. Given the fact that the "two natures remain unconfused and unaltered after the union," it is clear that Jesus in his humanity did not have direct access to the "content" of the divine mind. In this regard, the scholastic theologian states: "If there had not been in the soul of Christ some other knowledge besides his divine knowledge, he would not have known anything. Divine knowledge cannot be an act of the

human soul of Christ; it belongs to another nature" (*Summa Theologiae*, Part III, Question 9, article1 ad 1). Thus, Jesus human knowledge, necessarily followed the laws of human learning and human knowing.

27.*Summa Theologiae*, Part III, Question 9, articles 1 to 4.

28.See his article "How Much Did Jesus Know?" in *Jesus God and Man* (Milwaukee: Bruce Publ. Co., 1967), pp. 39-102 and his later revision of the same in *An Introduction to New Testament Christology* (New York: Paulist Press, 1994), pp. 31-102.

29.See "Dogmatic Reflections on the Knowledge and Self-Consciousness of Christ in *Theological Investigations*, Vol. V, trans. Karl-H. Kruger (Baltimore: Helicon Press, 1966), pp. 193-215.

30.See his "Christ as Subject: A Reply" in *Collection*, ed. F. E. Crowe (New York: Herder and Herder, 1967), pp. 164-197.

31.The author of the fourth Gospel, however, offers his readers a different image of Jesus: Jesus knows in the beginning who it is who will betray him (6:71, 13:11). Similarly, though he asks Philip where they might obtain enough bread to feed the hungry crowd, he asks only to test the Apostles, for he already knew what he would do (6:5f). These texts, however, do not lead us to conclude that Jesus had supra-human knowledge, for as Brown states: "All this is part of the Johannine tendency to picture Jesus without any element of human weakness or dependence" (*An Introduction to New Testament Christology*, p. 33). The author of the fourth Gospel crafts these texts so as not to mar his overall portrait of Jesus as "the ONE WHO IS," emphasizing the belief that it is the Eternal Word, God, who is made flesh.

32.See Chapter 3, pages 64-68, and Chapter 7, pages 185-189.

33.For example: Jn. 3:16-18, 5:19-30, 17:1; see 1:14.

34.For example: Jn. 3:12f, 5:19f, 8:54f; see 1:18.

35.*Introduction to New Testament Christology*, p. 89.

36.Brown deals with this question at some length. For fuller detail on the intricacy of the discussion, see *ibid.*, pp. 89-100.

37.After an extensive analysis in *An Introduction to New Testament Christology*, Brown concludes similarly:

> Nothing rules out the following possibilities: Jesus reached a firm conviction that if he were rejected and put to death as the prophets of old had been, God would bring about the divine kingdom by vindicating him against those who regarded him as a false spokesman and who rejected as diabolical the power over evil and sin that God had given him. In reflection on Dan. 7 and other OT passages (Ps. 110:1; perhaps Ps. 80:18) Jesus might have expanded the symbolic concept of "one like a son of man" to whom God would give glory and dominion. It became "the Son of Man," the specific human figure whom God glorifies and through whom God manifests the final triumph; and Jesus used it of himself seen as the instrument of God's plan. Early Christians, taking their clue from Jesus' own language, developed the idea further, applied it to different aspects of his life and used it frequently to describe Jesus' self-understanding (pp. 98-99).

38.Contemporary Christians often will ask: "Did Jesus know that he was God?" The difficulty in presenting the question this way lies in the fact that, as one asks it, the inquirer presumes that he or she knows who God is, giving a certain meaning to the name "God." Hence, the inquirer often means "Did Jesus know he was God in the way that I (or we) understand God to be?" For this reason, one can respond only by making a distinction:

If the questioner understands God to be best described as the immutable, all-powerful, unperturbed God as the Hellenistic mind conceived of God, the answer is "No; Jesus did not know himself to be God (in that sense)." That God does not exist. That is not the God Jesus revealed. But, if one means by God the One of unlimited love, the One who is utterly faithful to the demands of genuine love, the One who always embraces creation with forgiveness, the One who is always life-giving, then Jesus knew himself as the incarnation of such love; he knew himself to be one with God in ever increasing measure throughout his life; he knew himself to be God's very self-expression in the flesh.

At the same time, Jesus always knew himself to be the Son of God, not the Father. His self-consciousness always involved his awareness that he was from Another and for Another, the Father. His explicit awareness seems always to be much more directed to *Abba* than toward himself. He is always much more conscious of himself as receiving God's life (love and wisdom) and much more conscious of himself as handing that life on, than on holding anything for himself.

39."The Dignity and Freedom of Man," in *Theological Investigations*, Vol. II, trans. Karl-H. Kruger (Baltimore: Helicon Press, 1963), p.248

40.We say this even though as a person moves through life he or she may conclude with firm conviction that his or her particular religious commitment facilitates service of others and trust in the Transcendent more fully than other possible religious commitments do.

41.Any choices which do not foster and express these overriding values during the course of our lives will weaken our fundamental decision. Choices which are contradictory to our fundamental decision may even lead us to alter our most personal overriding foundational choices. For example, it is possible, in choosing an otherwise worthy profession, to make the choice largely for reasons of comfort, convenience, self-exaltation, or opportunity for gaining wealth. In this light, we can see that we also have the capacity to choose pleasure, material prosperity, or unbridled power over others as our absolute value. We are free, not only at the level of concrete choice, but also at the broader levels of choice, including the overriding level of personal all-embracing and foundational choice.

42.Even persons whom we love deeply and who love us similarly are limited in their capacities to offer us all the love and fullness of life which we desire.

43.Christian Tradition itself began to wrestle with this complex question in the aftermath of Chalcedon, manifesting once again the perennial difficulty of giving adequate account of both Jesus' divinity and his humanity. For, although Scripture affirmed that Jesus *did not* sin (Heb. 4:14), it did not affirm that he *could not* sin. The Second Council of Constantinople (553), however, took this biblical affirmation a step further: It declared that Jesus was impeccable.

It should be no surprise that, in the aftermath of this latter declaration (in a manner similar to the aftermath of Nicea and the aftermath of Ephesus), the integrity of Jesus' humanity was put in jeopardy. Sergius, the Patriarch of Constantinople, a man with decided monophysitic leanings, maintained that in Jesus there could be only one energy, one will. Otherwise, he argued, Jesus could have opposed the divine will. Should that have been the case, neither Jesus' sinlessness as a fact, nor our redemption, could have been secured in the incarnation of the Word made flesh. Sergius' position received the name *Monothelytism* (One Will). Thus, once again, the Christian Community found itself in need of reaffirming the integrity of Jesus' humanity: The Church condemned Monothelytism at the Third Council of Constantinople in the years 680-681, although it did not reverse the teaching of Constantinople II with regard to the impeccability of Jesus.

The current debate concerning the freedom and sinlessness of Jesus simply indicates that the Church must continually think through its understanding of Jesus, and particularly must give a meaningful account of the relationship of Jesus' divinity and his humanity, in every age. Every age must do Christology lest it lose sight of the genuine significance for us of God's having become alive for us in and through Jesus of Nazareth.

44.Daniel Helminiak argues from this position in his book *The Same Jesus*. After laying out an extensive treatment of human freedom and the nature of sin, he addresses the question of Jesus' impeccability and concludes: "Just because Jesus was who he was does not mean it was metaphysically impossible for him to sin. If it was not metaphysically impossible for him, a divine one, God, to die, it was not metaphysically impossible for him, a divine one, God, to sin. Jesus was sinless but not impeccable. His temptations were real." (p. 223)

45.Brian McDermott (*Word Become Flesh*, pp. 206f) and Gerald O'Collins (*Interpreting Jesus*, p. 194f) seek to honor this perspective in offering well-nuanced positions. In this vein, after offering several reflections taken from the Scriptures, McDermott writes: "Jesus' earthly life was that of the Son of God Incarnate, the definitive self-communication of God to the world. As such, he could not have sinned; he could not have chosen contrary to his deepest character as the authentically human and the incarnate self-expression of God. But given the supreme importance of his freedom for our salvation, when we consider Jesus as a *viator,* on the way before his resurrection, then we do better to say that as he continued to choose the Father's will through the various stages of his life, it became increasingly impossible *morally* for Jesus to sin; his human will became developmentally more and more confirmed in grace, more and more 'practiced' in choosing the values that pertained to God's reign...."

46.This should not be thought of in an egotistical or selfish sense. A person may estimate that, in the overall, a selfless act of love or service of neighbor, even at some personal cost, will be the most personally satisfying act which he or she could perform at a given moment.

47.Given the fact that the Gospel account of Jesus' going into the wilderness and confronting temptation is meant to be a paradigm of the whole of Jesus' historical journey, we can be sure that Jesus engaged in such "retreats" and in the difficult processes of important decision-making quite often.

48.The difficulties of expressing the unity of the divine *Logos* and human nature of Jesus, both as one in being and as one in his human activity, have led contemporary theologians to seek alternative ways of giving adequate and accurate answer to the question of who precisely Jesus is. As noted above (endnote 2), our contemporary culture does not easily distinguish person from nature. Hence, to speak of Jesus as a divine Person conveys to many the understanding that he is not human, particularly in his ways of knowing and choosing and loving.

For this reason, Walter Kasper, after commenting on the positions of a number of twentieth century theologians including those currently writing, offered his own formulation, striving faithfully to preserve the insight of the classical definition. Thus he writes: "Jesus' humanity is...hypostatically united with the *Logos* in a human way, and this means in a way which includes human freedom and human self-consciousness. Precisely because Jesus is no other than the *Logos*, in the *Logos* and through him he is also a human person. Conversely, the person of the *Logos* is the human person." He quotes Aquinas in support if his position: 'In Christ, human nature was assumed so that it might be the person of the Son of God' (*Summa Theologiae* III, q.2, a.10); 'The Word became flesh, that is human, in such a manner that the Word Itself is personally a man' (*Questiones Disputatae, V, De unione Verbi Incarnati*, a.1). To this, Kasper then adds: "We must also say that the indeterminate and open aspect that belongs to the human person is determined definitively by the unity of person with the *Logos*, so that in Jesus thorough the unity of person with the *Logos*, the human personality comes to its absolutely unique and underivable fulfillment." (*Jesus, the* Christ, p. 248).

This contemporary manner of understanding the concept of person in some ways has its origin in modern philosophy itself, beginning with John Locke. Rather than understand person as the center of the human dynamism preceding actual consciousness and freedom, person came to mean an autonomous human subject enjoying actual self-consciousness and freedom.

Recognizing this tendency in modern philosophy, the valuable insights of contemporary psychology, and the difficulties of reconciling these tendencies with classical ways of speaking of the unity of Jesus, Pius XII wrote of the permissibility of distinguishing between a distinct *psychological* personality in Jesus (embracing the human expression of the incarnation of the *Logos*) so long as one maintained the *ontological* unity and singularity of the one subject in Jesus (Encyclical *Sempiternus Rex*; printed in Neuner and Dupuis, p. 187, n. 663). Since the statement of Pius XII, twentieth-century theologians have reworked the classical formula, striving, in a manner intelligible to the modern mind, to give an adequate account of the unity of the *Logos* with the human nature of Jesus.

For a synthesis of a number of some of the modern positions, concerning the Personhood of Jesus, see Brian O. McDermott, *Word Become Flesh*, pp. 268-281.

49.*Adversus Haereses*, V, Preface.

50.See Chapter 7, pages 195-`98, where we have defined salvation in this manner.

51.As the author of Ephesians put it: "God likewise predestined us through Christ Jesus to be his adopted sons (and daughters), such was his will and pleasure" (1:5); we are sons and daughters in the Son. Moreover, we have been, in fact, created in, through and for the Word (Jn. 1:1; Col. 1: 15-17), so clearly so that Origen could say that in each of us lies "seeds of the *Logos*."

Select Bibliography

Benedict XVI, Pope. See Ratzinger, Joseph.

Best, Ernest. *Following Jesus: Discipleship in the Gospel of Mark.* Sheffield, England: University of Sheffield, JSOT Press, 1981.

Boff, Leonardo. *Jesus Christ Liberator: A Critical Christology for Our Time.* NY: Orbis, 1978.

Borg, Marcus J. *Jesus: A New Vision.* San Francisco: Harper,1987.

_____. *Meeting Jesus Again for the First Time.* San Francisco: Harper, 1994.

Borowitz, Eugene B. *Contemporary Christologies: A Jewish Response.* NY: Paulist Press, 1980.

Brown, Raymond E. *An Adult Christ at Christmas.* Collegeville, MN: Liturgical Press, 1978.

_____. *The Churches the Apostles Left Behind.* New York:Paulist Press, 1984.

_____. *A Coming Christ in Advent.* Collegeville, MN:Liturgical Press, 1988.

_____. *The Community of the Beloved Disciple.* New York:Paulist Press, 1979.

_____. *A Crucified Christ in Holy Week.* Collegeville, MN: Liturgical Press, 1986.

_____. *The Gospel according to John, I-XII, Anchor Bible, 29.* Garden City, NY: Doubleday, 1966.

_____. *The Gospel of John, XIII-XXI,* Anchor Bible 29A. Garden City: Doubleday, 1970.

_____. *Jesus, God and Man.* Milwaukee: Bruce, 1967.

_____. *An Introduction to New Testament Christology.* New York: Paulist Press, 1994.

_____. *The Virginal Conception and Bodily Resurrection of Jesus.* NY: Paulist Press, 1973.

Brown, Raymond E. and Meier, John P. *Antioch and Rome.* New York: Paulist Press, 1983.

Bibliography

Cook, Michael L. *The Jesus of Faith: A Study in Christology.* NY: Paulist Press, 1981.

Cullmann, Oscar. *The Christology of the New Testament.* Philadelphia: Westminster Press,1963.

de Jonge, Marinus. *Christology in Context.* Philadelphia: Westminster Press, 1988.

Dulles, Avery. *The Craft of Theology.* New York: Crossroad, 1995.

Dwyer, John C. *Son of Man and Son of God.* NY: Paulist Press, 1983.

Fitzmyer, Joseph A. *A Christological Catechism: New Testament Answers.* N.Y.:Paulist, 1982.

_____. *The Gospel According to Luke I-IX,* Anchor Bible 28. Garden City, NY: Doubleday, 1981.

Fuller, Reginald H. *The Foundations of New TestamentChristology.* N.Y.: Charles Scribner's Sons, 1985.

Fuller, Reginald H. & Perkins, Pheme. *Who Is This Christ? Gospel Christology and Contemporary Faith.* Philadelphia, PA: Fortress Press, 1983.

Haight, Roger. *Dynamics of Theology.* Mahwah, NJ: Paulist Press, 1990.

Haught, John F. *What is God? How to Think of the Divine.* Mahwah, NJ: Paulist Press, 1986.

Helminiak, Daniel A. *The Same Jesus.* Chicago: Loyola University Press, 1986.

Hill, Brennan. *Jesus the Christ: Contemporary Perspectives.* Mystic, CT: Twenty-Third Publications, 1991.

Johnson, Elizabeth A. *Consider Jesus.* New York: Crossroad, 1990.

Kasper, Walter. *Jesus the Christ.* NY: Paulist Press, 1976.

Kelly, J. N. D. *Early Christian Doctrines,* 2nd edition. New York: Harper and Row, 1960.

Lane, Dermot A. *The Experience of God: An Introduction to Doing Theology.* New York/Ramsey, NJ: Paulist Press, 1981.

_____. *The Reality of Jesus: An Essay in Christology.* NY: Paulist Press, 1977.

Latourelle, Rene. *The Miracles of Jesus and the Theology of Miracles,* translated by Matthew J. O'Connell. New York: Paulist, 1988.

Mackey, James P. *Jesus the Man and the Myth: A Contemporary Christology.* NY: Paulist Press, 1979.

McBrien, Richard P. *Catholicism,* Vol. 1 & 2. Minneapolis, MN: Winston Press, Inc., 1980.

McDermott, Brian. *Word Become Flesh.* Collegeville, MN: Liturgical Press, 1993.

McKnight, Edgar V. *What is Form Criticism?* Philadelphia: Fortress Press, 1969.

Meier, John P. "The Historical Jesus: Rethinking Some Concepts", *Theological Studies*, 51[1990], pp. 3-24.

_____. *The Marginal Jew,* Vol. 1 & 2. Garden City: Doubleday. 1991, 1994.

_____. *The Vision of Matthew.* New York/Ramsey, NJ: Paulist Press, 1979.

Monden, Louis. *Signs and Wonders.* New York: Desclee Company, 1966.

Nolan, Albert. *Jesus Before Christianity.* Maryknoll: Orbis Press, 1978.

Norris, Richard A., Jr., ed. *The Christological Controversy.* Philadelphia: Fortress, 1980.

Mann, C. S. *Mark.* Anchor Bible, Vol. 27. Garden City, N.Y.: Doubleday, 1986.

O'Collins, Gerald. *Interpreting Jesus.* NY: Paulist Press, 1983.

_____. *Jesus Risen.* N.Y.: Paulist, 1987.

_____. *The Resurrection of Jesus Christ.* Valley Forge: Judson Press, 1978.

Pawlikowski, John T. *Christ in the Light of the Christian-Jewish Dialogue* (A Stimulus Book) NY: Paulist Press, 1982.

Norman Perrin. *What is Redaction Criticism?* Philadelphia: Fortress Press, 1969.

Rahner, Karl. *Foundations of Christian Faith.* N.Y.: Seabury,1978.

_____. *On the Theology of Death.* NY: Herder & Herder, 1961.

_____. *Theological Investigations,* vols. 1, 4, 5. Baltimore: Helicon, 1963-1966.

Ratzinger, Joseph (Pope Benedict XVI). *Jesus of Nazareth: From the Baptism in the Jordan to the Transfiguration.* N.Y.: Doubleday, 2007.

_____. *Jesus of Nazareth: Holy Week: From the Entrance into Jerusalem to the Resurrection.* San Francisco: Ignatius Press, 2011.

Bibliography

Schillebeeckx, Edward. *Jesus: An Experiment in Christology.* NY: A Crossroad Book, The Seabury Press, 1979.

_____. *Christ: The Experience of Jesus as Lord.* NY: A Crossroad Book, The Seabury Press, 1980.

_____. *Interim Report on the Books Jesus and Christ.* A Crossroad Book, The Seabury Press, 1982.

Schillebeeckx, Edward and Metz, Johannes-Baptist. *Jesus, Son of God?* (Concilium Religion in the Eighties) NY: The Seabury Press, 1982.

Schoonenberg, Piet. *The Christ.* N.Y.: Herder & Herder, 1971.

Senior, Donald. *Jesus: A Gospel Portrait.* (New York: Paulist Press, 1992).

Sheets, John R., ed. *The Theology of the Atonement.* Englewood Cliffs, NJ: Prentice Hall, 1967.

Sloyan, Gerald S. *Jesus in Focus: A Life in its Setting.* Mystic, CT: Twenty-Third Publications, 1994.

Taylor, Vincent. *The Gospel According to Mark,* 2nd ed. London: Macmillan, 1966.

Thompson, William M. *The Jesus Debate.* NY: Paulist Press, 1985.

_____. *Jesus, Lord and Savior: A Theopathic Christology and Soteriology.* NY: Paulist Press, 1980.

Van Beeck, Frans Jozef. *Christ Proclaimed: Christology as Rhetoric.* NY: Paulist Press, 1979.

Index

Index